Guest Spot

SWING
Playalong *for* Trumpet

WISE PUBLICATIONS
London/New York/Paris/Sydney/Copenhagen/Madrid

Exclusive Distributors:
Music Sales Limited
8/9 Frith Street, London W1V 5TZ, England.
Music Sales Pty Limited
120 Rothschild Avenue, Rosebery, NSW 2018, Australia.

Order No. AM960575
ISBN 0-7119-7363-6
This book © Copyright 1999 by Wise Publications.

Book design by Michael Bell Design.
Music arranged by Paul Honey.
Music processed by Enigma Music Production Services.
Cover photography by George Taylor.
Printed in the United Kingdom by Page Bros., Norwich, Norfolk.

CD produced by Paul Honey.
Instrumental solos by Steve Waterman.
Engineered by Kester Sims.

Your Guarantee of Quality:
As publishers, we strive to produce every book to
the highest commercial standards.
The music has been freshly engraved and the book has been
carefully designed to minimise awkward page turns and
to make playing from it a real pleasure.
Particular care has been given to specifying acid-free, neutral-sized
paper made from pulps which have not been elemental chlorine bleached.
This pulp is from farmed sustainable forests and was
produced with special regard for the environment.
Throughout, the printing and binding have been planned to
ensure a sturdy, attractive publication which should give years of enjoyment.
If your copy fails to meet our high standards,
please inform us and we will gladly replace it.

Music Sales' complete catalogue describes thousands of
titles and is available in full colour sections by subject,
direct from Music Sales Limited.
Please state your areas of interest and send a
cheque/postal order for £1.50 for postage to:
Music Sales Limited, Newmarket Road, Bury St. Edmunds, Suffolk IP33 3YB.

Guest Spot

Trumpet Fingering Chart

MOUTHPIECE

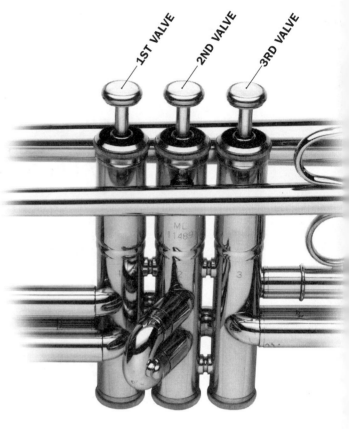

1ST VALVE   2ND VALVE   3RD VALVE

VALVES

SOUNDS	**B♭ TRUMPET CORNET FLUGELHORN**	e	f	f♯/g♭	g	g♯/a♭	a	a♯/b♭	b	c¹	c♯¹/d♭¹	d¹	d♯¹/e♭¹	e¹	f¹	f♯¹/g♭¹	g¹
	BARITONE	E	F	F♯/G♭	G	G♯/A♭	A	A♯/B♭	B	c	c♯/d♭	d	d♯/e♭	e	f	f♯/g♭	g

$\blacktriangleright$ Indicates the lower limit of the best playing range

WRITTEN

f♯/g♭   g   g♯/a♭   a   a♯/b♭   b   c¹   c♯¹/d♭¹   d¹   d♯¹/e♭¹   e¹   f¹   f♯¹/g♭¹   g¹   g♯¹/a♭¹   a¹

Transposition

The Bb trumpet, cornet and flugelhorn sound a major second below the written pitch.
Rule: **Written C sounds Bb**

Written:    Sounds:

The baritone sounds a major ninth below the written pitch. Rule: **Written C sounds Bb**

Written:    Sounds:

Pitch System

The letter names which appear at the top of the fingering chart indicate the relative octave as well as the name of each pitch, as shown below.

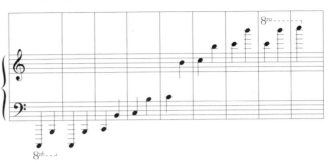

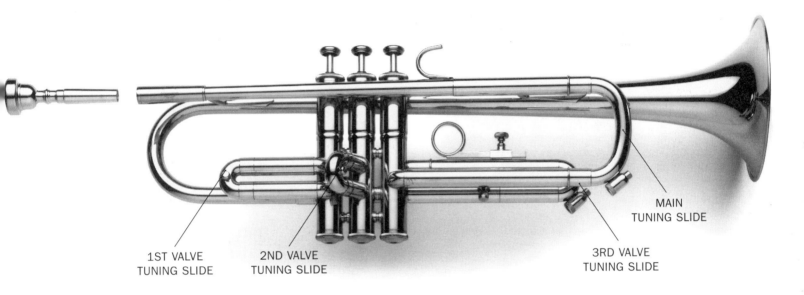

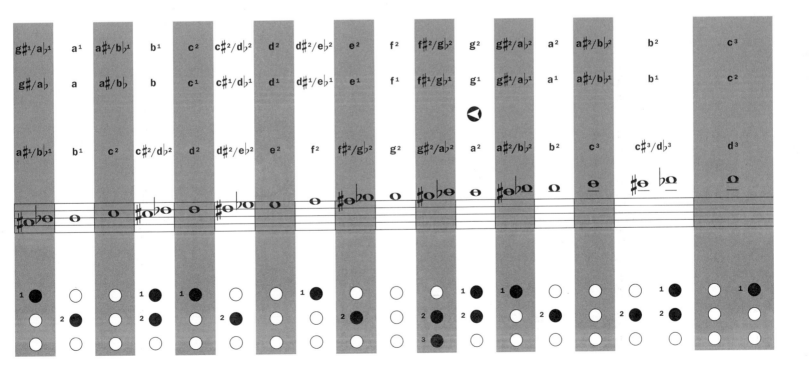

◄ Indicates the upper limit of the best playing range

Ain't Nobody Here But Us Chickens

Words & Music by Joan Whitney & Alex Kramer

I'm Getting Sentimental Over You

Words by Ned Washington
Music by George Bassman

Moderate swing

rall.

Flying Home

By Benny Goodman & Lionel Hampton

Medium swing

14

Jump, Jive An' Wail

Words & Music by Louis Prima

Bright swing

16

(straight quavers)

Hit That Jive Jack

Words & Music by John Alston & Campbell "Skeets" Tolbert

Bright swing

Swing That Music

Words & Music by Louis Armstrong & Horace Gerlach

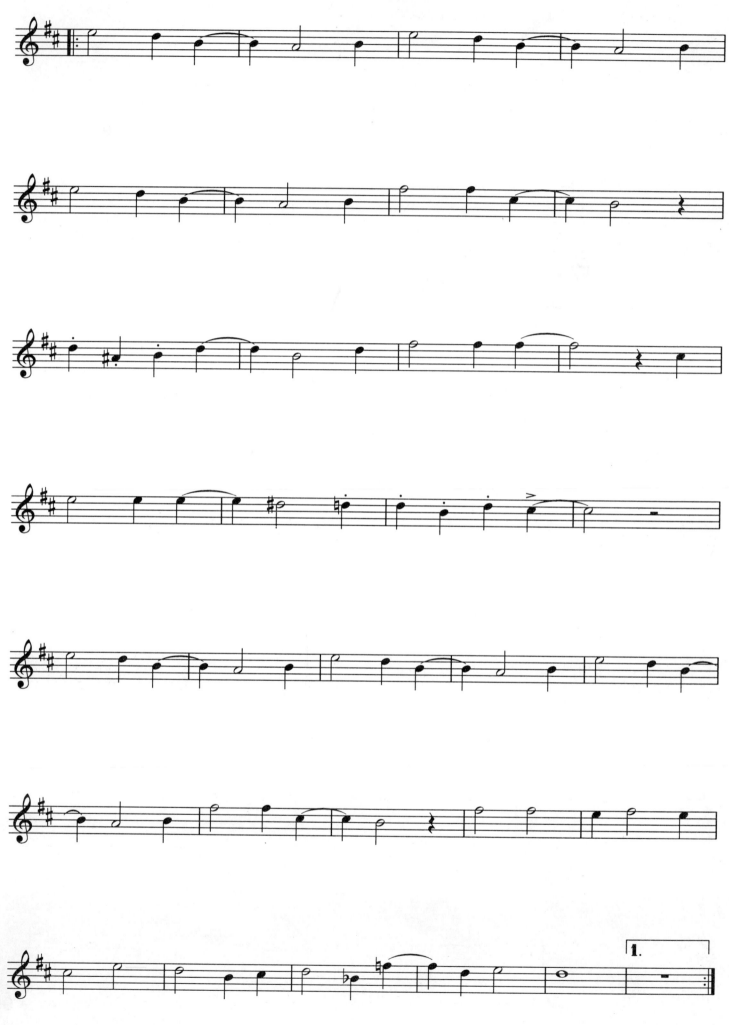

23

Is You Is Or Is You Ain't My Baby?

Words & Music by Billy Austin & Louis Jordan

Perdido

Music by Juan Tizol
Words by Harry Lenk and Ervin Drake

Easy swing

Tuxedo Junction

Words & Music by Buddy Feyne, Erskine Hawkins, William Johnson & Julian Dash

Moderate swing

Zoot Suit Riot

Words & Music by Steve Perry

Bright swing

11/00 (38752)

THE
IDEAL HOME
— DESIGN —
SOURCEBOOK

BARBARA CHANDLER

LAURENCE KING

To Ben Tewson, my mother Evelyn Simpson, and my daughters Catherine Morris
and Abigail Chandler. With thanks.

Research assistants
Olivia Aarons
Sanjive Chawla

Published 1992 by Laurence King

British Library Cataloguing in Publication Data

Chandler, Barbara
  Ideal Home Design Sourcebook. –
  2Rev.ed
  I. Title
  747.025
ISBN 1 85669 013 X

Designed by Barbara Mercer
Printed in England

For a complete catalogue, please write to:
Laurence King Publishing
71 Great Russell Street
London WC1B 3BN

Preface

by Sir Terence Conran

"People's tastes are formed and developed by what they see and are shown, so shops play a vital role in shaping the preferences of the nation. Of course, all forms of media—television, cinema, and especially books and magazines—provide visual stimulation and a source of global information. The media scour the world to bring the latest designs and styles to our notice, but unless the consumer is particularly entrepreneurial or determined, it is likely that he or she will buy only what is on offer, and that his or her tastes will be formed by the retailer's selection. Retailers, I believe, have a responsibility to understand the emerging tastes and aspirations of their customers, and to give them the opportunity to make a choice."

Sir Terence Conran (knighted in 1983) has done more to vitalise Britain's shopping for the home than any other single figure. He founded Habitat in 1964 and it grew from an outpost of good design on the borders of South Kensington and Fulham into a chain of stores selling well-designed furnishings in the UK, France, Belgium, Holland, the USA and Japan. During the 1980s, his retail interests snowballed to include Mothercare, British Home Stores (renamed BhS) and Heal's. He retired from the holding company Storehouse plc in May 1990 but still retains control of The Conran Shop, his always innovative home store in the beautifully restored Michelin Building, opposite the very first Habitat site, which now trades as Joseph. His vast contribution to the spread of good design in this country has included authorship of many books, notably *The House Book* and *Terence Conran's DIY By Design*, and the foundation of the Design Museum at Butler's Wharf, London.

Contents

INTRODUCTION

Welcome to the second edition of *The Home Design Source Book*, now flourishing under the patronage of *Ideal Home* magazine, whose "London Shops" section I founded 15 years ago. Over these years, I have amassed a vast amount of shopping information, which further increased when I started to write the weekly "Finishing Touches" home page for the London *Evening Standard*. I receive a large number of enquiring letters; often, people have seen a mention of what they want in something I have written, but the magazine or newspaper has gone the way of all such ephemera, so they need the information again.

This book is my attempt to supply such information in an unloseable form. It contains as much guidance as I can muster on where to go shopping for the home in London and the South East . . . putting you in touch with around 4,000 outlets for goods and services. Most people shop for their homes from multiple sources, ranging from huge department stores through to their own local High Streets. Then they make special journeys to specialists or to out-of-town superstores to meet particular needs or interests. I have tried to reflect this diversity.

I have been writing about design and decorating since my elder daughter was a babe-in-arms, and now she has a baby herself. I still believe that there is no place like home. At a time when the outside world is getting increasingly mass-produced, standardised, computerised, vandalised and polluted, we can at least control our own little environment, and surround ourselves—at home—with beauty, comfort and efficiency. We can try, anyway.

I would like to thank everyone who helped nurture the first edition into its bigger, healthier successor, particularly my friends in the trade who kept the idea alive by selling it. All information is as correct as I can possibly make it, but, being human, I cannot promise there are no mistakes. Things change very fast in retailing . . . shops close down, move, or alter opening hours and trading policies. So do please always telephone before making a special journey. Mentions cannot be taken as recommendations or endorsements of quality or services. No payments have been made for inclusion in this book. The choice of entries is mine and my researchers'. There is no advertising.

Now that everything I know about shopping is in this book I suppose no one will ever phone me up—or write—ever again. Which would be very sad . . . because you could tell me about who *you* would like to see included next time round, and make the exercise a very welcome two-way process. Write to me c/o *Ideal Home*, Kings Reach Tower, Stamford Street, London SE1 9LS.

Barbara Chandler   London 1992

1

INTERIOR DESIGN

Interior design is not a prerogative of the élite. It simply means having your home the way you want it: comfortable, attractive, efficient, stylish. In a sense therefore, the whole of this book is about interior design. This first chapter highlights specialist advice and services that are available, from sources as diverse as DIY superstores to upmarket design boutiques. The good news is that many interior designers today are friendly, accessible, and above all affordable; particularly those with shops, listed here.

"Simplicity is one thing needful in furnishing, of that I am certain. If only our houses were built as they should be, we should at all events take as our maxim the less, the better; the excess of furniture destroys the repose of a lazy man and it is in the way of an industrious one; and besides, if we really care for art we shall always feel inclined to save on superfluities that are forever in our way; but make work for servants and doctors. If you want a golden rule that will fit everybody, this is it: 'Have nothing in your houses that you do not know to be useful, or believe to be beautiful.'"

William Morris (1834–96)

"You wouldn't say an axe handle has style to it. It has beauty, and appropriateness of form, and a 'this-is-how-it-should be-ness'. But it has no style because it has no mistakes. Style reflects one's idiosyncrasies. Your personality is apt to show more to the degree that you did not solve the problem to the degree that you did."

Charles Eames (1907–78)

"The golden rule is that there are no golden rules."

George Bernard Shaw (1856–1950)

There are many good reasons why you should consult an interior designer.
1. **Function/planning:** a professional makes rooms work better. This is particularly relevant for kitchens and bathrooms, of course.
2. **Co-ordination:** a designer's special training/experience helps to pull a room together, even when the main ideas are your own.
3. **Colour, perspective, proportion:** the designer dovetails all these elements into a unified whole.
4. **Visualising:** a designer can help you to imagine what a room will look like when it is finished (this is tricky for the inexperienced).
5. **Access:** a designer puts you in touch with services/merchandise that you would otherwise not know about.
6. **Supervision:** a designer takes

charge, saving time and trouble.
7. **Money saving:** a designer can prevent costly mistakes. Many will deduct their initial charges if you follow a scheme through their shop. An excellent free leaflet is available from **The Interior Decorators' and Designers' Association (IDDA)**, entitled *Should I Use an Interior Designer?* The IDDA can also send a detailed register of members, with thumbnail portraits of style/experience (this costs £7.50). Many don't have shops/showrooms and are not included in this book. **The Interior Decorators' and Designers' Association** Crest House, 102/104 Church Road, Teddington, Middx TW11 8PY. *Tel:* 081-977 1105.

London Postal Districts

Allied Maples See **Floors 3. Carpets.** Free visits from home consultants.

Battersea Design Company 167 Battersea Rise, SW11 1HP. (5 mins Clapham Junction BR.) *Tel:* 071-228 3957. *Open:* Mon to Fri, 9.30am to 6.00pm, Sat 9.00am to 1.00pm. "The complete works", from planning/building through to the last accessory. Experienced in quality kitchens/bathrooms as well as living/bedrooms. All soft furnishings to order. Showroom packed with samples from around 70 suppliers. "From a metre of fabric to a £40,000 contract."

Bellhouse and Company 33 Kensington Park Road, W11 2EU. (5 mins Notting Hill Gate/Ladbroke Grove tubes.) *Tel:* 071-221 0187. *Open:* Mon to Fri, 9.30am to 5.30pm. Closed for lunch 1.00pm to 2.00pm. Open Sat by appointment.

Full interior design service: "From a few metres of cloth or a couple of rolls of paper, to an entire house." Vast range of pattern books; sample service. Own workshop for all soft furnishings. Curtains, blinds, pelmets, lambrequins. Frilling, piping, braids, tassels. Beautifully quilted bedcovers, bedhangings, valances. Own range of traditionally made upholstery, mostly buttoned. Carpets: cords/sisals, special colours, patterns/borders. Specialist paint finishes/stencilling by experienced artists. "No commission too insignificant."

Lucy Bellhouse Associates 26 Holland Park Villas, W14 8DH. (5 mins Holland Park tube.) *Tel:* 071-602 9225. *Open:* Mon to Fri, 9.30am to 5.30pm. Small, friendly showroom packed with samples: all top makes. Flexible, individual interior design service. All soft furnishings to order.

Clifton Interiors 10 Bristol Gardens, Little Venice W9 2JG. (3 mins Warwick Avenue tube.) *Tel:* 071-289 0902. *Open:* Mon to Fri, 9.30am to 5.30pm, Sat by appointment. Down-to-earth but decorative approach; free initial consultation. Lots of samples, plus ideas "library". Browsers welcome.

Colefax and Fowler See **Decorating Materials 2. Co-ordinated Collections.** Each branch has a resident interior designer who can be consulted on the premises by the hour.

Colour Counsellors 3 Dovedale Studios, 465 Battersea Park Road, SW11 4LR. *Tel:* 071-978 5023. *Open:* strictly by appointment. Showcase for products of the British Design Group. Also the headquarters of a network of "colour counsellors" who bring furnishing samples arranged in eight colour groups: red, blue, green, yellow, purple, brown, orange and neutrals. This brilliant idea of founder Virginia Stourton is now thriving nationwide. Full interior design/soft furnishings service.

Colour Counsellors for the London Area: Karen Allyson-Green, SW18/SW19. *Tel:* 081-870 3006. Susannah Harrison, N5. *Tel:* 071-226 6562. Carol Hearne, NW3. *Tel:* 071-435 2409. Ann Reynolds, SW7/W8. *Tel:* (0426) 917365. Susan Wauchope, SW1/SW4. *Tel:* 071-720 8253. Other postal districts. *Tel:* 071-978 5023.

Design Affair Tir-Na-Nog, 6 Springbridge Road, W5 2AA. (2 mins Ealing Broadway tube/BR.) *Tel:* 081-579 3688/3228. *Open:* Mon to Sat, 9.30am to 5.30pm. Full interior design/soft furnishings service. Specialist displays of bathrooms by Villeroy and Boch; kitchens by Leicht and Geba. Room settings to show curtains, upholstery.

Elizabeth Eaton 30 Elizabeth Street, SW1W 9RB. *Tel:* 071-730 2262. (Currently hunting for new showrooms.) *Open:* Mon to Fri, 9.00am to 6.00pm. Large displays fabrics/wall-coverings. Full design services, including architectural advice. Own exquisite papers/fabrics. Wonderful antique furniture, gleaned from all over the country.

Ellice Interiors Unit G6, Butler's Wharf Business Centre, 45 Curlew Street, Butler's Wharf SE1 2ND. (10 mins Tower Hill tube.) *Tel:* 071-403 7224. *Open:* Mon to Fri, 9.00am to 5.00pm, Sat by appointment. Personal service. Extensive samples. Full interior design service. Complete furnishing packages. Curtain/blind specialists. Paintings/prints of riverside London. Very convenient for new Docklands developments.

Fourteen Battersea Square 14 Battersea Square, SW11 3RA. *Tel:* 071-223 9174. *Open:* Mon to Fri, 10.00am to 5.30pm, Sat by appointment. One-stop shopping for interiors, with three designers. Fabrics/wallcoverings. Furniture/pictures/accessories/lighting. All services, from plumbing to curtain-making. Friendly atmosphere.

Harmony Interiors 128c George Lane, South Woodford E18 1AD. (1 min South Woodford tube.) *Tel:* 081-530 4944. *Open:* Mon to Sat, 9.15am to 5.30pm. Early closing Thu, 1.00pm. Complete interior design service. All soft furnishings/own workshops. Many clients from Essex.

Homebase See **DIY Superstores.** Colour schemes from £5 a room. Fill in form with details of room size, existing furnishings, preferences etc. Back comes the scheme—with a voucher to spend on paint!

Interior Designers' Showcase 26 Eaton Terrace, SW1W 8TS. *Tel:* 071-824 8999. *Open:* by appointment. For a fee, Marilyn Gross advises on the best interior designer/architect for your needs, showing portfolio/records of her previous work. Extensive magazine/book library.

Interior Space 22 Thackeray Street, W8 5ET. (2 mins High Street Kensington tube. NCP Young Street.) *Tel:* 071-937 4770. *Open:* Mon to Fri, 9.30am to 6.00pm, Sat by appointment. See the potential of *trompe l'oeil* in this beautifully decorated shop, with basement design studio offering complete services, from a pair of curtains to total refurbishments. Specialist fabrics/wallpapers/furniture. Gifts/*objets d'art*. Unique range of imported fabrics.

Interpretations 308 Worple Road, Raynes Park SW20 8QU. (3 mins Raynes Park BR.) *Tel:* 081-879 0103. *Open:* Mon to Sat, 9.30am to 5.30pm. Large, bright showroom, with three connecting rooms. Full range of samples. Fabrics/wallcoverings/carpets. Sofas, sofabeds; occasional furniture, mirrors. Personal, friendly service. Curtain-making, quilting, cushions, loose covers, upholstery, carpet fitting.

Jade 10 Porchester Place, Connaught Square, W2 2BS. (5 mins

Marble Arch tube. NCP.) *Tel:* 071-724 6222. *Open:* Mon to Fri, 9.30am to 5.30pm. Chartered designer Alexandra McMorran heads the interior design team of this family firm, founded in 1926. Elegant, ground-floor showroom: carefully selected, unusual pattern books. Wallpapers/fabrics/borders/trimmings/carpets. Curtain designs/room layouts. Scheme co-ordination. Custom-built joinery.

Kensington Design and Developments 12 Stratford Road, W8 6QD. (4 mins Kensington High Street tube.) *Tel:* 071-938 4388. *Open:* Mon to Fri, 9.30am to 5.30pm. Interior designers with own shop. Very relaxed atmosphere. Fabrics/wallpapers: book loans. Antiques. Import kelims direct from Turkey.

The Kinnerton Street Design Company 36 Kinnerton Street, Knightsbridge SW1X 8ES. (5 mins Hyde Park Corner tube.) *Tel:* 071-235 9315. *Open:* by appointment only. All interior design services, from repair work to complete refurbishments. Fabrics/wallpapers/borders etc. "We can get almost anything!"

Laura Ashley See **Decorating Materials 2. Co-ordinated Collections.** Home styling service. £50 (refundable).

The Little House 629 Watford Way, Mill Hill NW7 3JN. (15 mins Mill Hill BR.) *Tel:* 081-906 3117. *Open:* Mon to Fri, 9.00am to 5.00pm, Sat 10.00am to 4.00pm. Closed Thu. Pink-and-white doll's house for adults with latest samples, interior design and soft furnishing service. Specialists in handmade curtains and upholstery. Designer carpets with borderwork in any colour.

Mr Jones 175/179 Muswell Hill Broadway, Muswell Hill N10 3RS. (Highgate tube, plus bus.) *Tel:* 081-444 6066. *Open:* Mon to Sat, 9.30am to 5.00pm. Personal/dedicated service. Proprietor Susan Jones has over 20 years' experience of soft furnishings. Curtains/festoon blinds/swags/tails etc. Comprehensive sample swatches and books available. Upstairs, Martin Jones is manager of a showroom for hand-crafted, fitted kitchens and bedrooms.

Nova Interiors 168 Regent's Park Road, NW1 1XN. (5 mins Chalk Farm tube.) *Tel*: 071-586 2000/7772. *Open*: Mon to Fri, 10.00am to 6.00 pm, Sat 10.00am to 4.00 pm. Knowledgeable/friendly service. International ranges of fabrics/ wallcoverings. Full interior design service. Curtains, decorating, carpentry.

Pavilion Designs 49 Pavilion Road, SW1X 0HD. (4 mins Knightsbridge tube.) *Tel*: 071-245 6788/9. *Open*: Mon to Fri, 10.00am to 5.30pm. Well-established partnership; Karen Armstrong and Sarah van Gerbig trade from exceptionally pretty premises, with full interior design service by appointment. Specialists in decorative antiques, papier mâché lamps, coffee tables and pictures. Large fabric selections.

Peacock of Barnes 3 White Hart Lane, SW13 0PX. (Barnes BR.) *Tel*: 081-878 3012. *Open*: Mon to Fri, 9.30am to 5.30pm, Sat 9.30am to 1.30pm. Sunny, comfortable showroom with over 200 wallcovering pattern books/co-ordinating fabric samples. Total interior design/decorating service, including all building work.

Pullingers 224/226 York Road, Battersea SW11 3SD. (Clapham Junction BR.) *Tel*: 071-924 2400. *Open*: Mon to Sat, 10.00am to 6.00pm. 2,500 sq ft in old joinery factory, recently transformed into showrooms with 11 room settings. Fabrics/wallcoverings. Carpets/ upholstery/beds. Full interior design service.

R and V Interiors 10 Ashfield Parade, Southgate N14 5EJ. (2 mins Southgate tube.) *Tel*: 081-882 5653. *Open*: Tue to Sat, 9.15am to 5.00pm. Margaret Yates offers a

comprehensive interior design service, including all soft furnishings, upholstery, picture-framing etc. "We're friendly, but professional." Wallpapers/fabrics. Accessories.

Rose and Gorilla Design and Decorating 1 Lytton Close, Hampstead Garden Suburb N2 0RH. (8 mins Golders Green tube. Plentiful, free parking.) *Tel*: 081-458 0060. *Open*: by appointment. Personal, friendly advice in studio from Lindy Rose. Around 500 wallpaper/fabric collections. Full catalogues of trimmings/curtain styles/sofas and furniture. Speciality is accessories/soft furnishings. "Clean, helpful team" for all services from upholstery to picture-framing.

Sanderson of Berners Street See **Decorating Materials 2. Co-ordinated Collections.** Interior design service for modest fee, refundable against merchandise.

Schemes 56 Princedale Road, W11 4NL. (5 mins Holland Park tube.) *Tel*: 071-727 3775/1148. *Open*: Mon to Fri, 9.30am to 6.00pm. Small showroom, full of samples. Fabrics, papers, carpets, ceramic tiles, borders. Own linen union printed fabrics in fresh, Mediterranean colours have complementary handpainted tiles. Plus new co-ordinating pottery.

The Study 55 Endell Street, WC2H 9AJ. (5 mins Covent Garden tube.) *Tel*: 071-379 9303. *Open*: Mon to Fri, 11.00am to 7.00pm, Sat 11.00am to 5.00pm. Smallish shop. Full interior design service with lots of samples. Christopher Nevile's interior treatments combine the aesthetic avant-garde with professional panache. Brilliantly original art/craft accessories: furniture/lighting/textiles/ceramics/ glass.

Taylor and Marr 60 White Hart Lane, Barnes SW12 0PZ. (5 mins Barnes Bridge BR. Easy parking.) *Tel*: 081-878 1984. *Open*: Mon to Fri, 9.30am to 5.30pm, Sat 10.00am to 1.00pm. Part of a street packed

with furnishing interest: combine exploration with a river walk. Well established: "We can furnish your whole house in one go." Fabrics/ papers/carpets. Excellent fitters. Curtain-making. Sofas, beds blinds, headboards. Reupholstery.

Wesley-Barrell See **Upholstery and Suites 1. Chairs, Sofas and Suites.** Inspirational design ideas over two floors. Full interior design service by professionals Juliette Barrell and Diane Mullarkey: they can plan a room/house from scratch, or simply solve an awkward problem. Booking advisable. Refundable fee for a full scheme. Service available at all branches.

Home Counties/ South East

Allders of Croydon See **Department Stores.** Free interior decorating service from large department store (five floors), with good selections of home furnishings.

Berkshire Furnishings The Orchard Workroom, 1 Andover Road, Ludgershall, Andover, Hants SP11 9LU. (A342.) *Tel*: (0264) 790355. *Open*: Mon to Fri, 10.00am to 4.00pm, or by appointment. Experienced owner has 20 years' interior design experience. Very personal service. "We'll go anywhere, do anything." Through liaison with a local removals firm, they'll even move house for you! Small showrooms: large selection of fabrics/wallcoverings. All soft furnishing to order: particularly pelmets/swags and tails. Also carpets/antiques/furniture/*objets d'art.*

Bewl Interiors The Hall, Turners Green, Wadhurst, E. Sussx TN5 6TU. (6m South Tunbridge Wells.) *Tel*: (0892) 782028. *Open*: Tue to Fri, 9.30am to 5.00pm. Closed for lunch, 1.00pm to 2.15pm. Open Sat, 10.00am to 1.00pm. Peaceful, welcoming atmosphere conducive to browsing amidst plentiful samples from top makes. Wallpapers, fabrics, sofas, chairs, lamps and carpets. Experienced personal advice and full making-up services.

Chess Interiors   24 Market Place, Chalfont St Peter, Bucks SL9 9DU. (M40, junction 1.) Tel: (0753) 888422. Open: Mon to Fri, 9.30am to 5.00pm. Early closing Thu, 1.00pm. Open Sat, 10.00am to 5.00pm (closed for lunch Sat, 1.00pm to 2.00pm). Peter and Pam Lennon offer a wide variety of design services, including curtains and plaster mouldings (for which they have a matching service). Wallpapers/fabrics.

Alexi Church   11/13 High Street, Camberley, Surrey GU15 3RB. (4 mins Camberley BR. Multi-storey car park opposite.) Tel: (0276) 66104. Open: Tue to Sat, 9.00am to 5.30pm. Full interior design service. Lots of samples. Full soft furnishings service. Furniture/upholstery. Accessories: lamps, china, cushions and pictures. Decorating/stencilling.

Clover House at Home of Interiors   17/19 Frogmore, High Wycombe, Bucks HP13 5DH. Tel: (0494) 529128. Open: Mon to Sat, 9.00am to 5.30pm, evenings by appointment. Manager Sally Watt (a trained textile designer) really puts herself out for clients. Home visits (free locally) made with Ruth Richards, head of workroom. Full selection fabrics/papers. Accessories/prints/dried flowers.

Cobham Interiors   52 High Street, Cobham, Surrey KT11 3EF. (Cobham BR.) Tel: (0932) 64767. Open: Mon to Fri, 9.00am to 5.30pm, Sat 10.00am to 5.30pm, Wed 9.00am to 7.00pm. Fabrics, wallcoverings, furniture. Complete interior design/soft furnishing service.

Colour Counsellors See **London Postal Districts** above.
Sue Aiken, Alton. Tel: (0420) 541523. Sara Allday, Banbury. Tel: (0295) 811473. Anne Butterworth, Cholesbury. Tel: (0240) 29700. Fran Davies, Hastings. Tel: (0424) 420925. Francesca Evans, Woking. Tel: (0276) 857802. June Galczynski,

Newbury. Tel: (0635) 47691. Sheila Garcia, Upminster. Tel: (0402) 223517. Vanse Gethin, Maidstone. Tel: (0622) 743339. Lucienne Greig, Thames Ditton. Tel: 081-398 2661. Diana Harvey, Ham Street. Tel: (0233) 732796. Fiona Mills and Bobby Penny, Reigate. Tel: (0737) 241489. Anne Morrell, Sutton. Tel: 081-770 7948. Maggie Nitch-Smith, Winchester. Tel: (0962) 869591. Rosemary Palmes, Wormley. Tel: (0428) 682340. Nan Read, Ascot. Tel: (0344) 26866. Jane Sadler, Long Crendon. Tel: (0844) 201692. Pauline Shubrook, Woodford Green. Tel: 081-505 6876. Ann Smith, Middlesex. Tel: 081-907 2299. Pauline Sturgeon, Sudbury. Tel: (0787) 76634. Susan Troward and Nicola Anderson, Guildford. Tel: (0483) 60317. Kathryn Turner, Polegate. Tel: (0321) 25058. Penny Wicks, Chorleywood. Tel: (0923) 283174.

Cornucopia Interiors   40 Downing Street, Farnham, Surrey GU9 7PH. (Central Farnham, park behind showroom.) Tel: (0252) 716020. Open: Mon to Sat, 9.30am to 5.00pm. Three interlinked showrooms: 1,000 sq ft. Co-ordinated collections, top brand furniture. Cushions, rugs, exclusive Italian accessories. Soft furnishings service. Expert advice.

Decorum   1 Steward House, Sydenham Road, Guildford, Surrey GU1 3SR. Tel: (0483) 37077. Open: Mon to Sat, 9.30am to 5.30pm. Fine furniture/furnishings, keen prices. Comprehensive range of British, American and Continental wallpapers/fabrics. Prompt, professional curtain- and blind-making. Carpets, custom-made upholstery, headboards. Reupholstery, loose covers, quilting. Full track-fitting and installation services.

The Design Studio   39 High Street, Reigate, Surrey RH2 9AE. (10 mins Reigate BR.) Tel: (0737) 248228. Open: Mon to Fri, 9.00am to 5.30pm, Sat 9.30am to 5.00pm. Half-day Wed. Established by John and Heather Kemeys in 1983; busy, family-run interior design business:

"from a cloakroom to a whole house." Room sets for kitchens/bedrooms/bathrooms. Extensive fabric/wallpaper samples. Floor tiles in terracotta, stone, marble. Own soft-furnishing workrooms. Unusual decorative accessories/gifts. Garden/conservatory furniture. Italian ceramics.

Design Works   86 Queen's Road, Buckhurst Hill, Essex IG9 5BS. Tel: 081-506 0263. Open: Mon to Sat, 9.30am to 5.30pm (both branches). Closed all day Wed. "There's nothing we can't cover." Inspirational room settings with fabrics/papers/furniture. All soft furnishings, with own workrooms. Upholstery. Unusual floor tiles (agents for Paris Ceramics). Painted furniture/antiques.

Designers' Fountain   20 Heritage Close, High Street, St Albans, Herts AL3 4EB. (Secluded shopping precinct off High Street, next to Abbey, opposite car park.) Tel: (0727) 833390. Open: Mon to Sat, 10.00am to 5.00pm. Personal attention from owner. Lots of samples; soft furnishings service.

Ellis Designs   12 High Street, Sunninghill, Berks SL5 9NE. Tel: (0344) 291185. Open: Mon to Fri, 9.30am to 5.00pm, Sat 10.00am to 1.00pm (both branches). Friendly, expert advice. "No project too small or too large." Good samples/displays. Quick service for all soft furnishings.
Also at: 2 Station Parade, Virginia Water, Surrey GU25 4AA. (Next to Virginia Water BR.) Tel: (0344) 844522.

Epping Interiors   Campion Court, High Street, Epping, Essex CM16 4AO. (Epping tube. Own car park at rear.) Tel: (0378) 72829. Open: Mon to Sat, 9.30am to 5.30pm. Early closing Wed 2.00pm. All best brands. Family business/personal service. Home visits with samples. Curtains, loose covers, pelmets, blinds: all made-to-measure by hand in own workshop.

Fabrika of Teddington   6 Church Road, Teddington, Middx TW11 8PB.

(6 mins Teddington BR.) *Tel:* 081-943 2685. *Open:* Tue to Fri, 9.30am to 5.00pm, Sat 9.30am to 3.00pm. Full interior design services, with soft furnishings workroom on premises. Quality wallpapers/fabrics/blinds. Hand-sewn curtains, bedcoverings etc.

Fazeh Interior Design   33 King's Road, Brentwood, Essex CM14 4DW. (Set back in yard, off Brentwood High Street.) *Tel:* (0277) 213308. *Open:* Mon to Sat, 10.00am to 5.00pm. Closed Thu. Expert advice in shop from charming, sympathetic owner, with masses of samples. Home visits (chargeable).

Folly Interiors   North Lodge, Vyne Road, Sherborne-St-John, near Basingstoke, Hants RG26 5DX. *Tel:* (0256) 881794. *Open:* Tue to Fri, 10.00am to 6.00pm, Sat and Sun, 2.00pm to 4.00pm. Showroom with full library of samples, in the grounds of a National Trust property. Diane Giordmaine offers full interior design/consultancy services. All soft furnishings made-to-measure, from simple unlined curtains to decorator treatments. Friendly, personal service. "I cater for all budgets." Glass, pictures, mirrors, small *objets d'art.*

Galienne Schmidt Interiors and Design   37 Prospect Street, Caversham, near Reading, Berks RG4 8JB. *Tel:* (0734) 481283. *Open:* Mon to Fri, 9.00am to 5.00pm, Sat 10.00am to 5.00pm. Relaxed and friendly atmosphere for browsing amongst samples of fabrics/papers from all top makes. Full interior design service. No charge for home visits to local clients.

John Hall Interiors   58 Western Road, Tring, Herts HP23 4BB. (2m Tring BR.) *Tel:* (0442) 826966. *Open:* Mon to Sat, 9.00am to 5.30pm. Personal service/advice. John and Tina Hall have worked with soft furnishings for over 20 years. Wallpapers/borders/carpets/curtains. New upholstery/re-covering. Own workshops, carpet layers, blind and track fitters, floor layers. "We like to

get to know our customers over a period of time."

Ideas Unlimited   10 Russell Hill Parade, Russell Hill Road, Purley, Surrey CR8 2LE. *Tel:* 081-645 9762. *Open:* Mon to Sat, 9.30am to 5.00pm. Early closing Wed 1.30pm. Late night Tue, 8.00pm. Selections of co-ordinated furnishings; full interior design/soft furnishings service. Team of decorators, upholsterer, trackfitter, carpet-layer. "The whole works!"

Inspirations   18 High Street, Princes Risborough, Bucks HP17 9UD. (Plenty of parking.) *Tel:* (0844) 42598. *Open:* Mon to Fri, 9.15am to 6.00pm, Sat 9.00am to 5.30pm. Gina Varmuza practised in London before opening her shop four years ago. Complete design service, from building plans to finished interiors. Fabrics/wallpapers. China/glass/cushions/rugs/furniture. Very special gifts. "That something different."

The Interior Design and Decorating Workshops   Samuel Spencer's Emporium, 39 Jewry Street, Winchester, Hants SO23 8RY. (3 mins from car park.) *Tel:* (0962) 855763. *Open:* Mon to Sat, 9.30am to 5.30pm. Experienced designer; latest ranges, beautiful accessories. Handmade curtains, upholstery. Cabinet-making, special paint finishes. Period restoration/refurbishment.

Interiors of Ascot   The Old Bakehouse, Course Road, Ascot, Berks SL5 7HL. (5 mins Ascot BR.) *Tel:* (0344) 872443. *Open:* Mon to Fri, 9.00am to 5.30pm, Sat 10.00am to 1.00pm. Extensive ranges fabric/wallcoverings; inspiring displays. Friendly advice/professional schemes. Full interior design service. Comprehensive product library: furniture, lights, carpets, braids, gifts.

Libra Interiors   Northlands Farm, Oakwood, Chichester, W. Sussx PO19 3PY. (2m Chichester centre.) *Tel:* (0243) 527055. *Open:* by appointment only. Personal service from experienced owner/designer.

Showroom with window treatments in converted barn: lots of samples, undivided attention.

Merrow Interiors   117 Collingwood Crescent, Boxgrove Park, Guildford, Surrey GU1 2PF. (30 mins Guildford BR.) *Tel:* (0483) 506244. *Open:* Mon to Fri, 9.30am to 5.00pm, Sat 9.30am to 1.00pm. Experienced personal advice from carpet expert and soft furnishings specialist.

Mister Smith Interiors   1/3 The Parade, Croft Road, Crowborough, E. Sussx TN6 1DR. (Facing Waitrose, free car park.) *Tel:* (0892) 664152. *Open:* Tue to Sat, 9.00am to 5.30pm. Closed for lunch, 1.00pm to 2.00pm. Interior design service/samples. Handmade soft furnishings, own workroom. Furniture, lamps, pictures. Specialist ranges of plain carpets in any width or colour. Hand-carved borders and special designs.

Russell Moore Interiors   17 Springfield Road, Chelmsford, Essex CM2 6JE. (Town centre, opposite car park.) *Tel:* (0245) 257979. *Open:* Tue to Sat, 10.00am to 4.00pm. Complete interior design service (established 10 years). Large library with fabric/wallpaper books. Curtains/upholstery.

Northover Interiors   82 High Street, Reigate, Surrey RH2 9AP. (10 mins Reigate BR. Priory Car Park.) *Tel:* (0737) 242236. *Open:* by appointment. Personal service from experienced designer-owner. Complete design service with optional supply facility. Structural alterations and "green building" concepts a speciality.

Private Lives   The Old Parsonage, Church Street, Crondall, near Farnham, Surrey GU10 5QQ. *Tel:* (0252) 850527. *Open:* Mon to Fri, 9.30am to 5.00pm, Sat to 1.00pm. Full interior decorating service from renovated barn, packed with impressive samples and displays. Sophisticated soft-furnishing ideas backed by making-up/installation services. Special paint finishes;

fabric coverings for walls and ceilings.

Pullingers Interiors and Furnishing High Street, Bishops Waltham, Southampton, Hants SO3 1AA. (Car parks nearby.) *Tel*: (0489) 894546. *Open*: Mon to Sat, 9.00am to 5.30pm. Full interior design service. Three floors of modern/ traditional home furnishings, including carpets, flooring, upholstery/cabinets, fabrics, bed/ bedlinens, wallpapers. High standard of service/fitting/ making-up.
Also at: Sheet Green, Sheet, near Petersfield, Hants GU32 2AF. *Tel*: (0730) 66351.

Sage High Street, Ripley, Surrey GU23 6BB. (Village centre. Easy parking.) *Tel*: (0483) 224396. *Open*: Mon to Sat, 9.30am to 5.30pm. Complete interior/exterior design services and showroom (established 1971). Large town house in country

house style over two floors. Exclusive fabrics/wallcoverings. Tiles/carpets/ lighting/sofas. Accessories/fine linens. Kitchens/bathrooms/ bedrooms/libraries. Garden design. Stencilling/paint effects. Ironwork. Curtains/upholstery.

Suttons Furnishings High Street, East Grinstead, W. Sussx. *Tel*: (0342) 321695. *Open*: Mon to Sat, 9.30am to 5.00pm. New premises for designer/makers of fine furnishings. Family firm; huge range of samples. Trading for 40 years; own workrooms. Colour brochure available.
Also at: 6 Regent Arcade, East Street, Brighton, E. Sussx BN1 1HR. *Tel*: (0273) 723728.

Pamela Voice Decoration Bell Hall, Colne Engaine, Colchester, Essex CO6 2ES. *Tel*: (0787) 223874. *Open*: by appointment only. Personal service for private clients, from supply of accessories/

wallpaper to complete room schemes. Sample service/initial visit free. Often works with well-known local architect. Telephone enquiries welcome.

Wessex Interiors 25 Stockbridge Road, Winchester, Hants SO22 6RW. (Park outside.) *Tel*: (0962) 855165. *Open*: Mon to Fri, 9.30am to 5.30pm, Sat 9.30am to 12.30pm. Attractive showrooms with room settings. All best decorating brands. Porcelain lamps/silk cushions/ lacquerware. Expert advice. Complete decorating service. Decoration/soft furnishings/ furniture/lighting.

West London Galleries 12 Chobham Road, Sunningdale, Berks. *Tel*: (0344) 22254. *Open*: Mon to Fri, 9.15am to 5.00pm. Closed for lunch, 1.00pm to 2.00pm, Sat 10.00am to 12.00 noon. Fabric/ papers. All soft furnishings made-to- measure. Full interior design service. Re-upholstery/loose covers.

2
KITCHENS

The kitchen is the most overworked room in the home, so it is worth organising congenial surroundings for yourself. The shops listed in this chapter can cope with anything and everything, from a luxury refit to a simple new saucepan.

1. SPECIALISTS

"If you can't stand the heat, get out of the kitchen."

Harry S Truman, former US President (1884–1972)

There used to be two or even three kitchen specialists on every High Street, before the recession at least weeded out some of the cowboys. Nevertheless, there are still enough dealers to create a dilemma. So how do you choose between them? Membership of the **Kitchen Specialists' Association** (KSA) is reassuring (see **Help! 5. Helpful People**). This guarantees minimum standards of service/workmanship, and safeguards your money in the event of bankruptcy.

Top makers, whether British, German, Spanish or French, usually keep their stockists up to scratch and some offer limited financial guarantees/service standards. Companies that are not KSA members (which often have delightfully individualistic ranges) may also offer very good service. The best step, then, is to ask for local references and follow them up. It is not advisable to buy a kitchen if you have only seen it pictured in advertisements or brochures. Organising a kitchen is a tricky business; on larger projects you will certainly need some expert planning advice. Most of the companies below can offer total refits, including plumbing, electrics, decorating, and even structural alterations. Planning will be "free", but of course this service will be reflected in the price of merchandise—there's no such thing as a free scale drawing.

London Postal Districts

Alternative Plans   9 Hester Road, Battersea SW11 4AN. (Immediately over Battersea Bridge.) *Tel:* 071-228 6460. *Open:* Mon to Fri, 8.30am to 5.30pm, Sat 9.00am to 4.00pm.

Pleasant, enthusiastic service and a wide range of kitchen styles. Established 10 years. Speciality: Boffi Italian futuristic designs with stainless-steel tops/front. Experts in kitchens for the disabled.

B J Brown (London)   681/689 Holloway Road, N19 5SE. (5 mins Archway tube.) *Tel:* 071-281 4136. *Open:* Mon to Sat, 9.00am to 5.30pm. Family firm with spacious, sophisticated showrooms for kitchens/bathrooms. Italian Schiffini/Spanish Xey/British Framford. Worktops: Corian, laminate, solid wood, tiles, granite. Ceramic/marble floor tiles. Built-in appliances. Planning. Builders/DIY supplies at trade counter round corner.
Also at: 53/59 Hargrave Road, N19 5SH (trade counter). *Tel:* 071-272 2157.

Bruton Kitchens   3 Baker Street, W1M 1AA. *Tel:* 071-935 0217. *Open:* Mon to Fri, 9.00am to 6.00pm, Sat 10.00am to 4.00pm. "Experience is our forte," says manager Jonathan Atwood. Poggenpohl/SieMatic/Goldreif. Plan/design/install. "We do everything."

Bulthaup   37 Wigmore Street, W1 9LD. (5 mins Oxford Circus/Bond Street tubes.) *Tel:* 071-495 3663. *Open:* Mon to Fri, 9.00am to 5.00pm, Sat 9.30am to 5.00pm. Other times by appointment. Bulthaup is a top German make that's definitely different. Exclusive design centres offer a vast array of exciting colours (including really vivid hues). Interesting materials. Clever planning solutions. Justly famous is its unique kitchenwork bench in stainless steel: the Continent's answer to our "unfitted" kitchens. Expert advice. Design/supply/install.

Complete Kitchens   56 Springbank Road, Lewisham SE13 6SN. (Opposite Hither Green BR.) *Tel:*

081-852 5926. *Open:* Mon to Fri, 9.30am to 6.00pm, Sat 10.00am to 4.00pm. Early closing Thu 1.00pm. Family business, established 21 years. Design/supply/install. Middle price bracket. Bedrooms/bathrooms.

Gilway Kitchen Studio   81 Fortess Road, NW5 1AG. (3 mins Kentish Town/Tufnell Park tubes.) *Tel:* 071-482 4284. *Open:* Mon to Sat, 9.30am to 5.30pm. Kitchen showroom (four displays) for middle-of-range quality German/Danish makes. Supply/install Junckers wooden floors/worktops. Quality appliances. Qualified architects/planners offer exceptionally strong professional back-up. Full interior design/architectural services. Room lay-outs/complete schemes. Conversions/extensions. Planning applications/building regulations. Plans for DIY installations if required.

Hampstead Kitchens   3 The Market Place, Hampstead NW11 6LB. (A1.) *Tel:* 081-209 0042. *Open:* Mon to Fri, 9.30am to 5.30pm, Sun 10.00am to 1.00pm. Extensive modern kitchens by Allmilmö. Also English handpainted and wooden kitchens. Free measuring/planning. Full installations. Personal service/advice.

C P Hart and Sons   Newnham Terrace, Hercules Road, SE1 7DR. (5 mins Lambeth North/Waterloo tubes. Free parking.) *Tel:* 071-928 5866. *Open:* Mon to Fri, 8.30am to 5.30pm, Sat 8.30am to 5.00pm. Super displays underneath the grimy arches of Waterloo. A family business, trading for over 50 years. Pioneered a designer look for erstwhile trade-only showrooms, making the public welcome as well as builders/plumbers. Greg Hart is the grandson of the founder. Good stocks/immediate delivery (free within a 30-mile radius)/value for money/exclusive lines. Coffee shop.

Humphersons Heal's, 196 Tottenham Court Road, W1P 9ID. (3 mins Goodge Street tube.) *Tel:* 071-636 1390.
Also at: 227/229 High Road, Chiswick W4 2DW. (5 mins Turnham Green tube.) *Tel:* 081-995 0733.
And at: 164 Brompton Road, SW3 1HW. (5 mins Knightsbridge tube.) *Tel:* 071-581 2271.
See also **Home Counties/South East** below.

Interior Futures 35/37 Market Place, Hampstead Garden Suburb NW11 6JG. (10 mins East Finchley tube. Park outside.) *Tel:* 081-455 9013/4. *Open:* Mon to Fri, 9.30am to 5.30pm, Sat 10.00am to 4.00pm, Sun 10.30am to 2.00pm. Newly ensconced in their own showrooms, Jenny and Colin Morris have been forever in the trade: Colin has 19 years' experience of selling/fitting/planning. Jenny has been a qualified interior designer for 16 years. Personal, caring service; they put themselves out endlessly for customers. Large, elegant, airy room settings. SieMatic/Scottwood. Bathrooms/bedrooms. Plan/design/install, including building work, and full interior design/soft furnishing service. The most elegant loo in the business . . . and free coffee!

In-toto 186 Chingford Mount Road, Chingford E4 9BS. (15 mins Walthamstow tube.) *Tel:* 081-524 1039. *Open:* Mon to Sat, 9.00am to 6.00pm. Large, double-fronted modern showroom with six room sets. Wellman specialists/working appliances. Husband-and-wife team Jaz and Sue Bhogal are real enthusiasts and delight in a kitchen challenge. KSA members.
See also **Home Counties/South East** below.

Roma Jay Designs 8 Angler's Lane, Kentish Town NW5 5AA. *Tel:* 071-267 8886. *Open:* by appointment. Roma Jay is one of the few independent kitchen designers in the business. She offers impartial, objective design services: you pay for expertise rather than "free" design with profits on units/appliances. Efficient, pleasant,

practical and enthusiastic; she could actually save you money. Her consultants travel nationwide.

JU Kitchen Consultants 160/162 Notting Hill Gate, W11 3QG. (3 mins Notting Hill Gate tube. Parking on private road at back.) *Tel:* 071-221 0257. *Open:* Mon to Sat, 9.30am to 5.30pm. The delightful owner of this well-run shop (Mrs Ushi Quansah, who has 20 years' experience) understandably gets 80 per cent of her business through recommendations. Top-quality German Miele units, plus their splendidly robust appliances. Also Camargue kitchens, made in England. Plan/design/install. KSA members.

Just Kitchens 41/43 Wigmore Street, W1H 9DF. *Tel:* 071-486 9758. *Open:* Mon to Fri, 9.00am to 6.00pm, Sat 9.30am to 5.30pm. New prestige W1 showroom for SieMatic, a chic German brand.
Also at: 242/244 Fulham Road, SW10 9NA. (5 mins South Kensington tube.) *Tel:* 071-351 1616. *Open:* Mon to Fri, 9.00am to 6.00pm, Sat 9.00am to 5.30pm. Full displays. Poggenpohl top-quality German kitchens, plus Goldreif middle-market brand. Highly individual service; one person oversees an order from start to finish. Established for 17 years. Can simply deliver furniture, or carry out a job from beginning to end, including building work.
And at: 206/208 Upper Richmond Road, SW14 8AH. *Tel:* 081-876 6106.

KDA Hometeam Watford Way, Hendon, NW4 4UJ. *Tel:* 081-203 4162. Design and manufacture own range of kitchens and bathrooms, sold direct to the public.

Kitchen World 10 Alderman's Hill, N13 4PJ. (Arnos Grove tube, plus bus.) *Tel:* 081-882 5701. *Open:* Mon to Sat, 9.30am to 5.30pm. One of the oldest-established firms in the kitchen business, trading from its present premises for 17 years. Ten kitchens on display. Poggenpohl/Cuisines Schmidt/Pronorm. Plan/design/install, plus associated building work. KSA members.

Kitchens Etcetera 62/63 High Street, Wimbledon Village SW19 5EE. (10 mins Wimbledon tube/BR.) *Tel:* 081-946 3855. *Open:* Mon to Fri, 9.00am to 5.30pm, Sat 10.00am to 12.00 noon. Poggenpohl stockists. Plan/design/install. KSA members.

Linward Interiors 135 Chiswick High Road, W4 2EA. (10 mins Turnham Green tube.) *Tel:* 081-994 1030. *Open:* Mon to Sat, 9.00am to 5.30pm. Well-established family firm; personal service. Carmague/Jubilee fitted kitchens. Appliances by AEG, Neff, Bosch, Philips, Zanussi, Hotpoint. Complete installation service: from structural alterations to decorating.

Pennybee Interiors 53/54 Wimbledon High Street, SW19 5AX. (15 mins Wimbledon tube/BR.) *Tel:* 081-947 7224/5. *Open:* Mon to Fri, 9.30am to 5.30pm. Family firm with extensive 4,500 sq ft showrooms. Attractive displays of leading British/Continental kitchens. Very personal service. Adrian Shilton handpainted finishes. Bespoke solid wooden kitchens, from South London joinery firm. Branded appliances. Plan/design/install. Complete range of interior design/furnishing services, including fitted bedrooms/bathrooms, carpets, curtains. Extensive wallpaper/fabric samples. All necessary building/fitting. Refurbishments a speciality. Extensions/conversion. Justly proud of "a complete service". KSA members.

Rooms 49 Mottingham Road, Mottingham SE9 4QZ. *Tel:* 081-857 5699. *Open:* Mon to Sat, 9.00am to 5.00pm. Tony Whitcombe founded this business 14 years ago with his wife. "We pride ourselves on personal, professional service." Good mix of French/English kitchens in wood/laminates. Plan/design/install. Friendly welcome for the smallest job. "We are as happy to supply a worktop as a whole kitchen." KSA members.
See also **Home Counties/South East** below.

Julie Royce 114 St John's Hill,

Battersea SW11 1SJ. (5 mins Clapham Junction BR.) *Tel:* 071-924 3049. *Open:* Mon to Fri, 10.00am to 6.00pm, Sat 11.30am to 3.30pm. Highly personal service from owner, who is an experienced kitchen designer/interior decorator. Also fitted kitchens. Lots of pretty back-up merchandise; unusual tiles/fabrics.

Smith and Sons   Anvil House, Matthias Road, N16 8NU. (Dalston Junction BR.) *Tel:* 071-254 1200. *Open:* Mon to Fri, 8.00am to 5.30pm, Sat 8.30am to 4.30pm. Family firm with 126 years' experience—"The Professionals' Professional". Comprehensive, upmarket builders' merchants specialising in kitchens/bathrooms. Over 17,000 items under one rambling roof. Around 10 kitchen displays, including sinks, tiles, taps. Planning/installations. Interior design. Paint, gas, plumbing departments. Personal service; prompt deliveries.

Southway Contracts   Southway House, 964 North Circular Road, NW2 7JR. (Junction M1/North Circular. Free parking.) *Tel:* 081-452 8011. *Open:* Mon to Fri, 9.00am to 5.30pm, Sat 10.00am to 4.00pm. 15 years' experience in fitted kitchens for builders/developers. Stunning retail showroom (20,000 sq ft). Upmarket European designs. Fitted kitchens, major electrical appliances, lighting, bedrooms, bathrooms, hard flooring/carpets. Poggenpohl/Goldreif/Pronorm.

Ultimate Kitchens   107 Pimlico Road, SW1W 8PH. (5 mins Sloane Square tube.) *Tel:* 071-730 7927. See also **Home Counties/South East** below.

Home Counties/ South East

AB Designs   13 Church Street, Reigate, Surrey RH2 0AA. (M25, junction 8.) *Tel:* (0737) 249247. *Open:* Mon to Sat, 10.00am to 5.00pm. German Rational/Tiffany in

solid wood. Painted styles from England. Plan/install. KSA members.

James Allen Interiors
202 Moulsham Street, Chelmsford, Essex CM2 0LG. (Old town, off Parkway. Parking at rear.) *Tel:* (0245) 252325. *Open:* Mon to Sat, 9.00am to 5.30pm. Or by appointment. Established family business, offering German, French and English kitchens/hand-painted finishes/bedrooms. Personal service, with lots of advice. Plan/design/install. KSA members.

Cheam Home Centre   17/19 High Street, Cheam, Surrey SM3 8RQ. (2 mins Cheam BR. Customer car park at rear.) *Tel:* 081-642 1788. *Open:* Mon to Sat, 9.30am to 5.30pm. 30 room displays (20 kitchens); working appliances. Wall tiles, flooring (marble, wood, cork), suspended and beamed ceilings, two brick-built home extensions. Planning, installations. KSA members.

CML Kitchens   Unit 2, Apsley Industrial Estate, Kents Avenue, Apsley, Hemel Hempstead, Herts HP3 9XH. (A41, off M25. 1 min Apsley BR, 2 mins Hemel Hempstead BR.) *Tel:* (0442) 68914. *Open:* Mon to Sat, 10.00am to 5.00pm. Kitchen/bedroom specialists with upmarket French/German displays. Plan/design/install, plus all necessary building work. KSA members.

Contour Kitchens   Sheffield House, High Street, Cookham, Berks S16 9SF. (Near Maidenhead, by River Thames.) *Tel:* (0628) 524343. *Open:* Mon to Fri, 9.00am to 6.00pm, Sat 10.00am to 5.00pm. Paul and Josephine Francis have been established 10 years. Refreshingly robust approach. "We offer bloody good service . . . based on old-fashioned honesty!" Complete refurbishments. KSA members.

Design Matters   123 Albert Street, Fleet, Hants GH13 9RP. (Own car park.) *Tel:* (0252) 628605. *Open:* Tue to Sat, 9.30am to 5.00pm, Mon by appointment. Ian Wilson is a qualified interior designer (DipAD). SieMatic/Zeyko/Scottwood. Bedrooms/bathrooms.

Designer Kitchens   37 High Street, Potters Bar, Herts EN6 5AJ. (5 mins M25, junction 24. Free parking.) *Tel:* (0707) 50565. Specialises in French laminate/wood and English handmade, fitted kitchens. Family firm, established seven years. "We undertake the whole package, stripping out the old, fitting the new, and any work along the way." KSA members.

Dorking Kitchens and Bathrooms   42a West Street, Dorking, Surrey RH4 1BU. *Tel:* (0306) 887871. *Open:* Tue to Sat, 9.00am to 5.00pm. Quintessential family business, founded 11 years ago by Tony and Jean Dixon, now with son Robert and wife Mandy, and nephew Richard just learning. "Our strongest point is service." Rationale/handpainted Solent/Chippendale. Wood/laminates. Plan/design/install, plus tiling, electrics, plumbing etc. "We'll do as much or as little as you like." KSA members.

Harmony Interiors   46/50 Wellington Street, Luton, Beds LU1 2QH. (Close to town hall.) *Tel:* (0582) 25553. *Open:* Mon to Sat, 9.00am to 6.00pm. Closed all day Wed. Personal service. A family business, trading for 11 years. International displays from Germany/France/UK. Plan/install.

Hertford Kitchens   37 Railway Street, Hertford, Herts SG14 1BG. (Town centre.) *Tel:* (0992) 553290. *Open:* Mon, 10.00am to 2.00pm, Tue to Sat, 9.00am to 5.00pm. Closed for lunch, 12.00 noon to 1.00pm. Mr and Mrs Burnham run an upmarket studio with planning/installation service, plus all necessary building work. Established for eight years. Poggenpohl/Miele/Goldreif. Plan/design/install. KSA members.

Humphersons   11/17 Fowler Road, Hainault Industrial Estate, Ilford, Essex IG6 3UU. *Tel:* 081-500 9021. *Open:* Mon to Sat, 9.00am to 5.30pm. Kitchen/bedroom/bathroom specialists. High-quality ranges, many handpainted. Leicht/Nobilia. Design/plan/install.

See also **London Postal Districts**, above.

In-toto   2 The Links Business Centre, Raynham Road, off Dunmow Road, Bishops Stortford, Herts CM23 5NZ. (Near town centre. M11, junction 8. Ample parking.) *Tel:* (0279) 757260. *Open:* Thu to Tue, 9.30am to 5.00pm. Sun viewing, 11.00am to 4.30pm. Closed Wed. Showroom with 11 full room sets, some with working appliances. Roger and Joy Cunningham offer a full design service. Supply/install. Finance available.

In-toto   38 Castle Street, Guildford, Surrey GU1 3UQ. (10 mins Guildford BR.) *Tel:* (0483) 303341. *Open:* Mon to Sat, 9.30am to 5.00pm. Showroom with 10 room sets, some with working appliances. Frank John McIsaac offers a complete service: design/supply/fit. Finance available.

In-toto   6/7 Medwin Walk, Horsham, W. Sussx RH12 1AG. (Alongside new shopping centre. Multi-storey car park.) *Tel:* (0403) 66630. *Open:* Mon to Sat, 9.30am to 5.00pm. Modern showroom displays, 11 complete kitchens. Mike Hodge and Carol Carter design/supply/ install Wellman kitchens with Philips/ Bauknecht appliances. Also full tiling service for walls/floors. Ceiling redecoration/lighting.

In-toto   10/12 The Causeway, Teddington, Middx TE11 0HE. (2 mins Teddington BR.) *Tel:* 081-943 2293. *Open:* Mon to Sat, 9.30am to 5.30pm. Double-fronted exterior. Showroom contains 10 displays, including a full working kitchen. Owners Peter and Linda Ward design, free of charge, to individual requirements. Supply/install, including tiling/floors/ceilings. KSA members.

In-toto   Unit 7, Station Industrial Estate, Oxford Road, Wokingham, Berks RG11 2YQ. (5 mins Wokingham BR. Free car park.) *Tel:* (0734) 774949. *Open:* Tue to Fri, 9.30am to 5.00pm, Sat 9.30am to 1.00pm. Modern industrial unit.

Large showroom, nine kitchen displays. Laurie and Merial McGlone design/supply full Wellmann, Philips and Bauknecht range. Installations. Finance available. KSA members.

The Kitchen Centre   The Crossings, Core's End Road, Bourne End, Bucks SL8 5AL. *Tel:* (0628) 522237. *Open:* Tue to Sat, 9.00am to 5.00pm. French and English wood/laminate kitchens. Plan/design/install, including any necessary building work. KSA members.
Also at: The High Street, Princes Risborough, Bucks HP17 0AX. *Tel:* (0844) 43681.

The Kitchen Centre   136/140 High Street, Orpington, Kent BR6 0JS. *Tel:* (0689) 836411/2. *Open:* Mon to Sat, 9.00am to 5.30pm. "Our strong point is service; we get to know all our customers, and they come back to us." Cuisines Schmidt/Stoneham. Olympus Bedrooms. Plan/design/ install, plus ceilings, floors. Granite/ Corian worktops. KSA members.

The Kitchen Company   23/7 Belmont Road, Uxbridge, Middx UB8 1QS. *Tel:* (0895) 30600/58090. *Open:* Mon to Sat, 9.00am to 5.30pm. With 20 displays, this chic shop won French top brand Arthur Bonnet's award for the best UK stockist. Design/supply/install. Plumbing/tiling/electrics. Interior design advice. Floorings. Also central heating/windows/structural alterations. KSA members.

Kitchen Concept   138/140 Upper Wickham Lane, Welling, Kent DA16 3DP. (20 mins Welling/Bexley Heath BR.) *Tel:* 081-855 1298. *Open:* Mon to Sat, 9.30am to 5.00pm. Refurbished double-fronted showroom with six displays. Established 15 years. Design/supply/ install. Can advise on colours and co-ordination. Ceilings/tiles/floors a speciality.

Kitchen Pleasure   17 Greenhill Parade, Great North Road, New Barnet, Herts EN5 1ES. (Junction Great North Road/Station Road.) *Tel:* 081-449 0614/6734. *Open:* Mon

to Sat, 9.00am to 5.30pm. Top range kitchen/fitted furniture in 700 sq ft showroom. Plan/design/install.

Kitchen Projects   65 High Street, Ascot, Berks SL5 7HP *Tel:* (0344) 24829. *Open:* Mon to Sat, 9.00am to 5.00pm. Closed all day Wed. Family-run business, trading for 16 years. Poggenpohl/Bulthaup. Also Scottwood; English, with wood/ handpainted finishes. Plan/design/ install, with associated building works. Bedrooms/bathrooms, KSA members.
Also at: 73/75 King Street, Maidenhead, Berks SL6 1DU. *Tel:* (0628) 72788. *Open:* Mon to Sat, 9.00am to 5.00pm. Closed all day Mon.
And at: 61 Bell Street, Henley-on-Thames, Oxon RG9 2BA. *Tel:* (0491) 576626. *Open:* Mon to Sat, 9.00am to 5.00pm. Closed all day Mon.

Moneyhill Interiors   1 Moneyhill Parade, Rickmansworth, Herts WD3 2BQ. (M25, junction 17.) *Tel:* (0923) 773906/771778. *Open:* Mon to Fri, 9.00am to 5.30pm, Sat 9.30am to 4.30pm. Family business/established 10 years. Around 20 kitchens on display with appliances and tiles. Poggenpohl/Neff/Miele/Gaggenau. Full-time designer with especially good plans. Complete service; supply/fit. Plumbing/ electrics/tiling/plastering. All building work. Own factory for worktops and "fancy bits". KSA members.

Newbury Kitchen Studio   9 The Broadway, Newbury, Berks RG13 1AF. (Main shopping street, by clock tower.) *Tel:* (0635) 32550. *Open:* Mon to Sat, 9.00am to 5.30pm. Established for nine years, Lynda and David Buckingham offer friendly, caring service for Poggenpohl/Scottwood/Goldreif. Design/plan/install. KSA members.

The Pantiles Kitchen Studio   62 The Pantiles, Tunbridge Wells, Kent TN2 5TN. *Tel:* (0892) 22468. *Open:* Mon to Sat, 9.30am to 5.30pm. Pat Berryman and Jackie Evans provide a friendly, personal service. Poggenpohl/Goldreif. Plan/design/

install. Also bedrooms/bathrooms. Corian worktops. Wall/floor tiling. Amtico. KSA members.

Quintessence   London Road, Knebworth, Herts SG3 6EX. (3 miles A1. Free parking.) *Tel:* (0438) 814403. Bob and Veronica Edgell enjoy a good local reputation for their personal service. Displays include working kitchens/bathrooms. Allmilmö and English handmade collection. Complete service; plan/design/install. "Kitchens, bathrooms and beyond." Plumbing/tiling/heating. KSA members.

Rooms   65 High Street, Banstead, Surrey SM7 2NL. *Tel:* (0737) 361063. *Open:* Mon to Sat, 9.00am to 5.00pm. Closed all day Wed. See also **London Postal Districts** above.

Sigma Kitchens   47b Crown Road, St Margaret's, Twickenham, Middx. (St Margaret's BR/Richmond tube, plus bus.) *Tel:* 081-892 4593/891 3181. *Open:* Mon to Fri, 10.00am to 5.30pm, Sat 10.00am to 4.00pm. Evenings by appointment. French and English quality kitchens. Plan/install.

Ulteriors   80 High Street, Teddington, Middx TW11 8JD. (5 mins Teddington BR.) *Tel:* 081-977 8287. *Open:* Mon to Fri, 9.30am to 5.30pm, Sat 10.00am to 4.30pm. Flamboyant Italian Snaidero kitchens, plus handpainted British range. Owner David Smith, trained in architecture, advises on all aspects of design.

Ultimate Kitchens   120 South Street, Dorking, Surrey RH4 2EU. (15 mins Dorking BR.) *Tel:* (0306) 881814. *Open:* Mon to Sat, 9.00am to 5.30pm. Quality German brands: Poggenpohl/Goldreif. Laminates, wood veneers, solid woods, high-gloss polyesters. Full range of appliances, sinks, taps, accessories. AEG, Gaggenau, Miele, Neff. Design/estimating by friendly, professional staff. Full installation service. KSA members.
Also at: 45 South Street, Farnham, Surrey GU9 7RE. (1 min Farnham BR.) *Tel:* (0252) 727074.
And at: 78 High Street, Esher, Surrey KT10 9QS. (10 mins Esher BR.) *Tel:* (0372) 67776.
And at: 60 London Road, Southampton, Hants SO1 2AH. *Tel:* (0703) 334281.
Head office: Tel: 081-974 2494.

See also **London Postal Districts** above.

Windmill Kitchens and Bedrooms   53 The Broadway, Joel Street, Northwood Hills, Middx HA6 1NZ. (Next to Northwood Hill tube.) *Tel:* (0923) 835561/2/3. *Open:* Mon to Fri, 9.00am to 5.30pm, Sat 9.30am to 5.00pm. 5,000 sq ft, with 22 kitchens at the last count. Margaret and John Boon, with designer Stephen Davies, have been established for 11 years. Friendly welcome; play area for children. Miele/Mobalpa/Loddenkemper. Belgian diningroom furniture. Large area for freestanding appliances. Own tilers. Make up their own worktops: Corian/Duropal. Can install beamed ceilings. All building work/replastering/decorating. "People come to us because they know we can do anything." KSA members.

21st Century Kitchens   137/139 Station Road, Edgware, Middx HA8 7JG. (Opposite Edgware tube.) *Tel:* 081-905 7122. *Open:* Mon to Sat, 9.00am to 6.00pm. New glossy SieMatic showroom, with all the latest styles/finishes from this upmarket German brand. Plan/design/install.

2. BUDGET AND REFITS

Many kitchen specialists—see **1. Specialists** (above) and **3. Wooden Kitchens** (below)—run budget "flat-pack" lines alongside pricier ranges. Check out your High Street. **DIY Superstores** have ideas galore for budget kitchens, and have bought up famous British factories/brands. For example, MFI has Hygena/Schreiber; Texas has Wrighton.

London Postal Districts

Patriarch Furniture   Stratford Workshops, Burford Road, E15 2SP. *Tel:* 081-503 0885. *Open:* by appointment. Jonathan Davidson has a small joinery workshop, making high-quality replacement kitchen

doors to order. "Virtually anything is possible." Luxury look at (relatively) low cost.

Home Counties/South East

The Replacement Door Centre   231a South Street, Romford, Essex RM1 2BE. *Tel:* (0708) 731258. Wide variety of replacement door styles for kitchens/bedrooms, including pastel/ragrolled effects.

The Replacement Kitchen Door Company   1 Hollow Cottages, London Road, Purfleet, Essex RM16 1QP. *Tel:* (0708) 865386. *Open:* by appointment. Specialists in made-to-measure doors. Choice of designs

available, also made to match existing patterns. Fretwork, glazing bars etc. no problem. Oak, pine, maple, cherry—other timbers as required. Complete kitchen refits, friendly service.

▶ Bargains!

STC Warehouse   7 Stepfield Industrial Estate, East Witham, Essex CM8 3DJ. (Witham BR 1 mile.) *Tel:* (0376) 518715. *Open:* Tue to Sat, 9.00am to 4.00pm. Sun viewing 10.00am to 3.00pm. Slightly damaged or bankrupt, ever-changing stock. Units, worktops, taps, sinks, appliances. Warehouse showroom. Bring kitchen size/plan for help with complete kitchen package.

Most dealers listed under **1. Specialists** above offer British, French or German wooden kitchens; below are firms that specialise. You will also find wooden kitchens under **5. Luxury and Bespoke Kitchens** below.

London Postal Districts

The Danish Kitchen 106 Pitshanger Lane, Ealing W5 1QX. (15 mins Ealing Broadway tube.) *Tel:* 081-998 4176. *Open:* Mon to Sat, 10.00am to 6.00pm. Husband-and-wife team. Scandinavian solid wood styles (including worktops). Also granite/Corian worktops. Showroom recently enlarged. Plan/ install. KSA members.
See also **Home Counties/South East** below.

Magnet See **DIY Superstores.** One of the UK's largest retailers of fitted kitchens. Computers plan best layouts. Rigid kitchens made to order. No self-assembly. Independent installers. No payment until you are satisfied.

Jonathan Morton Design 21 Canterbury Grove, SE27 0NT. (5 mins West Norwood BR.) *Tel:* 081-670 8984. *Open:* by appointment only. Factory showroom. Kitchens in maple, mahogany, cherry, pine or oak, or made to your ideas. Timber work tops. Plan/install.

Paula Rosa Kitchens 25/29 Fulham High Street, SW6 3JH. (5 mins Putney Bridge tube.) *Tel:* 071-384 1813. *Open:* Mon to Fri, 10.00am to 6.00pm, Sat 10.00am to 5.30pm. Attractive, spacious double-fronted showroom.
See also **Home Counties/South-East** below.

Scandinavian Kitchens 717 Fulham Road, SW6 5UL. (2 mins Parsons Green tube.) *Tel:* 071-731 0659. *Open:* Mon to Fri, 10.00am to 5.00pm. All units made-to-measure in Sweden by largest kitchen manufacturer: takes around eight weeks. Twenty different woods, combined with clean lines of Scandinavian design. High quality, functional, incorporating very latest labour-saving Swedish gadgets/appliances. Measure/design/install.

Home Counties/ South East

Alpine Kitchens 713 Harrow Road, Wembley, Middx HA0 2LL. (Sudbury Town tube. Parking at rear.) *Tel:* 081-902 0855/0232. *Open:* Mon to Fri, 8.00am to 6.00pm. Beautiful woods, keen prices. Plan/install.

Bygone Fieldside Farm, Quainton, Aylesbury, Bucks HP22 4DQ. *Tel:* (0296) 75573. *Open:* Mon to Fri, 8.30am to 5.00pm. "We're very green: we only use reclaimed timber." All English woods, at least 100 years old. Handmade into whatever the customer wants. Limed or natural oak. Natural, limed or bleached pine.

Chartwell Design Company Brook Lane (off The Street), Plaxtol, near Sevenoaks, Kent TN15 0QR. (Sevenoaks 6 miles.) *Tel:* (0732) 810285. *Open:* Mon to Fri, 9.00am to 5.00pm, Sat 10.00am to 4.00pm. Kitchen furniture in solid pine or oak; or elegant handpainted finishes. Plan/install.
Also at: Thames Corner, Thames Street, Lower Sunbury, Middx TW16 5QW. (Opposite Lower Sunbury Swimming pool.) *Tel:* (0932) 765611. *Open:* Mon to Fri, 9.00am to 5.00pm, Sat 10.00am to 4.00pm.

Country Pine (Batchelor and Sons) The Old Saw Mills, Pluckley Road, Bethersden, Ashford, Kent TN26 3DD. *Tel:* (0233) 820691. *Open:* Mon to Fri, 9.00am to 5.00pm, Sat 9.00am to 4.00pm. Custom-built kitchen furniture: "anything you want: no set style." Plan/design/install from floor to ceiling, including tiling. Seven kitchens on display.

The Danish Kitchen 4 Eton Street, Richmond, Surrey TW9 1EE. (5 mins Richmond tube.) *Tel:* 081-332 2298. See also **London Postal Districts** above.

Naturally Wood Unit 4, Twyford Road, Bishops Stortford, Herts CM23 3JL. (5 mins Bishops Stortford BR.) *Tel:* (0279) 755501. *Open:* Mon to Fri, 9.00am to 5.30pm, Sat 9.00am to 12.00 noon. Set up six years ago by Andrew McBride and Jack Brown to provide the very best in customised kitchen design/traditional cabinet-making. Now there is a team of 26 dedicated craftsmen, including experienced fitters. Antique pine, oak, limed oak, maple, ash, limed ash and pretty painted finishes. All timbers are from the Appalachian mountains of N. America. Plan/install.

Pine Partners Interiors 91 High Street, Barkway, Royston, Herts SG8 8ED. (B1268.) *Tel:* (0763) 848764. *Open:* by appointment only. Purpose-built fitted furniture for kitchens/bedrooms/bathrooms. Country Diary National Trust Shorebirds collection of limed/handpainted finishes. Period properties a speciality. Very personal service.

Renaissance Building 13 Shamrock Quay, Northam, Southampton, Hants SO1 1QL. *Tel:* (0703) 632882. *Open:* Mon to Fri, 9.00am to 6.00pm, Sat 10.00am to 5.00pm. Bespoke handmade kitchens in variety of wood/handpainted finishes.

Revived Pine Unit 3, Bedford Road, Petersfield, Hants GU32 3LJ. *Tel:* (0730) 66128. *Open:* Mon to Fri,

8.00am to 5.00pm, Sat 9.00am to 12.30pm. Complete kitchen service. Kitchens in old and new pine, ash, oak, elm.

Paula Rosa Kitchens   131/132 North Street, Brighton, E. Sussx BN1 1RG. (Below clock tower.) *Tel:* (0273) 21516. *Open:* Mon to Sat, 9.00am to 5.30pm. Traditional and contemporary designs/colours. Attractive wood finishes include Victorian limed oak. Established over 25 years. Goods are made in own workshops in Storrington. Plan/install. KSA members.
Also at: 8/9 Friary Street, Guildford, Surrey GU1 4EH. (Off High Street.) *Tel:* (0483) 502818. *Open:* Mon to Sat, 9.00am to 5.30pm.
And at: 4 Phoenix Court, Guildford, Surrey GU4 3EG. (Off High Street.) *Tel:* (0483) 31060. *Open:* Mon to Sat,

9.00am to 5.30pm.
Factory showroom and brochures: Water Lane, Storrington, W. Sussx RH20 3DS. (Water Lane Industrial Estate.) *Tel:* (0903) 743322. *Open:* Mon to Fri, 9.00am to 5.30pm, Sat 9.00am to 5.30pm, Sun 10.00am to 4.00pm.
See also **London Postal Districts** above.

Shaston   Easton Lane, Winnall Industrial Estate, Winchester, Hants SO23 7SP. *Tel:* (0962) 632332. *Open:* seven days, Mon to Sat 9.00am to 5.00pm, Sun 10.00am to 4.00pm. "We do close on Christmas day!" Complete kitchen service. Plan/design/install. Work comes mostly by recommendation. Tiling etc. Gas/electrics to approved standards. Specialise in wood: limed or antique oak, ash, acacia, pine.

Painted finishes.
Also at: 6 Hambridge Road, Newbury, Berks RG14 5SS. *Tel:* (0635) 49700.

Splinters   22 Phillips Crescent, Headley, Bordon, Hants GU35 8NU. *Tel:* (0428) 713101. *Open:* by appointment. Peter Shuff is a cabinet-maker offering any kitchen furniture to customer's specification. Variety of woods/painted finishes.

Woodgoods   Unit 40, Woolmer Industrial Estate, Bordon, Hants GU35 9AZ. (south of Farnham 8 miles. Easy access M3, M25, M27, A3.) *Tel:* (0420) 477182/3. *Open:* Mon to Fri, 9.00am to 5.00pm, Sat by appointment. Limed old pine finishes. Solid wood inside/out: no chipboard. Personal attention. Plan/install.

4. PAINTED KITCHENS

The softer, more delicate tones of painted finishes are not as hardwearing as laminates or wood, but they are very fashionable. Factory-applied lacquered finishes are readily available from both Continental and British firms, but handpainted effects are uniquely British. Many of the companies listed under **1. Specialists** and **3. Wooden Kitchens** above can offer handpainted finishes, as can their more expensive counterparts listed under **5. Luxury and Bespoke Kitchens** below.

London Postal Districts

Eden Grove Handmade Kitchens   56 Eden Grove, Islington N7 8EJ. (10 mins Holloway Road tube.) *Tel:* 071-607 6376. *Open:* by appointment. Paul Veltman heads a small team, making individual kitchens to measure at affordable prices.

Harvey Jones   94 Waterford Road, King's Road, SW6 2HA. (3 mins

Fulham Broadway tube.) *Tel:* 071-736 1908/371 3302. *Open:* Mon to Fri, 9.00am to 5.30pm, Sat 10.00am to 4.00pm. Pioneered wood/painted finishes from 1977 onwards. Personal/individual service. Competitive prices.

Hygrove Kitchens   152/154 Merton Road, Wimbledon SW19 1EH. (3 mins South Wimbledon tube. Easy parking.) *Tel:* 081-543 1200/6520. *Open:* Mon to Sat, 10.00am to 6.00pm, or by appointment. Custom-made kitchens in dragged/marbled paint finishes. Pine, medium oak, limed oak. Spacious showroom. Attention to detail. Plan/install. Colour brochure available.
See also **Home Counties/South East** below.

Peter Leer Furniture   2 Vicar's Road, NW5 4NL. *Tel:* 071–267 0211. *Open:* by appointment. Trained as an architect, and now a cabinetmaker, Peter Leer offers kitchen cabinets with classical detail, wonderfully painted by Nicholas Vivian. "He's a wizard. Flowers, stencils, murals: you name it, he can do it."

Smallbone of Devizes See **5. Luxury and Bespoke Kitchens** below.

Westow Woodcraft   21 Westow Street, Crystal Palace SE19 3RY. (10 mins Gypsy Hill BR.) *Tel:* 081-771 5713. *Open:* Mon to Sat, 9.00am to 6.00pm. Individual bespoke kitchens handpainted in clients' homes. "The way it should be."

Home Counties/ South East

Crabtree Kitchens See **5. Luxury and Bespoke Kitchens** below. Special painted finishes.

Hygrove Kitchens   9/10 Woodbridge Road, Guildford, Surrey GU1 4PU.
See also **London Postal Districts** above.

John Lewis of Hungerford See **5. Luxury and Bespoke Kitchens** below.

Naturally Wood See **3. Wooden Kitchens** above. Painted finishes for handmade kitchens.

5. LUXURY AND BESPOKE KITCHENS

This is the top end of the trade. Bespoke is a word bandied around freely in the kitchen world. Some top-notch firms make goods to order in any size or finish, but still work within the confines of "standard" (albeit very exclusive) ranges. Others (usually smaller) sit down with clients and dream up a kitchen from scratch. Bear this in mind when selecting a company from those listed below.

Many of the firms listed under **1. Specialists** above supply luxury bespoke Continental kitchens (from standard ranges). Many companies listed under **3. Wooden Kitchens** and **4. Painted Kitchens** also offer bespoke services. Paradoxically, the more you pay, the longer you often have to wait, so check delivery dates. A further paradox is the fact that unfitted kitchens are now fashionable, so we are virtually back to what might have been ripped out in the first place! Several of the firms below cater for the unfitted trend. The architectural joinery firms listed in **Walls** and **Staircases** often offer bespoke kitchen services, as do companies listed in **Furniture 12. Made-to-Measure and Commissioned**.

London Postal Districts

Brotch Designs Woodman Works, 204 Durnford Road, Wimbledon SW19 8BR. (3 mins Wimbledon Park tube.) *Tel:* 081-944 1606. *Open:* by appointment. Designer/makers of bespoke kitchens. "Infinite attention to personal detail and unique concepts", from Victorian arches to Corinthian columns.

Hayloft Woodwork See **Furniture 12. Made-to-Measure and Commissioned.** Individual bespoke kitchens from reclaimed timbers.

Howdle Bespoke Furniture Makers 9 Marylebone High Street, W1M 3PB. (5 mins Baker Street tube.) *Tel:* 071-224 6453. *Open:* Mon to Fri, 9.00am to 6.00pm, Sat 11.30am to 4.00pm. Clive Howdle (trained furniture/interior designer) and his team make fine furniture, including fitted kitchens. Materials from MDF to best hardwoods: oak/cherry/maple. Strong architectural feel, with clean, simple lines, good proportions, symmetry, columns, porticoes and pediments. Reputation for making good use of small spaces. All ancillary furniture to match. Showroom.

John Lewis of Hungerford Liberty, Regent Street, W1R 6AH. (5 mins Oxford Circus tube.) *Tel:* 071-734 1234. *Open:* Mon to Sat, 9.30 am to 6.00pm, late night Thu 7.30pm. See **Home Counties/South East** below.

Newcastle Furniture Company 128 Walham Green Court, Moore Park Road, Fulham SW6 4DG. (2 mins Fulham Broadway tube.) *Tel:* 071-386 9203. *Open:* Mon to Fri, 9.30am to 5.30pm, Sat 10.00am to 2.00pm. Fitted/freestanding kitchen furniture in non-threatened woods/painted finishes. Maple/reclaimed pine/oak. Established for over 10 years. Each kitchen is individual; special features have included spice/wine racks, bookshelves, larders . . . even a baby gate. Complete service.

Probyn Padfield 1 Spring Place, Kentish Town NW5 3BA. (5 mins Kentish Town tube.) *Tel:* 071-482 3776. *Open:* by appointment. Jack Padfield and John Probyn trained at the Architectural Association and the Royal College of Art respectively. Genuine bespoke cabinetry. "We never repeat a kitchen." Refreshingly clean/elegant modern lines to highest standards of traditional craftsmanship in hardwoods such as cherry/maple/American black walnut.

Smallbone of Devizes 105/109 Fulham Road, SW3 6RL. (5 mins South Kensington tube.) *Tel:* 071-581 9989. *Open:* Mon to Fri, 9.00am to 5.30pm, Sat 10.00am to 6.00pm. *Brochure: tel:* (0380) 728000. Behind the hyped-up image Smallbone is indeed a trendsetter: it introduced the first kitchens in old pine, then painted finishes and the "unfitted" kitchen. Expect to pay substantially. The magic name of Smallbone has been known to add to the value of a house. The vast Fulham Road showrooms are a very palace of interior design—go if you can. Newer sycamore ranges inlaid with box/walnut, with willow baskets/teak draining boards, are excellently innovatory. The handpainted, barley-twist pilaster design has a neo-classical feel. Also beautiful freestanding pieces. Full interior design/installation service. See also **Home Counties/South East** below.

Mark Wilkinson Furniture 126 Holland Park Avenue, W11 4JA. (3 mins Holland Park tube.) *Tel:* 071-727 5814. *Open:* Mon to Fri, 9.30am to 5.30pm, Sat 10.00am to 5.00pm, or by appointment. *Brochures: tel:* (0380) 850004. Mark Wilkinson (co-founder of Smallbone) is a great kitchen innovator; he designed the original country kitchen (with that much-copied fishtail frieze), the green kitchen, and the frosted oak finish. Now there is "Provence" (with waxed finishes in singing shades of pinks/green/blues), and "Santa Fe", hot from New Mexico (with punched-tin doors and sun-burst cooker hoods). Superb details. Carvings, handpainted tiles. Complete personal service: plan/design/make/install. See also **Home Counties/South East** below.

Woodstock Furniture 23 Pakenham Street, WC1X 0LB. (5 mins Russell Square tube.) *Tel:* 071-837 1818. *Open:* Mon to Fri, 9.00am to

6.00pm, Sat 10.00am to 2.00pm. "We make genuine bespoke, one-off, real furniture for the kitchen." No standard ranges—they interpret customers' ideas. Each unit is a traditionally constructed piece of furniture in its own right. No "front framing"; no concealed joints/hinges. Replenishable hardwoods: maple/cherry/oak. Own workshop in Andover. Dressers, larders, chairs, benches, stools made to order. Complete service: plan/design/make/install.
Also at: 92 Lots Road, SW10 0QD. (10 mins Fulham Broadway tube.) *Tel:* 071-837 1818/3220. *Open:* Mon to Fri, 10.00am to 5.30pm, Sat 10.00am to 2.00pm.

Home Counties/ South East

Arena   Thomas Yard, 6 Rectory Road, St Clements, Oxford, Oxon OX4 1BP. *Tel:* (0865) 726505. *Open:* Mon to Fri, 9.15am to 5.30pm, Sat 10.00am to 1.00pm. Small group of designer/craftsmen, good at problem solving. Lots of experience in redesigning kitchen/breakfast/family living areas. Handle job from start to finish: design, planning permission, building work, installation. Floors/lighting/plumbing. Brochure available.

Crabtree Kitchens   The Twickenham Centre, Norcutt Road, Twickenham, Middx TW2 6SR. (Twickenham BR/Richmond tube plus bus. Own car park.) *Tel:* 081-755 1121. *Open:* Mon to Fri, 9.00am to

5.30pm, or by appointment. Family business (established for 16 years) run by John Crabtree, his son Patrick and daughter Alex. Very personal service. Individually designed kitchens, including new range with a Shaker feel. Maple/limed oak/ash. Marbling/stippling/dragging, or any other special effects. "Programme 90" is a new, high-gloss spray finish in plain/metallic/Hammerite colours.

Grafam Woodcraft   6 Church Farm Workshops, Hatley St George, Sandy, Beds SG19 3HP. *Tel:* (0767) 51776. *Open:* by appointment. Freestanding units in traditional Victorian designs, hand-crafted from solid hardwoods. "Virtually anything to order."

Johnny Grey   Fyning Copse, Rogate, Petersfield, Hants GU31 5DH. *Tel:* (0730) 821424. *Open:* by appointment. One of Britain's premier modern furniture designers, offering "the ultimate cook's kitchen". Fresh, innovative thinking, high craftsmanship. Exclusive/personal service. Rare/unusual woods.

John Lewis of Hungerford   High Street and Park Street, Hungerford, Berks RG17 0DN. (5 mins Hungerford BR.) *Tel:* (0488) 682066. *Open:* Mon to Sat, 9.00am to 5.30pm, closed for lunch 1.00pm to 2.00pm. One of the most sympathetic kitchen designers in Britain, with ranges in solid wood/painted finishes/gleaming lacquer. Unmatched for modern interpretations of traditional styles. Country inspirations worldwide, from Ireland and the South of France to

New England. Wonderful colour-washed/rubbed finishes. Inspirational room settings, tiled floors, lots of accessories. Plan/design/install.
See also **London Postal Districts** above.

Smallbone of Devizes   21 London Road, Tunbridge Wells, Kent TN1 1DA. *Tel:* (0892) 45918.
Also at: 17 Holywell Hill, St Albans, Herts AL1 1EZ. *Tel:* (0727) 37351.
See also **London Postal Districts** above.

Whitton Wood Designs   37 Crown Road, St Margaret's, Twickenham, Middx TW1 3EJ. (5 mins St Margaret's BR.) *Tel:* 081-891 6639. *Open:* Mon to Fri, 10.00am to 6.00pm, Sat 10.00am to 5.00pm. "We genuinely custom-build." Receptive to clients' ideas in any design/style: Georgian, The 50s, medieval, futuristic, Japanese, American. All furniture made to measure in Somerset workshops. Solid wood throughout. Cherry, ash, maple, oak, pine. Staining/liming/bleaching/painting. Worktops in wood, Corian, tiles, laminates. Dressers/plate-racks. Complete service.

Mark Wilkinson Furniture 13 Holywell Hill, St Albans, Herts AL1 1EZ. *Tel:* (0727) 40975. *Open:* Mon to Fri, 9.30am to 5.30pm, Sat 10.00am to 5.00pm.
Also at: 4 High Street, Maidenhead, Berks SL6 1QJ. *Tel:* (0628) 777622. *Open:* Mon to Fri, 9.30am to 5.30pm, Sat 10.00am to 5.00pm.
See also **London Postal Districts** above.

6. WORKTOPS

Worktops that work tops . . . to smarten an old or inherited kitchen. You can buy standard lengths from **DIY Superstores.** Most kitchen companies listed under **1. Specialists** will make up worktops; those listed under **3. Wooden Kitchens** will also usually make them up in solid wood.

London Postal Districts

Crocodile   257 Archway Road, N6 5BS. (Opposite Highgate tube.) *Tel:* 081-341 6220. *Open:* Mon to Fri,

10.00am to 6.30pm. Marble/granite worktops, teamed with original Belfast sinks.

Frederick   387/9 High Road, Wood Green N22 4JA. (15 mins Wood Green tube.) *Tel:* 081-888 8164. *Open:* Mon to Fri, 8.15am to

5.00pm. Closed all day Thu. Open Sat, 9.00am to 5.00pm. Made-to-measure or cut-to-size laminated worktops. Three hundred patterns/colours. Mitring/cut-outs for sinks/hobs. Will deliver anywhere in London/N. Home Counties.

Gilway Interior Designs See **Gilway Kitchen Studios, 1. Specialists** above. Design/fit solid wooden worktops: attractive oak/beech strips with oiled finish.

Norman Glenn Kitchens See **1. Specialists** above. Corian experts.

Just Kitchens See **1. Specialists** above. Corian experts.

Marble and Granite Trading Unit 4, Bush Industrial Estate, 15/25 Standard Road, Park Royal NW10 6DF. (7 mins North Acton tube.) *Tel:* 081-453 1166. *Open:* Mon to Fri, 9.00am to 8.00pm, Sat and Sun 9.30am to 5.00pm. Forty colours of marble/granite. Worktops cut to size, with cut-outs for sinks/hobs.

Patriarch Furniture See **2. Budget and Refits** above. Make up worktops for your own tiling. Also

laminated worktops with special wood lipping.

Quality Marble See **Tiles 3. Marble, Slate and Stone.** Work/vanity tops in marble/granite, cut to size. Cut-outs for sinks/hobs. Installations.

Star Ceramics See **Tiles 1. Specialists.** Large sheets of volcanic lava, cut to size and glazed in beautiful colours in France. Superb texture.

Zarka Marble 41a Belsize Lane, NW3 5AU. (5 mins Belsize Park/Swiss Cottage tubes.) *Tel:* 071-431 3042. *Open:* by appointment. Marble/granite worktops: samples in showroom. Also vanity tops, marble floor/walls etc. Supply/fix.

Home Counties/ South East

G E C Anderson See **7. Sinks** below. Stainless-steel worktops with integrated sinks.

Corian CD (UK) Whitehall Buildings, Whitehall Road, Leeds LS12 1BG. *Tel:* (0532) 439651 (for

local stockists/installers). Thick, solid, luxurious worktops that look like marble/granite. Made from natural minerals combined with acrylics. Sinks can be moulded-in for a one-piece, seamless finish. Highly resistant to staining/damage. Very hygienic. Non-porous.

Windmill Kitchens and Bedrooms See **1. Specialists** above. Corian experts.

▶ Mail Order

Kirkstone Skelwith Bridge, near Ambleside, Cumbria LA22 9NN. *Tel:* (0539) 433296. Nationwide deliveries. Cut-to-size worktops in beautiful green volcanic stone, found only in the Lake District and quarried since Roman times.

Viceroy Products Viceroy Works, Lowfields Road, Leeds, W. Yorks LS12 6BS. *Tel:* (0532) 441525. Nationwide deliveries. Small factory making worktops to measure in oak/ash/beech/maple. "Any length, any width, any shape." Built-in draining boards. Hand-finished with special oil; resists water and most chemicals.

---

7. SINKS

London Postal Districts

"... that kitchen-sink-revolutionary look that one cannot get unless one has been to a really good school."

Dame Rebecca West (1892–1983) of Shirley Williams in an interview with Jilly Cooper in *The Sunday Times*.

Whose turn is it to do the washing-up? Usually yours. Sinks in more common materials—the ubiquitous stainless steel, and the newer moulded resins—are easily found at home improvement specialists and **DIY superstores**. Larger sizes and more unusual materials are available from the specialists below. You may have to order by post to get exactly what you want. These companies offer nationwide deliveries. Try **Architectural salvage** merchants for genuine old sinks.

Aston Matthews See **Bathrooms 2. Sanitaryware.** Sink specialists with large stocks. Top-quality stainless steel. Plenty of large sizes. Enamelled cast iron. Wide choice of ceramic butlers' sinks, including waste disposal models.

Elon Tiles See **Tiles 1. Specialists.** Robust Kohler American cast-iron sinks in white/almond. Very deep, very resilient. Wide range of styles/sizes.

Home Counties/ South East

Drummond's of Bramley See **Architectural Salvage.** Original butlers'/Belfast/stoneware sinks.

Mail order

G E C Anderson 89 Herkomer Road, Bushey, Watford, Herts WD2 3LS. *Tel:* 081-950 1826. *Open:* by appointment only. Stainless-steel sinks/worktops made to measure. Any size/shape "quickly at sensible cost". Cut-outs for hobs/quick discs.

Bowls available separately, with flat flanges for mounting under granite/marble. Nationwide deliveries. Also stainless-steel shelves/drawers/cupboards for that fashionable, high-tech look.

Architectural Wall and Floor The Basement, Marsh House Mill, Marsh House Lane, Darwen, Lancs BB3 3JJ. *Tel*: (0254) 873994. *Open*: by appointment. Sanitaryware handmade by local craftsmen using 100-year-old methods. Belfast sinks/combination sinks/gamekeepers/French farmhouse/cleaners' sinks/waste-disposal Belfast. Fire-clay drainers, plus co-

ordinated taps/wastes. Nationwide deliveries.

Brass Traditional Sinks Devauden Green, near Chepstow, Gwent NP6 6PL. *Tel*: (02915) 738. Colour brochures. Old-fashioned, capacious and robust rectangular Belfast ceramic sinks. Also rectangular/round solid brass sinks. Nationwide deliveries.

David Emerson King's Close, Yapton, Arundel, W. Sussx, BN18 0EX. *Tel*: (0243) 552966 (24 hours). Made-to-measure worktops (take seven days) with optional fitting service. Duropal laminates, 56

colours/textures, exceptionally hard-wearing. Cut-outs for sinks, hobs etc. Colour brochure. Nationwide deliveries.

Farmhouse Sinks Inverfolla, Appin, Argyll PA38 4BQ. *Tel*: (0631) 73520. White French fire-clay. Robust/practical. Wide range of sizes/shapes. Nationwide deliveries.

Housekeeper Worktops Dryden House, Market Place, Hawes, N. Yorks DL8 3RA. *Tel*: (0969) 667111. Traditional wooden drainers/open bases for butler/Belfast sinks. For standard units, or to stand alone.

---

8. APPLIANCES

"The best wartime wedding presents were judged to be "a portable wireless or gramophone, a portable Electrolux refrigerator that works on oil, electricity or gas . . . a petrol coupon . . . honey in the comb . . . homemade jam."

Vogue magazine, summer 1941

Buy appliances from kitchen specialists as a package deal, or shop for bargains.

London Postal Districts

▶ Bargains!

All Gas 22 Lacy Road, Putney SW15 1NL. (5 mins Putney BR; Putney Bridge tube.) *Tel*: 081-785 7126. *Open*: Mon to Fri, 9.00am to 5.00pm, Sat 9.00am to 12.00 noon. New merchandise. Major brands. Discounts: 10 to 40%. Appliances (including cookers, boilers, fires) not in stock usually take 24 hours, maximum four days.

▶ Bargains!

Appliances Direct 5/6 Burlington Parade, Edgware Road NW2 6QQ. (Kilburn tube, plus bus.) *Tel*: 081-208 2672. *Open*: Mon to Fri, 10.00am to 6.00pm, Sat 10.00am to 5.00pm. New cookers, fridges, dishwashers etc. Discounts up to 15%. Philips, Neff, Westinghouse, AEG. Philips machines ex-exhibition: up to 40% off. New kitchens: plan/install.

▶ Bargains!

Buyers and Sellers 120/122 Ladbroke Grove W10 5NE. (Opposite Ladbroke Grove tube.) *Tel*: 081-229 1947/8468. *Open*: Mon to Sat, 9.00am to 5.00pm. Early closing Thu, 9.15am to 2.30pm. Cynthia Coyne, wheeler-dealer par excellence, has constant supplies of not-quite-perfect (tiny blemish) or end-of-line fridges, freezers, microwaves, ovens, hobs, washing machines etc. All brand new, guaranteed. All major brands: Electrolux/Zanussi/Philips/Ariston. Discounts up to 20%. Armchair shopping: Cynthia and partner David Nunes happily give advice/take orders over the 'phone.

▶ Bargains!

City Domestic Appliances 131 Essex Road, N1 2SN. (2 mins Essex Road BR.) *Tel*: 071-837 6668. *Open*: Mon to Fri, 9.00am to 5.30pm. Closed all day Thu. Open Sat, 9.00am to 4.30pm. Hoover near-perfect machines; full guarantee. Average 20% off. Also re-conditioned machines.

▶ Bargains!

Hot and Cold Inc 13 Golborne Road, Notting Hill W10 5NY. (5 mins Westbourne Park tube.) *Tel*: 081-960 1300. *Open*: Mon to Sat, 10.00am to 6.00pm. Very British, despite name. Smallish, rather scruffy, jam-packed shop. Owner Richard Fuchs tirelessly controls hundreds of appliances on display. Ninety brands—all discounted. Many bargains always in stock. Speciality: posh built-ins; Miele, Scholtes, Neff, Gaggenau, Bosch etc. New perfect superseded models from half-price.

▶ Bargains!

Icetech Appliances 1/3 Baron's Court Road, West Kensington W14

9DP. (Opposite West Kensington tube.) *Tel:* 071-381 2303/3119. *Open:* Mon to Fri, 9.30am to 6.00pm, Sat 9.30am to 5.00pm. Early closing Thu 1.00pm. All makes freestanding/ built-in appliances from budget through to top range. 1,000 lines in stock, including sinks, taps, waste disposers. Very competitive prices. Bosch appliances with slight "cosmetic" faults (eg small chip or scratch).

▶ Bargains!

JD Domestic Appliances   988/994 Harrow Road, Kensal Green NW10 5NT. (3 mins Kensal Green tube.) *Tel:* 081-968 8722. *Open:* Mon to Sat, 9.00am to 6.00pm. Reconditioned fridges, cookers, washing machines. Servicing/repairs. *Also at:* 56 Northfield Avenue, Ealing W13 6RR. (3 mins Northfields tube.) *Tel:* 081-566 3973. *Open:* Mon to Sat, 9.00am to 6.00pm.

JS Humidifiers   Dufton Industrial Centre, 238 Green Lane, SE9 3TL. (M25, junction 3.) *Tel:* 081-851 7521. *Open:* Mon to Fri, 8.30am to 5.30pm (showroom). Humidifiers to combat dry air. De-humidifiers to fight condensation. Also air purifiers/air conditioners. High-quality/low-cost water softeners.

Home Counties/ South East

▶ Bargains!

G D Evans   331/333 High Street, Slough, Berks SL1 1TX. (London side of Slough, near large Co-Op.) *Tel:* (0753) 24188/35138. *Open:* Mon to Sat, 9.00am to 5.30pm. Sun viewing 10.00am to 1.00pm. Ex-exhibition/ display/built-in/freestanding ovens, hobs, cookers, washing machines, fridges, freezers, all colours. Handsome discounts. Over 2,000 appliances in stock. Mainly Neff/ AEG/Siemens. Friendly service from family firm: trading since 1956. Phone for current offers. Nationwide deliveries.

Lawrence Kitchens   Unit C, Progress Road, Sands Industrial Estate, Lane End Road, High Wycombe, Bucks HP12 4JD. (M40 junction 4.) *Tel:* (0494) 443474. *Open:* Mon to Sat, 8.30am to 5.30pm. Built-in appliances/sinks at trade prices. Top brands, all models obtainable. Also self-assembly kitchens by Crosby, Kingswood, Symphony.

RDO Kitchens and Appliances
Bancroft Road, Reigate, Surrey RH2 7RP. (M25 junction 8. Town centre, own car park.) *Tel:* (0737) 240403. *Open:* Mon to Fri, 9.00am to 5.30pm, Sat 9.00am to 1.00pm. Trading over 30 years. Enormous comprehensive stocks of AEG, Neff, Gaggenau, De Dietrich. Even manufacturers come here when stuck for a particular model! Supply 50% trade, 50% public. Nationwide deliveries within three days.

Ruislip Appliances   116 Pembroke Road, Ruislip Manor, Middx HA4 8HW. (2 mins Ruislip Manor tube. Opposite Windmill Pub.) *Tel:* (0895) 633837. *Open:* Mon to Sat, 9.00am to 5.30pm. Early closing Wed 1.00pm. Most models Neff/De Dietrich in stock. Servicing.

Stellison Kitchen Centre   11/13 Kent's Hill Road, Benfleet, Essex SS7 5PN. (10 mins Benfleet BR. Own car park.) *Tel:* (0268) 793729/758820. *Open:* Mon to Sat, 9.00am to 6.00pm. Around 20 kitchen displays from France, Holland, and Britain. Built-in branded appliances at, they claim, unbeatable prices.

---

9. KITCHENWARE

"The way to a man's heart is through his stomach."

Fanny Fern, US writer (1811–72)

People are as different in the kitchen as anywhere else. Some burn pans so often that all they need are cheap and cheerful replenishable sources— see **Bargains!** below. Others aspire to a serious and long-cherished *batterie de cuisine*. It's fun taking time to browse round specialist cookware suppliers; the equipment can provide fresh culinary inspiration.

London Postal Districts

Bodum   24 Neal Street, WC2H 9PS. (5 mins Covent Garden tube.) *Tel:* 071-240 9176. *Open:* Mon to Sat, 10.00am to 6.00pm. "My idea is that good design should not be expensive," says Dane Jorgen Bodum, founder/director of this delightful shop. To which I would also add "fun". Designs have become classics. Glass/plastics/ metal combine in witty and useful coffee-makers, teapots and other cookware. The range is growing. Mail order catalogue available. *Also at:* Whiteley's, Bayswater W2. *Tel:* 071-792 1213. *Open:* Mon to Sat, 10.00am to 7.00pm.

Cookware and Cane   251 Upper Richmond Road West, East Sheen SW14 8QS. (10 mins Mortlake BR.) *Tel:* 081-878 8950. *Open:* 7 days, Mon to Fri 9.30am to 5.30pm, Sat 9.30am to 6.00pm, Sun 10.30am to 4.30pm. Cookware/glass/china/ earthenware. Cane chairs/shelves/ small tables.

Elizabeth David 3 North Row, The Market, Covent Garden WC2E 8RA. (3 mins Covent Garden tube.) *Tel:* 071-836 9167. *Open:* Mon to Wed, 10.00am to 6.00pm, Thu to Sat, 10.00am to 8.00pm, Sun 12.30pm to 5.00pm. Lives up to its famous name. Definitive source for the complete cook. Porcelain, earthenware, copper, stainless steel, aluminium, woodware, basketware. Knives, pans, utensils, gadgets. Specialised equipment. Personal service, friendly advice. Cake tin hire.

▶ Bargains!

Discount House 148 Kilburn High Road, NW6 4JD. (5 mins Kilburn/Kilburn Park tubes.) *Tel:* 071-328 4306. *Open:* Mon to Thu, 9.00am to 5.30pm, Fri and Sat 9.00am to 6.00pm. Happy hunting-ground for bargain kitchen/tableware.

Divertimenti 139/141 Fulham Road, SW3 6SD. (5 mins South Kensington tube.) *Tel:* 071-581 8065. *Open:* Mon to Fri, 9.30am to 6.00pm, Sat 10.00am to 6.00pm. Vibrant and colourful where **David Mellor** (see below) is restrained and elegant. London's kitchens are the richer for them both. Specialist cookware makes even advanced cooking seem easy. The very best for everyday tasks. Luscious tableware in shiny, plain glazes/hand-decorated patterns. Also cookbooks/herbs and spices. Beguiling and beautiful: batten down your wallet. Crockery brochure, £1. Mail order brochure, £2.50.
Also at: 45/47 Wigmore Street, W1H 9LE. (8 mins Bond Street tube.) *Tel:* 071-935 0689. *Open:* Mon to Fri, 9.30am to 6.00pm, Sat 10.00am to 5.30pm. Original, smaller branch: very jolly. Knife-sharpening, plus service for relining copper pans.

The French Kitchen and Tableware Supply Co 42/44a Westbourne Grove, W2 5SH. (Notting Hill Gate tube.) *Tel:* 071-221 2112. *Open:* Mon to Fri, 9.00am to 5.30pm, Sat 10.00am to 5.00pm. French cooking is alive and well and living in London. Professional kitchenware

from the finest names in Europe, for the seriously serious cook.

Leon Jaeggi and Sons 231 Tottenham Court Road, W1P 0BL. (3 mins Goodge Street tube.) *Tel:* 071-631 1080/580 1957. *Open:* Mon to Sat, 9.30am to 5.30pm (both branches). Caters for caterers, but individual shoppers welcome. Stacks of burnished copper, made by Jaeggi and Sons in Staines, stand beacon-like in the window. Most pans are lined with tin (retinning service available). But for very high temperatures (crêpes, omelettes) linings are silver. Also own-make black iron omelette/frying pans. Season on first use: sprinkle with salt, and heat gently for half an hour. Wipe out with kitchen paper. Rub over with cooking oil and more salt; heat again. Wipe out; thenceforth do not wash. Suits me!
Also at: 124 Shaftesbury Avenue, W1V 7DJ. (3 mins Leicester Square tube.) *Tel:* 071-434 4545.

Kerry's Kitchen Shop 119 King Street, Hammersmith W6 9JG. (5 mins Hammersmith tube.) *Tel:* 071-748 5946. *Open:* Mon to Sat, 9.15am to 5.30pm. Christopher Beresford keeps this supermarket-style shop strictly down-to-earth. Here there are lots of good ideas: brushes for teapot spouts/bottles; packs of dishcloths; kettle defurrers; vegetable parers. Crockery/glass is sold individually, with stocks for replacements. Sensible pans ("no over-floral sets"): stainless steel, aluminium, non-stick.

Peter Knight Cookshop 156 Walton Road, East Molesey, Surrey KT8 0HP. (10/15 mins Hampton Court BR.) *Tel:* 081-979 8371. *Open:* Mon to Sat, 9.30am to 5.30pm. Caters amply for the imaginative cook.

La Cuisinière 299 New King's Road, SW6 4RE. (5 mins Parsons Green tube.) *Tel:* 071-736 3696. *Open:* Mon to Sat, 9.30am to 6.00pm (both branches). Annie Price, a trained chef, says her shops are a "cook's paradise". Everything you could want is here, both functional and inspirational. Exclusive,

inexpensive Portuguese china in five bright designs. Baskets/picnicware. Wedding lists. Gift-wrapping/vouchers. Books. Hire of cake tins/fish kettles etc.
Also at: 81/83 Northcote Road, SW11 6PJ. (10 mins Clapham Junction BR. 49 bus stops outside.) *Tel:* 071-223 4487.

David Mellor 4 Sloane Square, SW1W 8EE. (3 mins Sloane Square tube.) *Tel:* 071-730 4259. *Open:* Mon to Sat, 9.30am to 5.30pm. Established 1969. One of London's first "designer" shops. Mellor is internationally famous for cutlery (see full displays of his modern classics). English crafts—baskets/ceramics/woodware—soften the effect of gleaming metal pans/knives. A high degree of excellence. Mail order catalogue, £1.50p.
Also at: 24 Shad Thames, Butler's Wharf SE1 2YD. (10 mins Tower Hill tube. Park outside.) *Tel:* 071-407 7593. *Open:* Tue to Sat, 10.30am to 6.00pm, Sun 11.30am to 5.30pm. Here, appropriately adjacent to The Design Museum, saucepans become art, aligned in elegant racks in a prestigious new building by Michael Hopkins. The best in European pots/pans, with copper from Birmingham. New, young English potters/woodturners/basket-makers. Superb English/Scottish studio glass. Fresh showing for classic artefacts: 1930s Finnish glass by Alvar Aalto; 1930s German porcelain; and Scandinavian pottery from the 1950s/60s. An essential pilgrimage for design purists.

Home Counties/South East

▶ Bargains!

Spoils Unit 22, Liberty II Shopping Centre, Mercury Gardens, Romford, Essex. (Town centre or Sainsbury's car parks.) *Tel:* (0708) 751413. *Open:* Mon to Sat, 9.00am to 5.30pm. Thriving 13-year-old chain:

21 stores nationwide. Commendable aim—"firsts" quality at "seconds" prices. Ideal for setting up home. Practical kitchenware and good basics. Pretty china/cutlery/glass. Woodware/baskets. Cane furniture. Gifts. Varied stock/excellent prices. *Also at:* 323/324 Chequers Centre, Duke's Walk, Maidstone, Kent ME15 6AR. (Town centre car park.) *Tel:* (0622) 678916. *Open:* Mon to Sat, 9.00am to 5.30pm.
And at: 145 High Street, Southend, Essex SS1 1LL. (5 mins Southend BR. Car park at rear.) *Tel:* (0702) 352733. *Open:* Mon to Sat, 9.00am to 5.30pm.

And at: Unit 54b, Eastgate Centre, Basildon, Essex SS14 1AE. (Next to bus terminal. Multi-storey car park.) *Tel:* (0268) 520827. *Open:* Mon 10.00am to 6.00pm, Tue to Fri 9.30am to 6.00pm, Sat 9.00am to 6.00pm.
And at: Unit 4, Corn Exchange, High Street, Bishops Stortford, Herts. (5 mins multi-storey car park.) *Tel:* (0279) 652210. *Open:* Mon to Sat, 9.00am to 5.30pm.
And at: 253/254 Lakeside Shopping Centre, West Thurrock, Grays, Essex RM16 1ZQ. (Free parking for 9,000 cars.) *Tel:* (0708) 890298. *Open:* Mon to Sat, 9.00am to 9.00pm.

And at: Store D, Marlowe's Centre, Hemel Hempstead, Herts. (1,200 space car park.) *Tel:* (0442) 235018. *Open:* Mon to Sat, 9.00am to 6.00pm. Late night Thu, 8.00pm.

Mrs Sykes Kitchenry   146 High Street, Teddington, Middx TW11 8HZ. (Teddington BR.) *Tel:* 081-943 2951. *Open:* Mon to Sat, 9.30am to 5.30pm. Well-designed kitchenware, keen prices: casseroles, Sabatier knives, glass, earthenware, tinware. Rental service for cake moulds/fish kettles. Interesting basketware. Extensive gifts/cards. Small shop: friendly, knowledgeable service.

10. ACCESSORIES

There is a lot you can do to make an ugly or inefficient kitchen prettier and more functional. Keep your eyes open for traditional ware in markets and junk shops. Old utensils/pans are rapidly becoming antiques. The shops listed in **9. Kitchenware** are packed with accessories (the dividing line between sections is blurred).

London Postal Districts

The Conran Shop See **Furniture 1. General.**   Particularly strong in imaginative cook/kitchenware.

Ikea See **Furniture 1. General.** Extremely good selections of well-designed, inexpensive kitchenware. Wood/metal/ceramics. Well worth a browse.

John Lewis of Hungerford See **5. Luxury and Bespoke Kitchens** above. Enchanting country style accessory range. Shelves, small cupboards,

pegs, plate racks, knife box etc. Six finishes: distressed pine, rubbed cream, cornflower blue, Provencal ochre, New England slate blue, and burgundy.

The Newcastle Furniture Company See **5. Luxury and Bespoke Kitchens** above. Attractive, freestanding food preparation trolleys.

Woodstock Furniture See **5. Luxury and Bespoke Kitchens** above.   Excellent trolleys, tables and workstations.

Home Counties/ South East

Grafam Woodcraft See **5. Luxury and Bespoke Kitchens** above.   Excellent freestanding food preparation trolleys, with lockable castors.

Mail Order

Domestic Paraphernalia   C/o Unit 15, Marine Business Centre, Dock Road, Lytham, Lancs FY8 5AJ. *Tel:* (0253) 736334. Traditional "up-and-down" ceiling pulley clothes-airer: cast-iron ends/wooden slats.

Lakeland Plastics   Alexandra Buildings, Windermere, Cumbria LA23 1BQ. *Tel:* (05394) 88100. Free catalogue. 101 bright ideas for the kitchen/home. Gadgets don't come any cleverer. Personal callers welcome at the Windermere Shop. *Open:* Mon to Fri, 8.00am to 6.00pm, Sat 9.00am to 5.00pm. Open bank holidays. Closed Sun. The Miller Howe Café (run by TV personality/chef John Tovey) has an adventurous and affordable menu. Worth a trip.

Rackmaster   43 Russell Street, Wilton, Salisbury, Wilts SP2 0BG. *Tel:* (0722) 744143. Leaflet available. Attractive plain design for plate racks with solid beech frames/birch dowels. For drainage or storage. Oiled finish.

Woodfit Kem Mill, Whittle-le-Woods, Chorley, Lancs PR6 7EA. *Tel*: (02572) 66421 (24 hours). Invaluable catalogue of professional kitchen/bedroom fittings to transform DIY/budget cupboards into streamlined storage/workstations.

The York Handmade Brick Co See **Tiles 2. Terracotta and Quarries**. York clay stacking wine racks keep wine at even temperature/right angles. Excludes damaging ultra violet light. Comes in two-bottle units. Natural terracotta colours.

3
BATHROOMS

Bathrooms caught the home improvement fever relatively recently, breaking out in a rash of fancy basins, whirlpools, gold taps, and pulsating showers. A heady mix. Stay cool and plan carefully. Harnessing water power for your home needs more than casual investigation.

1. SPECIALISTS

"Lying there in those strong arms of yours, slumbering in the hardened muscles, resting in the well-trained fingers and educated hands, lies the health of this leviathan city."

Attributed to Stevens Hellyer, Victorian plumbing pioneer.

Some bathroom specialists take over the whole job, including installations. Others will help you to plan, but will then pull out the plug. Usually, however, they can recommend plumbers. So decide at the outset the level of service you require, and shop accordingly. Many kitchen specialists now offer fitted bathrooms, so it's worth also skimming through the **Kitchens** section.

London Postal Districts

Absolute at Arnull of London 13/14 Queen Street, W1X 7PL. (5 mins Green Park tube.) *Tel:* 071-499 3231. *Open:* 9.30am to 5.30pm, Sat 11.00am to 2.00pm. Prestigious Mayfair showroom with chic interior; cool, elegant, sharply modern. Family firm trading for over 20 years. The manager is the founder's daughter, Sandy Arnull. Flagship (after extensive refurbishment) for Ideal-Standard's upmarket "Absolute" international bathroom concept. Two floors of bathrooms, with 17 luxurious settings. Working whirlpools/ showers. In-house interior design service. Tiles/fabrics/floor coverings/lighting. Installations. Very special—worth seeing when you're in the West End.

Aquatarian Bathrooms 17 Norwood Road, Herne Hill SE24 9AA. (Herne Hill BR.) *Tel:* 081-671 9222. *Open:* Mon to Fri, 9.00am to 5.30pm, Sat 9.30am to 5.30pm. Small studio/individual service. Purpose-built fitted bathrooms. Installations by own team of plumbers,

carpenters, tilers and painters. Marble bathrooms/period styles a speciality.

B J Brown See **Kitchens 1. Specialists**. One of biggest Ideal-Standard "Solutions" stockists. Super showrooms. A friendly welcome awaits you from David and Victor Bloom; these affable brothers are trained architects. Shirley Bloom helps with colour schemes. Super room settings. Steam enclosures/ whirlpools. Expert planning; can recommend plumbers. Worth knowing about.

Colourwash 65 Fulham High Street, SW6 3JJ. (5 mins Putney Bridge tube.) *Tel:* 071-371 0911. *Open:* Mon to Fri, 9.00am to 5.30pm, Sat 10.00am to 5.00pm, or by appointment. Owners Jane Gilchrist and Teeny Hickman provide a friendly, sympathetic service. "Every style from minimal modernism to turn-of-the-century pomp." Planning/full interior design. Lots of pretty accessories.

Durante Jacuzzi, Bath and Whirlpool Centre 255/259 Queenstown Road, SW8 3NP. (Opposite Queenstown Road BR. 137 bus from Sloane Square. Own car park.) *Tel:* 071-498 6800. *Open:* Mon to Fri, 9.30am to 5.30pm, Sat 10.00am to 1.00pm. Paula and Aubrey Durante used to be in posh Sloane Street, where they initiated the British public into the bathing rites of Jacuzzi whirlpools, first introduced from America in the 1960s. The new, 8,000 sq ft showrooms have more space in this underneath-the-arches converted warehouse. Fabulous room settings: Art Deco/ Victorian/modern. Full Jacuzzi range (23 models). Pulsating showers, Jacuzzi whirlpools and steam enclosures all on view. Personal, friendly service. Full interior design/soft furnishings service. Professional installations, including "qualified, caring carpenters".

Exclusive Bathrooms 303 Camberwell New Road, SE5 0TF. (8 mins Oval tube.) *Tel:* 071-708 0260. *Open:* Mon to Sat, 9.00am to 5.30pm. Speciality is extra large baths/whirlpools, in 40 shapes and unique finishes (such as mother-of-pearl and marble), made in the shop's own Yorkshire factory. Working Jacuzzi/spa systems—try them out. Any colour is matched, to order. 7,000 sq ft of showrooms, with around 70 displays. Sanitaryware from all main makes mostly in stock. Power/pressure showers/steam cabinets. Exclusive marble/granite/ceramic tiles. Vanity tops made-to-measure. Design service.

Godwins 28 Rushgrove Avenue, The Hyde, Colindale NW9 6QS. (10 mins Colindale tube.) *Tel:* 081-200 0508. *Open:* Mon to Fri, 8.00am to 5.00pm, Sat 9.00am to 4.00pm (all branches). David Godwin is a real bathroom fanatic, continually seeking new products. This address is one of the largest bathroom showrooms in NW London, with 80 settings and all the latest traditional designs. Wide selection of cast-iron baths/Jacuzzi whirlpools. Latest taps in brass/gold/chrome, including elegant waterfall model. Upmarket imports. Phone for colour brochures. Planning/specialist advice.
Also at: 49 Church Road, Hendon NW4 4DU. (Hendon Central tube. Restricted parking.) *Tel:* 081-203 1095. Specialist showroom for pumped showers, Jacuzzi whirlpools, upmarket taps. Expert technical advice.
And at: 176 High Road, East Finchley N2 9AS. (5 mins East Finchley tube. Restricted parking.) *Tel:* 081-444 2311. Large ranges, well displayed; specialist staff to advise on plumbing problems.
And at: 103 Lancaster Road, Ladbroke Grove W11 1QQ. (2 mins Ladbroke Grove tube.) *Tel:* 071-792 8091. Newest showroom: Godwin's central London showcase for all top

Continental makes. Large selections of cast-iron baths/showers/whirlpool baths.

C P Hart See **Kitchens 1. Specialists.** Extensive displays of latest fashions/technology. Exclusive merchandise/good stocks/free deliveries. Working whirlpools/taps/showers. Recommended trusty plumbers. Glossy brochure available. Definitely worth a visit. *Also at*: 103/105 Regent's Park Road, NW1 8UR. (Chalk Farm tube.) *Tel*: 071-586 9856. *Open*: Mon to Sat, 10.00am to 6.00pm. New designer showroom: three floors of the best bathroom products. Planning advice. Free delivery.

The London Bath and Tile Centre 20 Moxon Street, W1M 3JB. (7 mins Baker Street tube. NCP opposite.) *Tel*: 071-935 6590. *Open*: Mon to Fri, 8.30am to 5.30pm. Exclusively Twyford's stockist. Space galore on London's most fascinating site: a rescued, revamped subterranean air-raid shelter. Delightful room settings. Working Caradon Mira showers. Bathroom interior design: planning/colour schemes/ floorings/lighting. Exclusive Collexion accessories. Installations/renovations.

The Marble Bathroom 66 Mountgrove Road, N5 2LT. (10 mins Finsbury Park tube.) *Tel*: 071-354 1554. *Open*: Tue to Thu, 10.00am to 4.00pm, Sat 10.00am to 3.00pm. Imported baths sculpted from solid marble. Colours from white/cream to grey, with marked veining. Also basins/bidets/loos.

The David Neale Bathroom Centre 67/71 Abbey Road, St John's Wood NW8 0BU. (10 mins Swiss Cottage/St John's Wood tubes.) *Tel*: 071-624 8126. *Open*: Mon to Fri, 8.00am to 5.00pm, Sat 9.00am to 1.00pm. Top brand name bathroom displays, including whirlpools.

Max Pike Bathrooms 4 Eccleston Street, SW1W 9LN. (2 mins Victoria tube/BR.) *Tel*: 071-730 7216. *Open*: Mon to Fri, 10.00am to 6.00pm. Max Pike is a celebrity in the bathroom world. Bathrooms are his life; the

man himself glowers from the ads. The showroom reflects his dedicated, innovative approach and uncompromising commitment to the very best. (Prices accordingly.) Pressured massage shower. Hydromassage systems. Single/double baths. Spout/waterfall taps. Steam baths. "Environmental machines" to take you into another climate. Murals. Marble. Technical planning. Product design. Layout/colour schemes. Free deliveries in London area.

Pipe Dreams 72 Gloucester Road, SW7 4QT. (5 mins Gloucester Road tube.) *Tel*: 071-225 3978. *Open*: Mon to Fri, 9.30am to 5.30pm, Sat 10.00am to 5.00pm. Evening appointments by request. Owner/manager Robert Browne provides individual planning/design advice. Stylish room settings: Biedermeier, cottage, Victorian. Plus stark white steam room. Handmade, handpainted cloakroom basins. Tile murals, made-to-measure vanity units, cupboards, bath panelling. Marbles/granites. Installations/full interior design.

Southway Contracts See **Kitchens 1. Specialists.** Original Bathrooms provide stunning Italian displays.

West One Bathrooms 46 South Audley Street, Mayfair W1Y 5DG. (10 mins Bond Street/Marble Arch tubes. Car park behind shop.) *Tel*: 071-499 1845. *Open*: Mon to Fri, 9.30am to 7.00pm, Sat 9.30am to 4.00pm. Extraordinary, exclusive, extravagant, and expensive! Imported suites/accessories from Germany, Italy, Spain, USA. Planning service.

Home Counties/ South East

Atlantis Bathrooms and Kitchens 69/71 Bower Street, Bedford, Beds MK40 3RB. (Park outside.) *Tel*: (0234) 214113. *Open*: Mon to Sat,

9.00am to 5.30pm, Sat 9.00am to 5.00pm. Seventeen bathroom settings. Ideal-Standard "Solutions" stockist. Working whirlpools/airbaths/power showers. Design/install.

The Bath House 25 High Street, Purley, Surrey. (2 mins Purley BR.) *Tel*: 081-668 0600. *Open*: Mon to Sat, 9.00am to 5.30pm. Extensive showrooms with traditional/modern bathrooms. Showers/tiles/accessories. Knowledgeable staff. Large selections of whirlpool baths. Pumped shower specialists. Design/plan/install. *Also at*: 145 High Street, Epsom, Surrey. *Tel*: (0372) 742748.

The Bathroom Centre 1 Hotspur Top Lane, Beaconsfield, Bucks. (A40. Parking outside.) *Tel*: (0494) 675665. *Open*: Mon to Fri, 9.00am to 5.00pm, Sat 9.00am to 2.00pm. Ideal-Standard Solutions Design Centre. Smart displays of modern and traditional bathrooms by Ideal-Standard/Sottini. Working showers/ whirlpools. Showerlux/Nordic. Design/build/install. *Also at*: 10/12 Station Road, Gerrards Cross, Bucks. (Parking nearby.) *Tel*: (0753) 888888. *Open*: Tue to Sat, 9.00am to 5.00pm. This is an upmarket showroom, with Burg built-in furniture and Sally Anderson exclusive tiles.

The Bathroom Centre 194/196 High Road, Woodford Green, Essex IG8 9EF. (15 mins South Woodford tube.) *Tel*: 081-504 1765. *Open*: Mon to Sat, 9.00am to 6.00pm. Thirty room settings over three floors; exclusive ranges; all leading European makes. Plan/install. Complete service, including free coffee!

The Bathroom Shop 4 Chapel Street, Guildford, Surrey GU1 3UH. *Tel*: (0483) 573434. *Open*: Mon to Sat, 8.30am to 6.00pm (all branches). Personal service, good prices, wide range traditional/modern styles. Showroom displays. *Also at*: Unit 3, Wykham Estate, Moorside Road, Winnall, Winchester, Hants SO23 7RX. (Own car park.) *Tel*: (0962) 862554.

And at: 37 Queen Street, Maidenhead, Berks SL6 1NB. *Tel*: (0628) 32622.
And at: Unit 23, Arun Business Park, Shripney Road, Bognor Regis, W. Sussex PO22 9SX. (Own car park.) *Tel*: (0243) 841345.

Bathroom Visions   12 Duke Street, Princes Risborough, Bucks HP17 0AT. (Park at rear.) *Tel*: (0844) 42028. *Open*: Mon to Sat, 9.00am to 5.00pm. Comprehensive range of modern and traditional bathrooms; working whirlpools/steam enclosures available to try out. Plan/install. Trademark is elegant vintage van.

Bird Baths   13 Hainault Street, Ilford, Essex IG1 4EN. (5 mins Ilford BR. Opposite bus depot and multi-storey car park.) *Tel*: 081-478 8213. *Open*: Mon to Sat, 9.00am to 5.00pm. Family builders' merchants revamped into attractive bathroom specialist. Friendly, personal service. Styles from traditional Victorian to avant-garde Continental. Tiles, accessories. Many exclusive items.

Corniche Bathrooms   17/19 Elmshott Lane, Cippenham, Slough, Berks SL1 5QS. (M4 junction 7. Park at rear.) *Tel*: (0628) 666668. *Open*: Mon to Fri, 9.00am to 5.30pm, Sat

9.30am to 5.30pm. Co-ordinated bathroom room settings, upmarket merchandise, modern/traditional styles. Knowledgeable staff, friendly service. Plan/install. Computer-aided design. Handmade furniture in all styles. Whirlpool specialists. Licensed credit broker.
Also at: 9 Hill Avenue, Amersham, Bucks HP6 5BD. *Tel*: (0494) 433142.

County Bathrooms and Tiles
Northbridge Road, Berkhamsted, Herts HP4 1EH. (Industrial estate, A41 London Road.) *Tel*: (0442) 876244. *Open*: Mon to Sat, 8.30am to 5.30pm. Planning. Personal service. Large stocks, lots of choice. Working displays. Thousands of tiles.

DHS   The Bathroom Centre, 17 Radford Way, Billericay, Essex. (Parking at rear.) *Tel*: (0277) 655109. *Open*: Mon to Sat, 8.30am to 5.30pm. Ideal-Standard "Solutions". Plan/install.

Original Bathrooms   143/145 Kew Road, Richmond, Surrey TW9 2PN. (15 mins Richmond tube.) *Tel*: 081-940 7554. *Open*: Mon to Sat, 9.00am to 5.30pm. The Pidgeons are the oldest-established family selling bathrooms in the UK, having worked in the field through five generations

since 1876. Great-uncle Frederick was apprenticed in 1871 to Thomas Crapper, the celebrated WC inventor (and enricher of English language). "We offer unparalleled depth of knowledge and experience, plus the very best of service." Twenty displays of modern/traditional bathrooms in an attractive showroom. Working Jacuzzis/power showers. Planning service.

Walton Bathrooms   The Hersham Centre, The Green, Molesey Road, Walton-on-Thames, Surrey KT12 4HL. *Tel*: (0932) 224784. *Open*: Mon to Sat, 9.00am to 5.30pm. Plan/install. Over 25 quality bathrooms on display. Whirlpool/ power shower specialists. Member of the Federation of Master Builders. Colour brochure available.
Also at: Stanley House, High Street, Ripley, Surrey GU23 6AY. (Off A3. Free parking.) *Tel*: (0483) 211443.
And at: High Street, Ascot, Berks SL5 7HG. (5 mins Ascot BR. Near racecourse. Easy parking.) *Tel*: (0344) 874646. Converted supermarket provides 3,000 sq ft of space. "The most modern showroom in the UK." Designed with Villeroy and Boch, the top German modern make. Fitted bathroom furniture. Working power showers/whirlpool baths/steam enclosures. Latest colours/designs.

2. SANITARYWARE

"The biggest waste of water in the country by far. You spend half a pint and flush two gallons."

HRH The Duke of Edinburgh

"We have all passed a lot of water since then."

Samuel Goldwyn, US film producer (1882–1974)

As old-fashioned traders get more sophisticated, adding room settings to their displays and planning to their services, the line between "specialists" and "builders'

merchants" becomes increasingly blurred. Buy baths, basins, WCs, bidets etc from specialists above, from **DIY Superstores**, or from the suppliers listed below.

London Postal Districts

▶ Bargains!

Aston Mathews   143/147 Essex Road, Islington N1 2SN. (10 mins

Highbury and Islington tube.) *Tel*: 071-226 7220/3657. *Open*: Mon to Fri, 8.30am to 5.00pm, Sat 9.30am to 2.00pm. Established in Islington in 1823. Knowledgeable, enthusiastic, energetic staff. Large stocks, prompt deliveries. Excellent reputation. Wide-ranging, often exclusive designs, and low prices.

▶ Bargains!

Bathrooms Direct   764a Fulham Road, SW6 5SA. (5 mins Putney Bridge tube.) *Tel*: 071-736 3081.

Open: Mon to Fri, 9.00am to 5.00pm. Cheapest (they claim) for main brands. Also French imported styles.

H E Olby and Co   299/313 Lewisham High Street, SE13 6NW. (Opposite Ladywell BR. Own car park.) *Tel:* 081-690 3401. *Open:* Mon to Thu, 8.00am to 5.00pm, Fri 8.00am to 4.00pm. Closed for lunch, 1.00pm to 2.00pm. Open Sat, 9.00am to 12.00 noon. Twyfords Living Bathroom Centre, with seven room settings.

Potter Perrin   412 Streatham High Road, SW16 8EX. (5 mins Streatham BR. Park in side roads.) *Tel:* 081-677 5321. *Open:* Mon to Fri, 8.30am to 5.30pm. Late night Thu, 8.00pm. Twyfords Living Bathroom Centre. Nine room settings. Recommended plumbers.

Riverside Plumbers Merchants/ Bathroom Centre   180/188 Mile End Road, E1 4LS. (3 mins Stepney Green tube.) *Tel:* 071-790 1323. *Open:* Mon to Fri, 8.00am to 6.00pm, Sat 8.00am to 5.00pm. Keen prices. Quality sanitaryware: most leading makes. Full service for bathrooms: plan/supply/install (to include tiling, electrics, plastering etc). Phone for special seasonal offers.

▶ **Bargains!**

Simply Bathrooms   297 Munster Road, SW6 6BW. (10 mins West Brompton/Parsons Green tubes.) *Tel:* 071-381 4222. *Open:* Mon to Fri, 8.30am to 5.30pm, Sat 9.00am to 5.00pm, Sun 9.00am to 1.00pm. Newly revamped showroom. Wonderful prices for major brands: around 30% off. Ideal-Standard, Armitage Shanks, Twyfords. Orders

take around two to three days; deliveries are mostly free. Working shower/whirlpool displays. Powerjet whirlpools for any bath, old/new. See also **Home Counties/South East** below.

West One Bathrooms
60 Queenstown Road, SW8 3RY. (5 mins Clapham Common tube; parking outside shop.) *Tel:* 071-720 9333/6. *Open:* Mon to Sat, 8.30am to 5.30pm. Sharp prices, friendly service. Displays feature British top brands, plus imported exclusive suites from Italy, Germany and France (Porcelain de Paris). Quick, often free, deliveries.

Home Counties/ South East

Cakebread Robey and Co   318/326 Southbury Road, Enfield, Middx EN1 1TT. (Opposite Southbury BR. Own car park.) *Tel:* 081-804 8244. *Open:* Mon to Fri, 8.00am to 5.00pm. Closed for lunch, 12.30pm to 1.30pm. Open Sat, 9.00am to 4.00pm. Twyfords Living Bathroom Centre. Ten room sets. Recommended plumbers.

Drainage Systems   Cray Avenue, St Mary Cray, Kent BR5 3RH. *Tel:* (0462) 422611. *Open:* Mon to Fri, 9.00am to 5.15 pm. Twyfords Living Bathroom Centre, with 10 room settings. Recommended plumbers.

Gammon and Smith   Bedford Road, Petersfield, Hants. (Customers' car park.) *Tel:* (0730) 62233. *Open:* Mon to Fri, 8.00am to 5.00pm. Closed for lunch, 1.00pm to 2.00pm. Open Sat, 8.00am to 12.30pm. Builders' merchants: 16 bathroom settings. Ideal-Standard Solutions centre. Free planning/design. Recommended installers.

Miscellanea   Crossway, Churt, near Farnham, Surrey GU10 2JA. (A287.) *Tel:* (0428) 714014. *Open:* Mon to Fri, 8.30am to 5.00pm, Sat 8.30am to 4.00pm. "The largest selection of bathroomware in Britain." No-one has ever challenged them. Over 1,000 suites always in stock for immediate collection/delivery. Major British/ Continental makes. All new shades/ styles. Saunas/Jacuzzis/steam enclosures/pumped showers. Tiles/ marble/sinktops/worktops. Fitted kitchens/bedrooms. Plus rare and discontinued colours. Planning.

Only Bathrooms   27 London Road, Kingston-upon-Thames, Surrey KT2 6ND. (5 mins Kingston BR. Park in Cattle Market.) *Tel:* 081-549 6579. *Open:* Mon to Fri, 9.00am to 5.00pm, late night Thu, 6.30pm. Twyfords Living Bathroom Centre. 27 room settings, including fitted bathroom furniture. Tiles/ accessories. Design service/ recommended plumbers.

Simply Bathrooms   2 Bensham Lane, Croydon, Surrey CR0 2RQ. (10 mins West Croydon BR.) *Tel:* 081-689 6883. *Open:* Mon to Thu, 8.30am to 5.30pm. Late night Fri, 8.00pm. Open Sat, 9.00am to 5.00pm, Sun 9.00am to 1.00pm.
See also **London Postal Districts** above.

Skeet and Jeffes   Monument Way, East Woking, Surrey GU21 5LY. (Customers' car park.) *Tel:* (0483) 755005. *Open:* Mon to Sat, 8.15am to 5.00pm, Sat 8.30am to 4.30pm. Over 100 years old—the founder's grand-daughter is the sales director. Twyford's Living Bathroom Centre. Many room settings; suites/shower enclosures/vanitary units. Power showers/steam enclosures/ whirlpools. Tile shop. Samples available. Free planning. Recommended installers.

3. PERIOD BATHROOMS

Shop here for old-style elegance when restoring older homes, or for adding atmosphere to modern properties. Many bathroom specialists listed above also stock period-style ranges. For genuine fittings, comb **Architectural Salvage** merchants, but check with a plumber that your ideas are feasible! See also **5. Renovation** below.

London Postal Districts

Bathing Beauties   43 Muswell Hill Road, N10 3JB. (Highgate tube, plus bus.) *Tel:* 081-365 2794. *Open:* Mon to Sat, 8.00am to 5.30pm. This exceptionally pretty shop glows with polished wood, shiny ceramics and burnished brass. "We're not interested in veneers, substitutes or fakes." Specialists in fitted period-style bathrooms, in solid (sustainable) hardwoods. Plan/design/install. Good selections of refurbished taps/showers: exclusive finishes include tortoiseshell/marble.

Grove Green Antiques See **Architectural Salvage**.   Ever-changing selection of original Victorian fittings: very reasonable prices.

Sitting Pretty   131 Dawes Road, SW6 7EA. (5 mins Fulham Broadway tube.) *Tel:* 071-381 0049. *Open:* Mon to Fri, 10.00am to 5.00pm, Sat 10.00am to 2.00pm. James and Janice Williams pioneered the traditional bathroom revival 15 years ago. SP is still tops (bottoms?) for wooden loo seats, now made from joined sections of solid timber to save trees. Mahogany and English hardwoods such as oak/elm/ash/cherry. Plus your coat of arms, if you wish . . . Repro freestanding baths and sanitaryware, including Gothic styles. Wide range of taps. "The very best of service." Recommended plumbers.

The Water Monopoly   16/18 Lonsdale Road, NW6 6RD. (Queen's Park tube.) *Tel:* 071-624 2636. *Open:* by appointment only. Samantha von Daniken turns bathroom furnishing into an art. Fine English/French antique sanitaryware restored with inspired modern decorative touches, using colours from pastels/primaries to metallics/fluorescents. Freestanding roll-top baths lined with acrylic in white/cream/ivory, plus outer coating of matt polyurethane in virtually any colour. China basins in curlicues of wrought iron; wooden loo seats, bleached and stained. Baths from 2ft to 7ft long: cast iron, double-ended, copper, porcelain, marble, fireclay. Co-ordinated with porcelain basins, loo pans, bidets. Zinc, glass, copper-hooded canopy baths. All stock photographed—phone to discuss. Own shotblasters, metalplaters, recasters, engineers, enamellers and plumbers. Wonderful, and wonderfully expensive.

Home Counties/ South East

Bathshield   Blenheim Studio, London Road, Forest Row, E. Sussx RH18 5EZ. (3 miles East Grinstead BR. 8 miles Gatwick Airport. A22.) *Tel:* (0342) 823243. *Open:* by appointment only. Original Victorian baths/fittings. Reproductions. Restoration/re-enamelling of baths in workshops/in situ. Nationwide service.

Drummond's of Bramley See **Architectural Salvage**.   "The largest stock of original period bathroom fittings in the UK." Canopy/roll-top/plunger/soapdish baths. Showers/mixer taps. Marble-topped and pedestal basins. Loos/wooden seats. High- and low-level china/cast-iron cisterns. Bath/basin taps. Unusual fittings.

4. ACCESSORIES

"The next thing he saw was a washstand with ewers and basins and soap and brushes and towels; and a large bath, full of clean water—what a heap of things, all for washing! . . . Tom for the first time in his life found out that he was dirty, and burst into tears with shame and anger."

Charles Kingsley (1819–75), *The Water Babies*

Be wary: the dividing line between accessories and clutter is particularly narrow in bathrooms. Many specialists offer attractive bathroom accessories. The firms listed under **Doors 2. Door Furniture and Specialist Ironmongery** are also good places to look for them.

London Postal Districts

The Conran Shop See **Furniture 1. General**.   Smart accessories in white enamel/wood/chrome.

Czech and Speake   39c Jermyn Street, SW1Y 6DN. (5 mins St James's Park tube.) *Tel:* 071-439

0216. *Open:* Mon to Fri, 9.00am to 6.00pm, Sat 10.00am to 5.00pm. Exquisite bathroom boutique, redolent with Edwardian elegance. Reproduction designs for taps, mirrors, bath-racks, hooks and so on. Solid brass in three finishes: non-tarnish, chromium plate, or nickel plate with a warmer, silvery appearance. Cubist range is authentic Art Deco. Aromatic toiletries in beautiful bottles, including *No. 88 for Men*, packed in black opal glass.
See also **Home Counties/South East** below.

Danico Brass See **Doors 2. Door Furniture and Specialist Ironmongery.**   Elegant brass taps and tap/shower handsets. Towel rails/rings.

Floris   89 Jermyn Street, SW1Y 6JH. (5 mins Green Park tube.) *Tel:* 071-930 2885. *Open:* Mon to Fri, 9.30am to 5.30pm, Sat 9.30am to 4.00pm. Gracious, sweetly scented shop with gleaming mahogany showcases: family business for over 250 years. Famous fragrances/bath oils/essences, plus exquisite accessories: brushes, combs, porcelain boxes, glass perfume bottles, china soap dishes, pot pourris. Everything a gentleman needs to complete his toilet . . .

Gore Booker See **Accessories 1. General.**   Good selection of plain wooden accessories, including traditional bath-racks/shelves.

Habitat See **Furniture 1. General.** Unusual selections include elegant bronzed range; handpainted ceramics in bright primaries; stainless steel; and beechwood/metal made in Sweden.

Ikea See **Furniture 1. General.** Dax cabinets/shelves for neat storage solutions—a fitted look at an unfitted price. Lots of other well-designed ideas in chrome/white/black. Pine wall bars with slot-on fittings. Hooks/towel rails/soap dishes etc.

The Kite Store   48 Neal Street, Covent Garden WC2H 9PJ. (2 mins Covent Garden tube.) *Tel:* 071-836 1666. *Open:* Mon to Fri, 10.00am to 6.00pm, Sat 10.30am to 5.30pm. Make your own shower curtains from polyurethane-coated ripstop nylon in good colours such as black, white, pink, orange, purple, and primaries.

Knobs and Knockers See **Doors 2. Door Furniture and Specialist Ironmongery.**   Bathroom accessories in white china/brass/chrome. China cord pulls etc.

Locks and Handles See **Doors 2. Door Furniture and Specialist Ironmongery.**   Very good selections of unusual bathroom fittings, including enamelled French Art Nouveau designs in black or white.

Penhaligon's   41 Wellington Street, WC2E 7BR. (5 mins Covent Garden tube.) *Tel:* 071-836 2150. *Open:* Mon to Sat, 10.00am to 6.00pm. For mail order catalogue *tel:* 081-880 2050. The original fragrances of William Henry Penhaligon, a Jermyn Street barber of 1870, have essences/oils blended in glass vats. Pretty bottles in Victorian shapes with bows. Gentlemen's shaving accessories. *Also at:* 55 Burlington Arcade, Piccadilly, W1V 9AF. (5 mins Piccadilly tube.) *Tel:* 071-629 1416. *Open:* Mon to Fri, 9.30am to 5.30pm, Sat 9.30am to 5.00pm. *And at:* 20a Brook Street, W1Y 1AE. (3 mins Bond Street tube.) *Open:* Mon to Sat, 9.30am to 5.30pm. *And at:* 8 The Royal Exchange, EC3R 3ND. (3 mins Bank tube.) *Tel:* 071-283 0711. *Open:* Mon to Fri, 9.30am to 5.30pm.

Shearer Interiors   28 St Luke's Road, W11 1DJ. *Tel:* 071-727 3324. *Open:* by appointment. Exclusive shower screens in coloured, laminated glass.

The Tap Shop   1551 London Road, SW16 4AD. (1 min Norbury BR.) *Tel:* 081-679 1463. *Open:* Mon to Sat, 9.00am to 5.30pm. Closed all day Wed. "The best selections of taps in London . . . for baths, basins, sinks and bidets." Competitive prices. Eight styles of Victorian taps. Wide choice of coloured taps. Colour-

matching service. Lots of accessories—mirrors, rails, shelves, hooks. Sanitaryware at keen prices.

Home Counties/ South East

Czech and Speake   10 Tunsgate, Guildford, Surrey GU1 3QT. *Tel:* (0483) 506941. *Open:* Tue to Fri, 9.00am to 5.00pm, Sat 10.00am to 6.00pm.
See also **London Postal Districts** above.

The Design Studio   39 High Street, Reigate, Surrey RH2 9AE. (15 mins Reigate BR.) *Tel:* (0737) 248228. *Open:* Mon to Sat, 9.00am to 5.00pm. Useful range basic/classic bathroom accessories. Chrome/brass/pale gold plate. Folding shower/bath seat. Grab rails. Old-style shower sets in brass/chrome/bright nickel/antique nickel. Mail order catalogue.

▶ Mail Order

Collexion by Twyfords   *Tel:* (0782) 202716 for brochure, then order direct. Beautiful colours for surprisingly wide range of bathroom co-ordinates. Towels/tiles/borders/cornices. Essential viewing.

Hethecraft Pine Furniture   Old Station Yard, Metheringham, Lincoln LN4 3HD. *Tel:* (0526) 21926. Victorian towel racks in various woods or painted.

JAB Services   23 Oakwood, Partridge Green, Horsham, W. Sussx RH13 8JG. *Tel:* (0403) 710650. Corded bathroom light pulls in a range of colours, with tassel ends, or ceramic/wood/brass decorative knobs.

Limericks Linens See **Bedrooms 11. Bed linen.**   Victorian-style beech towel stands. Plain shower curtains with matching towels. Towelling by the metre (good for bathroom curtains). Attractive square linen baskets.

5. RENOVATION

Ideas for putting the beauty back into your bathroom, without full-scale replacements.

London Postal Districts

Bathroom Renovations 20 Moxon Street, W1M 3JB. (Baker Street tube. NCP opposite.) *Tel*: 071-935 6590. *Open*: Mon to Fri, 8.30am to 5.30pm. "We've made baths that are 50 or 60 years old look just like new," says Keith Morris. Speciality: removing limescale, iron stains etc. from enamelled cast-iron baths, using "grind and polish" technique. Chips repaired. Discoloured basins/loos cleaned. Re-coating in a virtually unlimited choice of colours. Countrywide service.

Born Again Baths 10 Barley Mow Passage, Chiswick W4 4PH. *Tel*: 081-995 3503. No showroom: visits by appointment. William Anstice offers personal service for on-site grind-and-polish for cast-iron baths. Chips/small blemishes repaired. Spraycoating (but first the bath is shot-blasted in West Drayton workshops) only worthwhile for "serious antiques"—such as early models by Doulton/Jennings, and Shanks; roll-tops c1890 to 1920;

Victorian/Edwardian baths over 6ft 4in long; models with plunge-pull wastes; or canopy baths. Also good quality secondhand refurbished baths.

H M James and Sons 736 Romford Road, Manor Park E12 6BT. (3 mins Manor Park BR. Close to A406, off M11.) *Tel*: 081-553 1521. *Open*: Mon to Fri, 9.00am to 5.30pm. Closed for lunch, 1.00pm to 2.00pm. Open Sat, 9.00am to 1.00pm. Closed Sat on BH weekends. Can supply obsolete colours for additions/replacements to sanitary ware.

Renubath 248 Lillie Road, SW6 7QA. *Tel*: 071-381 8337. Established 26 years. Repair/polish/resurface metal baths. Chipped enamel/acrylic repairs. Guaranteed for 12 months. Trained operators. Nationwide

Home Counties/ South East

Bath Renovations (Essex) 89 Water Lane, Purfleet, Essex RM16 1GX. No showroom: by appointment. *Tel*: (0708) 868155; or (mobile) (0836) 215235. Cast-iron/steel baths resurfaced; all sanitaryware chemically cleaned.

Fourteen years' experience, one-man business; mainly East London/Essex/Kent, but will travel further.

Bathshield See **3. Period Bathrooms** above. Re-enamelling service (nationwide).

Miscellanea. See **2. Sanitaryware** above. Specialist stocks of rare/discontinued colours.

Mail Order

The Bath Re-enamelling Company Chapel Court, Hospital Street, Nantwich, Ches CW5 5RF. *Tel*: (0270) 626564. In situ spray enamelling or factory stove enamelling. Operatives sent to homes anywhere in mainland Britain. Baths also collected/delivered. Brochure available.

Bathroom Ceramics Beansheaf, Kirby Misperton, Malton, Yorks YO17 0UF. *Tel*: (065 386) 437. Not open to callers. Despatch anywhere in British Isles, Jersey, IOW, IOM. White sanitaryware reglazed to match discontinued colours: same make (where possible) as original range. 35 discontinued colours as standard. Brochure/samples available.

4
BEDROOMS

You may thrive on a quick kip like Napoleon and Mrs Thatcher—reputedly just four hours a night. Or you may need nine hours, like me. Never mind the length, feel the quality: for this you need a good, comfortable bed. A bedroom isn't just a sleeping compartment. It's a place to undress, store your clothes, dress again (all rather tiresome), and generally prepare your private face for a public world. A place to read, relax, make love. Is yours the stuff that dreams are made on?

1. BEDS: GENERAL

"Be guided by expert advice, comfort and support—not price."

Patrick Quigley, chief executive, National Bed Federation

The golden rule is to lie before you buy. Quality is essential. Buy the best, even if you must arrange credit. You can also try out beds at many of the stores listed in **Furniture 1. General**, and at **Department Stores**.

London Postal Districts

Adams and Son   36/38 Hatch Lane, Chingford E4 6LQ. (10 mins Woodford tube.) *Tel*: 081-524 1821. *Open*: Mon to Sat, 8.30am to 5.30pm. Early closing Thu, 12.00 noon. Forty beds on display, 25 brands, large stock. Mattresses sold separately if required. Discounts. Free same-day local delivery. Free fitting for OAPs/disabled. Free disposal of old bed.

Angel Foam Company   104/106 Pentonville Road, N1 9JB. (1 min Angel tube.) *Tel*: 071-837 7553. *Open*: Mon to Fri, 10.00am to 5.00pm, Sat 10.15am to 4.00pm. Specialist manufacturers of foam mattresses: any shape, any size (circular or even heart-shaped!)

Beaumont Beds   238/240 Lewisham High Street, Lewisham SE13 6JU. (10 mins Lewisham BR. Plentiful parking.) *Tel*: 081-852 4515. *Open*: Mon to Sat, 9.30am to 6.00pm. Good stocks/same day or 24-hour deliveries. Mattresses/divans sold separately. Custom-made beds. Special/odd sizes. Brass/pine. Experienced advice. See also **Home Counties/South East** below.

Bed Shop UK   14 Baker Street, W1M 1DA. (10 mins Marble Arch.) *Tel*: 071-935 3354. For advice/prices *tel freephone*: (0800) 581109. *Open*: Mon to Sat, 9.00am to 6.00pm. 3,000 sq ft of beds: hardwoods, slatted, brass/iron, divans, sofabeds, space-savers, children's beds, bunks. "Odd beds are our speciality." Established for 10 years. Free deliveries within 40 miles. "Wedding list" service—a computer keeps a list of contributions towards the happy couple's bed. See also **Home Counties/South East** below.

Beds, Beds, Beds London   313/321 North End Road, SW6 1NN. (10 mins Fulham Broadway/West Brompton tubes.) *Tel*: 071-385 4550/2000. *Open*: 7 days, Mon to Sat 9.30am to 7.00pm, Sun 10.00am to 4.00pm. "The largest selection of beds in London." 250 beds on display, 1,000 in stock, from the bottom to the top end of the market. Sales every 2 months. Sizes from 2ft 6in to 9ft square. Same-day delivery. Pocket-sprung/orthopaedic/drawer divans/zip-and-link etc.

Bedworld Bedding Centres   470/472 Kingsland Road, Hackney E8 4AE. (5 mins Dalston Junction BR.) *Tel*: 071-254 2534. *Open*: Mon to Sat, 9.00am to 5.30pm. Early closing Thu 1.00pm.
Also at: 95 Fore Street, Edmonton N18 2TW. (Lower Edmonton BR.) *Tel*: 081-807 3331.
See also **Home Counties/South East** below.

C W Burrows   79 Leonard Street, EC2A 4QY. (6 mins Old Street tube.) *Open*: Mon to Fri, 9.00am to 5.00pm. Family business established 50 years. "Friendly, old-fashioned service." 4,000 sq ft warehouse. Leading brands, full range of styles/prices. Free local delivery. Custom-made beds.

City Beds   38 Jupp Road (off Carpenters' Road), Stratford E15 1AF. (3 mins Stratford tube.) *Tel*: 081-534 9000. *Open*: Mon to Sat, 8.30am to 5.30pm. Discount warehouse for all branded makes. Divans. Brass, wood, four-posters, bunks. Orthopaedic beds. 1,500 beds in stock for immediate delivery. Free bed disposal. 5% discount for OAPs who pay in cash. See also **Home Counties/South East** below.

Foamplan See **Upholstery and Suites 1. Chairs, Sofas and Suites.** Quality mattress specialists. Cut-to-size service for fire-retardant, combustion-modified foam mattresses. Mattress recovering service. Pine beds/bunks.

▶ **Bargains!**

S and M Myers See **Floors 3. Carpets.**   Government/hotel surplus beds/bedding, soft furnishings. Constantly changing stocks.

▶ **Bargains!**

Myers Warehouse   39/49 The Broadway, Crouch End N8 8DT. (5 mins Finsbury Park tube.) *Tel*: 081-340 9488. *Open*: Mon to Sat, 9.00am to 5.30pm. Discounts for branded beds: Slumberland, Relyon, Myers, Sleepeezee. Orthopaedic/pine beds; king-sizes. Large pine showroom, pine bedroom furniture. Sofabed specialists.

Tulleys of Chelsea See **Upholstery 1. Chairs, Sofas and Suites.**   Ground-floor bedding department with 35 beds on show. Brass beds, pine beds, folding beds, sofabeds, bunks, storage beds, ottomans, headboards, firm beds, mattresses, mattress covers, pillows. Wide range sizes/prices; hundreds in stock for immediate delivery.

Home Counties/ South East

Beaumont Beds   85/87 Church Street, Croydon, Surrey. *Tel:* 081-688 4776.
Also at: 137/139 High Street, Orpington, Kent. *Tel:* (0689) 890089. See also **London Postal Districts** above.

Bed Shop UK   7 South Parade, Summertown, Oxford OX2 7JL. *Tel:* (0865) 511369. *Open:* Mon to Sat, 9.00am to 5.30pm.
See also **London Postal Districts** above.

The Bedpost   7 Station Approach, Hayes, Bromley, Kent BR2 7EQ. (Opposite Hayes BR.) *Tel:* 081-462 5544. *Open:* Mon to Sat, 9.00am to 5.30pm. Discount prices, major brands: Relyon, Sleepeezee, Sealy, Silent Night, Myers. 2,500 sq ft; divan bases, mattresses, brass/lacquered bedsteads, headboards. From spare room models to luxurious pocket springs.

Beds Are Uzzz   490/492 Greenford Road, Greenford, Middx UB6 8SH. (Off A40, Western Avenue.) *Tel:* 081-578 2883. *Open:* Mon to Sat, 9.15am to 5.30pm. Specialist family business with large range, including custom-made. Same-day delivery/installation. Free removal of old bed. "We'll refund the difference if you can find it cheaper."
Also at: 73 High Street, Old Hemel, Hemel Hempstead. *Tel:* (0442) 66148.
And at: 11 Cobham Road, Ferndown Industrial Estate, Wimborne, Dorset BH21 7PE. (3 miles East of Wimborne. A31.) *Tel:* (0202) 891897. *Open:* 7 days, Mon to Sat, 9.00am to

5.30pm, Sun 10.00am to 5.00pm. "One of country's largest bed showrooms."

Bedworld Bedding Centres   26/28 East Barnet Road, Barnet, Herts EN4 8RQ. (2 mins New Barnet BR.) *Tel:* 081-441 7875. *Open:* Mon to Sat, 9.00am to 5.30pm. Early closing Thu 1.00pm. Bed specialists: family business, established for 11 years. 2,000 sq ft, with all top makes. Full range of bunks/storage beds. Headboards/pillows/duvets.
Also at: 336 High Road, Harrow Weald, Middx HA3 6HF. (15 mins Harrow and Wealdstone BR.) *Tel:* 081-861 5892. *Open:* Mon to Sat, 9.00am to 5.30pm. Early closing, Wed 1.00pm.
See also **London Postal Districts** above.

Bedworld (Chesham Furniture)
11 High Street, Chesham, Bucks HP5 1BG. (5 mins Chesham tube.) *Tel:* (0494) 775509. *Open:* Mon to Sat, 9.00am to 5.30pm. Late nights Wed, Thu and Fri, 8.00pm. Established for 16 years. 3,000 sq ft with 65 models on display. Energetic service: "If we can't supply you, who can?" Middle-market brands. Bunks/divans. Special lengths/sizes.
Also at: 46 Frogmore, High Wycombe, Bucks HP13 4DG. (A40.) *Tel:* (0494) 473325. *Open:* 7 days, Mon to Sat 9.00am to 5.30pm, Sun 10.00am to 4.00pm (all branches).
And at: 12 Churchgate, Hitchin, Herts SG5 1DN. (A1M.) *Tel:* (0462) 434471.
And at: 176 Queensway, Bletchley, Bucks MK2 2SW. (M1, junction 14.) *Tel:* (0908) 640799.
And at: 161a Dunstable Road, Luton, Beds LU1 1BW. *Tel:* (0582) 411312.

City Beds   Unit B, 11/17 Fowler Road, Hainault, Ilford, Essex IG6 3UU. (Opposite Hainault Forest on

Romford Road.) *Tel:* 081-501 2426. *Open:* Mon to Sat, 8.30am to 5.30pm.
See also **London Postal Districts** above.

County Bedrooms   45/47 St Peter's Court, High Street, Chalfont St Peter, Bucks SL9 9QQ. (A413. Free car park.) *Tel:* (0753) 889795. *Open:* Mon to Sat, 9.00am to 5.30pm. 4,500 sq ft showroom with 20 room settings. "The biggest selection of beds in Britain." Middle to top ranges. Electric beds. Sofabeds/storage beds. Free bedroom design service. Top makes of fitted furniture: woods/lacquers/handpainted.

Hertfordshire Bedding and Sofabed Centre   46 Bell Street, Sawbridgeworth, Herts CM21 9AN. (Sawbridgeworth BR/M11.) *Tel:* (0279) 722923. *Open:* Mon to Sat, 9.00am to 5.30pm. Family business, established 10 years. 2,500 sq ft showing full range of middle-to-upper-price beds. Headboards, pillows, duvets, children's beds. Custom-made beds. Pocket-sprung beds a speciality. Free delivery within 50 miles. Free disposal of old beds/suites.
Also at: 9 The Green, Kingsway, Ware, Herts SG12 0QW. (Ware BR/A10.) *Tel:* (0920) 465727. 1,000 sq ft of beds only; all top brands.

Weldons   11 High Street, Barnet, Herts EN5 5UN. (1 min High Barnet tube.) *Tel:* 081-440 3174. *Open:* 7 days, Mon to Thu, 9.00am to 5.30pm, Fri and Sat, 9.00am to 6.00pm, Sun 10.00am to 2.00pm. Family business, trading since 1947. Expert advice. 5,000 sq ft, 40 beds on show. Top bed brands "at cheaper prices than the big stores". Sofabeds/bunks/pine furniture. Free delivery anywhere in mainland UK.

2. FITTED FURNITURE

You can't take it with you when you move. It may add value to your house, but not nearly as much as you paid. On the other hand, fitted furniture is the way to maximise space in smaller rooms. Specialist firms will design/make or supply/ install. Browse also through the **Kitchens** and **Bathrooms** sections: many of these specialists now offer a service for bedrooms, too. Joinery firms listed under **Furniture 12. Made-to-Measure and Commissioned** can fulfil more ambitious fitted bedroom schemes, as can the joinery firms listed in the **Staircases** section.

London Postal Districts

Cosmos Fitted Bedrooms 1180 High Road, Whetstone N20. (Opposite B and Q: 5 mins Totteridge and Whetstone tube.) *Tel:* 081-446 2416/1332. *Open:* 7 days, Mon to Sat, 9.00am to 5.30pm, Sun 10.00am to 2.00pm (all branches). *Also at:* 5 Hall Lane, Chingford, E4. (Next to Sainsbury's. Shared car park.) *Tel:* 081-524 7888/9. See also **Home Counties/South East** below.

Domain 42 Newman Street, W1P 3PA. (8 mins Goodge Street tube.) *Tel:* 071-255 3264. *Open:* Mon to Fri, 9.00am to 5.30pm, Sat 9.30am to 2.30pm. The Living Bedroom Centre for B&B Italia stylish lacquered beds; plus sheets, duvets, quilts, bedspreads.

Duxiana 46 George Street, W1H 5RF. (5 mins Baker Street tube.) *Tel:* 071-486 2363. *Open:* Mon to Fri, 10.00am to 6.00pm, Sat 10.00am to 5.00pm. Ultra-stylish Swedish bedrooms; slimline Dux beds, with double-layer springs for firm but resilient support. All-cotton bed linens. Down-filled pillows/duvets. Headboards include upholstered/

stained cane. Bedside tables match overall scheme. Brochure available.

Exclusive Bedrooms 489 Finchley Road, NW3 6HS. (10 mins Finchley Road tube.) *Tel:* 071-431 1222/0418. *Open:* Mon to Sat, 9.30am to 5.30pm, Sun viewing 11.00am to 2.00pm. Fitted, mirrored wardrobe specialists. Sliding/folding/hinged. Competitive prices, myriads of models. Plan/make/install. Free brochure available, *tel:* (0927) 427514. *Also at:* 448 Chiswick High Road, W4 5RG. (2 mins Chiswick Park tube.) *Tel:* 081-994 2513. See also **Home Counties/South East** below.

Harvey Jones See **Kitchens 4. Painted.**

Hayloft Woodwork See **Furniture 12. Made-to-Measure and Commissioned.** Imaginative ideas for bespoke bedroom designs.

Hulsta 22 Bruton Street, W1X 7DA. (5 mins Green Park tube.) *Tel:* 071-629 4881. *Open:* Mon to Fri, 9.00am to 5.00pm. German modern fitted furniture/beds. Also living/ dining rooms. Wood veneers/ lacquers. Sophisticated, flexible high quality systems. *Also at:* Southway Contracts. See **Kitchens 1. Specialists.** *And at:* Geoffrey Drayton Interiors, See **Furniture 1. General.** *And at:* EKO Furnishings, 130/132 Fortess Road, NW5 2HP. *Tel:* 071-485 2735. *And at:* Harrods. See **Department Stores.** *And at:* Heal's See **Furniture 1. General.**

Magnet See **DIY Superstores.** Comprehensive range of fitted bedrooms. Free design service.

Master Bedrooms 39 Burnt Ash Hill, Lee SE12 9JQ. (2 mins Lee BR.) *Tel:* 081-851 5533. *Open:* Tue to Sat, 9.30am to 5.30pm, Mon to 3.00pm.

Everything for the bedroom, from their own workshops. Friendly, unpressurised design advice. Fitted wardrobes. Matching stools, chairs, ottomans, headboards, chaises longues in velvets, moirés or your own fabrics. Eleven finishes, hundreds of mouldings. Window seats. Fitted dressing tables.

Mirrorglide 356 Upper Richmond Road West, SW14 7JT. (10 mins Mortlake BR. Park outside.) *Tel:* 081-878 4989. *Open:* Mon to Sat, 9.30am to 5.30pm (all branches). Floor-to-ceiling sliding-door specialists, with wide choice of mirrors/surrounds. Plus matching hinged cupboards, overbed storage, bedside cabinets etc. Flexible, adaptable, willing, sensibly priced. Plan/design/ make/install. See also **Home Counties/South East** below.

Rails 448 Chiswick High Road, W4 5RG. (2 mins Chiswick Park tube.) *Tel:* 081-994 2513. *Open:* Mon to Sat, 9.30am to 5.00pm. Specialists in sliding-wardrobe systems, with upmarket choice of doors. Attractive showroom also has brass beds/co-ordinated fabrics. Plan/design/ install. Takes from 2½ weeks.

Southway Contracts See **Kitchens 1. Specialists.** Huge new showroom with fitted furniture from Hulsta/Interlubke/Wiemann.

Staton Fitted Furniture Ltd 719 North Circular Road, NW2 7AH. (Near Brent Cross.) *Tel:* 081-450 6581. *Open:* Mon to Fri, 9.00am to 5.30pm, Sat 9.00am to 5.00pm, Sun 10.00am to 4.00pm. Factory showroom, selling direct. Well-established, enthusiastic, reliable. Fitted wardrobes with backs, shelves, double hanging and shoe rails. Various door styles, with mirrors, mouldings, etc. Plan/fit. "Our new extension makes us the largest fitted bedroom showroom in London."

Home Counties/South East

Olaf Ahrens   128 Malden Road, New Malden, Surrey KT3 6DD. (Just off A3. Parking. New Malden BR.) *Tel:* 081-949 9226. *Open:* Mon to Sat, 9.00am to 5.30pm. Other times by appointment. Founder/owner/manager is John Ahrens, who has been trading for 30 years. 4,000 sq ft showroom/accessorised room settings. System storage specialists: all individually planned. Bedrooms/living/diningrooms. Studios/children's rooms. The home office. Electrically adjustable beds/fold-down wallbeds. Hinged/sliding door wardrobes. Plan/install.

Classic Bedrooms   61/63 South Street, Dorking, Surrey RH4 2JU. *Tel:* (0306) 880330. *Open:* Mon to Sat, 9.00am to 5.00pm. Specialists in quality fitted furniture since 1976. Mainly Hulsta (sophisticated, elegant German brand). Also French cherry traditional designs. Plus French linens/German pillows, duvets. Plan/install.

Cosmos Fitted Bedrooms   5/7 High Road, Chadwell Heath, Romford RM6 6PU. *Tel:* 081-590 2642/598 9022. *Open:* 7 days, Mon to Sat 9.00am to 5.30pm, Sun 10.00am to 2.00pm. Very wide choice from fitted furniture makers. Established 1978. Made-to-measure mirrors (bronze/silver/peach) with solid wood frames. Sliding "designer panels":

veneers/laminates/handpainted. Also hinged styles, including glazed doors with fabric linings. £50 deposit—no more to pay until order is completed satisfactorily. Plan/design/install.
See also **London Postal Districts** above.

Exclusive Bedrooms   81 Joel Street, Northwood Hills, Middx HA6 1LU. *Tel:* (0927) 427514.
See also **London Postal Districts** above.

Gibbons Built-in Furniture   Unit 2, Station Industrial Park, Oxford Road, Wokingham, Berks RG11 2YQ. (Adjacent Wokingham BR.) *Tel:* (0734) 793911. *Open:* Mon to Fri, 9.00am to 4.00pm, Sat 9.00am to 12.00 noon. Fitted bedroom, kitchen, lounge furniture; melamine, medium density fibreboards, natural woods.

Mirrorglide   6/8 London Road, Guildford, Surrey GU1 2AF. (Opposite civic hall, with large public car park.) *Tel:* (0483) 63123. *Open:* Mon to Sat, 9.30am to 5.30pm (all branches).
Also at: 94 The Broadway, Tolworth, Surrey KT6 7HT. (5 mins Tolworth BR. Park outside.) *Tel:* 081-390 5214.
See also **London Postal Districts** above.

Personal Touch   55 Beckenham Lane, Bromley, Kent BR2 0DA. (2 mins Shortland BR.) *Tel:* 081-464 2196. *Open:* Mon to Sat, 9.00am to 5.00pm. Craft-based bespoke furniture, individually designed/made to measure. Personal service.

Plan/fit. Colour brochure available.

Sharps Bedrooms   Albany Park, Frimley, Camberley, Surrey GU15 2PL. *Tel:* (0276) 685366. Claim to be the UK's largest maker of fitted bedroom furniture. Over 90 stores nationwide. Wide variety of styles. Plan/make/install. Five year guarantee. Colour catalogue, *tel freephone:* (0800) 789789.

Solite   337/339 Baker Street, Enfield, Middx EN1 3LF. (20 mins Enfield Town BR. Park nearby.) *Tel:* 081-366 1460. *Open:* Mon to Sat, 10.00am to 5.00pm. Early closing Wed, 1.00pm. Sliding/hinged doors for wide range of budgets. Mirrors/veneers/laminates/simulated effects. Takes from two to six weeks. Plan/design/make/install.

Mail Order

David Emerson See **Kitchens 6. Worktops.**   Tailor-made sliding/bi-fold door wardrobes in wide choice of finishes. In-home visits. Design/supply/install.

Sovereign Sliding Mirror Wardrobes   33a Torton Hill Road, Arundel, W. Sussx BN18 9HF. *Tel:* (0243) 552123. Free catalogue. Made-to-measure sliding mirror wardrobe fronts. Bottom track fits to floor, top to ceiling. Doors fit gap exactly. Mirror safety backing to BS 6262. DIY installation, or hire local carpenter.

3. PINE BEDS

London Postal Districts

Alphabeds   8/9 The Colonades, Waterloo Road, SE1 7LY. (2 mins Waterloo tube/BR. Easy parking.)

Tel: 071-620 2988. *Open:* Mon to Fri, 10.00am to 7.00pm, Sat 10.00am to 6.00pm. Strong jointed bolted frames, guaranteed for 15 years. Free delivery. Own make spring-interior mattresses. Also mattresses made with natural fibres. Own make futons. Also unbleached Egyptian

cotton sheeting. Illustrated price list. *Also at:* 8 Foscote Mews, W9 2HH. (2 mins Royal Oak tube.) *Tel:* 071-289 2467. *Open:* Tue to Sat, 10.00am to 6.00pm.
And at: 16 Broadway Market, Hackney E8 4QJ. (10 mins Bethnal Green tube.) *Tel:* 071-249 6100.

Open: Mon to Sat, 10.00am to 6.00pm. Closed Thu.

Big Table Furniture Co-op
56 Great Western Road, W9 3NT. (1 min Westbourne Park tube.) *Tel:* 071-221 5058/229 6032. *Open:* 7 days, Mon to Sat 10.00am to 6.00pm, Sun viewing 12.00 noon to 5.00pm. Late night Thu, 10.00pm. Well-established maker of pine beds (despite name!). Brochure available.

Litvinoff and Fawcett   238 Grays Inn Road, WC1 8JR. (10 mins Chancery Lane/King's Cross tubes.) *Tel:* 071-278 5391. *Open:* Mon to Sat, 10.00am to 6.00pm. Julian Litvinoff is justly famous for his sturdy, strong plain pine beds (from stock). Other designs to order; various colours/finishes. Guaranteed. Splendid value. Choice of handmade mattresses. Brochure available. Send sae.
Also at: 9 Chalk Farm Road, NW1 8AA. (5 mins Chalk Farm tube.) *Tel:* 071-482 0066. *Open:* 7 days, 10.00am to 6.00pm.

McQueen Pine   725 Garratt Lane, SW17 0PD. (10 mins Tooting Broadway tube/Earlsfield BR.) *Tel:* 081-879 7324. *Open:* Mon to Sat, 10.00am to 6.00pm, closed Wed (all branches). Handmade solid pine beds direct from workshop. Underbed drawers, blanket boxes, bedside tables, wardrobes and chests. Any size to order. Sprung/foam mattresses. Free illustrated leaflet available. Nationwide deliveries.
Also at: 365 St John Street, EC1V 4LB. (3 mins Angel tube.) *Tel:* 071-278 6905.
And at: The Viaduct Workshops, St James's Lane, Muswell Hill N10 3AX. (Highgate tube.) *Tel:* 081-883 4811.

Taurus Pine Beds   333 Kilburn High Road, NW6 7QB. (2 mins Kilburn tube.) *Tel:* 071-624 3024. *Open:* Mon to Sat, 10.00am to 6.00pm. Small family business. Handmade solid pine bed frames direct from workshop. Self-assembly, but assembly service available. Quality mattresses.

Warren Evans   1A Hawley Road, NW1. (10 mins Camden tube.) *Tel:* 071-267 5354/6198. *Open:* 7 days, Mon to Sun, 9.30am to 5.30pm. Late nights Mon and Wed, 7.30pm. Workshop/showroom quality pine beds. Various styles/finishes. Futons, futon sofabeds, pine furniture, orthopaedic mattresses. Also bedroom/kitchen furniture handmade to order within four days.

▶ **Worth a Trip**

Moriarti's Workshop   High Halden, near Ashford, Kent TN26 3LY. *Tel:* (0233) 850214. *Open:* Mon to Sat, 9.00am to 5.00pm. Master craftsman Ian de Fresnes (alias "Moriarti") masterminds country showroom/workshop: designer-maker par excellence. Thirty-eight bed styles, each in up to eight sizes. Solid pine, slatted bases. Space-saving pine storage bed specialists—with drawers and cupboards. Exclusive mattresses. Goldpine bedroom furniture. Brochure available. Mail order.

4. SPACE-SAVING BEDS

London Postal Districts

Ever-Reddy Beds See **8. Beds for Bad Backs**, below. Economy folding beds. Foam/sprung mattresses. Widths: 2ft 3in, 2ft 6in, 3ft, 4ft. Folding "Sleep chair".

Ikea See **Furniture 1. General**. Low-priced folding guest beds.

The London Wall Bed Company 263 The Vale, Acton W3 7QA.

(Customer collection service from Acton Town/Shepherd's Bush tubes.) *Tel:* 081-743 1174. *Open:* Mon to Fri, 9.00am to 5.00pm, Sat 11.00am to 4.00pm. Small showroom with folding wall beds, mirrored wardrobes, fitted bedrooms. Personal service.

Rest-Rite Bedding   51/55 High Road, Willesden Green NW10 2SX. (2 mins Willesden Green tube.) *Tel:* 081-459 6138. *Open:* Mon to Fri, 9.30am to 5.00pm. Half-day Thu, 12.30pm. Open Sat, 10.00am to 4.30pm. Strongly made metal beds which fold flat (vertically or

horizontally) against wall, complete with bedding. Spring bases/mattresses for regular use. Brochures. Mail order.

Mail Order

Golden Plan   P.O. Box 768, London, SW1P 1NB. *Tel:* 071-834 5692. Beds fold (fully made-up) flat against wall vertically (on end) or horizontally (widthways). Firm-based with proper mattresses to take standard bedding. Five-year guarantee. Catalogue available.

5. BRASS BEDS

"Love is not the dying moan of a distant violin—it is the triumphant twang of a bedspring."

S J Perelman, US humorist (1904–79)

Redolent of Victorian values, antiques are still plentiful; reproductions also proliferate.

London Postal Districts

And So To Bed 638/640 King's Road, Fulham SW6 2DU. (10 mins Fulham Broadway tube.) *Tel*: 071-731 3593. *Open*: Mon to Sat, 10.00am to 6.00pm. Best known for brass beds: originals, and reproductions made in own factory. Also beautiful wooden bedsteads. Divans and mattresses. Wonderful linens (many natural fibres), bedcoverings and accessories. Interior design service.
Also at: 96b Camden High Street, NW1 0LT. (5 mins Camden Town tube.) *Tel*: 071-388 0364. *Open*: Mon to Fri, 9.30am to 5.30pm. Closed Thu. Open Sat, 10.00am to 6.00pm. For sumptuous *Book of the Bedroom*, telephone 071-731 3593, or write to 638/640 King's Road, SW6 2DU. See also **Home Counties/South East** below.

Brass Victorian Bedsteads 48 Bell Street, NW1 5BU. (2 mins Edgware Road tube.) *Tel*: 071-262 2036. *Open*: Mon to Sat, 11.00am to 7.30pm. Antique brass/iron bedsteads; new mattresses. Also reproductions.

Dreams 34 Chalk Farm Road, NW1. *Tel*: 071-267 8107/8194. *Open*: Mon to Fri, 10.30am to 6.00pm, Sat and Sun 11.00am to 6.00pm. Two floors of hand-crafted brass beds/head boards, made in own workshop. Large selection of antique iron/brass bedsteads. Renovation service for brass/iron bedsteads/brass fittings. Top quality mattresses. "We have no connection with Dreams Ltd. of High Wycombe," say long-established owners Louis and Pat Amato.

Home Counties/ South East

And So To Bed 5 The Pantiles, Tunbridge Wells, Kent TN1 5TZ. (10 mins Tunbridge Wells BR.) *Tel*: (0892) 515099. *Open*: Mon to Sat, 9.00am to 5.30pm. Closed Wed. See also **London Postal Districts** above.

The Victorian Brass Bedstead Company Hoe Copse, Cocking, W. Sussex. (A286 Midhurst/Chichester Road.) *Tel*: (0730) 812287. *Open*: Seven days, by appointment. 18th-century, 60ft Sussex barn filled with hundreds of Victorian bedsteads. Full restoration service. New bed bases and mattresses if required.

Victorian Brass Bedsteads 37a Broad Street, Canterbury, Kent. (7 mins Canterbury East BR.) *Tel*: (0227) 69055. *Open*: Mon to Sat, 9.00am to 5.00pm. Iron/brass antique bedsteads.

▶ Worth a Trip

The Antique Bedstead Company The Baddow Antique Centre, The Bringy, Church Street, Great Baddow, near Chelmsford, Essex CM2 7JW. (A12 from London.) *Tel*: (0245) 71137. *Open*: Mon to Sat, 10.00am to 5.00pm, Sun 11.00am to 5.00pm. Large selections original Victorian bedsteads, brass, black, white. Singles; or 4ft/4ft6in/5ft widths. Good investments. Modern spring bases/mattresses to fit. Photo sheet of current stock. Nationwide deliveries.

Mail Order

Brass Bed Manufacturing Co Jubilee House, West Street, Sowerby Bridge, Halifax, W. Yorks HX6 3AP. *Tel*: (0422) 834457/839759. *Showroom open*: Mon to Sat, 9.00am to 5.30pm. Brochure. Traditional brass bedsteads, four-posters, half-testers, headboards. Mattresses/bedbases. "One of the largest collections of antique and Deco original bedsteads in the country."

6. TRADITIONAL WOODEN BEDS

"And so home again, staying nowhere, and then up to her chamber, there to talk with pleasure of this day's passages and so to bed."

Samuel Pepys (1633–1703)

"I believe the greatest asset a head of state can have is the ability to get a good night's sleep."

Baron Harold Wilson of Rievaulx

London Postal Districts

And So to Bed See **5. Brass Beds** above. Beautiful wooden traditional style bedsteads, complete with head/foot boards, imported from France.

Beaudesert   8 Symons Street, SW3 2TJ. (2 mins Sloane Square tube.) *Tel:* 071-730 5102. *Open:* Mon to Fri, 9.30am to 5.30pm. Joinery workshop for expensive upmarket four-posters, in hand-crafted mahogany, complete with hangings. Interior design. Own range of country-house style fabrics.

Ever-Reddy Beds See **8. Beds for Bad Backs**, below.   Handmade traditional pine beds, new/antique finish, matching wardrobes/chests.

Simon Horn Furniture   117/121 Wandsworth Bridge Road, Fulham SW6 2TP. (Entrance in Broughton Road. 5 mins Parsons Green tube.) *Tel:* 071-731 1279. *Open:* Mon to Sat, 9.30am to 6.00pm. Friendly, knowledgeable family business. Spacious showrooms. Large, impressive collection of French wooden classical beds. The famous "lit bateau" daybed has a curved head and foot of equal height. Place the single version along a wall, and dress it with a sweep of fabric suspended from a central wooden coronet. Cherrywood, oak, rosewood, caned or upholstered. English reproductions and most provincial French copies. "The largest collection of styles in Europe, we think!"

Ikea See **Furniture 1. General**. Attractive bedsteads in white lacquered metal with brass. Also wood "folk" designs. "Just lie back and think of Sweden."

Laura Ashley See **Decorating Materials 2. Co-ordinated Collections**.   Original designs in wood/metal.

Moriarti's Workshop See **3. Pine Beds** above. English Country Collection includes hand-carved solid pine bedsteads, plus four-posters.

Warren Evans See **3. Pine Beds** above. Selection of attractive bedstead styles in light/stained woods.

Home Counties/ South East

Beds of Distinction   190/192 High Street, Hornchurch, Essex. (7 mins Hornchurch tube. 12 mins Upminster BR.) *Tel:* (0402) 477096. *Open:* Mon to Sat, 9.00am to 6.00pm. Design/make/deliver/assemble hardwood four-poster beds. Up to 10ft wide. Can incorporate water beds. Mail order.

Post 4 Beds   14 Thorney Lane North, Iver, Bucks SL0 9JY. (1 mile Iver BR/M25, M4 or M40.) *Tel:* (0753) 654874. *Open:* by appointment. Wooden four-posters, elegant drapes made to order. Posts can be simply hand-turned in pine or mahogany; reeded, fluted or carved with acanthus leaves. Brass rods take drapes in various styles. Painted, distressed, stencilled finishes to order. Leaflets available. Mail order.

▶ Worth a Trip

Seventh Heaven   Chirk Mill, Chirk, Clwyd. (About 3 hours' drive from London. M1, M6, M54, A5.) *Tel:* (0691) 777622/773563. *Open:* 7 days, Mon to Sat, 9.00am to 5.00pm, Sun 10.00am to 5.00pm. Possibly the

largest UK selection of antique beds. Wooden, upholstered, painted, brass, iron. Bedsteads, four posters and half-testers. Beautifully restored. New bases/mattresses. Also wardrobes and bedside cabinets. Exclusive bed linens. National deliveries. Catalogue available.

Mail Order

Barco Joinery See **Windows 1. Replacements**.   Self-assembly kit to convert 4ft 6in double bed into four-poster. Finishes: dark oak/mahogany/pine. Turned 4in-thick posts with ball finials. White cotton canopy; white lace drapes with matching tie-backs. Shaped headboards. Parts also available separately. Leaflet on request.

J and J Cottage Industries   103 Hallcroft Road, Retford, Notts DN22 7PY. *Tel:* (0777) 702026. Individually made solid pine four-poster beds with curtain-making service. Plus bedsteads/pretty, traditional bedroom furniture.

Knight Time   Woodlea Green, Goonearl Lane, Redruth, Cornwall TR16 5BH. *Tel:* (0209) 821197. Hand-built wax-finished four-posters in choice of hardwoods. Individually designed. No chipboard/plywood. Good heirloom potential.

Pinecraft Beds   9 Wingate Drive, Didsbury, Manchester M20 8RT. *Tel:* (061) 434 1432/446 2372. Established makers of pine four-posters; sturdy self-assembly design, lacquered plain; or stained any colour. Choice of head/foot boards/mattresses. Colour brochure. To order: four to eight weeks.

7. HEADBOARDS AND CORONAS

Without a headboard, a bed is rather boring and slab-like. Many standard bed ranges feature headboards: see **1. Beds: General** above. Designs on the whole are unimaginative. Brass bed specialists sell some headboards without the whole bed—see **5. Brass Beds** above. You can also buy headboards from the shops listed in **Furniture 7. Cane** and **9. Painted**. Firms in **Soft Furnishings 3. Made-to-Measure** or in **Interior Design** will help with upholstered headboards in fabrics to match the rest of your furnishings. There are some other ideas below.

London Postal Districts

Allied Maples See **Floors 3. Carpets**.   Larger stores have good displays. Upholstered headboards in 12 colours, plus pleated/buttoned styles. Also mahogany/teak/pine, and brass. Headboards with co-ordinating pillowcases.

Robert and Colleen Bery Designs See **Furniture 9. Painted**.   Stunning stencilled headboards.

Deanguard Drapes See **Walls 1. Fabric Lining**.   Upholstered headboard experts.

Hutson Designs See **Furniture 9. Painted**.   Exquisite painted headboards: flowers/fruits/classical motifs.

John Lewis See **Department Stores**. Kits/brass fittings for sweeping drapes at head of bed.

Tempus Stet See **Lighting 2. Traditional and Antique**. Ornate coronas for elaborate drapes.

Home Counties/ South East

Duskminster See **Furniture 9. Painted**.   Headboards painted to match fabrics/wallpapers.

Mail Order

The Dormy House See **Accessories 10. Occasional Furniture**. Headboards in four shapes, upholstered with flame-retardant foam. Upholstery service. Plus made-to-order frilled/piped slip-over headboard covers, lined with flame-retardant interliner. Or the prettiest idea I've seen: rectangular cushion pads suspended from hardwood poles, with optional frilled covers. Also classic kidney-shaped dressing tables with frilly fabrics.

Grandisson Doors See **Doors 1. Front and Interior**. Distinctive carved wooden headboards with ornate scrolls, fretwork, etc.

8. BEDS FOR BAD BACKS

"Back pain is one of the country's most widespread and misunderstood complaints. The DHSS calculate that it costs Britain some 59.6 million working days a year. A bed cannot cure back pain, but it can make life more comfortable and provide relief from discomfort."

The National Back Pain Association, 31/33 Park Road, Teddington, Middx TW11 0AB. *Tel:* 081-977 5474. Send sae for information.

London Postal Districts

Anatomia   21 Hampstead Road, NW1 3JA. (2 mins Warren Street tube.) *Tel:* 071-387 5700. *Open:* Mon to Sat, 9.00am to 5.30pm. Swedish Lattoflex beds. Anatomically designed pillows for an ideal neck position. Snore-stop pillows (I am assured they work). Balans chairs.

The Back Shop   24 New Cavendish Street, W1M 7LH. (7 mins Bond Street/Baker Street tubes.) *Tel:* 071-935 9120/9148. *Open:* Mon to Fri, 10.00am to 6.00pm, Sat 10.00am to 2.00pm. "We're a comfort shop." Beds tailored to height/weight of partners. Trained adviser will visit, by appointment. Thirty-night trial. Pillows. Ergonomically designed chairs/desks. Lumbar wedges for cars/chairs.

The Back Store   330 King Street, Hammersmith W6 0RR. (5 mins Stamford Brook tube.) *Tel:* 081-741 5022. *Open:* Mon to Fri, 10.00am to 6.00pm, Sat 10.00am to 4.00pm. Complete bedroom on display. Handmade beds to suit partners' height/weight. Advisers will visit. Pillows/mattress toppers. Chairs.

Chester-Care   16 New Englands Lane, NW3 4TG. (8 mins Belsize Park tube.) *Tel:* 071-586 2166. *Open:* Mon to Fri, 9.00am to 5.00pm. Aids for greater comfort in bed. Products to help the disabled in kitchen/bathroom, and all around the house. New mail order catalogue available *tel:* (0623) 757955.

Ever-Reddy Beds   125 Essex Road, Islington N1 8LU. (10 mins Highbury and Islington tube). *Tel:* 071-226 1207/354 4044. *Open:* Mon to Sat, 9.00am to 5.00pm, or by appointment. "London's leading specialist bedmakers." Same day deliveries. Back care bed specialists. Twelve-year guarantee/built-in spineboard. Home visits with advice. Thirty-day satisfaction guarantee. Change your mind, change your bed.

Home Counties/ South East

Back In Action   PO Box 1457, Bourne End, Bucks SL8 5YU. *Tel:* (0628) 527659. Ring for directions. The postal address is Bucks, even though the firm is over the river in Cookham, Berks. David Newbound and Linda Pearce run a popular consultancy service for back-pain sufferers and carers. Postural training. Bed/chair selection. Chiropractor-designed King Koil beds, with strengthened middle section. Hydrobeds.

Essex Bedding Centres   44 East Walk, Basildon, Essex SS14 1HE. (2 mins Basildon BR. Free car park.) *Tel:* (0268) 522209. *Open:* Mon to Sat, 9.00am to 5.30pm. 2,000 sq ft, with around 60 beds on show, plus warehouse backup of nearly 1,000. All major brands. Fifty per cent of stock is pocket-sprung backcare

beds. Sizes from 2ft 3in to 7ft square. Handmade beds to order. For quotation/advice ("anytime") *tel:* (0860) 863503 (mobile).
Also at: 15 Farnham Road, Romford, Essex RM3 8ED. *Tel:* (04023) 45611. *Open:* Mon to Sat, 9.00am to 5.30pm.
And at: 254/56 London Road, Hadley, Essex SS7 2DE. *Tel:* (0702) 557972. *Open:* Mon to Sat, 9.00am to 5.30pm. Closed all day Wed.
And at: 62 London Road, Southend SS2 1PG. *Tel:* (0702) 430422. *Open:* Mon to Fri, 9.00am to 5.30pm. Closed all day Wed. Open Sat, 9.00am to 5.00pm.

The Keep Able Centre   2 Capital Interchange Way, Brentford, Middx TW8 0EX. (10 mins Gunnersbury tube/Kew Bridge BR. Easy parking.) *Tel:* 081-742 2181. *Open:* Mon to Fri, 9.00am to 5.00pm, Sat 10.00am to 5.00pm. Fully adjustable bed with built-in massage. Lift/recline armchairs. Plus over 2,000 products for making life easier for the handicapped/disabled.

9. WATERBEDS

Popular in the USA, sleeping on water is now gaining acceptance in Britain.

London Postal Districts

The London Waterbed Company 99 Crawford Street, W1H 1AN. (5 mins Baker Street tube.) *Tel:* 071-935 1111. *Open:* Mon to Fri, 10.00am to 6.00pm, Sat 11.00am to 6.00pm. Late night Thu, 7.00pm. "The widest range of waterbeds in the country", including Japanese, pine, American Colonial, brass. Some are like divans; they don't need a frame. All

price ranges. Matching furniture and accessories. Mail order service for accessories. Friendly, helpful service. "Come in and lie around, take as long as you like."

The Waterbed Company   57 New King's Road, SW6 4SE. (5 mins Fulham Broadway tube.) *Tel:* 071-731 0606. *Open:* Mon to Fri, 10.00am to 6.00pm, Sat 11.00am to 4.00pm. Waterbeds are an acquired taste: converts are addicted. All mattresses have heaters, and are stabilised for different support/heat requirements. Favoured by back sufferers. Mattress weight makes special frames essential: 40 different frame styles in a good choice of

wood/colour finishes. Mattress/heater guaranteed five years; fill with garden hose. Add water conditioner twice a year. Nationwide delivery/installation service.

Home Counties/ South East

Back In Action See **8. Beds for Bad Backs** above. Experienced back-pain therapists recommend Hydrobed for relieving back-pain in many situations. Keeps back warm all through the night.

10. FUTONS

A firm feel, natural fibres, and simple styling provide oriental allure.

London Postal Districts

Futon Company 138 Notting Hill Gate, W11 3QG. (2 mins Notting Hill Gate tube.) *Tel:* 071-221 2032. *Open:* Mon to Sat, 10.30am to 6.00pm (all branches). Late night Thu, 7.00pm. Sun viewing 11.00am to 5.00pm. Robert Pearce pioneered futons in Britain, at first making them himself with friends. Now his shops sell futons/sofabeds, duvets, bed linen. Natural fibres. Elegant modern furniture. 300 furnishing fabrics; trendsetting glassware, ceramics, gifts. Most available immediately. Interior design service/wedding lists. *Also at:* 169 Tottenham Court Road, W1P 9LH. *Tel:* 071-636 9984. *And at:* 654a Fulham Road, SW6

5RU. *Tel:* 071-736 9190. *And at:* 32/38 Battersea Rise, South Circular, SW11 1EE. (3 mins Clapham Junction BR.) *Tel:* 071-228 4546. *And at:* 147 Chiswick High Road, W4 4DT. (5 mins Turnham Green tube.) *Tel:* 081-994 9399.

Futon Express 23/27 Pancras Road, NW1 2QB. (2 mins King's Cross tube.) *Tel:* 071-833 3945. *Open:* Mon to Sat, 10.00am to 6.00pm. Futons: 100 per cent cotton fillings, simple pine bases in brown/black stain, or unvarnished at low cost. Chunky good-looking sofabeds, your fabric or theirs. Home assembly if access is restricted. Stain-protection service. *Also at:* 149 St John's Hill, SW11 1TQ. (5 mins Clapham Junction BR.) *Tel:* 071-924 2517. *Open:* Tue to Sat, 10.00am to 5.30pm. *And at:* 56 Chalk Farm Road, NW1 8AN. (4 mins Chalk Farm tube.) *Tel:*

071-284 3764. *Open:* Tue to Sun, 11.00am to 5.30pm.

Futon South 109 Balham High Road, SW12 9AP. (5 mins Balham tube.) *Tel:* 081-675 6727. *Open:* Mon to Sat, 10.00am to 6.00pm, Sun viewing 11.00am to 4.00pm. Slatted base plus six-layer cotton futon/cover at reasonable price. Curtains to match; cotton cushions, bolsters, pillows to order in any size. Also Indian rugs.

Take 45/46 Chalk Farm Road, Camden Lock NW1 8AJ. (4 mins Chalk Farm tube.) *Tel:* 071-267 3937. *Open:* 7 days, 10.00am to 6.00pm (both branches). Futon sofabeds; removable cotton satin covers. Also porcelain, tableware and china. *Also at:* 14/15 New College Parade, Finchley Road, Swiss Cottage NW3 5EP. (5 mins Swiss Cottage tube.) *Tel:* 071-586 0064.

11. BED LINEN

Widely available, of course, from department stores and furnishing stores. Often offered as part of co-ordinated furnishing ranges: see **Decorating Materials, Interior Design, Soft Furnishings,** and **Department Stores.**

London Postal Districts

Boutique Descamps 197 Sloane Street, SW1X 9QX. (3 mins Knightsbridge tube.) *Tel:* 071-235 6957. *Open:* Mon to Sat, 9.30am to 6.00pm. Late night Wed, 7.00pm. Exclusive bed linens/towelling collections by talented French designer Primrose Bordie. Baby accessories. Also furniture.

Futon Company See **10. Futons** above. Bed linens in natural fibres.

John Lewis See **Department Stores.** Sheeting by the metre; ground floor, Oxford Street.

The Linen Cupboard 21 Great Castle Street, W1N 7AA. (1 min Oxford Circus tube.) *Tel:* 071-629 4062. *Open:* Mon to Sat, 9.00am to 6.00pm. Late night Thu, 8.00pm. Small, but well-stocked. Bed linen, towels, table linen at very reasonable prices. Specialists in baby linen.

Lunn Antiques See **Soft Furnishings 2. Lace, Nets and Voiles.** Bed/table linen, mainly in white. Well-known for antique lace.

Monogrammed Linen Shop 168 Walton Street, SW3 2JL. (7 mins South Kensington tube.) *Tel:* 071-589 4033. *Open:* Mon to Fri, 10.00am to 6.00pm, Sat 10.00am to 5.00pm. Linen, cotton, cotton satin sheets. Bedspreads, blanket covers. Creams, whites, patterns, plains with coloured bindings. Baby pillowcases and children's clothes. Monogramming service takes three days.

▶ Bargains!

Pillow Talk Kingsbury Circle, Kenton Road, NW9 9QH. (3 mins Kingsbury tube.) *Tel:* 081-204 3366. *Open:* 7 days, Mon to Sun, 9.00am to 6.00pm. Late nights Thu and Fri, 8.00pm. Ongoing promotions/discounts on wide selections branded sheets, duvet covers etc. Plain dyes/prints/frills/children's designs. Perfects/good-quality seconds. Telephone orders also.

The Sleeping Company
143 Fulham Road, SW3 6RT. (5 mins South Kensington tube.) *Tel*: 071-581 2058. *Open*: Mon to Sat, 10.00am to 6.00pm. Late night Thu, 7.00pm. Georgina Sant's devotion to bedlinen comes out in her beautiful stock: an exclusive/extensive choice of sheets, duvet covers, pillowcases etc., all in natural fibres. Linens, cottons, seersuckers, stripes, lace, frills, patterns. Lots of white. Large selection of exquisite cutwork. Exclusive "green" range in unbleached cotton (actually it's very soft and creamy in colour). Duvets,

pillows, cushions, bolsters. Made-to-measure service for unusual sizes. Monogramming. Brides list.

The White House   51/2 New Bond Street, W1Y 0BY. (5 mins Oxford Circus/Bond Street tubes.) *Tel*: 071-629 3521. *Open*: Mon to Fri, 9.00am to 5.30pm, Sat 9.00am to 1.00pm. Established 1906; London's premier stockist of fine (but expensive) bed linens. Printed, embroidered luxury sheet sets, co-ordinating with towels. Bedcovers, tablecloths, tablemats. Monogramming. Commissions.

Mail Order

Keys of Clacton   Stephenson Road, Gorse Lane Industrial Estate,

Clacton-on-Sea, Essex CO15 3AJ. (5 mins Clacton BR.) *Tel*: (0255) 432518. Catalogue: send stamp. Warehouse/shop for personal callers: 132 Old Road, Clacton. *Open*: Mon to Sat, 9.00am to 5.00pm. Family business, trading for 40 years. Bed linen for hard-to-get bed sizes/shapes. Luxury percales, cosy flannelettes (including duvet covers). Twenty sizes in fitted bottom sheets. Mattress cover specialists.

Limericks Linens   Guildford Road, Hayle, Cornwall, TR27 6BR. *Tel*: (0736) 756054. Newly emerged old favourite: profits now go to Dr Barnardos. Incredibly useful catalogue. Lots of hard-to-get items: sheeting by the metre, mattress covers etc.

12. DUVETS, QUILTS AND SPREADS

Duvets are also known as continental quilts. Buy the best you can afford. Find selections also at department and furnishing stores. The warmth of duvets is measured in "tog" values: the higher the tog, the warmer the quilt. Summer weight is 4.5. 12 is warm; 13.5 extra warm. Fillings can be synthetic or natural. At the bottom end of the market the cheapest synthetics are made from low-grade polyesters; at the upper end, branded polyesters have hollow fibres for greater warmth and lightness. Natural fillings vary from cheaper feathers/down to down/feathers and the luxury of pure down. It's all a matter of personal preferences and budget. But a quality quilt is virtually a life-long investment. Watch out for bargains in the sales. Some people still prefer old-fashioned quilts topped by a bedspread. So there are ideas for these, too, below.

London Postal Districts

Museum Quilts   Susan Jenkins, 254/258 Goswell Road, EC1V 7EB.

(5 mins Angel tube.) *Tel*: 071-490 7732. *Open*: Mon to Fri, 12.00 noon to 6.00pm. Other times by appointment. Original antique American quilts; each tells a story. Finest workmanship; good investment.

Nice Irma's See **Ethnic Crafts and Furnishings**.   Possibly one of the best ranges of quilts/spreads in London, at very reasonable prices. Prints, weaves, embroidered crewelwork. Traditional designs/modern colourings. Colour mail order catalogue available, *tel*: 071-284 3836.

Mail Order

Keys of Clacton See **11. Bed Linen** above.   Huge range of bedspreads, including non-standard widths: 2ft 6in, 4ft, 6ft. Four valance drops cover bulky duvets or deep drawer divans. Also luxurious pure new wool blankets.

Limericks See **11. Bed Linen** above.   DIY duvets: containers to fill yourself. Fillings: down/feather

and down/polyester/feathers. Tickings.

Patchwork Quilts by Teresa Bell
Top House, Burn, Selby, N. Yorks YO8 8LR. *Tel*: (0757) 270343. Charming, traditional square-blocked designs, wadded/quilted, backed. 100 per cent cotton fabrics, all top names: Warner, Colefax and Fowler, Osborne and Little etc. Definitely heirlooms.

Sundown Quilts   200 Kirk Clough, Brogden, Barnoldswick, Colne, Lancs BB8 5XE. *Tel*: (0282) 813741. Excellent explanatory leaflets. Twelve (many shops only stock three) standard sizes continental quilts. Natural fillings from duck feather to luxury white goose down. Any size quilt/bed linen made to order. Also quilt recovering and alterations. Send sae for price list/material samples.

5
FLOORS

We rarely consider the things we walk over: pavements, colleagues, spouses . . .
and floors. This area of the home is the hardest-done-by; positively down-
trodden, in fact. Make sure you choose materials that can cope with wear, and
then give them the encouragement, appreciation and care they deserve.

1. WOOD

"The white-washed wall, the nicely
  sanded floor,
The varnished clock that clicked
  behind the door;
The chest contrived a double debt to
  pay,
A bed by night, a chest of drawers
  by day."

Oliver Goldsmith (1728–74)

Firms specialising in wooden floors usually offer services for stripping/ renovating older wood surfaces. Many firms listed under **Architectural Salvage** can supply reclaimed wooden floors. Buy DIY wooden floors from **DIY superstores**, and some home improvement stores. Get help with laying/sanding/sealing etc. from firms listed under **Services 6. Floors: Stripping and Repolishing**.

London Postal Districts

Robert and Colleen Bery Designs See **Furniture 9. Painted.** Colour-washed, wooden floor tiles, plain/ stencilled. Stunning designs.

Campbell Marson and Co Unit 34, Wimbledon Business Centre, Riverside Road, SW17 OBA. (10 mins Tooting Broadway tube/ Earlsfield BR.) *Tel*: 081-879 1909. *Open*: Mon to Fri, 9.00am to 5.00pm, Sat 9.30am to 5.30pm. Old family business specialising in hardwood flooring: elaborate parquetry panels/borders, blocks, strips, rustic oak boards, pre-finished solids/laminates. Installations.

The Hardwood Flooring Company Canada House, Blackburn Road, West Hampstead NW6 1RZ. (West Hampstead tube/BR. Parking outside.) *Tel*: 071-328 8481. *Open*:

Mon to Fri, 8.30am to 5.30pm. "Hardwood costs about the same as good-quality carpet, but lasts much longer," says Geoffrey Hales, proprietor and wood enthusiast. Reclaimed timbers from cotton mills, churches, warehouses, schools: strip/block, maple/oak/redwood. Junckers beech/oak/ash/elm. Maple unfinished strip/block. Exquisite French oak wide-board planking. Laying service.

Tudor Flooring 2 Avenue Parade, Ridge Avenue, N21 2AX. (Southgate/Wood Green tubes. Grange Park/Winchmore Hill BR. Ample parking.) *Tel*: 081-360 4242. *Open*: Mon to Sat, 9.00am to 5.00pm. Proprietor Allan Ling trained under French/Italian parquet craftsmen. Wood specialists. Junckers/Kahrs/Tarkett. Amtico and other vinyls. Cork, ceramics, quarry tiles. Armstrong, Marley, Nairn, Wicanders.

Victorian Wood Works 139 Church Walk, N16 9PA. (Manor Park tube.) *Tel*: 071-241 2230. *Open*: Mon to Sat, 9.00am to 5.00pm. "New" floors from reclaimed timber. "We're very green and don't use forest hardwoods," says director Declan Malloy. Repairs/refinishing for old wooden floors. Will travel anywhere—as far as Russia for prestige restoration projects!

Home Counties/ South East

The First Flooring Company Pells Farm, Pells Lane, West Kings Down, Kent TN13 2AU. *Tel*: 071-738 4760. *Open*: by appointment. Specialists in reclaimed hardwood flooring.

Patey and Sons 110 Stafford Road, Wallington, Surrey SM6 9AY. (10 mins Wallington BR.) *Tel*: 081-647 8163. *Open*: Mon to Fri, 8.00am to 5.00pm. Sanding/sealing, parquet renovations. New hardwood floors/ cork floors/sheet vinyl and tiles.

Peter Robinson Deans Yard, Unit 12/13, rear Orchard Way, Fontwell, Arundel, W. Sussx BN18 0SJ. *Tel*: (0243) 552708. *Open*: Mon to Fri, 9.00am to 5.00pm, Sat 9.00am to 1.00pm. Wide selection secondhand floorboards. Window/doorframes/ timber.

Woodfloors and Woodstripping 15 Orleans Road, Twickenham, Middx TW1 3BJ. *Tel*: 081-891 2539. *Open*: by appointment. Mike Weatherall supplies/lays all types of new floors, or restores old ones. Colleague Malcolm Connell adds special effects: liming/bleaching/ stencils. London/Home Counties.

Mail Order

Heritage Woodcraft 14 Carlyon Road, Atherstone Industrial Estate, Atherstone, Warks CV9 1JE. *Tel*: (0827) 714761. All types of hardwood floor manufactured/ supplied nationwide. Blocks, strips, overlays, mosaics, panels, sports and dance floors. Exclusive custom-made designs.

Woodstock Hardwoods Ponsharden, Falmouth, Cornwall TR10 8AB. *Tel*: (0326) 76555. Specialist suppliers of all hardwood floors, nationwide deliveries. Easy lay, tongued-and-grooved strips. Twenty varieties of hardwood machined to any size for restorations/replacements.

2. VINYL, LINO AND CORK

So-called hard floors are attractive enough to bring into soft living/dining situations. Vinyls are stocked by many carpet retailers (see below), and at furnishing stores/department stores, but a specialist widens the scope. **DIY superstores** have budget ranges of vinyl, cork and wood.

London Postal Districts

▶ Bargains!

The Direct Bargain Centre See **Decorating Materials 1. Paints and Papers.** Changing stock often includes floor coverings e.g. cork/vinyl tiles/carpets.

First Floor 174 Wandsworth Bridge Road, SW6 2UQ. (15 mins Fulham Broadway/Parsons Green tubes.) *Tel*: 071-736 1123. *Open*: Mon to Fri, 9.30am to 5.30pm, Sat 10.00am to 2.00pm. Upmarket individual designs for linoleum/vinyl. Inlays/borders. Also rubber, cork, wood. Bordered carpets, special rugs.

Graham Floorings 20 Queens Parade, Friern Barnet Road, N11 3DA. (Arnos Grove tube. Ample parking. Opposite town hall.) *Tel*: 081-361 0983. *Open*: Mon to Fri, 8.30am to 5.00pm, Sat 9.00am to 4.00pm. Friendly family firm. Directors Terry Wolfe, the founder's son, and Brian Peack each have over 25 years' flooring experience. Wide range of vinyl sheet/tiles. Importers/installers of parquet/all-wood floors. Accessories/screeds/adhesives. Free estimating. Expert installations.

Laura Ashley Home See **Decorating Materials 2. Co-ordinated Collections.** At Last! Decorator designs for mass-market vinyls.

Printed self-adhesive tiles in charming patterns.

Sinclair Till 791–793 Wandsworth Road, SW8 3JQ. (5 mins Clapham Junction BR.) *Tel*: 071-720 0031. *Open*: Mon to Fri, 9.30am to 5.30pm, Sat 10.00am to 4.00pm. Suzie Sinclair/Alastair Till have a spacious corner showroom. Inspirational samples/examples of work. Speciality is inlaid lino. Made from linseed oil, wood flour, and cork, lino is very "green"—it's also warm, natural, hard-wearing and practical. Also innovative designs for wood. Plus good selections of natural-fibre mattings.

Victoria Flooring 4 Croxted Road, Dulwich SE21 5SW. *Tel*: 081-670 3322. *Open*: Mon to Fri, 9.00am to 5.30pm, Sat 10.00am to 4.00pm. Recently refurbished showroom for vinyls/wood/cork. Amtico. Carpets. Own fitters.

Home Counties/South East

All Floors 307/309 Brighton Road, South Croydon, Surrey CR2 6EQ. (A235 South of Croydon. 100 yds South Croydon bus garage. Parking in roads opposite.) *Tel*: 081-688 6969/5474. *Open*: Mon to Fri, 8.30am to 5.30pm, Sat 8.30am to 5.00pm. "Largest ranges, best prices." 1,000-sq ft showroom for one-stop flooring. Fifty years' flooring experience. Vinyl tiles, Heuga carpet tiles, wood mosaic panels, cork tiles. Amtico display centre. Hundreds of sheet vinyls. Accessories: floor sealer/floor paint/non-slip floor polish/self-levelling screed.

Completely Covered 30 Victoria Road, Farnborough, Hants GU14 7PG. (5 mins Farnborough BR. M3, junction 3. Three large car parks

nearby.) *Tel*: (0252) 541754. *Open*: Mon to Fri, 9.30am to 5.30pm, Sat 9.30am to 5.00pm. Amtico specialists: large displays. Ceramic tiles (walls/floors). Carpets, wood floorings, cork. Family business. Free measuring/estimating.

Dorking Floors 324 High Street, Dorking, Surrey RH4 1QX. (M25, junction 9. Park in side streets.) *Tel*: (0306) 883388. *Open*: Mon to Sat, 8.00am to 5.30pm. Closed for lunch from 1.00pm to 2.00pm. Specialise in original/unusual designs. Amtico specialists. Cork/wood. Trained staff/personal service: John Sutton has been trading for over 25 years.

Thames Flooring 612 Woodbridge Road, Guildford, Surrey GU1 4RF. (5 mins Guildford bus station. Park outside.) *Tel*: (0483) 65461. *Open*: Mon to Fri, 9.00am to 5.00pm, Sat 9.00am to 1.00pm. Established nearly 40 years. Good-size showroom. Cork/vinyl/carpets/ceramics. Friendly specialist staff. Free estimating. Skilled installations. Design service.

Mail Order

Northern Cork Supplies Unit 303, Phoenix Close, Haywood, Lancs OL10 2JG. *Tel*: (0706) 627255. Cork/hardwood specialists. Warehouse prices. Personal callers welcome. Nationwide deliveries. Samples 50p.

Siesta Cork Tiles Unit 21, Tait Road, Gloucester Road, Croydon, Surrey CR0 2DP. *Tel*: 081-683 4055. Leaflets/samples (two 2nd class stamps). Acrylic-sealed/pvc-surfaced cork tiles. Thicker tiles for insulation/pinboards. White and coloured cork tiles.

3. CARPETS

Carpets must combine soft surfaces with hard wear. Solve this problem by taking specialist advice, and buying the best you can afford, even if you have to wait for your furniture. Check out grading schemes and fibre qualities. Never put down a carpet until all building, plumbing and electrical work is completed.

London Postal Districts

Afia Carpets   The Design and Decoration Building, 107a Pimlico Road, SW1W 8PH. (5 mins Sloane Square tube.) *Tel:* 071-483 2439. *Open:* Mon to Fri, 10.00am to 6.00pm, Sat 11.00am to 5.00pm, Sun by appointment. Late night Wed, 7.00pm. David and Judy Afia are carpet experts. They design/custom-make fine quality fitted carpets, in a variety of textures. Exclusive range of needlepoint rugs. Brochure available.

Allied Maples   For details of nearest store, tel: 081-200 0200. *Star store:* Unit 1, Eley Road, off Angel Road, Edmonton N18 3BH. (3 mins Angel Road BR.) *Tel:* 081-884 2596. *Open:* 7 days, Mon to Fri, 10.00am to 6.00pm. Late nights Mon and Fri, 8.00pm. Open Sat, 9.00am to 6.00pm, Sun 10.00am to 5.00pm. Over 200 stores nationwide: now incorporates Allied Carpets. You can exchange goods within 14 days for any reason (including a change of mind): even fitted carpets, and made-to-order curtains/upholstery. Carpets/floor coverings. Readymade/custom curtains. Furniture/beds/linens/rugs. Around 3,000 carpets, 2,700 curtain fabrics. Free home delivery for most items. In-home furnishing advice. Low price guarantee. Free fitting on carpets over £9.99 sq yd. Free measuring/estimating. Fitting guarantee for 12 months. Wearability guarantee on all carpets. Mastershield Protection Plan protects carpets/upholstery against accidental stains.
Also at: 90/100 Edgware Road, W2 2HX. (3 mins Marble Arch tube.) *Tel:* 071-402 2233.
And at: Brixton, Wood Green, Wembley, Guildford, Putney, Reading, Colchester, Luton, Ilford, Watford, Crawley, Bracknell, Thurrock, Woking, Harlow, Maidenhead, Burnt Oak, Croydon, Epsom, Bromley, Chadwell Heath, Hayes, Holloway, Lewisham, Walthamstow, West Ealing.

▶ Bargains!

Budget Carpets   390 Walworth Road, Camberwell SE17. (5 mins Elephant and Castle tube.) *Tel:* 071-701 4460. *Open:* Mon to Sat, 9.00am to 5.30pm (all branches). Room-size remnants, low prices, plus many cut-price ranges. Free measuring, same-day deliveries. Cut-price fitting. Vinyls also.
Also at: Murphy's Yard, 30 Power Street, Woolwich, SE18. (3 mins Woolwich BR.) *Tel:* 081-855 7359.
And at: 19/21 Atlantic Road, Brixton SW9. (1 min Brixton tube.) *Tel:* 071-737 3268.

Capitol Carpets   98/100 Northcote Road, Battersea SW11. (10 mins Clapham Junction BR.) *Tel:* 071-228 7167. *Open:* Mon to Sat, 9.00am to 5.30pm. Family business. Supply/fit all major makes carpets/hard floors. Member of Metro group: competitive prices.
Also at: 437/439 Upper Richmond Road West, East Sheen SW14. *Tel:* 071-878 2051.
See also **Home Counties/South East** below.

The Carpet Showroom   111 High Road, East Finchley N2 8AG. (7 mins East Finchley tube.) *Tel:* 081-444 9911. *Open:* Mon to Sat, 9.00am to 6.00pm. Early mornings/evenings by appointment. Elegant upmarket showroom for all flooring, except ceramics. Amtico specialists. Careful service. Own fitters.

Carpet Tile Centres
227 Woodhouse Road, Finchley N12 9BD. (15 mins Arnos Grove tube.) *Tel:* 081-361 1261. *Open:* Mon to Sat, 9.00am to 5.00pm. Comprehensive stock of carpet tiles, including Heuga at cheapest prices.
Also at: 150 Pinner Road, Harrow. *Tel:* 081-863 9551. *Open:* Mon to Fri, 9.00am to 11.00am only.

Decorum Carpets   17/21 Pavilion Road, SW1. (5 mins Knightsbridge tube.) *Tel:* 071-235 0104/5 and 071-235 7384/5. *Open:* Mon to Sat, 9.00am to 5.30pm. Huge choice plain carpets/borders/runners: 48-hour delivery.

▶ Bargains!

Discount Carpet Company   290 West Green Road, N15 5TB. (10 mins Wood Green tube.) *Tel:* 081-889 6366. *Open:* Mon to Sat, 9.00am to 5.30pm (both branches). Early closing Thu, 1.00pm. Cut-price carpets/vinyls/mattings.

▶ Bargains!

Europa International   Europa House, Meaford Way, Oakfield Road, Penge SE20 8RA. (Near Sainsbury's Homebase.) *Tel:* 081-676 0064. *Open:* Mon to Fri, 9.00am to 5.00pm, Sat 9.30am to 5.00pm. Ex-exhibition carpets. Carpet your house for £100 (they say).

▶ Bargains!

Falcon Carpet Tiles   278 Upper Richmond Road, Putney SW15 6SQ. (10 mins East Putney BR.) *Tel:* 081-788 9075. *Open:* Mon to Sat, 9.30am to 5.30pm. Ex-contract industrial carpet tiles.

John Lewis, Peter Jones and other stores in John Lewis Partnership. See Department Stores. Plain carpets, all qualities, clearly displayed according to colour; super value Jonelle cord. Jonelle stock carpets laid within 14 days.

Marlows Carpets   67 East Hill, Wandsworth SW18 2QE. (5 mins Wandsworth Town BR/East Putney tube, plus bus.) Tel: 081-871 1169. Open: Mon to Sat, 8.30am to 6.00pm. Supply/fit carpets and vinyls, including Amtico. Carpet-/upholstery-/curtain-cleaning service.

▶ Bargains!

S and M Myers   100/106 Mackenzie Road, N7 8RG. (5 mins Caledonian Road tube.) Tel: 071-609 0091. Open: Mon, Wed, Fri 10.00am to 5.30pm, Sat 9.30am to 2.00pm. Remarkably good value plain/wool carpets sold off the roll.

Palace Floorings   20 Palace Gates Road, N22 4BN. (Alexandra Place BR opposite shop. Wood Green/Finsbury Park tubes, plus W3 bus.) Tel: 081-881 2538. Open: Mon to Sat, 9.15 am to 5.30pm. Family carpet business. Home visits with carpet samples. Vinyls: Nairn/Tarket/Armstrong.

▶ Bargains!

Posners Carpet Centre   9 Westbourne Grove, W2 4UA. (10 mins Bayswater tube.) Tel: 071-229 4304. Open: Mon to Sat, 9.00am to 5.30pm. Room-size remnants, seconds, discontinued ranges and perfect goods at keen prices. Also vinyl flooring. Fitting, free estimates.

Resista Carpets   255 New King's Road, Fulham SW6 4RB. (10 mins Parsons Green tube.) Tel: 071-731 2588. Open: Mon to Sat, 9.00am to 5.30pm (all branches except Sheen). Late night Wed, 7.30pm. Large stocks plain colour quality carpets. Twists, loops, velvets, plains, patterns, Axminster, Wilton, tufted. Also sheet vinyls, Amtico, woodblocks. Free plan/fit within 48 hours from stock. Expert advice. Free samples. Half-price carpet remnants.
Also at: 148 Wandsworth Bridge Road, Fulham SW6 2UH. (10 mins Parsons Green tube.) Tel: 071-731 3368.
And at: 584/586 Fulham Road, SW6 5NT. (10 mins Parsons Green tube.) Tel: 071-736 7551.
And at: 182 Upper Richmond Road West, East Sheen SW14 8AW. (10 mins Mortlake BR.) Tel: 081-876 2089. Early closing Wed, 12.00 noon.
And at: 207 Haverstock Hill, NW3 4QG. (2 mins Belsize Park tube.) Tel: 071-794 0130.

Waldorf   Whiteleys (first floor), 101 Queensway, W2 4YH. (5 mins Bayswater/Queensway tubes.) Tel: 071-792 3344. Open: Mon to Sat, 10.00am to 8.00pm. Long-established family business. Sophisticated, upmarket merchandise. Ritzy atmosphere, well-developed design sense. Exclusive carpet colours (well over 1,000). Special colours/designs to order. Borders. Parquet/vinyl tiles. Unusual modern rugs. Latest international furniture. Free interior design advice.

Expert fitting. Worth exploring.
Also at: 278/280 Brompton Road, SW3 2AN. (5 mins South Kensingon tube.) Tel: 071-589 5245. Open: Mon to Fri, 9.30am to 5.30pm, Sat 10.00 am to 4.00pm.

West End Carpet Co   1 Baker Street, W1M 1AA. (5 mins Marble Arch tube.) Tel: 071-224 6635. Open: Mon to Sat, 8.30am to 5.00pm (both branches). "Quality with economy." Top grade carpets plus wood/vinyl/cork. Own fitters.
Also at: 922/928 High Road, N12 9RW. (10 mins Woodside Park tube.) Tel: 081-446 5331.

Home Counties/South East

Capitol Carpets   34 Beddington Lane, Croydon, Surrey. Tel: 081-688 6209. Open: Mon to Fri, 8.00am to 5.00pm, Sat 9.00am to 5.00pm. See also London Postal Districts above.

▶ Bargains!

Carpet Town   Unit 1, Great Western Industrial Park, Armstrong Way, Windmill Lane, Southall, Middx UB2 4SD. (Off Uxbridge Road, close to Ealing Hospital.) Tel: 081-571 9333. Open: Mon to Fri, 10.00am to 8.00pm, Sat 9.30am to 5.30pm, Sun 10.00am to 5.00pm. Huge variety, low prices. Lots of remnants/ends of ranges. West London's largest carpet superstore, they claim. Measure/estimate within 24 hours. Fitted from stock within 72 hours.

4. MATTINGS

Not necessarily cheap these days, mattings can be chic, and blend well with natural materials such as wood and terracotta.

London Postal Districts

Crucial Trading   77 Westbourne Park Road, W2 4BX. (Paddington tube/BR. Bayswater/Royal Oak tubes.) *Tel:* 071-221 9000. *Open:* Tue to Sat, 10.00am to 6.00pm. Natural floorings attain design status. Sisal, seagrass, coir, rush. Pleasant showroom. New, chic colours/weaves. Samples. Expert fitting/stain-proofing. Special price offers. Mail order.

▶ Bargains!

Eaton's   30 Neal Street, Covent Garden WC2H 9PS. (5 mins Covent Garden tube.) *Tel:* 071-379 6254. *Open:* Mon to Fri, 10.00am to 5.00pm, Sat 12.00 noon to 6.00pm. The quaint little Eaton's Bag Company used to trade incognito alongside Foyles. Now it's a chic shell boutique in a tourist high-spot. Persevere to the back to find inexpensive natural mattings. Coarsely woven raffia (lay straight on boards; join with double-sided tape). Philippine/Chinese rush mats. Many others. Various weaves. Panels for roller blinds/furniture trim/wall decor. Samples. A very special shop.

Mail Order

Rooksmoor Mills   Bath Road, Stroud, Glos GL5 5ND. *Tel:* (0453) 872577. *Open:* 7 days, 9.00am to 5.00pm. Cotswold stone mill (parts date back to 17th century) with the Nailsworth Stream underneath. 9,000-sq ft showroom for cane furniture and budget-priced mattings: natural/bleached/herringbone. Latex-backed seagrass. Samples. Café.

5. MARBLE, SLATE AND STONE

See also **Tiles 3. Marble, Slate and Stone.**

London Postal Districts

Castelnau Tiles See **Tiles 1. Specialists.**   Natural stone slabs, slates and marbles.

Stone Age   The Studio, 40 St John's Hill Grove, SW11 2RG. *Tel:* 071-738 2554. *Open:* by appointment. Wide variety of sandstones/limestones from Spain/Italy. Free colour brochures. Samples. Recommended installers.

Worlds End Tiles See **Tiles 1. Specialists.**   Good selections marble floor/wall tiles in spacious settings.

Zarka Marble See **Kitchens 6. Worktops.**   All marble/granite, slate, French/English limestone, Yorkstone, sandstone. Stone carving/lettering/sand-blasting. Supply/fix.

Home Counties/ South East

Art Marbles, Stone and Mosaic Co Dawson Road, Kingston-upon-Thames, Surrey KT1 3AX. *Tel:* 081-546 2023/3240. *Open:* Mon to Fri, 9.00am to 5.00pm. Closed from 1.00pm to 2.00pm. Marble craftsmen: trading for over 50 years. Their installations have included The London Hilton and The Geological Museum. Complete service: design/manufacture/install marble/granite/slate. Plus technical advice. Can supply/process marble "for almost any use". Specialise in large projects, where stone is used for cladding, flooring, sills, jambs, copings and stair treads; but can also supply and fix marble for paving, vanity unit tops, bathroom wall linings, paving and fireplaces. Around 90 samples on view at Building Centre, 26 Store Street, WC1. Colour brochure/small samples available.

Just Tiles   84/88 Headley Road, Woodley, Reading, Berks RG4 4JE. (M4, junction 10. Signs to Reading, then Woodley. Ample parking.) *Tel:* (0734) 697774. *Open:* Mon to Sat, 8.30am to 5.30pm, Sun 10.00am to 1.00pm. Handmade terracottas/marble/granite/ceramics. 3,500 sq ft showroom. Family firm trading for 20 years. Expert fixing. 24-hour service for tile-cutting.

6
WALLS

Walls have pots of decorating potential. After all, they are the biggest single area of your home. This chapter suggests specialist treatments. For wallpapers, paints, stencils and the like, see **Decorating Materials**, which also lists suppliers of co-ordinated collections. And **Tiles** have their own chapter, too.

1. FABRIC LINING

Walls covered with fabric, pleated or stretched tight, are expensive and difficult to clean. If fabric is suspended from expanded wires top and bottom, or poles, it can be taken down for cleaning. However this treatment conceals really bad wall surfaces and/or insulation for a cosy room. For other firms that carry out "soft lining", see **Interior Design** and **Soft Furnishings**.

London Postal Districts

Bellhouse and Company See **Interior Design**. Specialists in fabric walling.

Deanguard Drapes 62/64 Choumert Road, SE15 4AX. *Tel*: 071-252 8264. *Open*: by appointment only. Soft furnishing experts (established over 25 years). Specialise in "fabricated walling", using traditional methods with battens/interlining, with flat or pleated fabric.

Lewis and Fell *Tel*: 081-992 0046. *Open* (telephone enquiries only): Mon to Fri, 9.00am to 5.00pm. Mother-and-son business (established 1945) catering for the top end of the trade. Experts at lining walls with fabric in traditional fashion.

Material Effects See **Ceilings 3. Tented**. All soft furnishings to a very high standard, including wall lining.

2. TAPESTRIES AND HANGINGS

In medieval times, tapestries were essential for insulation, and of course they were decorative, too. Revive a forgotten charm from shops below. You will find more suppliers of antique tapestries in **Soft Furnishings 9. Antique Textiles**. You can also hang bedspreads and rugs effectively on walls: see **Accessories**. Or stitch your own: suppliers are suggested in **British Crafts 4. Craft Supplies**.

London Postal Districts

Sarah Collins See **Soft Furnishings 10. Commissioned Fabrics**. Handpainted brightly coloured cotton/silk wall hangings in captivating, often amusing, domestic designs.

Belinda Coote Tapestries 29 Holland Street, Kensington W8 4NA. (2 mins Kensington High Street tube.) *Tel*: 071-937 3924. *Open*: Mon to Sat, 10.00am to 6.00pm. Reproduction tapestry wall hangings, tapestry fabrics, tapestry borders, tapestry cushions, handpainted furniture, wooden firescreens; small gifts.

Home Counties/ South East

Liza Collins 79A Leigham Court Drive, Leigh-on-Sea, Essex SS9 1PT. *Tel*: (evenings) 081-517 6449. *Open*: by appointment. Handwoven tapestries, one-off pieces and commissions.

Hines of Oxford Weavers Barn, Windmill Road, Headington, Oxford OX3 7DE. (Off London Road in Headington.) *Tel*: (0865) 741144. *Open*: by appointment, Mon to Fri, 9.00am to 5.00pm. Closed for lunch 1.00pm to 2.00pm. Closed Sat and Sun. Tapestry/wall hangings, importers from 10 Continental weavers. Reproductions from medieval times to 18th century, woven in wool/cotton/artificial silk. Hundreds of panels always in stock, from small to large, including handweave. Full colour catalogue. Travelling representatives may visit your area: ring for details.

Thursley Textile Designs 1 Moushill Lane, Milford, Godalming, Surrey. (A3 from London.) *Tel*: (0483) 424769. *Open*: Mon to Sat, 10.00am to 5.30pm. Handwoven tapestries from designer workshop. Furnishings, toys, clothes. Exhibitions/courses.

▶ Worth a Trip

Stuart Interiors See **Furniture 11. Reproduction**. Antique/reproduction 16th-/17th-century period tapestries.

3. WOODEN MOULDINGS

Once ripped untimely from period properties, restoration is now the order of the day for skirting boards, and picture and dado rails. Many firms make to order, and will copy your patterns. Specialist joinery firms are also listed under **4. Panelling**, below and **Staircases 1. Wooden**. Add mouldings to plain skirtings with scotia or quadrant beadings pinned along the top edge. Fit the dado rail at waist height, with co-ordinating papers/paint above/below (this cuts tall walls down to size). Rescue the once-despised picture rail and suspend paintings/prints in fine frames, with parallel fine brass/chrome chains fixed at each corner.

Now that mouldings are back in fashion, you will find reasonable selections at **DIY Superstores**. For restorations, try **Architectural Salvage** firms.

London Postal Districts

Court Davis Joinery   Block D, Imperial Works, Ryland Road, NW5. (Next to Kentish Town BR. 10 mins Kentish Town tube.) *Tel:* 071-485 8538. *Open:* Mon to Fri, 8.30am to 5.00pm, Sat 8.30am to 1.00pm. Manufacturer of specialist and standard joinery. Victorian mouldings. Stairs/handrails made to order.

General Woodwork Supplies 76–80 Stoke Newington High Street, Stoke Newington N16 5BR. (Seven Sisters/Finsbury Park tubes.) *Tel:* 071-254 6052. *Open:* Mon to Fri, 8.00am to 6.00pm, Sat 9.00am to 6.00pm. Closed Thu, 3.00pm. Wide range timber/mouldings cut to order.

W R and A Hide See **Staircases 1. Wooden**. Made-to-measure skirtings, architraves, mouldings.

Latham's Timber and Building Materials   Leaside Wharf, Mount Pleasant Hill, Clapton E5 9NG. (Clapton tube.) *Tel:* 081-806 1236/7. *Open:* Mon to Thu, 8.00am to 5.00pm, Fri 8.00am to 4.00pm, Sat 8.00am to 12.00 noon. Mouldings/architraves machined to order. Extensive selection of new timber: lime, sycamore, walnut, ash, oak, chestnut, elm, beech.

W H Newson   61 Pimlico Road, SW1W 8NF. (7 mins Sloane Square tube.) *Tel:* 071-730 6262. *Open:* Mon to Fri, 8.00am to 5.00pm, Sat 8.00am to 12.30pm. Timber/DIY specialists trading for 150 years. The original John Newson was a Victorian entrepreneur par excellence, graduating from being a road sweeper to a carpenter, and then a house builder. Fine timber/mouldings, door/windows, fencing, hardware, home improvement materials for trade/private customers. Mouldings matched to any specification. Trained staff. Speedy, free deliveries. Free colour catalogue is a DIY bible: make sure you get your copy.
Also at: 491 Battersea Park Road, SW11 4NH. *Tel:* 071-223 4411.
And at: 61/79 Norwood High Street, SE27 9JS. *Tel:* 081-670 0112.
See also **Home Counties/South East** below.

Tempus Stet See **Lighting 2. Traditional and Antique**.   Classical reproduction carvings/decorations in moulded quality resins, variety of finishes. Fruit and flower garlands, swags and drops, circular cherub plaques.

Home Counties/ South East

Alderage Timber Products   Old Park Farm Yard, Main Road, Kingsley, Hants GU32 9LU. *Tel:* (04204) 88245. *Open:* no set times, please phone to check. Old pine: cut/plain/moulded. New English hardwoods.

A W Champion   Champion House, 205/207 Burlington Road, New Malden, Surrey KT3 4NB. *Tel:* 081-949 1621. *Open:* Mon to Fri, 8.00am to 5.30pm, Sat 8.00am to 5.00pm. Timber merchants. Mouldings/ready-made staircases.

J R Nelson   The Sawmill, Newchurch, Romney Marsh, Kent TN29 0DT. *Tel:* (0233) 733361. *Open:* Mon to Fri, 9.00am to 5.00pm, Sat 9.00am to 12.00 noon (but phone first). Antique pitch pine sawn from 18th-/19th-century timbers. Exclusive range of architectural mouldings/ turnings.

W H Newson   Campaspe Trading Estate, Fordbridge Road, Lower Sunbury-on-Thames, Middx TW16 6AT. *Tel:* (0932) 780633/4.
Also at: Burr Street, Luton LU2 0HN. *Tel:* (0582) 27707.
And at: Heathside House, Brighton Road, Burgh Heath, Reigate KT20 6BE. *Tel:* (0737) 362111.
See also **London Postal Districts** above.

RGS Joinery   Paldre, Rucklers Lane, Kings Langley, Hemel Hempstead, Herts. (1 mile from A41.) *Tel:* (0442) 61394. *Open:* Mon to Sat, 8.30am to 6.00pm. Mouldings, skirtings, coving etc. in unusual shapes and sizes to order. Also traditional staircases. Installations.

4. PANELLING

Panelling is a perfect panacea for ugly pipework/electrics: but remember to leave removeable sections for maintenance access. In addition to wood, panelling can be made from plastic (to simulate white-painted planking or dark, aged timbers), or from fretted hardboard.

Bespoke joinery firms listed in other sections can usually help with panelling: see **3. Wooden Mouldings** (above), and **Staircases 1. Wooden**. Or find old panelling at **Architectural Salvage** merchants.

London Postal Districts

Bella Figura See **Lighting 2. Traditional and Antique.** Extensive displays of oakleaf panellings/mouldings made from rigid polyurethane. From simple fielded squares to intricate linenfold. Fine detailing/finish: attractive/realistic effects. Light and easy to cut/fix. Colourings: from Jacobean oak to light/limed/weathered oaks and mahogany. Also imitation, brightly coloured panels and leather-bound "books". A revelation in the aesthetic potential of "fake".

Roger Board Designs 273 Putney Bridge Road, SW15 2PT. (5 mins Putney Bridge tube. Putney BR.) *Tel:* 081-789 0046/946 5251. *Open:* by appointment. Traditional, well-established joinery company. Panelled rooms using only antique timber. Built-in fitments including bookcases/cupboards.

Charles Hurst Workshop See **Furniture 12. Made-to-measure.** Traditional Victorian decorative tongue-and-groove boarding ("matching").

W H Newson See **3. Wooden Mouldings** above. Reliable central London source for "matchboarding"

(pine panelling), pinboards, noticeboards. Plus Screenlite fretted hardboard panels in five decorative designs.

▶ Bargains!

TMW Timber and Builders Merchants 19/20 Latona Road, Peckham SE15 6RX. (15 mins Queens Road BR.) *Tel:* 071-358 0076. *Open:* Mon to Sat, 8.00am to 5.30pm. Closed from 12.30pm to 1.30pm. Timber/boards at discount prices (architraves, skirting, pine cladding) plus doors and other building materials.

Wansdown Joinery Works See **Staircases 1. Wooden.** Traditional panelled rooms.

Woodstock Furniture See **Kitchens 5. Luxury and Bespoke Kitchens.** Custom-made panelling in pitch pine or limed oak.

Home Counties/ South East

Roy Blackman Associates 150/152 High Road, Chadwell Heath, Essex RM6 6NT. (5 mins Chadwell Heath BR.) *Tel:* 081-599 5247. *Open:* Mon to Fri, 9.00am to 5.30pm, Sat 10.00am to 5.00pm. Simulated oak linenfold/Jacobean wall panelling. Reproduction oak beams, fireplaces, cocktail bars. Decorative plate-rack, carved friezes, cornices. Lightweight, durable, convincing—unless you touch them! Colour brochure available.

Peter H Blomfield Willow Wood, Bit Lane, Luggershall, near Aylesbury, Bucks HP18 9NZ. (Off A41.) *Tel:* (0844) 238278. *Open:* by appointment. Fitted panelled libraries in English/foreign woods. Bedrooms. Custom-made furniture.

JJ Bunker and Sons 73 Common Road, Chandlers Ford, Eastleigh, Hants SO5 1HE. *Tel:* (0703) 268176. *Open:* Mon to Fri, 9.00am to 6.00pm. Sat 9.00am to 12.00 noon. Specialists in replacement and restoration joinery. Staircase manufacturers.

Dove Bell Enfield Works, Jeffreys Road, Enfield, Middx EN3 7UB. (5 mins Brimsdown BR.) *Tel:* 081-805 1548. *Open:* by appointment. Made-to-measure service for panelled rooms. Purpose-made joinery.

Samuel Elliott and Sons 61 Gosbrook Road, Caversham, Reading, Berks RG4 8BP. (1 mile Reading BR.) *Tel:* (0734) 476622. *Open:* by appointment. Made-to-measure joinery. Fitting service.

Exquisite Interiors See **Furniture 12. Made-to-measure and Commissioned.** Specialists in pine-panelled rooms.

James Longley and Co East Park, Crawley, W. Sussx RH10 6AP. (5 mins Crawley BR.) *Tel:* (0293) 561212. *Open:* by appointment. Made-to-measure panelling/woodcarving. Fitting service.

Oakwood Joinery Orchard Works, Church Lane, Wallington, Surrey SM6 7ND. (15 mins Wallington BR.) *Tel:* 081-773 2141. *Open:* Mon to Fri, 7.00am to 6.00pm. Made-to-measure joinery; oak furniture and fittings. Wall panelling and doors.

Private Lives See **Interior Design.** Bespoke joinery. Panelled rooms/wall-to-wall bookcases to the highest standards.

Wallis Broadmead Works, Hart Street, Maidstone, Kent ME16 8RE. *Tel:* (0622) 690960. *Open:* by appointment. Made-to-measure panelling/joinery/fitting service. Doors/staircases/kitchens/fittings. Brochure available.

5. MURALS AND SPECIAL EFFECTS

"I will make a palace
fit for you and me
Of green days in forest
and blue days at sea."

Robert Louis Stevenson (1850–94)

The past decade has seen an amazing resurgence for older types of painted wall decorations, such as special paint effects, murals and *trompe l'oeil*. The impecunious (and mildly talented) can take such decorating challenges on board with the help of **Decorating Materials 3. Stick-ons** and **5. Stencils and Paint-Effect Kits**. Otherwise, you'll have to hire an artist. Thanks to the proficiency of art schools and an abundance of natural talent, no shortage exists. Prices vary widely, according to age/experience/nature of job/fame and so on. But always check whether you are paying a flat fee for the job or by the hour: the former is preferable. Most artists will visit you with their portfolio by arrangement, once they are assured that yours is a genuine enquiry. Before employing an artist, try to see actual examples of his or her work. Full sketches/drawings of proposed murals are desirable. Many of the firms listed under **Interior Design** can put you in touch with specialist painters/muralists. But artists come and go as inspiration ebbs, so check out current Michelangelos on the list below. Most are prepared to travel, providing a job is worth their while.

London Postal Districts

Tim Bizley   *Tel*: 081-349 0195. Stencils, murals, frescos, faux.

Brushstrokes   *Tel*: 071-737 6876. Simon Bingle and Roger Merricks trained at Camberwell School of Art. They have four years' experience of murals and *trompe l'oeil*, plus intricate special paint effects involving up to eight shades.

Nigel Crawley   Unit 17, Carew Street, SE5 9DF. *Tel*: 071-733 1276. Speciality: classical murals/Italian scenes.

Douglas Druce   *Tel*: 071-722 4581. Murals, *trompe l'oeil*, interior wall paintings. Also portraits and marbling.

Colin Failes   *Tel*: 071-274 2093. *Trompe l'oeil* murals and frescos.

Diana Finch   *Tel*: 071-352 0131. Specialist stencil/mural designer. Also furniture painting/fabric stencilling.

William Grantham   *Tel*: 071-249 9120. *Trompe l'oeil* artist with special interest in Italianate style.

Sally Jubb Divine Walls   *Tel*: 081-874 3568. Freehand style for flowers, animals, children's rooms: five years' experience.

Fiona Latta   *Tel*: 071-585 3035. This experienced artist (15 years) can paint *trompe l'oeil* onto walls or moveable panels. Sky ceilings/arcadian vistas/jungles. Furniture/blinds.

Catherine Lovegrove Murals   *Tel*: 081-960 8141. "Plagiarism a speciality!"

Sheena Magill   *Tel*: 071-607 6561. Any size mural, from a small panel to complete rooms, including ceilings. Original pictorial designs, *trompe l'oeil*, vistas, skies. Children's designs for nurseries in bright colours.

The Painted Ladies   *Tel*: 081-840 0416. Graphic designer Debbie Seed and textile artist Pavala Henshaw offer "a bit more than rag-rolling". Painted surface patterns for walls, furniture and even fridges.

Home Counties/ South East

Jenny Sacha Haine   *Tel*: (0460) 30292. Skilled, experienced stenciller. Imaginative interpretation of all decorative ideas.

7

CEILINGS

What goes up must not come down—structural stability is a first priority. But ceilings are also large, flat spaces, just begging to be decorated with mouldings, murals, timbers, fabric or whatever. If, however, you prefer to apply just a couple of coats of emulsion, all you need do is refer to **Decorating Materials** for details of paint suppliers.

1. MOULDINGS AND RESTORATION

Firms abound to help restore ceilings to their former glories. Many will copy mouldings and install them in your home. You can also add a rose or cornice to a modern room. Adding mouldings (ceiling rose, cornice etc.) can improve a bleak, featureless room. Many shops sell lightweight easy-to-fix versions (e.g. **DIY Superstores**, **Interior Design** specialists). Ready-made plaster mouldings are also available. Restoring existing mouldings is trickier, but the specialists listed below can help with home service.

London Postal Districts

H and F Badcock   Unit 9, 57 Sandgate Street, Old Kent Road, SE15 1LE. (Elephant and Castle tube, plus bus/New Cross BR, plus bus.) *Tel*: 071-639 0304. *Open*: Mon to Fri, 7.00am to 5.00pm. Large, specialist workshop. Fibrous plastering/mouldings. Can restore any moulded plasterwork. Prestige jobs have included the Foreign Office and Westminster Abbey.

Butcher Plastering Specialists 8 Fitzroy Road, Primrose Hill NW1 8TX. (10 mins Chalk Farm tube.) *Tel*: 071-722 9771. *Open*: Mon to Thu, 8.00am to 5.00pm, Fri 8.00am to 4.00pm. Twenty-five-year-old family business. Specialists in decorative mouldings/walls/arches. Able to match existing mouldings. Brochure available.

Decorative Plasterwork 385 Ladbroke Grove, North Kensington W10 5AA. (10 mins Ladbroke Grove tube.) *Tel*: 081-960 0448. *Open*: Mon to Fri, 9.00am to 5.30pm, Sat 9.00am to 1.00pm.

Plaster mouldings. Installation/restoration specialists.

FGS Interiors   350 Cricklewood Lane, NW2 2HQ. (10 mins Golders Green tube.) *Tel*: 081-458 7478. *Open*: Mon to Fri, 9.00am to 5.30pm. Family business, established for 10 years. Plaster architectural mould specialists. Manufacture/restore/install anything made of plaster. Also soft furnishing specialists. Brochure available on request.

Green and Veronese   Interior House, Linton Road, Crouch End, N8 8SL. (10 mins Highgate tube.) *Tel*: 081-348 4461. *Open*: by appointment. Fibrous plaster corniche manufacturers/suppliers. "We can make anything," they say. Their work has included the Royal National Theatre. Free brochure available.

Hodkins and Jones   23 Rathbone Place, W1P 1DB. (5 mins Tottenham Court Road tube.) *Tel*: 071-636 2617. *Open*: Mon to Fri, 9.30am to 5.30pm. Showroom for large, Sheffield-based company. Installations/restoration. Catalogue available.

J D McDonough   347 New King's Road, SW6 4RJ. (5 mins Parsons Green/Putney Bridge tubes.) *Tel*: 071-736 5146. *Open*: Mon to Thu, 8.00am to 5.00pm, Fri 8.00am to 4.00pm, Sat 8.00am to 1.00pm. Closed for lunch from 12.00 noon to 1.00pm. Family business, established for 50 years. Fibre fire-surrounds/centre pieces/niches/mouldings. Supply/fit. Their "high class work" has included Windsor Castle.

Michael F O'Reilly   46 Cumbrian Gardens, NW2 1EF. *Tel*: 081-458 2736. *Open*: by appointment.

Plasterwork/restoration. Outside stucco work, columns, pillars.

Home Counties/South East

Clark and Fenn   Unit 19, Mitcham Industrial Estate, Streatham Road, Mitcham, Surrey CR4 2AJ. (Tooting Broadway tube plus bus.) *Tel*: 081-648 4343. *Open*: Mon to Fri, 8.30am to 4.45pm. Impeccable pedigree: founded in 1780 by the Brothers Adam. Some 18th-century moulds still exist. Varied stocks. Install/restore.

GC Mouldings   10 West End Lane, Barnet, Herts EN5 2SA. (7 mins High Barnet tube. Own car park.) *Tel*: 081-449 2247. *Open*: Mon to Fri, 8.00am to 4.30pm, Sat 8.00am to 12.00 noon. Workshop for fibrous plaster mouldings. Supply/fix. Repairs, commissions.

Ornamental Design Plastering Co   Unit 2, Johnson's Ind. Est., off Silverdale Road, Hayes, Middx UB3 3BA. (5 mins Hayes BR.) *Tel*: 081-573 3129. *Open*: Mon to Fri, 7.00am to 5.00pm. Specialists in fibrous plaster mouldings. Cornices/niches. Nationwide service available.

Mail Order

Rainford House of Elegance Wentworth Street, Birdwell, Barnsley, S. Yorks S70 5UN. (M1 junction 36.) *Tel*: (0226) 350360. *Open*: Mon to Sat, 9.00am to 5.30pm, Sun 10.00am to 5.30pm. Late night Thu 8.00pm. Ornamental plaster mouldings: fireplaces, niches, cornices, wall panels, coving. Nationwide delivery service and installations.

2. TIMBERS AND BEAMS

Add a touch of olde England. This section tells you where to shop for timbers, old or fake. Explore also firms listed in **Architectural Salvage**, for the real thing.

London Postal Districts

W H Newson   61 Pimlico Road, SW1W 8NF. (7 mins Sloane Square tube.) *Tel*: 071-730 6262. *Open*: Mon to Fri, 8.00am to 5.00pm, Sat 8.00am to 12.00 noon. Timber beams distressed/stained by hand for effective aged look. Matching wall panelling, mouldings, corbels, shelving, plate racks, architraves, skirtings and chair rails.

Home Counties/ South East

Antique Buildings   Dunsfold, Surrey GU8 4NP. *Tel*: (0486) 49477. *Open*: any day, by appointment. Large stocks of ancient oak beams, all under cover. Handmade bricks/peg tiles/walling stone. Dismantled barns for re-erection.

Roy Blackman Associates See **Walls 4. Panelling.**   Finely crafted reproduction exposed oak beams. Lightweight, durable. Colour brochure available.

Glover and Stacey. See **Architectural Salvage.**   Oak beams. Many different sections: 5in by 5in most popular. Also seasoned English joinery oak. Various lengths of pine beams.

Petit Roque See **Heating 2. Fireplaces.**   Softwood beams distressed for traditional Tudor look. Real oak sometimes available.

Piltdown Architectural Salvage Oak Ferrars Farm, Piltdown, near Uckfield, E. Sussx. *Tel*: (0825) 723668. *Open*: Mon to Fri, 9.00am to 5.30pm, Sat 9.00am to 1.00pm. Oak timber/beams. Bricks/ tiles/slates.

Romsey Reclamation See **Architectural Salvage.**   Reclaimed beams.

Symonds Brothers   Colts Yard, Pluckley Road, Bethersden, Kent TN26 3DD. *Tel*: (0233) 82724. *Open*: Mon to Fri, 8.30am to 5.00pm, Sat 8.30am to 12.30pm. Reclaimed oak beams/bricks/tiles/slates.

Mail Order

Aristocast   Bold Street, Sheffield, S. Yorks S9 3TW. *Tel*: (0742) 561156. Reproduction oak beams. Design service. Colour brochure available. Nationwide deliveries. Own transport.

▶ Worth a Trip

Colin Baker, Timber Merchant Crown Hill, Halberton, Tiverton, Devon EX16 7AY. (Near Halberton Village.) *Tel*: (0884) 820152/821007. *Open*: by appointment ("any reasonable time"). Half an acre of beams and planks, mainly in English oak at very reasonable prices. Specialists in restoration of building timbers. Nationwide delivery service. Cut to size. Phone for advice/quote.

3. TENTED CEILINGS

A tented ceiling has draped fabric billowing from centre to walls. This treatment hides anything unpleasant above, including layers of insulation for a cosy room. But it's also a dust trap and a fire hazard. Keep fabric well away from light/heat sources. Cut-price fabrics keep costs down: see **Soft Furnishings 1. Fabrics.** Most firms listed in **Interior Design**, and some in **Soft Furnishings 3. Made- to-measure** can tackle tented ceilings.

London Postal Districts

Bellhouse and Company See **Interior Design.** Specialists in tented ceilings.

Deanguard Drapes See **Walls 1. Fabric Lining.** Tented ceiling experts.

Group   Jubilee House, Bedwardine Road, SE19 3AP. (10 mins Crystal Palace BR. Own car park.) *Tel*: 081-771 3641. *Open*: Mon to Fri, 9.30am to 5.00pm. Specialists in tented ceilings. All kinds of blinds/bespoke curtains.

Lewis and Fell. See **Walls 1. Fabric Lining**. Tented ceiling experts.

Material Effects   15 Bellevue Road, SW17 7EG. (1 min Wandsworth Common BR.) *Tel*: 081-767 2241. *Open*: Mon to Fri, 9.30am to 5.30pm.

Specialists (established 10 years) in tented ceilings: flat panels, pleated, gathered, festooned. Centre sunbursts/rosettes/chandeliers. "You name it, we've done it," says Penny Broom. All quality soft furnishings to order.

Home Counties/ South East

Private Lives See **Interior Design**. Lining rooms with fabric is a speciality; the crowning glory is a full-blown tented ceiling, with a decorative lighting pendant as centrepiece.

8
Doors

Estate agents sometimes remark that a house sale can be made or broken by the front door. In between moves, there may be other people you want to impress: friends (enemies even more), neighbours, relatives, rivals, the vicar, the postman. . . is your door up to such a demanding role? More important than who you let in is who you keep out: see **Security** for details of specialists who can help keep burglars at bay.

1. FRONT AND INTERIOR

"A door is what a dog is perpetually the wrong side of."

Ogden Nash (1902–71), *A Dog's Best Friend Is His Illiteracy*

For genuine old doors, hunt through the yards of **Architectural Salvage** merchants. See also **Walls 4. Panelling** and **Staircases 1. Wooden** for firms specialising in bespoke joinery, many of whom can make special sizes/designs of doors, and may be able to install them.

London Postal Districts

Cotswood Door Specialists
5 Hampden Way, Southgate N14 5DJ. (10 mins Southgate tube.) *Tel:* 081-368 1664. *Open:* Mon to Sat, 9.00am to 5.30pm. Supply fine-finish, and install a wide range of domestic doors: external, internal, plus matching garage doors. Design advice available. Gold-plated door furniture/high-security fittings.

Haslemere Design   12 Flitcroft Street, WC2H 8DJ. (3 mins Leicester Square/Tottenham Court Road tubes.) *Tel:* 071-379 7804. *Open:* Mon to Fri, 9.30am to 5.30pm. Made-to-measure traditional oak doors. Aged/patinated finish. Ironwork fittings.

Hearns Specialised Joinery See **Staircases 1. Wooden**.   Specialist makers of circular doors.

Just Doors   126 West Green Road, Tottenham, N15 5AA. (5 mins Seven Sisters tube.) *Tel:* 081-800 3118. *Open:* Mon to Sat, 8.30am to 5.30pm. New external/internal doors in stock/to order. Pine, mahogany, glass. Fitting service. Security fittings.

The London Door Company   165 St John's Hill, SW11 1TQ. (5 mins Clapham Junction BR.) *Tel:* 071-223

7243. *Open:* Mon to Sat, 9.30am to 5.30pm. Comprehensive supply/fit service for exterior/interior doors made to high standards in own workshops. Decorative glazing in etched/bevelled/brilliant cut/stained glass. Door furniture. Security products.

W H Newson See **Walls 3. Wooden Mouldings**.   These old-established Pimlico timber merchants are door doyens. Explore a myriad of options in their free catalogue. Wood folding doors for dividing rooms. Bifolds: louvred/panelled. Made-to-measure: bi-folds/mirrored (silver/bronze)/panelled.

Peco of Hampton   72 Station Road, Hampton, Middx TW12 2BT. (Hampton BR.) *Tel:* 081-979 8310. *Open:* Mon to Sat, 9.00am to 5.15pm. Closed for lunch from 1.00pm to 2.00pm. Family business, trading for over 20 years. 2,500-plus period doors in stock: stained/etched glass. Pine-stripping service. Workshop makes/repairs stained glass. Also cast-iron Victorian/reproduction fireplaces, plus pine surrounds.

Victorian Pine   298 Brockley Road, Brockley SE4 2RA. (Brockley/Crofton Park BR.) *Tel:* 081-691 7162/639 7226 (evening, phone first). *Open:* Mon to Sat, 9.00am to 6.00pm, Sun 10.00am to 2.00pm (phone first). Husband-and-wife team. Secondhand ("reclaimed") period doors, shutters, old pine kitchens. Traditional stripped pine architectural fittings/doors. Also stripping service for huge range of items, including woodwork and metal. "Buy a door and save a tree."

Home Counties/ South East

Classic Joinery   132 Vaughan Road, Harrow, Middx HA5 4HR. (1

min West Harrow tube.) *Tel:* 081-864 9396. *Open:* Mon to Fri, 9.00am to 5.00pm, Sat 9.00am to 1.00pm. Any size or shape of door made: 100 on display. Vast selection of brass handles/fittings. Break-in repairs/security products. Catalogues available.

Cotswood   63a Park Road, Kingston Hill, Kingston-upon-Thames, Surrey KT2 6DE. (8 mins Norbiton BR.) *Tel:* 081-546 3621. *Open:* Mon to Fri, 9.00am to 5.30pm, Sat 9.30am to 1.00pm. Family business, installing hardwood front, internal and garage doors of any size/shape. Installation/security service. Portfolio/photos available.

In Doors   Invicta Works, Malling, Kent ME19 6BP. (M20, junction 4.) *Tel:* (0732) 841606. *Open:* Mon to Fri, 9.00am to 5.00pm, Sat 9.00am to 12.30pm. Around 2,500 old doors in stock: about half already stripped. Also repro doors from reclaimed pine. Delivery/shipping services. Stripping. Made-to-measure panel doors.

Sunningdale Oak   83 Chobham Road, Sunningdale, Berks SL5 0HQ. (A30.) *Tel:* (0344) 26504. *Open:* Mon to Sat, 9.00am to 5.00pm. Other times by appointment. Solid oak 17th-/18th-century style interior doors from stock. Or made-to-order in any size. Established three years. Also wide range of solid oak furniture. Catalogue available.

Sussex Oak Doors   39 High Street, Billingshurst, W. Sussx RH14 9PP. (At intersection of A272/A29. 2 mins Billingshurst BR.) *Tel:* (0403) 782090. *Open:* by appointment. Solid oak vertical planked ledged internal doors for cottages/barns/ houses. 15th- to 18th-century styles. Made to order to fit existing doorways or new surrounds (four to six weeks). Rich wax distressed/ patinated finish. Everything looks authentic, including hinges/latches. Colour brochure available.

Toddoors   22/24 Mandeville Road, Northolt UB5 5BL. (3 mins Northolt tube.) *Tel*: 081-845 2493/9271. *Open*: Mon to Sat, 8.00am to 5.30pm. Hardwood doors, exterior/interior. Flushed/panelled. Full fitting/finishing service.

Mail Order

Barco Joinery See **Windows**
1. Replacements.   Standard doors in a wide choice of hardwoods, including attractive panelled designs and stable doors. Also good choice of models with feature glazing. Direct-from-factory prices are claimed to save 50%. Made-to-measure service. Nationwide deliveries.

Grandisson Doors   The Old Hall, West Hill Road, West Hill, Ottery St Mary, Devon EX11 1TP. *Tel*: (0404) 812876/815400. Exclusive, unique range of doors/fire surrounds, hand-carved by craftsmen in mahogany/oak/rosewood. Designs range from simple Victoria, with long oval cutout for glazing, to intricate Balmoral, where eight panels each feature an elaborate acanthus-leaf design. Colour brochure.

2. DOOR FURNITURE AND SPECIALIST IRONMONGERY

"As an apprentice antique restorer in the mid-1930s one of my tasks was to take a bus trip to the City every so often, with a list of 'wants' in my pocket—fittings for work on hand. There were just two names which stood out as suppliers of quality reproduction brasswork and other cabinet fittings: Beardmore of Cleveland Street and Cluse of Percy Street. Between these two firms practically every conceivable item for use by antique restorers and cabinetmakers could be obtained. In the 1960s Cluse Ltd became part of the Beardmore Group, and in turn Beardmore moved to premises in Percy Street."

Harold Carson, who served his apprenticeship with John Fredericks Old English Furniture, then at 92 Walton Street, SW3.

Door furniture is a strange term that covers knobs, handles, knockers, letter boxes and the like: the important finishing touches to set off your doors . . . and windows, too. London has a rich vein of suppliers, whose history is part of furniture-making itself.

London Postal Districts

A and H Brass   201/203 Edgware Road, Paddington W2 1ES. (10 mins Edgware Road tube.) *Tel*: 071-402 3981. *Open*: Mon to Sat, 9.00am to 6.00pm. Locks/handles for doors/windows, various finishes: brass, bronze, copper, pewter, antiqued, shiny modern. Commissions. Restorations. Key cutting. Engraving. 24-hour locksmith service. Architectural ironmongery, light fittings, door closers/locks, decorative grilles. Polishing/restoration. Catalogue £2.50. Mail order.

Barry Bros See **Security**.
Architectural ironmonger. Fittings for doors/windows: brass, chrome, antique, iron and mercury.

J D Beardmore   3/4 Percy Street, W1P 0EJ. (5 mins Tottenham Court Road tube.) *Tel*: 071-637 7041. *Open*: Mon to Fri, 9.00am to 5.30pm. Closed Fri, 5.00pm. Open Sat, 10.00am to 4.00pm. Established in 1860, well before brass knobs became trendy! Courteous, knowledgeable service. Large range, from tiny brass handles/knobs to

wrought iron rings for gates. Splendid brochure.

Brass Tacks   50/54 Clerkenwell Road, EC1M 5PS. (Barbican tube.) *Tel*: 071-250 1971. *Open*: Mon to Fri, 9.00am to 5.30pm. Make/sell brass door/window furniture, locks, hinges, bathroom accessories, electrical fittings etc.

F W Collins   14 Earlham Street, WC2H 9LN. (5 mins Leicester Square tube.) *Tel*: 071-836 3964. *Open*: Mon to Fri, 8.30am to 4.45pm. Trading over 150 years: a Mr Collins is still in charge. All kinds ironmongery crammed into tiny shop. Key cutting.

Comyn Ching   19 Shelton Street, Covent Garden WC2H 9JN. (5 mins Covent Garden/Leicester Square tubes.) *Tel*: 071-379 3026. *Open*: Mon to Fri, 9.00am to 5.30pm. Trading since 1723 from same premises! Arguably Britain's leading architectural ironmonger. Trade prices. Wide variety door/window fittings. Cheap aluminium to brass/antique-style black iron. Locks, hinges, sliding door gear etc. Engraving. Catalogue available. *Also at*: 110 Golden Lane, EC1Y 0SS. (Barbican/Old Street tubes.) *Tel*: 071-253 8414. *Open*: Mon to Fri, 8.30am to 5.30pm.

Danico Brass   31/33 Winchester Road, NW3. (Swiss Cottage tube.) *Tel:* 071-586 7398. *Open:* Mon to Fri, 9.30am to 6.00pm. Late night Thu 8.00pm. Excellent displays, comprehensive brass range. Trading since 1979. Door, window and electrical fittings, plus bathroom accessories, mixers, valves.

Fulham Brass and Ironmongery 905 Fulham Road, SW6 5HP. (10 mins Parsons Green tube.) *Tel:* 071-736 3246. *Open:* Mon to Fri, 9.00am to 5.00pm, Sat 10.00am to 4.30pm. Friendly service from partners established in 1985. Useful port of call for lever locks, handles, letter plates, radiator grilles. Twenty different styles of door handle. Brass, chrome, bronze, black, antique iron. Antique-style cabinet fittings. Chubb Security Centre. Bathroom accessories/curtain fittings. Picture lights. Engraving service.

Charles Harden   14 Chiltern Street, W1M 1PO. (5 mins Baker Street tube.) *Tel:* 071-935 2032. *Open:* Mon to Fri, 9.30am to 5.00pm. (Please telephone first; Saturday by appointment.) A one-man business, established for 33 years. Brass/ china/glass door furniture. China range is "as big as any in the country". Window/bathroom fittings. Samples copied. "Cheaper than competitors."

Knobs and Knockers   385 King's Road, Chelsea SW10 0LR. (Sloane Square tube, plus bus.) *Tel:* 071-352 5693. *Open:* Mon to Sat, 10.00am to 5.30pm. Company established over 20 years ago. There are now 50 stores nationwide. Brass door/ window furniture, hearthware, occasional furniture, bathroom accessories, gifts. Catalogue 95p, refundable for orders over £10. *Stores in Greater London:* Harrods/Knightsbridge; Notting Hill Gate; Bromley. *All enquiries:* Unit 2, Glory Farm House, Murdoch Road, Bicester,

Oxfordshire OX8 0TG. *Tel:* (0689) 321771.

Locks and Handles   8 Exhibition Road, SW7. (1 min South Kensington tube.) *Tel:* 071-584 6800. *Open:* Mon to Fri, 9.00am to 5.00pm, Sat 9.00am to 3.30pm. Easy to get to: a good place for an inspirational browse. Modern door furniture. Good displays/stocks of authentic period brass door/window furniture. Bathroom accessories. Radiator/ ventilator grilles. Security fittings. All to high decorative standards. Friendly, knowledgeable service.

A Touch of Brass   210 Fulham Road, SW10 9PJ. (5 mins South Kensington tube.) *Tel:* 071-351 2255. *Open:* Mon to Fri, 9.00am to 5.00pm, Sat 10.00am to 5.00pm. Good displays/stocks door/window fittings/lock fittings. Catalogue available. Mail order.

Yannedis   25/27 Theobalds Road, Holborn WC1X 8SR. (10 mins Holborn tube.) *Tel:* 071-242 7106. *Open:* Mon to Fri, 8.30am to 5.00pm (all branches). Trade prices, comprehensive stock. Traditional brass, modern stainless steel, colour-coated aluminium. Catalogue. Lock installation.
Also at: 27 Payne Road, E3 2SS. (Bromley-by-Bow tube.) *Tel:* 081-981 0031.
And at: Riverside House, Southend Road, Woodford Green, Essex IG8 8HQ. (Grants Hill tube, plus bus.) *Tel:* 081-550 8833.

Home Counties/ South East

Forgeries   Old Butchery, High Street, Twyford, Hants SO21 1RF. *Tel:* (0962) 712196. *Open:* by appointment. Reproduction period nails/hinges/bolts/handles.

Bryen Rose   8 London Road, Aston Clinton, Bucks HP22 5HQ. *Tel:* (0296) 631547. *Open:* by

appointment (ring first for samples). Handmade ironmongery. Rose-head cut nails.

Mail Order

Erme Wood Forge See **Heating 4. Fireside Accessories**.   Hand-wrought gates with delicate iron tracery. Standard patterns adapted/made-to-measure.

House Name Plate Company 18 Park Road, Rhosmedre, Wrexham, Clywd LL14 3EF. *Tel:* (0978) 822772. All types supplied: aluminium, solid brass, engraved wood/stone, ceramic, handpainted designs. Brochure available.

House of Brass   122 North Sherwood Street, Nottingham, Notts NG1 4EF. *Tel:* (0602) 475430. Solid brass door/window fittings. Also switches, sockets, dimmers, taps and mixers. Brass beds, headboards, designer rail systems, gifts. Worldwide mail order service.

Signs of the Times   Tebworth, Leighton Buzzard, Beds LU7 9QG. *Tel:* (05255) 4185. Oval or domed handpainted house signs based on 19th-century floral designs, or your own. Weather/corrosion-proof. Brochure available (send sae).

Tebworth Letter Boxes   Tebworth, Leighton Buzzard, Beds LU7 9QD. *Tel:* (05255) 4599. Attractive, painted zinc-plated steel letter boxes with locks. Ideal if you have a double-glazed door, or a dog that eats your mail. Brochures available (send sae).

True Value   95 High Street, Orpington, Kent BR6 0LF. (5 mins Orpington BR.) *Tel:* (0689) 873886. *Open:* Mon to Sat, 9.15am to 5.30pm. Georgian/Victorian-style solid brass door furniture, lion knockers, hooks; brass-plated electrical fittings, locks and bolts, solid brass bathroom accessories. Catalogue available.

9

WINDOWS

Windows, the eyes of a home, make or mar its exterior, so consider their style carefully before rushing to buy replacements. Inside, windows admit light and are vital for ventilation, of course, but also let out warmth and threaten privacy. This chapter deals with the structural aspects of window improvement. Ideas for curtains, blinds, etc. appear in **Soft Furnishings.**

1. REPLACEMENTS

"I remember, I remember,
The house where I was born,
The little window where the sun
Came peeping in at morn."

Thomas Hood (1779–1845)

Window firms are legion: the double-glazing cowboy is a national joke. Nevertheless, new windows can add substantially to comfort and exterior appearance, but rarely to market value. And be warned: glaringly modern windows can ruin the façade of period homes. Materials offered include UPVC (plastic in white, brown, or even woodgrain); aluminium, usually in white; softwood or hardwood. Take time to investigate; don't be pressured. Membership of **The Glass and Glazing Federation** (**GGF**) is essential. See **Help!** for their address. For credit agreement rights, also see **Help!** Many large firms operate nationally. Below is a selection of smaller firms offering specialist services. For made-to-measure replacement windows in hardwoods, consult the specialist joinery firms listed under **Staircases 1. Wooden** and **Walls 4. Panelling**.

London Postal Districts

Sutton Associates 19 Lonsdale Road, Chiswick W4 1ND. *Tel*: 081-995 5561. *Open*: by appointment. Derek Sutton is the sash doctor: "anything from mending cords and weights to full replacements."

Home Counties/ South East

Architectural and Display Woodwork Valley Road, Hughenden, High Wycombe, Bucks HP14 4LG. (A404.) *Tel*: (0240) 242551/243992. *Open*: by appointment. Made-to-measure joinery/fitting service. "Extremely high-class." Designs and drawings for approval.

Elphick Joinery 77 Mill Road, Hailsham, E. Sussx BN27 2HU. (A22 from London/3 miles Polegate BR.) *Tel*: (0323) 840471. *Open*: by appointment. Made-to-measure windows/bespoke joinery service. Also staircases/doors, architectural special joinery.

Haywards 73 Holland Pines, Bracknell, Berks. *Tel*: (0344) 424469. *Open*: by appointment. Peter Hayward specialises in repair/ refurbishment/replacement of all traditional box sash windows. Draught-proofing service.

Hearns Joinery See **Staircases 1. Wooden**. Specialists in circular windows; fitting service.

The Loft Shop See **Staircases 1. Wooden**. Specialists in windows for loft conversions.

The Original Box Sash Window Company Freepost 28, Windsor, Berks SL4 1BR. *Tel*: dial 100, ask for Freefone Box Sash. *Showroom open*: Mon to Fri, 9.00am to 5.30pm, or by arrangement. *Showroom*: 279 Lillie Road, SW6. (10 mins West Brompton tube.) *Tel*: 071-381 1226. *Open*: Mon to Sat, 10.00am to 6.00pm (phone first). Replacement traditional box sash windows: pine with hardwood sills. Single glass or double-glazed. Finishes: natural wood, long-lasting stain/seal, or painted. Colour brochure.

Rosewood Period Joinery 119 Westmead Road, Sutton, Surrey SM1 4JH. *Tel*: 081-773 3156/770 7415. *Open*: by appointment. Specialists in period property restoration, including custom-made windows.

Sashy and Sashy 5 Phoenix Lane, Ashurst Wood, New Forest Row, Sussex RH19 3RA. *Tel*: (0342) 823408. *Open*: by appointment (24-hour answerphone). Full restoration service by Michael Davis, antique restorer. Old glass, old-style catches.

Wickes See **DIY Superstores**. Made-to-measure window frames in pine, Philippine mahogany, mahogany traditional sliding sash, aluminium, UPVC. Sealed double-glazing units. Ready assembled, delivered.

Mail Order

Barco Joinery 59 King Street, Darlaston, W. Mids WS10 8DE *Tel*: (021) 526 7409 (24 hours). *Office open*: Mon to Fri, 9.00am to 5.00pm. Closed for lunch from 1.00pm to 1.30pm. Early closing Fri, 4.00pm. Open Sat, 9.00am to 1.00pm. Small family business (established 17 years), nationwide deliveries. Standard/made-to-measure joinery, windows/doors/frames at trade prices: claim 50% savings. Fit yourself or employ local builder. Fax requirements on (021) 568 6005. You will receive an answer "in about half an hour".

Thomas Rhodes and Son See **Staircases 1. Wooden**. Made-to-measure windows in traditional styles, including sash for old/listed properties.

2. STAINED AND DECORATIVE GLASS

"It was a blonde. A blonde to make a bishop kick a hole in a stained-glass window."

Raymond Chandler (1888–1959), *Farewell, My Lovely*

Sunlight streaming through coloured glass is as beautiful today as ever, a permanent and individual enhancement for your home, outside and in. Numerous firms can restore older windows, or make you new panels.

London Postal Districts

Leo Amery Stained Glass 110/116 Kingsgate Road, NW6 2JG. (West Hampstead tube.) *Tel*: 071-624 3240. *Open*: by appointment. Modern/abstract style (often incorporating antique glass fragments). Windows, and panels which are lit behind to hang on a wall. A hefty design fee is deducted from the final fee, if a commission progresses. Installations.

Philip Bradbury 83 Blackstock Road, N4 2JW. (5 mins Finsbury Park tube.) *Tel*: 071-226 2919. *Open*: Mon to Fri, 9.30am to 5.30pm, Sat 10.00am to 2.00pm. Etched patterns on new glass. Door/sash/fanlight restoration.

Ray Bradley 3 Orchard Studios, Brook Green W6 7BU. (7 mins Hammersmith tube.) *Tel*: 071-602 1840. *Open*: by appointment only. Stained glass and variations of the medium for all situations on any scale, including some restoration of good period glass. Also decorative work on sheet glass with sand-blast engraving, acid etching, enamelling, guilding and silvering. Work has been undertaken in this country and abroad, for private collections and the V&A Museum, London. Slides of work in situ can be seen on the Crafts Council selective index, 44a

Pentonville Road, Islington N1 9BY. *Tel*: 071-278 7700.

Susan M Cook The Stained Glass Studio, Unit 117, 31 Clerkenwell Close, EC1R 0AT. *Tel*: 071-263 8481. *Open*: 10.00am to 7.00pm (appointment only). Design/make/install stained glass windows/panels/screens. Traditional/modern/restoration. Commissions. Small design fee with estimate.

The Glasshouse 11 Lettice Street, SW6 4EH. (5 mins Parsons Green tube.) *Tel*: 071-736 3113. *Open*: Mon to Fri, 8.00am to 4.00pm, Sat and Sun by appointment. Stained-glass panels designed/made/installed to order. Restoration/repairs. Individual attention. See Caroline Benyon's samples in workshop office. Brochure available.

Goddard and Gibbs 41/49 Kingsland Road, E2 8AD. (15 mins Old Street tube.) *Tel*: 071-739 6563. *Open*: Mon to Fri, 9.00am to 5.00pm. The biggest/oldest name in British stained glass, established in 1868, and creator of windows for prestigious commissions . . . the Houses of Parliament and St Paul's Cathedral, no less. But private clients are welcome, with a promise of close attention. Shop (Stained Glass Supplies) at same address. Huge range of antique/decorative glass. DIY stained glass and lamp accessories. *Open*: Mon to Fri, 8.30am to 6.00pm, Sat 9.00am to 6.00pm.

Lead and Light 22 Camden Lock, NW1 8AP. (5 mins Camden Town tube.) *Tel*: 071-485 4568. *Open*: Sat to Sun, 10.00am to 5.00pm. Workshop for leaded window designs, with coloured glass sheets on display. Supplies for DIY. Also lighting.
Also at: 35a Hartland Road, Camden, NW1 8DB. (3 mins Chalk Farm tube.) *Tel*: 071-485 0997. *Open*: Mon to Fri, 10.00am to

5.00pm. 2,500 sq ft stained-glass studio/warehouse.

Matthew Lloyd Stained Glass Studios 63 Amberley Road, Palmers Green N13 4BH. (10 mins Southgate tube.) *Tel*: 081-886 0213. *Open*: by appointment. Design/make stained-glass windows/lights. Personal service. Contemporary/period reproduction and restoration work. Free estimates.

Maria McClafferty Design 11 Hillside Road, SW2. *Tel*: 081-671 6782. *Open*: by appointment. Designs/makes stained and/or etched/engraved panels for doors, windows, screens, skylights etc. Reproductions/original designs. Install/repair/restore. Nationwide service.

Stoney Parsons 203 Southgate Road, N1 3LD. (15 mins Highbury and Islington tube. Angel tube, plus bus.) *Tel*: 071-354 0892. *Open*: by appointment only. From her home studio, Stoney creates windows/panels in coloured glass and sympathetic to surroundings (mainly handblown). Modern designs, veering towards abstract. Favourite themes: landscapes, flowers. Installations.

James Preece Stained Glass 11 Portobello Green, 281 Portobello Road, W10 5TD. *Tel*: 081-968 8807. *Open*: Mon to Sat, 9.30am to 6.00pm. Original, modern window designs with panels of mouthblown glass.

Prisms Stained Glass Design 34 Boundary Road, NW8 0HG. (5 mins Swiss Cottage tube. 1 min South Hampstead BR.) *Tel*: 071-624 5812. *Open*: by appointment. Using traditional leading and Tiffany techniques, Beverly Bryon creates windows/sky-lights/door panels/mirrors in modern/period designs. Commissions undertaken. Repairs and restoration.

Shades of Light   Unit 3A, Wellington Road, Wimbledon SW19 8EQ. (5 mins Wimbledon Park tube.) Tel: 081-946 9101. Open: Mon to Fri, 8.30am to 5.00pm. Commissions/repairs for stained-glass/lead lights. Lavish colour brochure. Licensed to carry out Ritec's "clear-shield" protection and cleaning system.

Caroline Swash   88 Woodwarde Road, SE22 8UT. (North Dulwich BR.) Tel: 081-693 6574. Open: by appointment. Glassmaking runs in the family: Caroline, well-known as a glass artist, is the third generation. Repairs/restorations can be arranged. Also at: The Glass Studio, Gabriel's Wharf, SE1. Tel: 071-620 0245.

Victorian Stained Glass   83 Stamford Hill, N16 5TP. Tel: 081-800 9008. Open: Mon to Fri, 9.00am to 5.00pm, Sat 9.00am to 1.00pm. Large new studio. All stained-glass repairs. In-home service.

Home Counties/ South East

Contemporary Stained Glass Art 28 Westfield Road, West Green, Crawley, W. Sussx RH11 7BT. Tel: (0293) 536188. Open: by appointment. Christine Kirby creates modern stained glass panels/windows. Commissions.

Glass Studio   31 Tunfield Road, Hoddesdon, Herts EN11 9LQ. (Broxbourne BR, plus bus.) Tel: (0992) 460665. Open: by appointment. Stained-glass commissions.

The Glassery   83 East Barnet Road, New Barnet, Herts. (3 mins New Barnet BR. Adjacent car park.) Tel: 081-449 7971. Open: Mon to Fri, 8.00am to 5.30pm, Sat 8.00am to 5.00pm. Family business, established 1846. Stained glass, any design. Handmade and reproduction bullions. Leaded lights, real/imitation. Tabletops/mirrors cut and polished to shape. In stock, clear, coloured, patterned glass, mirrors, double-glazing systems, antique/cathedral glass.

Tudor Leaded Light Co   Rembrant House, Whippenell Road, Watford WD1 7WD. Tel: (0923) 36932. Measure/make/fit genuine leaded lights with stained-glass inserts. "No job too large or too small," they say. Repairs. Colour brochure available.

3. SHUTTERS, AWNINGS AND GRILLES

More of a Continental/American habit, shutters are well worth consideration. A durable way to furnish windows, they also insulate and provide security. Awnings shade and protect furnishings from the fading effects of sunlight, and keep rooms/patios cool on hot days. Many of the specialists listed under **Soft Furnishings 5. Blinds** make awnings. Fixed inside the room, shutters replace curtains and are ideal for bays. Well-chosen exterior shutters can improve the exterior appearance of your home even when folded back, and can guard your windows against intruders when closed.

London Postal Districts

Deans Blinds and Awnings See **Soft Furnishings 5. Blinds**.   Awnings specialists.

DLS Metalworkers   18 Ashwin Street, Hackney E8 3DL. Tel: 071-241 0715. Open: Mon to Fri, 9.00am to 6.00pm. Daniel Spring, trained silversmith/general metalworker, can make/fit decorative security grilles.

Putney Blinds See **Soft Furnishings 5. Blinds**. Awnings specialists.

Victorian Pine See **Doors 1. Front and Interior**. Original stripped pine shutters.

Home Counties/ South East

Continental Awnings   Unit 21, Headley Park 10, Headley Road East, Woodley, Berks RG5 4SW. (M4, junction 10.) Tel: (0734) 699655 (24 hour answerphone). Open (showroom): Mon to Fri, 9.00am to 5.00pm. Patio awnings/exterior Dutch blinds made-to-measure. Wide choice colours/designs. Manual or electric push-button operation. Aluminium frames; rot-proof fabrics. Three-year guarantee. In-home service for samples/measure/fit. Exterior window roller shutters, made-to-measure. Foils burglars, conserves energy, reduces condensation, absorbs noise. Made from aluminium filled with foam (for maximum insulation/protection) or from PVC. Installations.

Godington Forge   Godington, Bicester, Oxon OX6 9AF. Tel: (0869) 277423. Home visits in the London area by appointment. Richard List is the blacksmith who specialises in security. Offer a fine tracery of metalwork for window/door grilles, inside or out.

The Shutter Shop   Queensbury House, Dilly Lane, Hartley Witney, Hants RG27 8EQ. (M3, junction 5.) Tel: (0251) 264575/6. Open: Mon to Fri, 9.00am to 6.00pm. Custom-made shutters: any size, shape, style, colour. Made from pine/cedar/hardwood in US. Personal service: measure/fit. London/Home Counties.

Mail Order

American Shutters 72 Station Road, SW13 0LS. *Tel*: 081-876 5905. Exclusive US designs in wood stains/colours. Arched tops to order. Adjustable louvres in choice of slat widths. Also traditional solid panel designs. All panels custom-made to order. Colour brochures available.

The London Shutter Co St Martins Stables, Windsor Road, Ascot, Berks. *Tel*: (0344) 28385. Pine shutters with moveable slats, from America. Any colour/stain. Design/supply/install.

Plantation Shutters 93 Antrobus Road, Chiswick W4 5NQ. *Tel*: 081-994 2886. Kate and Peter Evans pioneered the moveable louvre shutter trend, founding their business seven years ago. Their American shutters come in standard sizes, or made-to-order with narrow or wide slats. Expert fitter available. Viewing by appointment.

J and C R Wood (Metalcraft) 303 Hull Road, Anlaby Common, Hull HU4 7RZ. *Tel*: (0482) 51915 (24 hours). DIY tools/metal supplies for window grilles, fancy/plain. Joints are riveted; no welding needed. Colour brochure available.

10
STAIRCASES

Your staircase is the vital link that holds your home together. It must be well designed and structurally sound, or family safety and convenience are endangered. Good looks are important, too, to cheer you up as you charge up and down.

1. WOODEN

"Halfway up the stairs
Isn't up and isn't down.
It isn't in the nursery,
It isn't in the town.
And all sorts of funny thoughts
Run around my head:
'It isn't really anywhere!
It's somewhere else instead!'"

A A Milne (1882–1956), *When We Were Very Young*

Traditional wooden staircases are vulnerable to wear and tear: traditional joinery shops will put them to rights. All will make-to-measure, and many stock standard staircase components. For the handy DIY person, **DIY Superstores** meet the vogue for restoration with good selections of old-style stairway components.

London Postal Districts

Gifford-Mead   The Furniture Cave, 533 King's Road, SW10 0TZ. (10 mins Fulham Broadway tube.) *Tel*: 071-352 6008. *Open*: Mon to Sat, 10.00am to 6.00pm. High quality, traditional staircase components. Manufacturing woodturners. Garden ornaments/English fireplaces.

Goodwood Systems   20 Tanners Hill, SE8 4PJ. (New Cross BR.) *Tel*: 081-691 4311. *Open*: Mon to Thu, 8.00am to 4.00pm, Fri 8.00am to 4.00pm. Standard/made-to-measure/fitting.

W R and A Hide   161 Dalling Road, Hammersmith W6 0ES. (5 mins Ravenscourt Park tube.) *Tel*: 081-743 2589. *Open*: Mon to Fri, 7.00am to 4.30pm. Closed for lunch, 12.45pm to 1.30pm. Made-to-measure staircases/doors/windows.

E A Higginson and Co   Unit 1, Carlisle Road, NW9 0HD. (15 mins Burnt Oak tube.) *Tel*: 081-200 4848. *Open*: Mon to Fri, 9.00am to 5.30pm,

Sat by appointment. Family business. Architectural joinery manufacturers. In stock: staircase components. Keen prices. Replacements to order. Import Italian spirals.

Magnet See **DIY Superstores**. Sweeping staircase or straight runs in mahogany/Parana pine. Spiral staircase kits. Free in-store computer design service for staircase planning: by appointment with staircase designers.

Mullen and Lumsden   39 East Smithfield, E1 9AP. (5 mins Tower Hill tube.) *Tel*: 071-481 8261. *Open*: Mon to Fri, 7.00am to 5.00pm. Made-to-measure staircases. All purpose-made architectural joinery.

Rees-Hart   16/22 Martello Street, London Fields, E8 3PE. (15 mins Bethnal Green tube.) *Tel*: 071-249 3631. *Open*: Mon to Fri, 8.00am to 4.30pm. Purpose-made wooden staircases. General building work.

Staircase Solutions   10 Crescent Road, N22 4RS. (5 mins Alexandra Palace BR.) *Tel*: 081-881 9600. *Open*: Mon to Fri, 9.00am to 5.30pm, Sat by appointment. Specialist staircase manufacturers/importers, with retail showroom. Straight flights/spirals. Installations/home visits with advice.

Stairways Products   102 Chingford Mount Road, E4 9AA. (Walthamstow Central tube.) *Tel*: 081-527 6180. *Open*: Mon to Fri, 10.00am to 6.00pm, Sat by appointment. Manufacturers of traditional and open plan stairways/spindles. Home surveys. Reproduction period joinery.

Stairwell   Cambridge Works, 2 Bedford Road, East Finchley N2 9DA. (5 mins East Finchley tube.) *Tel*: 081-883 7885. *Open*: Mon to Fri, 9.00am to 6.00pm. Bespoke wooden staircases. Wood turning.

Architectural joinery manufacturers. Spiral staircase importers.

Wansdown Joinery Works 327 and 339 Lillie Road, Fulham Cross SW6 7NR. (20 mins Fulham Broadway tube.) *Tel*: 071-385 0351. *Open*: Mon to Thu, 8.00am to 5.30pm, Fri 8.00am to 4.30pm. Period staircases/panelled rooms. Purpose-made architectural joinery.

Home Counties/ South East

Ampthill Joinery   Flitwick Industrial Estate, Malden Road, Flitwick, Bedford MK45 5BS. *Tel*: (0525) 716603. Purpose-made joinery.

Ashby and Horner Joinery 795 London Road, West Thurrock, Grays, Essex RM16 1LH. *Tel*: (0708) 866841. *Open*: by appointment. Make/fit staircases to order. All purpose-built architectural joinery.

Beazer Construction   Abridge Depot, Ongar Road, Abridge, Romford, Essex RM4 1UR. *Tel*: 081-508 5622. Standard/made-to-measure/fitting. Purpose-made joinery.

Bespoke Britannia Joinery (Extend a Home)   Unit 32, Industrial Estates, Leagrane Road, Luton, Beds LU8 1SD. *Tel*: (0582) 400707. Standard made-to-measure fitting.

E J Bushell   453 Sunleigh Road, Wembley, Middx. (Alperton tube.) *Tel*: 081-900 2905. *Open*: Mon to Fri, 8.00am to 5.00pm. Joinery manufacturers. Staircases/windows.

Cane End Joinery   Rowsham Road, Bierton, Aylesbury, Bucks HP22 5DZ. (A418.) *Tel*: (0296) 88207. *Open*: Mon to Thu, 7.30am to 5.00pm, Fri 7.30am to 4.30pm. Specialists in all types of manufactured joinery.

Cox Brothers Builders (Kent)
80/82 Peel Street, Maidstone, Kent
ME14 2SP. *Tel*: (0622) 64255.
Standard/made-to-measure fitting.
Specialist joinery manufacturers.
Associate companies for building
and electrical work.

Crockett and Eaton Charfleets
Road, Charfleets Estate, Canvey
Island, Essex. (2 miles Benfleet) *Tel*:
(0268) 696480. *Open*: Mon to Fri,
7.30am to 5.30pm, Sat 8.00am to
1.00pm. Standard/made-to-
measure/fitting. Extensions/
refurbishments.

Hearns Specialised Joinery 1a St
Mark's Road, Teddington, Middx
TW11 9DE. *Tel*: 081-977 0032.
Purpose-made architectural joinery.
Make/fit staircases to order.

Herriard Joinery The Station,
Bagmore Lane, Herriard,
Basingstoke, Hants RG25 2PY. (10
mins M3.) *Tel*: (0256) 83414. *Open*:
Mon to Fri, 8.00am to 5.00pm.
Standard/made-to-measure.

Hunkins and Frewin
14/22 Middleton Road, Banbury,
Oxon OX16 8QN. *Tel*: (0295)
251931. *Open*: Mon to Fri, 8.45am
to 5.15pm. Standard/made-to-
measure fitting. Purpose-made
joinery: stairs/windows/doors—
anything for the home. Speciality is
ornate restoration work for Oxford
colleges.
Also at: 53 West Way, Botley,
Oxford OX2 0QB. *Tel*: (0865)

723221. *Open*: Mon to Fri, 8.30am
to 5.00pm.

Input Joinery Enham Arch,
Newbury Road, Andover SP10 4DU.
(M3, A303.) *Tel*: (0264) 355858.
Open: Mon to Fri, 8.30am to
6.00pm. Made-to-measure
staircases/architectural joinery.

J Jarvis and Sons 133 Stansted
Road, Bishops Stortford, Herts CM23
2AN. *Tel*: (0279) 755962. Makers of
purpose-built architectural joinery.

JSR Joinery Poole Street, Great
Yeldham, Halsted, Essex CO9 4HN.
Tel: (0787) 237722. *Open*: Mon to
Thu, 8.00am to 4.30pm, Fri 8.00am
to 3.30pm, Sat by appointment. To
order: quality turned balusters/
handrails/staircases.

Lafford and Leavey Arrowhead
Road, Theale, Reading, Berks RG7
4AZ. *Tel*: (0734) 303333. *Open*: Mon
to Fri, 9.00am to 5.30pm, Sat 8.00am
to 12.00 noon. Sun (merchants only):
8.00am to 12.00 noon. Architectural
joinery manufacturers and builders'
merchants.

The Loft Shop Progress Way,
Croydon, Surrey CR0 4XP. *Tel*: 081-
681 4060. *Open*: Mon to Fri, 8.00am
to 5.30pm, Sat 8.00am to 12.00
noon. Specialists in all types of stairs
for loft access. Supply/install.
Also at: Chelmsford, Chertsey,
Fareham, Henley-on-Thames,
Ringwood, Rochford.

R Mansell Roman House, 13/27

Grant Road, Croydon, Surrey CR9
6BU. *Tel*: 081-654 8191. *Open*: Mon
to Fri, 8.30am to 5.00pm. Made-to-
measure; fitting service.

William Newman Unit No 6,
Jubilee End, Station Road, Lawford,
Essex CO11 1UR. *Tel*: (0206) 396280.
Open: Mon to Fri, 7.30am to
5.30pm, Sat 7.00am to 1.00pm.
Architectural joinery.

**T F Smith (Newland) Joinery
Works** 150 Newland, Witney,
Oxon OX8 6JH. (Witney–Oxford
road.) *Tel*: (0993) 702740. *Open*:
Mon to Fri, 8.00am to 5.00pm.
Standard/made-to-measure/fitting.
All purpose-made joinery: specialise
in technically difficult items.

Sunningdale Joineries The Mill,
Church Road, Bagshot, Surrey GU19
5EQ. (200 yds Bagshot BR.) *Tel*:
(0276) 76222. *Open*: Mon to Fri,
7.30am to 5.00pm, Sat 7.30am to
12.30pm. Made-to-measure
joinery/fitting service.

Mail Order

Thomas Rhodes and Son
Whitworth Yard, Red Lane,
Rochdale, Lancs OL12 9DB. *Tel*:
(0706) 46704. Wooden staircases
made to measure/design in
softwood/Parana pine/mahogany.
Spindles, newel posts, handrails
always in stock. Also all windows,
including tilt sliding sash, leaded
lights. Specialists in preservation
order, listed building commissions.

---

2. SPIRAL AND METAL

The archetypal solution to space
problems, spirals can also be
supremely decorative. Shop from a
specialist who will inform you on
important building regulations.

London Postal Districts

R Bleasdale 394 Caledonian
Road, Islington N1 1DN. (7 mins
Caledonian Road tube.) *Tel*: 071-609
0934. *Open*: Mon to Fri, 10.00am to
6.00pm, Sat 10.00am to 1.00pm.

Reproduction Victorian cast-iron
spiral staircases. Also railings/
balconies. Catalogues available.

Capricorn Architectural Ironwork
Tasso Forge, Tasso Yard, 56 Tasso
Road, W6 8LZ. (5 mins Barons Court
tube.) *Tel*: 071-381 4235/6/7. *Open*:
Mon to Fri, 8.00am to 6.00pm, Sat
9.30am to 1.30pm. The promise from

one of London's most famous metalworkers is "absolutely anything", from a candlestick to a large spiral staircase. Your design or theirs. Railings/gates etc.

Higginson Staircases   See **1. Wooden** above. Elegant range of wood/metal spiral staircases; choice of colour/wood finishes.

Metalcraft (Tottenham)   6/40 Durnford Street, N15 5NQ. (2 mins Seven Sisters tube.) *Tel:* 081-802 1715/1258. *Open:* Mon to Fri, 8.00am to 5.30pm. Architectural metal manufacturer: staircases/balconies/gates/railings. Mostly bespoke, with some standard items. Mild steel/cast iron. Restoration service for Victorian railings—they worked on the Tower of London. Cast-iron planters.

Home Counties/ South East

Kensington Traders   27 Ribocan Way, Progress Park, Leagrave, Luton, Beds LU4 9TR. (10 mins Leagrave BR.) *Tel:* (0582) 491171. *Open:* Mon to Fri, 8.30am to 5.00pm, Sat mornings by appointment. Spiral staircases/wrought-iron balusters.

Safety Stairways   Unit 45, Owen Road Industrial Estate, Owen Road, Willenhall, W. Mids WV13 2PX. (M6, junction 10.) *Tel:* (021) 526 3133. Britain's largest maker of cast-iron staircases. 168 models, wide variety of designs, over 20 years' experience. Nationwide installation network, or cash and carry direct from factory.

11
ARCHITECTURAL SALVAGE

The rescued interiors of demolished buildings are now grandly called architectural salvage, along with anything remotely useful or decorative from the outer structure. Architectural salvage includes beams, doors, window frames, panelling, stained glass, paving stones, bricks, fireplaces, slates, tiles, bathroom fittings. . . virtually everything, including the kitchen sink. It is cheaper to buy actually on demolition sites if possible; approach the foreman and offer to pay in cash. Or raid builders' skips—but ask permission first.

My listings range from restored "architectural antiques" at the top end of the trade to rougher demolition merchants, who are invaluable sources of building materials. Architectural Salvage (AS) merchants often have useful workshops/contacts for restoration services.

London Postal Districts

Churchill's Architectural Salvage 212 Old Kent Road, SE1 5TY. (5 mins Elephant and Castle tube.) *Tel:* 071-708 4308. *Open:* Mon to Fri, 9.30am to 5.30pm, Sat 9.00am to 6.00pm. Mainly fireplaces. Also decorative ironwork/bathroom fittings/sinks. Reclaimed door furniture: knobs, knockers etc. Sinks/pedestals. Garden furniture/ornaments/urns/statues/benches. Occasionally some pine furniture. "Impartial advice."

City Roofing 28 Aldermans Hill, Palmers Green, N13 4PN. (Next to Palmers Green tube.) *Tel:* 081-882 1905. *Open:* Mon to Fri, 6.30am to 4.30pm, Sat 6.30am to 12.00 noon. Large stocks of secondhand tiles/slates. Plus all roofing materials. Contractors and merchants. Free deliveries.

T Crowther and Sons 282 North End Road, Fulham SW6 1NH. (250 yds from Fulham Broadway tube. Free nearby car park in Coomer Place.) *Tel:* 071-385 1375. *Open:* Mon to Fri, 9.00am to 5.30pm. Closed weekends. Well-known company catering for top end of the trade: more architectural antiques than salvage. Visited regularly by Bond Street dealers. Don't confuse it with Crowthers of Syon Park: they are separate businesses, although originating from same family. Extensive premises include gardens and a 15,000 sq ft internal showroom. Wrought-iron gates/chimney pieces/panelling/fireplaces. Specialise in garden "features": statues/columns/fountains/well heads. Furniture (limited). Valuations. Deliveries/

installations/shipping. Own team of masons/carvers. Services for making up hearths/adapting panelling.

Davis and Davis Architectural Antiques Arch 226, Urwin Street, Camberwell SE5 0NF. (15 mins Elephant and Castle tube.) *Tel:* 071-703 6525. *Open:* Tue to Sat, 9.30am to 5.00pm. Friendly welcome from husband-and-wife team in 1,200 sq ft premises under a railway arch. "We concentrate on everyday practical needs." Doors/fireplaces. Bathroom fittings/taps. Decorative ironwork, including gates/railings. Chimney pots. Stained glass. Garden benches/edging tiles/balustrades. Free deliveries. Reasonable charges for fitting fireplaces/stripping doors.

Fens Restoration 46 Lots Road, Chelsea SW10 0QF. (Sloane Square tube, plus bus. Chelsea Harbour river buses.) *Tel:* 071-352 9883. *Open:* Mon to Fri, 9.00am to 5.30pm, Sat 9.00am to 1.00pm. Reclaimed doors, bathroom fittings, mouldings. Services for stripping/restoration/repairs.

Floyds 349–357 Ilderton Road, SE15 1NW. (Corner of Old Kent Road. New Cross Gate/New Cross tubes.) *Tel:* 071-639 6991/635 8977. *Open:* Mon to Fri, 8.00am to 5.30pm, Sat 8.00am to 1.00pm. Reclaimed yellow and mixed London stock bricks; old Welsh slates. General builders merchants.

Fortress 23 Canonbury Lane, N1 2AS. (5 mins Highbury and Islington tube.) *Tel:* 071-359 5875. *Open:* Tue to Sat, 10.00am to 5.30pm. Fashionable high Gothic, with an ecclesiastical flavour: fonts/stained glass/statues. All fully restored. Wrought ironwork, mirrors, decorative pieces for inside/outside. Hunt here for very special features.

William Fry and Co Mitre Works, Neasden Goods Depot, Neasden Lane, NW10 2UG. (2 mins Neasden tube.) *Tel:* 081-459 5141. *Open:* Mon to Fri, 8.00am to 5.00pm. Closed for lunch, 12.30pm to 1.30pm. Open Sat, 8.00am to 12.00 noon. Secondhand rolled steel joists (RSJs) for through

lounges, extensions etc. Deliveries arranged.

Grove Green Antiques 108 Grove Green Road, Leytonstone E11 4EZ. (10 mins Leytonstone tube.) *Tel:* 081-558 7885. *Open:* 7 days, 9.30am to 5.30pm. Bathroom fittings including Victorian baths/loos. Sinks. Fireplaces/chimney pots. Stained glass/panelled doors. Lanterns/leaded lights. Gardenware. Country furniture.

The Hardwood Flooring Company See **Floors 1. Wood.** Reclaimed flooring/doors, planks 6 to 8in wide, ¾in thick, kiln dried.

The House Hospital 68 Battersea High Street, SW11 3HX. (10 mins Clapham Junction BR. Easy parking.) *Tel:* 071-223 3179. *Open:* Mon to Sat, 10.00am to 5.00pm. Open site, plus shop features. Broad range of salvaged goods. Doors/brass handles. Bathroom fittings: baths/basins/taps. Victorian gates/railings. Door-stripping service.

House of Steel 400 Caledonian Road, N1 1DN. (Caledonian Road tube. Free courtyard parking.) *Tel:* 071-607 5889. *Open:* Mon to Fri, 10.30am to 5.30pm, Sat by appointment. Large warehouse, showrooms, workshops. Around 350 cast-iron fireplaces. Railings, gates, staircases, door knobs, etc. Also light-fittings, cast-iron and steel garden and interior furniture, fire accessories. Antiques, or reproductions.
Also at: Judy Cole and Son, 28 Camden Passage, N1. (5 mins Angel tube.) *Open:* Wed, Fri and Sat, 10.00am to 4.30pm. Metal antiques and reproductions.

Lazdan 218 Bow Common Lane, Bow Common E3. (5 mins Mile End tube.) *Tel:* 081-981 4632. *Open:* Mon to Fri, 8.00am to 5.00pm. Used bricks/slates in large quantities.

London Architectural Salvage and Supply Co (LASSCO) St Michaels Church, Mark Street, off Paul Street, EC2A 4ER. (5 mins Old Street tube.) *Tel:* 071-739 0448/9. *Open:* Mon to

Sat, 10.00am to 5.00pm. These deconsecrated church grounds provide an unusual setting for vast stocks of architectural salvage. Panelling, gates, fencing, chimney pieces, bathroom/kitchen fittings. Reclaimed wooden floorings/floorboards. Flagstones, stonework, sculptures, garden furniture. Period shop fittings. Marble/tiled floors.

Pub Farm/Turnpin Contracts
161/165 Greenwich High Road, SE10 8JA. (Greenwich BR.) *Tel:* 081-853 2658. *Open:* Mon to Fri, 8.30am to 6.00pm. Original Victorian/Edwardian architectural items, plus reproductions. Large warehouse with panelling, doors, seating, pews, benches, leaded lights, etchings, glass, lighting, mirrors, prints, signs. Installations/restorations by skilled craftsmen.

Reclaimed Building Material Supplies
Railway Goods Works, Morden Road, Mitcham, Surrey. (5 mins Morden tube. 1 min Mitcham BR.) *Tel:* 081-646 0467. *Open:* Mon to Fri, 9.00am to 5.30pm, Sat 9.00am to 5.00pm. Secondhand building materials: "anything and everything for building a house". Doors, tiles, slates, bricks, timber, railings, fences etc.

Townsends
81 Abbey Road, NW8 0AE. (15 mins Swiss Cottage/Kilburn tubes.) *Tel:* 071-624 4756. *Open:* Tue to Sat, 10.00am to 6.00pm. Restored fireplaces: wood, cast iron, marble. Reproduction fire grates, firebacks, coal scuttles. Gas coal/log fires. Installations (London area).

Tsar Architectural
487 Liverpool Road, Islington N7 8PG. (5 mins Highbury and Islington tube.) *Tel:* 071-609 4238. *Open:* Mon to Sat, 10.30am to 7.00pm, Sun 11.00am to 4.00pm. Tiles/period fireplaces. Own foundry makes reproduction brass fittings/garden furniture/statues/urns. Restoration service for marble fireplaces. Fireplace installations.

Whiteway and Waldron
305 Munster Road, SW6 6BJ. (10 mins Barons Court tube.) *Tel:* 071-381 3195. *Open:* Mon to Fri, 10.00am to 6.00pm, Sat 10.00am to 5.00pm. Ecclesiastical atmosphere and a wonderful source of unusual decorative architectural fittings, salvaged from more pious times. Stained glass/church furnishings/statuary/doors.

Home Counties/ South East

A1 Demolition
Jack's Yard, Nathan's Lane, Writtle, Chelmsford, Essex CM1 3RF. *Tel:* (0245) 422422. *Open:* Mon to Fri, 7.30am to 6.00pm, Sat 7.30am to 12.00 noon. Salvaged building materials.

Alden Reclamation
Old Mill Yard, off Craythorne Close, Horn Street, Hythe, Kent CT21 5SR. *Tel:* (0303) 261949. *Open:* by appointment. Handmade reclaimed 2in bricks/clay tiles. Welsh roofing slates/red brick pavers/flagstones.

Beckman and Hambleton
Jury Lane, Sidlesham Common, Chichester, W. Sussex PO20 7PX. *Tel:* (0243) 641614. *Open:* Mon to Fri, 7.30am to 5.00pm, Sat 7.30am to 12.00 noon. Reclaimed bricks/tiles/slates/oak beams/timber.

Bram-Coy Demolition
Hawkins Road, Colchester, Essex CO2 8XJ. *Tel:* (0206) 760342. *Open:* Mon to Fri, 7.00am to 5.00pm, Sat 7.00am to 12.00 noon. Reclaimed building materials (large purchaser/supplier, with domestic/commercial clients.)

Brants Salvage Yard
White House Farm, Silchester Road, Tadley, Hants RG26 6RA *Tel:* (0734) 701336. *Open:* by appointment. Salvaged building materials. Timber/flooring/doors.

Brickmart
Brimsdown Railway Sidings, Green Street, Brimsdown, Enfield, Middx EN3 7QN. *Tel:* 081-805 8411/524 2414. *Open:* by appointment. Secondhand building materials. Yellow stock bricks/clay tiles.

Brighton Architectural Salvage
33/4 Gloucester Road, Brighton, E. Sussex BN1 4AQ. *Tel:* (0273) 681656. *Open:* Mon to Fri, 10.00am to 5.30pm, Sat 9.30am to 4.30pm. Specialities: fireplaces/stained glass. Over half the stock is restored and ready to take away. Workshop makes Victorian-style pine surrounds. Full installation service.

Bromley Demolition Co
70 Siward Road, Bromley, Kent BR2 9JY. *Tel:* 081-464 3610. *Open:* Mon to Fri, 9.00am to 5.00pm, Sat 9.30am to 12.00 noon. Reclaimed bricks/timber.

Brookers
Kelstall, Brooker Hill, Shinfield, Reading, Berks RG2 9BX. *Tel:* (0734) 884247. *Open:* weekdays by appointment, and Sat 9.00am to 12.00 noon. Large supplies of secondhand roofing/bricks.

Building Insulation Supplies
Brooks Way, Sevenoaks Way, St Paul's Cray, Orpington, Kent BR5 3BB. *Tel:* (0689) 35637. *Open:* Mon to Fri, 9.00am to 5.00pm, Sat 9.00am to 1.00pm. Large stocks new/secondhand building materials. Rolled steel joists (RSJs)/guttering. Victorian doors.
Also at: 67a Bourne Road, Bromley, Kent.

Bygones Building Supplies
Broadland, Whitstable Road, Blean, near Canterbury, Kent CT2 9JQ. *Tel:* (0227) 767453. *Open:* by appointment. Salvaged period household fittings. Fireplaces/small ranges. Old water pumps/roll-top baths. Decorative ironwork.

Alfred G Cawley
Havering Farm, Worplesdon, Surrey GU4 7QA. (A320, Woking to Guildford, turning to Havering Farm.) *Tel:* (0483) 232398. *Open:* Mon to Fri, 8.00am to 5.00pm, Sat 8.00am to 2.00pm. Demolished building materials include bricks/tiles/windows. Bathroom fittings. Doors. Phone to check stocks.

Cromwell Reclamation
Rear of 12 High Street, Ware, Herts SG12 9BX. *Tel:* (0920) 468358. *Open:* Thu, Fri

and Sat, 9.30am to 4.30pm. Mainly Victorian through to 1930s. Bathroom fittings: baths/basins. Staircase components. Fireplaces/ surrounds. Ironmongery/garden items. Leaded glass/panelling/ mouldings.

Drummonds of Bramley   Birtley Farm, Horsham Road, Bramley, Guildford, Surrey GU5 0LA. *Tel:* (0483) 898766. *Open:* Mon to Sat, 9.00am to 6.00pm, Sun 10.00am to 6.00pm. Director Drummond Shaw aims "to offer anything and everything in architectural salvage . . . it's irritating when you go somewhere and only get half the materials." Heavy goods yard for old weathered materials: bricks/tiles/chimney pots. Stone window-sills. Stone floor/wall tiles. Beams/floorboards/mouldings/ staircases. Cast-iron radiators/ guttering. One of the best-stocked showrooms for restored bathroom fittings in the country. Architectural antiques include fireplaces/grates/ firebacks/guards. Stained glass/ unusual windows. Chandeliers/ lights/light switches. Gilt/decorative mirrors. Columns/pillars. Garden items include fountains/sundials/ birdbaths/busts. Urns/gates/ decorative ironwork. Arches/ railings/paving. Photographs on request. Service for shotblasting/ stripping/renovation.

Glover and Stacey   Grange Farm Buildings, Grange Road, Tongham, Farnham, Surrey GU10 1DN. *Tel:* (02518) 2939. *Open:* Mon to Sat, 9.00am to 5.00pm. Beams/panelling in mahogany, pine, oak. Stairs. Stained glass/Georgian sash windows/leaded lights. Wood block/strip floors. Building materials: hand-made peg/machine tiles/ slates/bricks. Tudor/oak beams/ stanchions. Cobbles/setts/roof finials. Large selections stripped/ unstripped/glazed doors. Ironwork. Craft workshop offers services for stonemasonry, sandblasting, joinery, stripping: they do around 2,000 doors a year.

J and W Demolition and Salvage Sandy Lane, Fair Oak, Hants SO5

7GH. (Phone with enquiries, please.) *Tel:* (0703) 684777. Stock varies according to demolition contracts. I was offered 350,000 bricks from a redundant church.

K and R Demolition   Hammonds Industrial Estate, Stubbington Lane, Stubbington, Fareham, Hants PO14 2NF. (M27, Titchfield turn-off, then follow signs to Stubbington. Ample parking.) *Tel:* (0329) 667143. *Open:* Mon to Fri, 9.00am to 5.30pm, Sat 9.00am to 1.30pm. General salvaged goods. Reclaimed timber/bricks/ tiles/slates. Fireplaces. Doors.

Oxford Architectural Antiques   The Old Depot, Nelson Street, Jericho, Oxford OX2 6BE. *Tel:* (0865) 53310. *Open:* Mon to Sat, 10.00am to 4.00pm. Closed Wed. Relatively new business; three directors are keen to help individual home-owners to renovate/restore period homes. Salvaged building materials, period fixtures/fittings. Bathroom fittings, doors, woodblock floors, fully restored fireplaces, Victorian and earlier. Recommended installers. Telephone enquiries welcome.

P C N Reeves Demolition Contractors
Hazelwood Farm, Hensting Lane, Owlesbury, Winchester, Hants SO21 1LE. (M3, Twyford turn-off. Ample parking.) *Tel:* (0962) 74323. *Open:* Mon to Fri, 8.00am to 4.30pm, Sat 8.00am to 12.00 noon. Wide range of salvaged goods for restoration. Reclaimed bricks/slates/tiles. Oak doors. Architectural items for the home/garden.

Roger's Demo and Dismantling Service   1 Spring Close, Scholing, Southampton, Hants SO2 7NW. *Tel:* (0703) 449173. *Open:* by appointment. Good selection salvaged architectural items. Doors/ fireplaces/bathroom fittings.

Romsey Reclamation   Station Approach, Railway Station, Romsey, Hants SO51 8DU. (M3, Winchester turn-off to Romsey. Ample parking.) *Tel:* (0794) 524174. *Open:* Mon to Fri, 8.00am to 5.00pm, Sat 9.00am to 12.00 noon. Reclaimed slates/bricks/ tiles/beams.

Southern Architectural Salvage Oaktree Farm, Bashley Cross Road, Bashley, New Milton, Hants BH25 5SY. *Tel:* (0425) 612587. *Open:* by appointment. Period reclaimed building materials. Bricks/slates/ tiles/fireplaces.

Sussex Demolition Services   Mint Walk, Warlingham, Surrey CR3 9EH. (Ample parking.) *Tel:* (0883) 626122. *Open:* Mon to Fri, 8.00am to 5.00pm, Sat 8.00am to 4.00pm. Demolition/site clearance specialists offer good choice of salvaged materials. Secondhand timber (hardwoods/softwoods); bricks; doors, stripped pine/painted (cheaper); tiles. Stair spindles. Rolled-steel joists (RSJs), paving slabs. Deliveries.

Tyrone Demolition Contractors 1 West View Villas, School Road, Rayne, Braintree, Essex CM7 8SR. *Tel:* (0376) 27939. *Open:* by appointment. Salvaged building materials bought and sold.

Whitehall Brick and Tile Works Sheerlands Road, Aborfield, near Reading, Berks RG2 9ND. *Tel:* (0734) 760244. *Open:* Mon to Fri, 7.00am to 4.15pm. Reclaimed bricks; large or small quantities.

Yapton Metal Co   Bundell Road, Yapton, near Arundel, W. Sussx. (Near Littlehampton. A259/A3. Ample parking.) *Tel:* (0243) 551359. *Open:* Mon to Sat, 9.00am to 5.00pm. Modern, old, unusual salvaged goods. Fixtures/fittings for home/garden.

Mail Order

The York Hand Made Brick Co Forest Lane, Alne, N. Yorks/YO6 2LU. *Tel:* (03473) 8881. Reclaimed bricks and clay roof pantiles. Will deliver direct anywhere in the country.

▶ Worth a Trip

Architectural Antiques   Savoy Showrooms, New Road, South

Molton, Devon EX36 4BH. (M4, M5, junction 27.) *Tel*: (07695) 3342/4167 (warehouse). *Open*: Mon to Sat, 9.00am to 5.00pm. André Busak claims this is the "best-organised architectural salvage business in the country". He could be right. Fax (07695) 4363 an enquiry, and the computer checks the stock. Housed in an old cinema (6,000 sq ft), with warehouse nearby. Substantial constantly changing stock from home/abroad. Fireplaces, tiles, bathroom fittings. Ironwork, marble, stone. Panelling, doors. Workshop restoration service.

Architectural Heritage Taddington Manor, Taddington, near Cutsdean, Cheltenham, Glos GL54 5RY. (4 miles Broadway, 8 miles Stow-on-the-Wold.) *Tel*: (038) 673 414. *Open Eas to Oct*: Mon to Fri, 9.30am to 5.30pm. *Oct to Eas*: Mon to Fri, 9.30am to 5.00pm. Chimneypieces, original/ antique garden statuary, complete panelled rooms, oak/mahogany doors, stained glass, "bizarre decorative items".

Baileys Architectural Antiques The Engine Shed, Ashburton Industrial Estate, Ross-on-Wye, Hereford & Worcs HR9 7BW. (M5, M40, A40.) *Tel*: (0989) 63015. *Open*: Mon to Fri, 9.00am to 5.00pm, Sat 10.00am to 5.00pm. Don't let the address put you off. A magnificent Brunel engine shed houses Mark and Sally Bailey's treasures, all beautifully restored. There is also a friendly welcome from manageress Sian Richards. Upstairs showroom for reproduction bathroom fittings. Fireplaces/stained glass/doors. Staircases/panelling.

The Original Choice
1,340 Stratford Road, Hall Green, Birmingham B28 9EH. (M42, junction 4, plus 4½-mile drive.) *Tel*: (021) 778 3821. *Open*: Mon, Thu and Fri, 9.30am to 5.30pm, Sat 10.00am to 6.00pm. Or by appointment. "We're strongest for fireplaces" says glass-restorer Pete Thorington, who has around 35 on display. Ring first, and they'll check out stock. Plus well-restored stained glass, and other bits and pieces. Everything fully repaired/renovated, with full installation service by own employees. Restoration services for customers' items.
Also at: 56 The Tything, Worcester WR1 1JJ. *Open*: Mon to Sat, 10.00am to 6.00pm. Late nights Thu and Fri, 7.30pm. Open Sun, 11.00am to 5.30pm. Around 80 fireplaces on display.

Solopark The Old Railway Station, Station Road, near Pampisford, Cambridge CB2 4HB.

Tel: (0223) 834663. *Open*: Mon to Thu, 8.00am to 5.00pm, Fri 8.00am to 4.00pm. Closed for lunch, 1.00pm to 2.00pm. Open Sat, 8.00am to 12.00 noon. One of largest suppliers in the UK of reclaimed building materials; 6 acres of storage/ buildings. Up to 2.5 million bricks, over 4,000 internal/external doors. Brick types include soft reds, handmades, Tudors etc. Roofing tiles/slates. Stripped pine, mahogany, teak timbers. Staircases, window frames, rolled steel joists (RSJs). Oak/elm/chestnut rafters. York stone pavings/tiles. Search service: leave your phone number and they'll try to find what you want.

Walcot Reclamation 108 Walcot Street, Bath, Avon BA1 5BG. (10 mins Bath BR. Car park.) *Tel*: (0225) 444404. International traders in architectural antiques with over 20,000 sq ft of showrooms, including yard and restoration workshops. New bathroom showroom.
Also at: 8a Riverside Business Park, Riverside Road, Lower Bristol Road, Bath. *Tel*: (0225) 335532. *Open*: Mon to Fri, 8.30am to 5.30pm, Sat 9.00am to 4.00pm (both branches). Reclaimed building materials. Flagstones/setts/ bricks/stone/quarry tiles. Pine floorboards/old oak/elm beams. Woodstrip/woodblock.

12

DECORATING MATERIALS

Paper and paint . . . these are the things that make a room, the most basic elements of interior decoration. Go without furniture if you must, and leave the floor bare (maybe even sleep on it). Have a central light bulb, shove a blanket over the window. But do something about the walls, even if it's only a simple coat of emulsion. It doesn't take long, costs very little, and makes a terrific difference. The choice of colours now available is kaleidoscopic, from brilliant white to splendid, hand-printed papers and special paint effects. In between there is enough to keep the most discerning decorator happy for a lifetime.

"It's beige! My colour!"

Elsie De Wolfe (1865–1950), US designer and leader of fashion, on first sighting the Acropolis.

"Either that wallpaper goes, or I do."

Last words of Oscar Wilde (1856–1900).

Decorating successfully is a tricky combination of "let's-do-it now" enthusiasm and the more sophisticated, satisfying effects that come from careful planning. Both motivations play a part in paint-licking a house into shape. Many of the shops listed below have stocks ready to hand for indulging in spur-of-the-moment enthusiasms. As do **DIY Superstores**. Then there are specialists for more considered schemes, some of whom appear below. Others may be found in **2. Co-ordinated Collections** and in **4. Period Papers**. See also **Interior Design**.

London Postal Districts

▶ Bargains!

Bernard Allen Wallpapers   72 High Street, Walthamstow E17 7LD. (2 mins Walthamstow Central tube/BR.) *Tel*: 081-509 1381. *Open*: Mon to Sat, 9.00am to 5.45pm (all branches). Own-brand paints. Good wallpaper selections.
Also at: 74 East Street, SE17 2DQ. (5 mins Elephant and Castle tube.) *Tel*: 071-703 9629.
And at: 29 High Street North, East Ham E6. (2 mins East Ham tube.) *Tel*: 081-471 9015.
See also **Home Counties/South East** below.

Bellevue Interiors   1 Bellevue Parade, Bellevue Road, Wandsworth Common SW17 7EQ. (Tooting Bec tube/Wandsworth Common BR.) *Tel*: 081-767 6659. *Open*: Mon to Sat, 9.00am to 5.30pm. Extensive wallpaper/fabric selections. Stencils/borders/speciality children's ranges. Curtain-making: instant computerised quotes, even on Saturday. Sanderson Spectrum paint mixing.

▶ Bargains!

Alexander Collins Homecare Centre 59/60 Stratford Centre, Stratford E15 1XF. (Stratford tube/BR.) *Tel*: 081-534 0770. *Open*: Mon to Sat, 9.00am to 5.30pm (both branches). Low prices for quality brand paint/wallpapers/vinyls (in stock). Over 3,000 specialist wallcoverings to order. "Staff trained and willing to help: just ring."
Also at: Alexander Collins Interior Design, 17 High Street, Wanstead E11 2AA. (Wanstead/Snaresbrook tubes.) *Tel*: 081-989 9058. Wallcoverings/paint.

The Colour Centre   184 Seven Sisters Road, N7 7PX. (2 mins Finsbury Park tube.) *Tel*: 071-272 3138/9144. *Open*: Mon to Sat, 8.15am to 5.30pm. Early closing Thu, 1.00pm. Paint at trade prices. Monthly special offers. Wallpaper discounts: from 10% for quality collections to 50% mass-market brands. 25% off Amtico vinyl flooring. Full range of tools/brushes/materials for all specialist painting techniques: including "how-to-do-it" videos/books. You too can imitate woodgrain/marble!
Also at: 514 Holloway Road, N7 6JD. (6 mins Holloway Road tube.) *Tel*: 071-272 4300. *Open*: as above.
And at: 29a Offord Road, N1 1EA. (5 mins Caledonian Road tube.) *Tel*: 071-609 1164. *Open*: Mon to Fri, 7.45am to 5.00pm, Sat 8.15am to 1.00pm.

Compton Colour Centre 30 Bellevue Road, SW17 7EF.

(Tooting Bec tube/Wandsworth Common BR.) *Tel*: 081-672 3328. *Open*: Mon to Fri, 8.30am to 5.30pm. Good paint selections. Dulux Dimensions computerised paint mixing. Brushes/rollers for special paint effects.

L Cornelissen and Son   105 Great Russell Street, WC1B 3RY. (5 mins Tottenham Court Road tube.) *Tel*: 071-636 1045. *Open*: Mon to Fri, 9.30am to 5.30pm, Sat 9.30am to 5.00pm. Specialists in traditional decorating materials for paint-effect finishes.

▶ Bargains!

Daves DIY   296 Firs Lane, Palmers Green N13 5QQ. (5 mins junction A10/North Circular Road.) *Tel*: 081-807 3539. *Open*: Mon to Sat, 9.00am to 6.00pm. Early closing Thu, 1.00pm. Friendly family business: heavily discounted prices. Top quality wallpapers at discount prices (400 books). 40% off thousands of stock designs. 50% off 12 rolls of the same design and anaglyptas. Latest Dulux computerised paint-mixing machines at both branches.
See also **Home Counties/South East** below.

Direct Bargain Centre   69/79 Mile End Road, Stepney E1 4TT. (2 mins Stepney Green tube.) *Tel*: 071-790 1094. *Open*: Mon to Fri, 8.00am to 5.00pm. Late night Thu, 8.00pm. Early closing Fri, 3.30pm. Closed Sat. Open Sun, 10.00am to 4.00pm. "Great bargains for your home": their catchy radio jingle sums up constantly changing stock. Decorating materials usually include: paint, wall-coverings, ceramic tiles. Also, large range of carpets/furniture.

Discount Decorating   157/159 Rye Lane, Peckham SE15 4TL. (1 min Peckham Rye BR.) *Tel*: 071-732 3986. *Open*: Mon to Sat, 9.00am to 5.30pm.

Discounts: paint, wallpapers, ceramic tiles.

Hoe Street Bargain Stores 78 Hoe Street, Walthamstow E17 4PG. (10 mins Walthamstow Central tube/BR.) *Tel:* 081-520 7075. *Open:* Mon to Sat, 9.00am to 5.30pm. Large stock of wallpapers half-price or less, from this old-established shop. Good value paint/decorating equipment.

JT Keep (Bollom) 13/15 Theobalds Road, WC1 8SN. (15 mins Holborn tube.) *Tel:* 071-242 0313. *Open:* Mon to Fri, 8.00am to 5.00pm, Sat 8.00am to 12.00 noon (all branches). Quality own-brand Bromel paints. Full range BS colours; specialist paints/varnishes. Before paint effects became fashionable, this was where professionals went (and still go) for scumble glazes/tints.
Also at: 314/316 Old Brompton Road, SW5 9JH. (1 min West Brompton tube.) *Tel:* 071-370 3252. See also **Home Counties/South East** below.

▶ Bargains!

Leslux 148 High Road, East Finchley N2 9ED. (4 mins East Finchley tube.) *Tel:* 081-883 9522/2419. *Open:* Mon to Sat, 8.15am to 5.30pm. For 25 years this energetic shop has undercut all prices. Wallpapers/fabrics up to 50% off, including exclusive makes. Paints: Dulux/Crown/Sandtex. Tiles: Amtico/Cork o'Plast/ceramics (up to 40% off). Nationwide deliveries.

Leyland 424 Edgware Road, W2 1EG. (10 mins Edgware tube.) *Tel:* 071-723 8048. *Open:* Mon to Sat, 7.00am to 6.00pm. Own-brand paints, good colours. Wallpaper discounts: up to 35% off. Cut-price Bosch power tools. Computerised paint mixing: over 4,000 colours. Very good selection of specialist products including Craig and Rose varnishes, Liberon waxes/polishes, Le Franc artists' oil colours. "Probably the best paint shop for miles and miles and miles!"

Also at: 6 Upper Tachbrook Street, SW1 1QE. (2 mins Victoria tube/BR.) *Tel:* 071-828 8695.
And at: 683/685 Finchley Road, NW2 2QS. (15 mins Golders Green tube.) *Tel:* 071-794 5927.

▶ Bargains!

Lomax Wallpapers and Paints 283/285 New North Road, Islington N1 7AA. (10 mins Essex Road tube.) *Tel:* 071-226 1516. *Open:* Mon to Sat, 8.00am to 5.30pm. Good paint prices: Leyland, ICI. Large shop: 2,500 wallpapers in stock, some discounted up to 50%. Enormous pattern book bar. Free paste on all wallpaper sales over 1 roll. Money refunded on unused stock rolls. Friendly, knowledgeable advice from family business, established for 25 years. New ceramic tile showroom. Marble insets for fire surrounds (cut to size).

John Oliver 33 Pembridge Road, W11 3HG. (2 mins Notting Hill Gate tube.) *Tel:* 071-221 6466/727 3735. *Open:* Mon to Sat, 9.30am to 5.30pm. The man and his shop have stayed engagingly the same for an incredible three decades: London needs them. Products change to suit the times . . . but not dramatically. John Oliver (elegant and affable as ever) is one of the great innovators who brought interior colour/design to London in the swinging sixties. Inimitable hand/machine-printed wallpapers: all kept on file, so you can have a reprint 20 years later ("and many do"). Any colourway to order: "we're always very flexible." Metallics are a speciality: no-one else in Britain does them. Particularly popular: marble papers with shimmery metallic grounds. Exclusive paints in 40 colours regularly up-dated (new collections are eagerly awaited by the colour-conscious). Plus authentic shades from the *Historical Book of Colours.* Matt/vinyl silk/flat oil (for walls and woodwork)/eggshell/gloss. Floor paint in any colour. John's matt emulsion is really flat: "look, no sheen". Paints can be mixed to these exclusive finishes in any colour: "we

match fabrics, loo seats, and even knickers . . . yes, really." Papers that resemble bookcases. Stick-on balusters. Wonderful new scattered star design. Need I say more?

Palmers 79 Chiswick High Road, W4 2EF. (3 mins Turnham Green tube.) *Tel:* 081-994 6569. *Open:* Mon to Sat, 8.00am to 5.30pm. Trade prices: major paint brands. All BS colours Dulux/Sandtex.

Papers and Paints 4 Park Walk, SW10 0AD. (15 mins Gloucester Road tube.) *Tel:* 071-352 8626. *Open:* Mon to Fri, 8.00am to 5.30pm. Family business, trading over 30 years. Patrick Baty has meticulously researched the history of colour to produce two unique paint ranges. Historical Colours are based on decorative artefacts (eg tapestries, pottery) through the ages. And Traditional Colours are based on shades used by house-painters up to 300 years ago. Set of hand-painted colour cards: £7.50. Sanderson paint stockists. Varnishes, glazes, brushes, tools, pigments, books for special paint effects.

Putnams See **Soft Furnishings 1. Fabrics.** Exclusive imported water-based paints in bright Mediterranean colours: lime, cerise etc. Good for colour washing furniture.

Simpsons Paints 354 Edgware Road, W2 1EB. (2 mins Edgware Road tube.) *Tel:* 071-723 3762. *Open:* Mon to Sat, 8.30am to 5.30pm. Huge selection of paints, wallpapers, decorative mouldings, ceiling roses. Radiator covers made to measure. Or buy decorative panels to make your own. Most items in stock, or within 24 hrs. *Also at:* 122/124 Broadley Street, NW8 8BB. (3 mins Edgware Road tube.) *Tel:* 071-723 6657. *Open:* Mon to Fri, 7.30am to 5.30pm, Sat 7.30am to 1.00pm.

Specialist Paper Hanging 31 Daws Lane, NW7 4SD. (Mill Hill Broadway tube. Park in adjacent garden centre.) *Tel:* 081-959 1061/1294. *Open:* Mon to Fri,

9.00am to 5.00pm, Sat 10.00am to 4.00pm. Good selection of papers. Hanging. Old-established family firm/personal service. Special welcome for elderly customers. Plus (with sister firm KPM Furnishings) carpets/curtains/furniture.

▶ Bargains!

G Thornfield   321 Gray's Inn Road, WC1X 8PX. (Opposite King's Cross tube.) *Tel:* 071-837 2996/2771/071-278 2515. *Open:* Mon to Sat, 7.15am to 2.00pm. Wallpapers up to 50% off; up to 30% off co-ordinating fabrics. All best brands: phone to check prices. Delivery from stock or within few days of order. Super value. Experienced advice: family firm trading over 35 years.

Top Layer   5 Egerton Terrace, SW3 2BX. (5 mins South Kensington tube.) *Tel:* 071-581 1019/1102. *Open:* Mon to Fri, 8.30am to 6.00pm, Sat 10.00am to 1.00pm. "Anything for walls," says Anthony Evans. Small, well-arranged, friendly showroom: 350 wallpaper books. Speedy supplies. Good selection of period papers: wallpaper design history specialists. Unique sample index arranged in colour groups. Handpainted Chinese silk panels. Matching plain silk wallcoverings. Highly recommended.

Peter Topp Wallcoverings 343 Fulham Palace Road, SW6 6TD. (10 mins Putney Bridge tube.) *Tel:* 071-736 4821/731 5322. *Open:* Mon to Fri, 9.30am to 5.30pm. Peter Topp's family have been trading in Chelsea and Fulham since 1853. Wallcovering specialists; bright,

comfortable showrooms. Heaps of samples/display panels, all top makes. Fabrics/soft furnishings to order. Trimming service for wallpapers. A very personal service: "Most of our customers just keep on coming back." One of my favourites.

Home Counties/ South East

▶ Bargains!

Bernard Allen Wallpapers   King George Avenue, Newbury Park, Ilford, Essex IG2 7SH. (2 mins Newbury Park tube. Next to Sainsbury's.)
See also **London Postal Districts** above.

Bromley and Company   44 Hayes Street, Hayes, Bromley, Kent BR2 7LD. (Hayes/Bromley North BRs.) *Tel:* 081-462 3830. *Open:* Mon to Sat, 8.30am to 5.00pm. Closed for lunch Mon to Fri, 1.00pm to 2.00pm. Early closing Thu, 1.00pm. Family firm. Sanderson fabric/wallcoverings specialist. All other top names. Full making-up service. Curtains/soft furnishings. Recommendations for paper-hangers.

Bytrend Interiors   2 Thames Street, Walton-on-Thames, Surrey KT12 2PU. (Easy free parking.) *Tel:* (0932) 225481. *Open:* Mon to Sat, 8.30am to 5.30pm. Personal service. All Sanderson ranges in stock. Speciality wallcoverings from top names. Three paint-mixing services. Making-up services: curtains/blinds/all soft furnishings. Can recommend good paper-hangers.

▶ Bargains!

Daves DIY   4 Enfield Road, Enfield, Middx EN2 7HW. (Oakwood tube/ M25, junction 24. Opposite Jolly Farmers.) *Tel:* 081-363 1680. *Open:* Mon to Sat, 9.00am to 5.00pm. Early closing Wed, 1.00pm.
See also **London Postal Districts** above.

JT Keep (Bollom)   Croydon Road, Beckenham, Kent BR3 4BL. (Elmers End BR.) *Tel:* 081-658 7723/4/2299. See also **London Postal Districts** above.

RV Tass   382 Richmond Road, Twickenham, Middx TW1 2DX. (10 mins Richmond tube/BR.) *Tel:* 081-892 3643. *Open:* Mon to Fri, 7.00am to 5.00pm, Sat 9.00am to 5.00pm. Paint/papers good prices; DIY advice from professional decorator. Full colour mixing. Crown/Dulux/ Sandersons.

Mail Order

National Trust (Farrow and Ball) Uddens Trading Estate, Wimborne, Dorset BH21 7NL. *Tel:* (0202) 876141. Colours (57 in all) based on Trust properties: eg "Picture Gallery Red" from Attingham Park, Shropshire. "Berrington Blue" is based on scrapes of old paint from an original boudoir at Berrington Hall, Derbyshire. Lots of off-whites/ neutrals as well as stronger shades. Seven paint types, including flat oils/distempers.

---

2. CO-ORDINATED COLLECTIONS

Taking the agony out of mix-and-match, this is where you'll find the real goers. Nowadays you can see big name pattern books in most specialist decorating shops. But a

visit to showrooms is always worthwhile. You benefit from informed help and advice, inspirational displays, and instant samples. A stroll along King's Road,

in particular, is a furnishing essential. Here are **Osborne and Little**, **Designers' Guild** and **Anna French** (see entries below), all within walking distance.

London Postal Districts

Nina Campbell   9 Walton Street, SW3 2JD. (7 mins South Kensington tube.) *Tel:* 071-225 1011. *Open:* Mon to Fri, 9.30am to 5.30pm, Sat 10.00am to 4.00pm. Nina achieved celebrity as Fergie's decorator. Don't let that put you off. She has exquisite taste. Originally apprenticed to John Fowler (see Colefax and Fowler, below), she is established as a decorating grande dame. Her colour palette is unique, now expressed in her own papers/fabrics/carpets. Old sources vibrantly re-worked: yellows, blues, singing greens, dusky pinks, aubergine. Lots of lovely linen fabrics: fresh/clear, not faded—a break from chintz. Plus the prettiest accessories in town: exquisite French porcelain/glass from famous names/ small workshops. Maybe you don't have a mansion, but a visit to Nina's is as essential as an objects lesson: how to choose them, where to place them, how to group them.

Jane Churchill   135 Sloane Street, SW1X 9BZ. (5 mins Sloane Square tube.) *Tel:* 071-730 6379. *Open:* Mon to Sat, 9.30am to 5.30pm. Late night Wed, 7.00pm. Essentially English look for fabrics, papers, borders, furniture, rugs, lamps, bed linens. Jane Churchill herself is renewing her career as an interior decorator; her shops were sold to Colefax and Fowler.
Also at: Liberty (3rd Floor), Regent Street, W1R 6AH. (5 mins Oxford Circus tube.) *Tel:* 071-734 1234. *Open:* Mon to Sat, 9.30am to 6.00pm. Late night Thu, 7.30pm. See also **Home Counties/South East** below.

Colefax and Fowler   39 Brook Street, W1Y 2JE. (5 mins Bond Street tube.) *Tel:* 071-493 2231. *Open:* Mon to Fri, 9.30am to 5.30pm. Closed for lunch, 1.00pm to 2.00pm. Perhaps the most famous name in English decorating, influencing upper-class taste for nearly 50 years. John Fowler was in partnership first with Lady Colefax, and then with Nancy Lancaster. They originated/refined the English country house style with its emphasis on elegance/comfort. They have, of course, been widely copied. Traditional, exclusive chintzes are their forte. Also damasks/weaves/trimmings. Furniture. Wallpapers from hand-blocked originals; decorative borders. Colour brochure available. *Also at:* 110 Fulham Road, SW3 6RL. (7 mins South Kensington tube.) *Tel:* 071-244 7427. *Open:* Mon to Fri, 9.30am to 5.30pm, Sat 10.00am to 4.00pm.
And at: 151 Sloane Street, SW1X 9BX. (5 mins Sloane Square tube.) *Tel:* 071-730 9847. *Open:* Mon to Fri, 9.30am to 5.30pm, Sat 10.00am to 4.00pm.

Danielle   33 Elystan Street, SW3 3NT. (10 mins South Kensington tube.) *Tel:* 071-584 4242/1900. *Open:* Mon to Fri, 10.00am to 5.00pm. Closed for lunch, 1.00pm to 2.00pm. Danielle is a grande dame of decorating, with her own ranges of hand-printed silks, moirés, cottons, and plain colours. Colour is her forte: fresh, original combinations that people travel miles for. To order: clients' own colours. Plus wallpapers/bedlinens. Full interior design service.

Designers' Guild   271 and 277 King's Road, SW3 5EN. (12 mins Sloane Square tube.) *Tel:* 071-351 5775. *Open:* Mon to Fri, 9.30am to 5.30pm, Wed and Sat, 10.00am to 5.30pm. Tricia Guild is the formidable lady in charge. Through the seventies/eighties she shaped her shops into an influential force in international decorating. Her special flair is co-ordination: stripes/checks/ plains/florals and abstracts go together in happy colour harmony. Fabrics/papers/borders/trimmings in jewel shades you don't find elsewhere. Whacky window displays. Don't miss. 277 concentrates on fabrics/papers, while at 271 there are furniture, ceramics, lighting and unique accessories, many from new artists/craftworkers straight from college.

Ehrman Wallpaper and Fabric Shop   21/22 Vicarage Gate, W8 4AA. (7 mins High Street Kensington tube.) *Tel:* 071-937 5077. *Open:* Mon to Fri, 9.30am to 5.30pm, Sat 10.30am to 4.30pm. Knitting supremo Kaffe Fassett produces original papers/fabrics. Evocative imagery/ striking colourings. Worth a look. Available by mail order.

Anna French   343 King's Road, Chelsea SW3 5ES. (Sloane Square tube, plus bus.) *Tel:* 071-351 1126. *Open:* Mon to Fri, 9.30am to 5.30pm, Sat 10.00am to 5.00pm. Anna's special gift is up-to-the-moment collections of printed/woven fabrics, with papers/borders in fabulous colourings . . . at reasonable prices for decorator merchandise. Curtains/accessories made to order. Friendly atmosphere. Essential viewing.

Hill and Knowles   133 Kew Road, Richmond, Surrey TW9 2PN. (10 mins Richmond tube/BR.) *Tel:* 081-948 4010. *Open:* Mon to Fri, 9.30am to 5.30pm. Some of the prettiest co-ordinated collections of wallpapers/ fabrics/borders on the market, including their well-known stencil and rag-roll designs.

Laura Ashley   *Tel:* (0628) 770345 for details of nearest branch. *Star stores:* 7/9 Harriet Street, SW1 9JX. (3 mins Knightsbridge tube.) *Tel:* 071-235 9797. *Open:* Mon to Sat, 9.30am to 6.00pm. Late night Wed, 7.00pm. Open Sat, 9.00am to 6.00pm. *Also at:* 256–258 Regent Street, W1 5DA. (3 mins Oxford Circus tube.) *Tel:* 071-437 9760. *Open:* Mon to Sat, 9.30am to 6.00pm. Late night Thu, 8.00pm. Open Sat, 9.00am to 6.00pm. Laura Ashley floral co-ordinates are in a class of their own. They are famous worldwide, and still going strong, to the delight of country-cottage owners everywhere. Also more sophisticated alternatives: checks, stripes, large-scale florals. Their catalogue is a decorating bible: one of the best explanations of mix-and-match I've seen. Extensive home merchandise offer now includes furniture, lighting, flooring and accessories. *Also at:* Aylesbury, Banbury, Bedford, Brighton, Bromley,

Canterbury, Chelmsford, Colchester, Croydon, Farnham, Guildford, High Wycombe, Hitchin, Horsham, Maidstone, Oxford, Reading, Richmond, Watford, Windsor.

Next Interiors   72 Kings Road, Chelsea SW3 4UG. (5 mins Sloane Square tube.) *Tel:* 071-584 1982. *Open:* Mon to Sat, 9.30am to 6.00pm. Late night Thu, 8.00pm. Co-ordinated fabrics/papers/borders/upholstery with fashion flair. Also good for accessories: china/glass/vases. Made-to-measure window-dressing/upholstery. Bedroom furniture. Mail order Next Directory, £3. *Tel:* (0345) 100500.
Also at: 54/58 Kensington High Street, W8 4PE. (5 mins Kensington High Street tube.) *Tel:* 071-938 4211. Café.
And at: 160 Regent Street, W1R 5TA. (5 mins Oxford Circus tube.) *Tel:* 071-434 2515.
Also at: Wimbledon, Putney, Richmond, Romford, Lakeside Shopping Centre (West Thurrock), Kingston-upon-Thames.

Osborne and Little   304 King's Road, SW3 5UH. (15 mins Sloane Square tube.) *Tel:* 071-352 1456. *Open:* Mon to Fri, 9.30am to 5.30pm, Sat 10.00am to 5.30pm. Peter Osborne and his brother-in-law Tony Little were initially famous for unique wallpapers; they now produce fabrics/borders/trimmings in many ranges/styles, from flamboyant to discreet. Twice winner of British Design Awards. Their prestigious premises in King's Road (like Topsy) "just growed." Several

shops now combine into a spacious showcase for a mass of own-design extras: lamp-bases/shades, quilts, throws, cushions, rugs, stationery, bed linen, bathroom accessories, tableware, luggage. Plus upholstered furniture. Don't decorate until you've been here.

Paper Moon   53 Fairfax Road, NW6 4EL. (10 mins Finchley Road/Swiss Cottage tubes.) *Tel:* 071-624 1198. *Open:* Mon to Fri, 9.30am to 5.30pm, Sat 10.00am to 5.00pm. Specialists in exclusive USA/Canadian designs. Contemporary/classic/country styles. Wallcoverings, co-ordinated fabrics, borders.

Sanderson   52 Berners Street, W1P 3AD. (10 mins Oxford Circus tube.) *Tel:* 071-636 7800. *Open:* Mon to Fri, 9.30am to 5.30pm, Sat 9.00am to 5.30pm. Inimitable world-famous co-ordinated collections, including William Morris hand blocks. Fabrics, papers/vinyls, borders, bed linens from the people who invented co-ordination. Elegant, spacious building with famous stained-glass window and splashing fountains. Fabrics, wallcoverings, carpets, accessories, cabinet/upholstered furniture. Paint mixed on the spot. Ten fully furnished room sets. Knowledgeable staff, excellent service. Coffee shop. Resident interior designer available by appointment. Everyone should visit at least once in a decorating lifetime. See their samples anywhere, but this is the real thing . . .

Spencer Churchill Designs See **Soft**

Furnishings 1. Fabrics.   Chintz papers/fabrics.

Timney-Fowler See **Soft Furnishings 1. Fabrics**.   Ultimate chic. Abundant classical motifs in black and white: Roman heads/coins/columns/urns. Modern classics.

Today Interiors   122 Fulham Road, SW3 6HU. (5 mins South Kensington tube.) *Tel:* 071-244 6661. *Open:* Mon to Fri, 9.30am to 5.30pm, Sat 10.00am to 5.00pm. Charming shop, taking no end of professional trouble to help with colour schemes. Fresh up-to-the-minute colourings for exclusive British co-ordinates. Friendly, non-patronising approach: inspirational displays. Generous free samples. Cotton fabrics for curtains/upholstery. Free pencils/sweeties. Recommended.

Home Counties/ South East

Jane Churchill   13/14 Christopher Place, St Albans, Herts AL3 5DQ. *Tel:* (0727) 60293.
See also **London Postal Districts** above.

K and K Designs   Unit 8, Cranborne Industrial Estate, Cranborne Road, Potters Bar, Herts EN6 3JN. *Tel:* (0707) 49300. *Open:* Mon to Fri, 9.00am to 5.30pm. Original fresh collections vinyls/papers, borders, fabrics, including popular mini-prints, and moiré fabrics, plus co-ordinating tiles.

3. STICK-ONS

The quickest way to add just a touch of high-dec panache to a plain wall is to stick it on. Most collections of paper/fabric co-ordinates now include borders: see **2. Co-ordinated Collections** above. I have highlighted some special favourites below. "Print rooms" are an 18th-century idea that is back in fashion: prints (or even magazine cuttings) are glued to the

wall and ornamented with fancy borders. *Trompe l'oeil* deceives the eye with clever perspectives for views, architectural features etc., and should really be painted by an artist (see **Walls 5. Murals and Special Effects**). But you can now also buy stick-ons for instant effect . . . if you know where to go.

London Postal Districts

Arc   26 North Street, Clapham Old Town, SW4 0HB. (10 mins Clapham Common tube.) *Tel:* 071-720 1628. *Open:* Mon to Fri, 9.30am to 6.00pm, Sat 11.00am to 6.00pm.

Classic narrow border patterns, plus "embellishments": swags, ropes, ribbons, chains. Sold on sheets to cut out. Use to frame their hand-coloured copies of 17th- to 19th-century engravings and to create a fashionable "print room" in your house. Exclusive and unusual.

Cole and Son See **4. Period Papers** below. Authentic early border designs.

Nicholas Gibbs 81 Queenstown Road, SW8 3RQ. *Tel:* 071-720 7415. *Open:* by appointment. Talented muralist markets marvellous packs of stick-on balusters/columns. Mail order.

National Trust Blewcoat School Gift Shop, 23 Caxton Street, SW1

0PY. (2 mins St James's Park tube.) *Tel:* 071-222 2877. *Open:* Mon to Fri, 10.00am to 5.30pm. Late night Thu, 7.00pm. Decorative "print room" borders inspired by the Print Room at Blickling Hall, Norfolk. Plus swags/ribbons/bows/braids.

The Nursery Window See **Children's Rooms.** Simple plain, scalloped borders to team with checked papers. Delightful deep teddybear frieze.

Ornamenta PO Box 784, SW7 2TG. *Tel (for stockists):* 071-584 3857. Or buy by mail order (catalogue/cuttings £1). Instant stick-on *trompe l'oeil* by inspired designer Jane Gordon Clarke. Fashionable colourings: they really do look handpainted. Twisted ropes/

cherubs/rosettes/Gothic motifs etc. Brilliantly successful.

Timney-Fowler See **Soft Furnishings 1. Fabrics.** Enhance plain white (or black) walls with stunning black-and-white classical borders, from a simple Greek key to a deep frieze of caryatids.

Home Counties/ South East

Alexander Beauchamp See **4. Period Papers** below. The "Dado and Border" collection ranges from high Victorian through Art Nouveau/Deco to the thirties.

4. PERIOD PAPERS

Some decorating shops cater specifically for period authenticity. Good decorating shops (see **Interior Design**) also stock pattern books with authentic period papers/fabrics.

London Postal Districts

Baer and Ingram Wallpapers 13 Crescent Place, Brompton Road, SW3 2EA. (5 mins South Kensington tube.) *Tel:* 071-581 9077. *Open:* Mon to Fri, 10.00am to 5.30pm, Sat by appointment. Specialist suppliers of traditional/hand-printed papers. Hundreds of pattern books. Damasks, moirés, stripes, flowers, special effects.

Cole and Son 18 Mortimer Street, W1A 4BU. (10 mins Oxford Circus/ Goodge Street tubes.) *Tel:* 071-580 1066. *Open:* Mon to Fri, 9.00am to 5.00pm. Founded in 1910, and still very much a family firm. The shop's Islington factory (known as John

Perry's) has vast archives and a cellar full of 2,330 wood blocks, some dating from 1780. Original sycamore/pear wood blocks are still used for hand-printing. Other designs are screen printed, but still by hand. Archive names include Adam/Pugin/Crace. Hand-printed designs produced in any colours to order: minimum 10 rolls. Elegant W1 showroom has over 400 fabrics/chintzes, plus 1,200 wallpapers . . . some French, with companion fabrics. Staff are unfailingly courteous. A visit is an exquisite experience.

Colefax and Fowler See **2. Co-ordinated Collections** above. Wallpapers from hand-blocked originals: florals, stripes, medallions, small-scale sprigs. "Musée des Arts Decoratifs" collection, based on famous French museum archives.

Habitat See **Furniture 1. General.** Co-ordinating papers/fabrics faithfully based on originals in the V&A; subdued and pretty small-scale prints.

Sanderson See **2. Co-ordinated Collections** above. Guardian of William Morris's inestimable legacy of pattern. Faithful, original handblocks. Also smaller-scale collection to suit cramped rooms.

Top Layer See **1. Paints and Papers** above. Owner Anthony Evans backs his passionate concern for wallpaper history with specialist sample books.

Watts of Westminster 7 Tufton Street, SW1P 3QE. (5 mins Westminster/St James's Park tubes.) *Tel:* 071-233 0424/1328. *Open:* Mon to Fri, 9.00am to 5.00pm. "Quite the most beautiful papers," said Sir John Betjeman. In the comforting shadow of the Abbey nestles a rich abundance of large-scale pattern/colour. Sumptuous damasks/tapestries/brocades/papers in original Watts' designs. Established at the end of the 19th century by three eminent Gothic Revival architects: the younger Gilbert Scott, George Bodley and Thomas Garner. Now owns an extensive archive of period patterns: many in constant production from 1874. Unique Pugin patterns with heraldic colourings/ Gothic detail. Viewing is spiritually uplifting . . . even if you do not buy.

Zoffany   63 South Audley Street, W1Y 5BF. (5 mins Bond Street tube.) *Tel:* 071-629 9262. *Open:* Mon to Fri, 9.00am to 5.30pm. Designs based on 18th-/19th-century originals, many with large, bold pattern repeats, plus co-ordinating chintzes. Also gentler "livable-with" designs in softer colourways. The public are welcome to browse/buy at this elegant trade showroom.

Home Counties/ South East

Hamilton Weston   18 St Mary's Grove, Richmond, Surrey TW9 1UY. (10 mins Richmond tube/BR.) *Tel:* 081-940 4850. *Open:* Mon to Fri, 9.30am to 6.00pm, Sat 10.00am to 1.00pm. Layers of wallpaper (dreaded by amateur decorators) thrill building conservator Robert Weston. Carefully peeled apart, they give fragmented inspiration for delightful period paper copies. "My best discovery was 22." He and his wife Georgina are an inexhaustible fount of specialist knowledge on period homes. Own collections of 18th-/19th-century document papers, taken from London town houses. The restored Victorian corner shop also sells period fabric/papers/borders from other suppliers. Clients' designs can be reproduced. Reference

books, lists of craftsmen, paints for restored interiors. Curtain-making/ upholstery. Friendly and accessible: *the* place for the dedicated home restorer.

▶ Worth a Trip

Alexander Beauchamp   Griffin Mill, Thrupp, near Stroud, Gloucester GL5 2AZ. *Tel:* (0453) 884537. *Open:* Mon to Fri, 8.30am to 5.30pm. Remarkable patterns from the past in wallpapers/fabrics. "The Archibald Knox Collection": 1897 designs by leading light of Arts and Crafts Movement. "The 17th-century Collection": designs c.1680, from Bourne Hall Museum in Ewell. "The Hampton Court Collection": late-18th/early 19th-century designs. Any colourways to special order. Hand-brushed backgrounds available.

5. STENCILS AND PAINT-EFFECT KITS

London Postal Districts

House Style   Unit 3, Huguenot Place, 17a Heneage Street, E1 5LJ. (3 mins Aldgate East tube/5 mins Liverpool Street tube/BR.) *Tel:* 071-247 9462. *Open:* by appointment. Jocasta Innes (author of *Paint Magic*) offers kits for colourwash, liming, antiquing, crackleglaze, marbling, verdigris, woodwashing, and porphyry. *A–Z of Paint Effects* video. Classes/courses.

Laura Ashley See **2. Co-ordinated Collections** above.   Traditional brass stencils in pretty patterns: durable and easy to use.

Paperchase   213 Tottenham Court Road, W1P 9AF. (5 mins Tottenham Court Road tube.) *Tel:* 071-580 8496. *Open:* Mon to Sat, 9.30am to

6.00pm. Late night Thu, 7.00pm. The store that started the stencil craze. Although overtaken by specialists they still have a fair selection. American Dover books with cut-and-use stencils, plus pre-cut designs (Christmas, Early American, Folk Art, American Indian, Teddy Bears). Extensive stencil range from Pavilion/Jocasta Innes. Cards, stationery, decorations, paper tableware.
Also at: 167 Fulham Road, SW3 6SN. (5 mins South Kensington tube.) *Tel:* 071-589 7839.
And at: 199/202 Oxford Street, W1R 1AH. (5 mins Oxford Circus tube.) *Tel:* 071-437 2476.
And at: Waterloo Station, SE1 7NQ. *Tel:* 071-928 5067.

Antonia Spowers   Designs Unit 3, Ransome's Dock, 35/37 Parkgate Road, SW11 4NP. *Tel:* 071-622 3630. *Open:* by appointment. Sophisticated, subtle stencil motifs/

borders based on a variety of traditional/ethnic sources. Brochure available.

The Carolyn Warrender Stencil Store   91 Lower Sloane Street, SW1W 8DA. (5 mins Sloane Square tube.) *Tel:* 071-730 0728. *Open:* Mon to Fri, 10.00am to 5.30pm, Sat 10.00am to 4.00pm. Unique shop for enthusiasts. Stencils from baby bunnies to Greek key. Brushes/ paints for various surfaces including fabrics/china. Advice/tuition/ workshops. Materials for cutting your own stencils. Stencils cut to order. Stencilling service. Paint-effect kits with pre-tinted glazes for sponging, dragging etc. Colour catalogue: £1.50 (inc p&p). Mail order.
See also **Home Counties/South East** below.

Home Counties/ South East

Felicity Binyon Stencil Design   9, Buckingham Street, Oxford OX1 4LH. *Tel*: (0865) 245243. Professional stenciller offers kits/courses.

Hang-It Walls and Windows 2A Church Lane, Banbury, Oxon. (M40, junction 11.) *Tel*: (0295) 276338. *Open*: Mon to Sat, 9.15am to 5.00pm. Early closing Tue 1.30pm. Stencilling materials specialist: Sue Appleton teaches at the local tech. Paints/brushes/stencils. Stencils cut to order. Chipboard tables. Cushion pads/covers. Curtain-making.

The Carolyn Warrender Stencil Store   20 Heronsgate Road, Chorleywood, Herts WD3 5BN. (1 min M25, junction 17.) *Tel*: (0923) 285588. *Open*: Mon to Fri, 9.00am to 5.30pm, Sat 10.00am to 5.00pm. See also **London Postal Districts** above.

Wonham Reid Retail See **Soft Furnishings 3. Made-to-Measure**. Jocasta Innes House Style kits/ stencils. Phone for details of courses/demonstrations.

Mail Order

Lyn Le Grice Stencil Design   The Stencilled House, 53 Chapel Street, Penzance, Cornwall TR18 4AF. *Tel*: (0736) 64193. Lyn deservedly has devotees worldwide for her very special stencils: send an A4 sae for details. Designs include "Sea Shore", "Willow Pattern", "Noah's Ark", "Jacobean". Large-scale wall-panel stencils to order. *Shop open* Mon to Sat, 10.00am to 5.30pm, with house tours Mon to Fri, at 11.00am to 3.00pm. Stencil day courses in London/Penzance.

For details of short courses in paint effects and stencils, contact the following:

Broken Colour Techniques *Tel*: (0255) 503039.

KLC *Tel*: 071-602 8592.

Harry Levinson *Tel*: 081-348 2811. (Timetable is geared to suit women with children at school.)

Gaby McCall *Tel*: 071-603 0837.

Pardon School of Specialist Decoration *Tel*: 071-245 1049.

Annie Sloan *Tel*: (0993) 812590.

Spitalfields Studio *Tel*: 071-247 9462.

13
SOFT FURNISHINGS

Fabric is the key to the new interiors of the nineties: draped, swathed,
stretched, pleated, frilled . . . the possibilities are legion. The ingenious can do
it themselves . . . creating curtains, blinds, and other desirable accessories at
the drop of a needle. Otherwise, a multitude of made-to-measure merchants
await your every command.

1. FABRICS

"We just sold coloured silks from the East—nothing else. The sort of thing that William Morris, Alma Tadema and Burne-Jones and Rossetti used to come in and turn over and rave about."

William Judd, long-serving Liberty employee, speaking of the early days.

It's getting more difficult to buy fabrics from stock—I've indicated where shops offer this useful facility. Also look at **Interior Design** shops, and shops listed below under **3. Made-to-Measure**. (You can order fabrics from these outlets from pattern books; they arrive in around three days). It's worth ordering samples, or even a sample length, to avoid expensive mistakes.
Department Stores often have useful stocks, suitable for immediate needs, and markets can provide bargains. Fabrics with matching papers can be found at outlets listed under **Decorating Materials 2. Co-ordinated Collections** (you'll also find samples at **Interior Design** shops). See also **2. Lace, Nets and Voiles; 6. Archive Fabrics; 9. Antique Textiles;** and **10. Commissioned Fabrics,** all below.

London Postal Districts

Alexander Furnishings 51/61 Wigmore Street, W1H 9LF. (Corner Wigmore Street and Marylebone Lane.) *Tel:* 071-935 2624/7806/8664/1678. *Open:* Mon to Sat, 9.00am to 6.00pm. Late night Thu 7.00pm. Six interconnecting shops: huge choice of ex-stock curtain/upholstery fabrics. Keenest prices (many discounted). Co-ordinated collections, including wallpapers. Tracks, poles, cushions, trimmings, nets. Sofas, sofabeds. Trading for 37 years. Personal service, friendly atmosphere. Free advice/samples. Curtains: measure, make, fit and

hang. Made-to-measure blinds. Loose covers/reupholstery. Bed-covers, headboards, quilting to order.

Anta 141 Portland Road, W11 4LR. *Tel:* 071-229 5077. *Open:* Mon to Sat, 9.30am to 5.30pm. Closed Wed, 1.00pm. Check out these classy tartan specialists, where fabrics line the walls of a cosy corner shop. Exclusive zingy high-fashion renderings of tartan themes (mostly in stock). Pure cotton/wool/silk. Also complementary stripes. Made-up accessories. Cuttings.

Celia Birtwell 71 Westbourne Park Road, W2 5QH. (5 mins Royal Oak/Westbourne Park tubes.) *Tel:* 071-221 0877. *Open:* Mon to Fri, 10.00am to 5.00pm. Celia Birtwell is a true original: her delicate, imaginative designs have a fantasy touch, ideal for sheers and floaty voiles. Also cotton/linen/silk prints. Very special.

▶ Bargains!

Corcoran and May 161 Lower Richmond Road, SW15 1HH. (15 mins Putney Bridge tube.) *Tel:* 081-788 9556. *Open:* Mon to Fri, 10.00am to 5.30pm, Sat 10.00am to 6.00pm (both branches). Closed for lunch, 1.00pm to 2.00pm. Seconds in top make furnishing fabrics. Curtains/blinds made to measure. *Also at:* 11 The Green, Ealing W5 5DA. (5 mins Ealing Broadway tube.) *Tel:* 081-567 4324.

The Final Curtain Company *Tel:* 081-699 3626. Natural fibres. Calico/ticking/cotton duck. Can be dyed to order.

Christian Fischbacher 27 Chelsea Garden Market, Chelsea Harbour, Lots Road, SW10 0XE. (C3, C4 buses) *Tel:* 071-351 7281. *Open:* Mon to Fri, 9.00am to 5.30pm, Sat 10.00am to 5.00pm. See show lengths of all

designs from this famous manufacturer's complete range of top contemporary fabric design, plus Pallu and Lake, Interior Selection and Charles Hammond. Samples. Fabrics to order. Papers in stock. Collier Campbell, Munro and Tutty, Jack Prince, Gianni Veresace. Beautifully brilliant and brilliantly bold.

Pierre Frey 253 Fulham Road, SW3 6HY. (5 mins South Kensington tube.) *Tel:* 071-376 5599. *Open:* Mon to Fri, 9.30am to 5.30pm, Sat 10.00am to 5.00pm. Leading upmarket French fabric house, with around 4,000 exclusive, sophisticated designs—tapestries, weaves, hand-prints. Curtains/upholstery. Fabric accessories include bags/luggage. Atmosphere is excessively exclusive.

Java Cotton Co See **Ethnic Crafts and Furnishings.** Cotton batiks from Indonesia. Wonderful authentic patterns and colour. Essential viewing.

John Lewis (and other stores in the John Lewis Partnership) See **Department Stores.** Own studio/printers/weavers for Jonelle brand furnishing fabrics. Outstanding designs/colours. Good quality, low prices. Traditional and modern. Curtaining, upholstery, loose cover fabrics, with some matching wallcoverings. Coloured/ insulated linings. Jonelle Duracolour fabrics will be replaced if they fade. I never buy fabrics until I've seen what's in JL first.

▶ Bargains!

P N Jones Trading 18 Holly Grove, SE15 5DG. (3 mins Peckham Rye BR.) *Tel:* 071-639 2113. *Open:* Mon to Fri, 9.30am to 5.00pm. Closed for lunch, 12.00 noon to 2.00pm. Open Sat and Sun by appointment. Warehouse for quality Indian fabrics. Lots of natural fibres/good colours. Masook cotton. Noil silk. Gopi lightweight cotton for linings. Cotton/silk mixtures. Dupion silk.

K and K Fabrics See **3. Made-to-Measure** below. Moirés/printed cottons etc. bought in bulk for stock, so prices are keen.

Les Olivades   16 Filmer Road, Fulham SW6 7BW. (5 mins Fulham Broadway tube.) *Tel:* 071-386 9661. *Open:* Mon to Fri, 10.00am to 6.00pm. Provençal fabrics from 17th-/18th-century archives of the Boudin family. Unique florals, paisleys, stripes, plaids. Rich, saturated colours: yellow ochre, vibrant crimson, midnight blue. Furnishing cottons 150cm wide. Matching/co-ordinating papers/linens. Patterned oil-cloths for pretty, practical tables that wipe clean with Gallic ease. Trays/fashion accessories. New, unusual French upholstery prints/weaves. Francophiles need go no further.

Liberty See **Department Stores**.   New Collier Campbell shop on third floor has full range from this famous design duo. Susan Collier sold her first design to Liberty in 1961. The 1973 Bauhaus pattern is still in production and a modern classic.

Liberty Prints   340a King's Road, SW3 5UR. *Tel:* 071-352 6581. *Open:* Mon to Sat, 9.30am to 6.00pm. A chance to explore at leisure beautiful curtain/upholstery fabrics from the famous parent store in Regent Street (see **Department Stores**). Plus other famous brands: Warner/Romo etc. Interior design service.

MacCulloch and Wallis   25 Dering Street, W1R 0BH. (3 mins Oxford Circus/Bond Street tubes.) *Tel:* 071-629 0311. *Open:* Mon to Fri, 9.00am to 5.15pm. Good stocks of basic furnishing fabrics: gingham, calico, muslin, cambric. Also linen canvas. Useful haberdashery.

▶ Bargains!

Ian Mankin   109 Regent's Park Road, Primrose Hill NW1 8UR. (5 mins Chalk Farm tube.) Tel: 071-722 0997. *Open:* Mon to Fri, 10.00am to 5.30pm, Sat 10.00am to 4.00pm. Natural fibres reign supreme in the quiet decorum of an old-fashioned drapers. No synthetics here: just rolls of mainly cotton turned into unbleached calico, gingham, muslin, scrim, and own exclusive weaves. There are 250 fabrics in total, many in exclusive colourways: plains, stripes, checks, tartans. No flashy florals or fluorescent brights: all very tasteful and understated. Nothing under £10 per metre. Thirty colourways: send £1 for samples. *Also at:* 271 Wandsworth Bridge Road, SW6 2TX. (10 mins Parsons Green tube.) *Tel:* 071-371 8825. *Open:* Mon to Fri, 10.00am to 5.30pm.

Andrew Martin   200 Walton Street, SW3 2JL. (5 mins South Kensington tube.) *Tel:* 071-584 4290. *Open:* Mon to Fri, 10.00am to 5.30pm, Sat 10.00am to 4.00pm. Particularly popular for exclusive kelim designs: wonderful glowing cotton prints that look like weaves: "we sell it to the world." Silk specialists. Exclusive, classy upholstery.

Mrs Monro   16 Motcomb Street, SW1X 8LB. (5 mins Knightsbridge/Sloane Square tubes.) *Tel:* 071-235 0326. *Open:* Mon to Fri, 9.30am to 5.30pm. Miss Jean Monro is semi-retired from the Knightsbridge decorating business her mother founded in 1926. Her traditional chintzes in original old colourings are loved the world over.

Muraspec Wallcoverings   78/89 Pentonville Road, N1 9LW. (5 mins Kings Cross/Angel tubes.) *Tel:* 071-278 0161. *Open:* Mon to Fri, 8.00am to 5.30pm. Find here (at the trade counter) extra-wide felts (72in) in 70 glorious colours (they used to be at the Felt and Hessian shop in Holborn, sadly now defunct). Not so many people know about this. Use them as table covers for card-sharps, or as thick, instant curtains.

A big plus point is that felt doesn't fray, so you needn't hem. The big minus is it's not washable: dry clean only.

Nice Irma's See **Ethnic Crafts and Furnishings**.   Wonderful imported furnishing fabrics for curtains/upholstery, all natural fibres. Wide selections ikats, cut lace, textured plains and cotton embroidered with wool Kashmiri crewel-work. Essential viewing.

Putnams   55 Regents Park Road, NW1 8UR. (10 mins Chalk Farm tube.) *Tel:* 071-431 2935. *Open:* Mon to Sat, 10.00am to 6.00pm. Antoinette Putnam sells exclusive prints based on her stocks of antique china. Upholstery weight 100 per cent cotton. This shop is as pretty as a traditional dresser, full of cups and plates.

Russell and Chapple   23 Monmouth Street, WC2H 9DE. (5 mins Leicester Square/Covent Garden tubes.) *Tel:* 071-836 7521. *Open:* Mon to Fri, 8.30am to 5.00pm. Busy shop catering for artists and theatrical trade. Three qualities natural hessian, 72in wide. Fourteen shades dyed hessian (warning: it tends to fade). Fire-retardant gauzes for filmy drapes. Butter muslin, cotton duck, calico, linens. Samples/price list. Mail order.

Souleiado   171 Fulham Road, SW3 6JW. (2 mins South Kensington tube.) *Tel:* 071-589 6180. *Open:* Mon to Fri, 10.00am to 6.00pm, Sat 10.00am to 5.00pm. For South of France sunshine, immerse yourself in authentic Provençal cottons printed from original traditional woodblocks. Fabrics by the metre, or made-up accessories. Table linens. Catalogue available.

Spencer-Churchill Designs   55 Hollywood Road, SW10 9HX. (5 mins Earls Court tube.) *Tel:* 071-376 3525. *Open:* Mon to Fri, 9.00am to 4.00pm. Aristocratic chintz. Lady Henrietta Spencer-Churchill, daughter of the Duke of Marlborough, is inspired by watercolours from Blenheim Palace library; wallpapers available to match.

▶ Bargains!

Stocks   157 Munster Road, SW6 6DA. (5 mins Parsons Green tube.) *Tel:* 071-736 4088. *Open:* Tue to Sat, 10.00am to 6.00pm, Sat 10.00am to 1.00pm. The shop reflects the abundant talents and friendly nature of its designer/owner, Sue West. Keenest prices for smartest fabrics. Chic tartans/plain glazed cottons. Seconds. Inexpensive silks. Well-priced own collections. Delightful gifts. Recommended.

Timney-Fowler   388 King's Road, SW3 5UZ. (12 mins Sloane Square tube.) *Tel:* 071-351 6562. *Open:* Mon to Sat, 9.30am to 6.00pm. RCA graduates Sue Timney and Graeme Fowler create the ultimate black-and-white fabric show: essential viewing. Famous for classical/baroque motifs. All fabrics in stock. New, richly Gothic printed crushed velvets. Wallpapers/borders. Also elegant mugs, plates, scarves, throws . . . even socks.

Home Counties/ South East

▶ Bargains!

Hang-It Walls and Windows See **Decorating Materials 5. Stencils.** Discontinued designer fabrics at rock-bottom prices.

▶ Bargains!

Material World   87 High Street, Tunbridge Wells, Kent TN1 1XZ. *Tel:* (0892) 20883. Designer fabrics at often less than half price. Job lots, ends of lines, discontinued ranges, seconds.
Also at: 35 North Hill, Colchester, Essex CO1 1QR. *Tel:* (0206) 575200. *And at:* 7 Weavers Walk, Northbrook Street, Newbury, Berks RG13 1AL. *Tel:* (0635) 529016.

Materialistic   Curtain Studio, 60 Hampton Road, Twickenham, Middx TW2 5QB. (5 mins Strawberry Hill BR.) *Tel:* 081-898 2212. *Open:* Mon to Sat, 9.30am to 5.30pm. Evenings by appointment. Around 100 rolls of furnishing fabrics, with masses more to order. Plus all tapes, tracks, etc. for DIY. Or they can fit tracks, make curtains etc. at well below West End prices. Samples, advice. Furniture, carpets, interior design.

▶ Bargains!

Catherine Russell   8 Connaught Avenue, Frinton-on-Sea, Essex CO13 9PW. (10 mins Frinton BR.) *Tel:* (0255) 674759. *Open:* Mon to Sat, 9.00am to 5.30pm. Early closing Wed, 1.00pm. Large, well-stocked shop. Sanderson fabrics: slight seconds at substantially reduced prices. Fabrics for DIY curtains can be cut with matching pattern repeats. Or have curtains made-to-measure on premises.

Mail Order

A number of firms can supply cut-price designer fabrics by mail order.

When you've found the fabric you want, telephone the numbers below for quotes on discounted prices, with nationwide deliveries. Understandably, interior design/ furnishing shops do not like the way these companies trade. A specialist shop/department may take a lot of trouble to help you with colour/style advice, estimating, and hints for making-up. It's not fair to take your trade elsewhere, and you have to ask yourself if the money you save is really worth the trouble. On the whole, making-up services are more satisfactory if a firm helps to choose/supplies the fabric, so that its choice can be taken into account for the overall style. Telephone with exact fabric details (maker, design number/name, colourway, quantities) and compare quotes:

Jenny Clarke Fabrics   Church Street, Windemere, Cumbria. *Tel:* (05394) 44686. Fabrics/papers from well-known makers. Making-up service.

Sue Foster Fabrics   57 High Street, Emsworth, Hants PO10 7YA. *Tel:* (0243) 378831. Curtain/loose cover/upholstery fabrics.

Just Fabrics   PO Box 1, Launceston, Cornwall PL15 7YZ. *Tel:* (0566) 776279. Top name fabrics/papers. Making-up service. Bargain prices for plain chintz, candy-striped chintz (20 colours), striped tickings (54in wide, nine colours), "loomstate" calico. Also sheetings: polycottons/cottons (94in wide), super percale (108in wide). Also linings, interlinings, tapes, piping cord, cushion pads, sheers. Quilting service.

---

2. LACE, NETS, AND VOILES

"Good taste is better than bad taste, but bad taste is better than no taste."

Arnold Bennett, British novelist (1867–1931)

London's windows need privacy from the prying eyes of London's pavements. Nets needn't be dowdy. There are many choices other than sad grey Terylene—crisp cotton lace; filmy voile; plain sheers. Read on. Many co-ordinated collections now include voiles, so browse through samples in **Interior Design** shops, or in shops listed in **1. Fabrics**, above, or 3. **Made-to-Measure**, below, or in **Decorating Materials 2. Co-ordinated Collections**.

London Postal Districts

Celia Birtwell See **1. Fabrics** above. Divine, floaty voiles with overprinted designs.

Anna French See **Decorating Materials 2. Co-ordinated Collections**. Wonderful cotton la from original Victorian looms. Mail order catalogue: £3.50.

John Lewis See **Department Stores**. Good net selections, including cotton macramé.

▶ Bargains!

Just Fabrics See **1. Fabrics** above. Plain cream/white Trevira sheers at keen prices: plain, fine/heavy slubs, stipe, open weave.

Laura Ashley Home See **Decorating Materials 2. Co-ordinated Collections**. Good selections cotton lace/voile white/ivory made on 19th-century looms.

Lunn Antiques 86 New Kings Road, Parsons Green, SW6 4LU. (5 mins Parsons Green tube.) *Tel:* 071-736 4638. *Open:* Mon to Sat, 10.00am to 6.00pm. "Our shop is a sea of lace," enthuses Stephen Lunn. He has run this delightful boutique with his wife since 1976. All types of old lace. Antique linen and lace laundry restoration service.

▶ Bargains!

Russell and Chapple See **1. Fabrics** above. Inexpensive muslin and gauze.

3. MADE-TO-MEASURE

"When the tea is brought at five o'clock,
And all the neat curtains are drawn with care,
The little black cat with bright green eyes
Is suddenly purring there."

Harold Monro (1879–1932)

Soft furnishings designed and made for your home are an affordable luxury, and will guarantee an exclusive touch. It's worth finding a maker you really get on with, in terms of design ideas, type of service and price. A wide variety is listed below. You will also find firms offering made-to-measure soft furnishings listed under **Interior Design**. **Department Stores** also frequently offer these services.

London Postal Districts

Albany Furnishings 4 Chester Court, Albany Street, NW1 4BV. (10 mins Regent's Park/Great Portland Street tubes.) *Tel:* 071-486 2085. *Open:* Mon to Fri, 9.00am to 5.00pm, Sat 9.00am to 4.00pm.

Specialise in electrically operated curtains and in black-out curtains. Tracks, poles, fabrics. Curtain-making. Pelmets, swags, tails. Nets, blinds, quilted bedspreads.

Austin Curtain Contracts Rookery Way, The Hyde, West Hendon NW9 6QG. *Tel:* 081-958 1602/205 0061. *Open:* by appointment. Home visits with samples. Experts in hand-sewn curtains. Festoons/Austrians. Swags/tails.

Avery Interiors (L Posner) 98 George Lane, South Woodford E18 1AD. *Tel:* 081-530 4677/081-989 8354. *Open:* Mon to Sat, 9.00am to 5.30pm (all branches). Early closing Thu, 1.00pm. Small family business (established for 54 years), run by two brothers. All top makes. Curtains/blinds. Tracks, poles, fitting. Visit/advise/estimate. Upholstery. Very personal service.

Pam Ballard Furnishings 9 Bedford Corner, The Avenue, Chiswick W4 1HA. (3 mins Turnham Green tube.) *Tel:* 081-995 4465. *Open:* Mon to Fri, by appointment. Wide selections fabrics. Full personal professional soft furnishings service.

Bennett and Cameron 88 Stoke Newington Church Street, N16 0AP. *Tel:* 071-254 9835. *Open:* Mon to Sat, 10.00am to 6.00pm. Closed all day Wed. Other times by appointment. "It's a very personal service: I like to put myself out for my clients," says Patricia Bennett. Children welcome. Soft furnishing/interior design specialists. Packed with fabric/paper samples. Upholstery/loose covers. Candlesticks/cushions. Own workroom. Will make up customers' own fabrics.

Bradleys 184 Kentish Town Road, NW5 2AE. (10 mins from Kentish Town tube.) *Tel:* 081-485 0029. *Open:* Mon to Sat, 9.00am to 6.00pm. Curtain-making/track-fitting; free estimates. Net curtains, household linens.

Fiona Campbell 259 New Kings Road, SW6 4RB. (3 mins Parsons Green tube.) *Tel:* 071-731 3681. *Open:* Mon to Thu, 9.30am to 5.30pm, Fri 9.30am to 4.30pm. Established for over 25 years. Well-stocked showroom offers professional help on all aspects curtain/carpet design. Lots of examples of past work. Fabrics, trimmings, wallpapers, blinds, lamps. Tracks, poles, fitting. New furniture/headboards.

Cedar Interiors 68 Pembroke Road, Kensington W8 6NX. *Tel:* 071-602 8388. *Open:* Mon to Fri, 9.30am to 5.30pm. All curtains, blinds, pelmets, swags and tails etc. made-to-measure. Mrs Audrey Burgess has been trading for over 30 years. Decorating/joinery. Headboards/bedspreads. Modern/traditional furniture. Linens/carpets.

Chamberlains Furnishings 221 Regent's Park Road, N3 3LD. (10 mins Finchley Central tube.) *Tel:* 081-346 8565. *Open:* Mon to Sat, 9.30am to 5.00pm. All made-to-measure soft furnishings. Fabrics/wallcoverings.

Curtain Contracts 47 Church Road, NW4. (15 mins Hendon tube.) *Tel:* 081-203 3772. *Open:* Mon to Fri, 9.30am to 4.15pm. Trading for 35 years. Specialist makers curtains, bedspreads, blinds, headboards. Poles/tracks (including electric/remote control).

The Curtain Corporation 119 Broadhurst Gardens, NW6. *Tel:* 071-372 0111. *Open:* by appointment. "We only do challenging work." Difficult windows catered for. Swags, tails, rosettes etc. Fully electrified tracks.

The Curtain Gallery 48 Brunswick Crescent, N11 1EB. *Tel:* 081-368 4593. *Open:* by appointment. Individual style/colour advice on in-home visits. All curtains/soft furnishings, including loose covers. Three-week turnaround.

Devon House Interiors 3/4 Devon House, Hermon Hill, Wanstead E11 2AW. (2 mins Snarebrook tube. Easy parking.) *Tel:* 081-518 8112. Large triple-fronted showroom. Over 35 years in the soft furnishing business. Own workrooms. Fabrics/papers. Lighting, furniture, carpets, accessories. Complete interior design package.

De Winter 223 Kensington Church Street, W8. (2 mins Notting Hill Gate tube.) *Tel:* 071-229 1918/4949. Mr and Mrs De Winter have been Kensington curtain-makers for over 50 years: the quintessential family business. All soft furnishings made on premises: from a simple blind to swags/tails for stately homes. Design service/interior design advice. Carpets/furniture. Stacked to ceiling with fabrics, all top makes, with bargains in seconds (eg Sanderson): "never knowingly understocked!"

Elite Curtains Rookery Way, The Hyde, West Hendon NW9 6QG. (10 mins Colindale/Hendon Central tubes.) *Tel:* 081-205 0061. *Open:* Mon to Fri, 8.00am to 5.00pm. Curtain-making; nets, shears, handsewn headings and pelmets. Made-to-measure festoons, Austrian, Roman, Venetian, vertical, roller blinds. Tracks installed. Curtains cleaned. Repairs/adaptations.

Exclusive Fabrics (Mainbury) 186 Kilburn High Road, NW6. *Tel:* 071-624 4741/9256. Established 40 years. Home service with samples. Design/estimate. All curtain/blinds: own factory. Pelmets, swags, tails, nets. Specialist in fitting awkward tracks (eg round bay windows).

The Final Curtain Company *Tel:* 081-699 3626. Susan McMullan visits with natural fabric samples (cream, grey, black) which can be dyed to any colour/effect. Full curtain-making service: curtains can be hung anywhere in the country. Unusual poles/trimmings.

Bruno Galetti 72 Haverstock Hill, NW3 2BE. *Tel:* 071-267 6936. *Open:* Mon to Fri, 8.30am to 5.00pm, Sat 9.00am to 1.00pm. Fabric/wallpaper sample library; track/pole samples. Blinds/trimmings. Curtain/upholstery workshops; personal, reliable service.

Interiors 454 Chiswick High Road, W4 5TT. (5 mins Chiswick Park tube.) *Tel:* 081-994 0073. *Open:* Mon to Fri, 8.30am to 6.00pm. Late night Thu, 8.00pm. Open Sat, 9.00am to 6.00pm. Friendly family business (two brothers). Spacious (over 3,000 sq ft) airy showroom; lots of samples/curtain styles. Sensational window displays: packed with inspiration. Advice/measuring. Track fitting. Hang/dress/steam curtains. Own workrooms for all soft furnishings. Curtain cleaning: take down/rehang. Upholstered headboard, screens, ottomans, 5,000 paint colours ex-stock: Crown, Dulux, Sanderson. Recommended.

Interiors by Greens 78/84 Seven Sisters Road, Holloway Road, N7 6AE. (5 mins Finsbury Park tube.) *Tel:* 071-607 6310/6128. Family-run business, established 54 years. Custom-made curtains in your fabrics or theirs. Blinds, pelmets, swags, tails. Tracks/poles. Measuring-up service free of charge.

John Lewis, Peter Jones and other stores in the **John Lewis Partnership**. See **Department Stores** and **1. Fabrics** above. Professional making-up for curtains, pelmets, loose covers, from these famous workrooms. By hand or machine. Blinds, continental quilt covers, tablecloths to order.

K and K Fabrics 33 Mill Lane, West Hampstead NW6. (7 mins West Hampstead/Kilburn tubes.) *Tel:* 081-908 4675/071-794 1781. *Open:* Mon to Fri, 8.30am to 6.00pm, Sat 8.30am to 5.00pm. Friendly, efficient husband-and-wife team. Curtains/blinds. Tracks, tapes, swags, tails. Your material or theirs: very flexible. Fabrics in stock at good prices.

Material Effects See **Ceilings 3. Tented**. All soft furnishings, to a very high standard. Loose covers. Upholstery. Tapestry-stretching and making into cushions.

Mr Nicholas Curtain Service 442 Church Lane, Kingsbury NW9 8AB. (10 mins Kingsbury tube.) *Tel:* daytime 081-205 7996; evenings 081-205 0415. *Open:* Mon to Fri, 9.00am to 5.00pm. Work/showroom supplies wide range of fabrics. Tracks etc. fitted. Curtains made by hand and hung in your home: plus swags/tails, pelmets, pinch pleats, blinds. Advise, measure, estimate.

Paine and Co   49/51 Barnsbury Street, Islington N1 1TP. (10 mins Angel tube.) *Tel*: 071-607 1176. *Open*: Tue to Fri, 10.00am to 6.00pm, Sat 10.00am to 3.00pm. Melanie Paine, interior designer, is famous for her books on fabrics and curtain treatments. Her designs are always original, sometimes unorthodox, using fabric for fluid drapes and swags. From a single blind to a whole house. Fabrics/ wallcoverings. Full interior design service.

Penbrice Interiors   The Studios, 165 Lanark Road, W9 1NZ. (2 mins Maida Vale tube.) *Tel*: 071-328 3546. *Open*: Mon to Fri, 9.00am to 5.30pm. Closed for lunch 1.00pm to 2.00pm. Open Sat by appointment. Personal/enthusiastic service from Mrs Penny Dixon. Showroom filled with soft furnishing inspirations to order. Sit in pleasant, quiet surroundings and peruse a 25-year-old collection of pictures, books, and drawings filled with ideas, from traditional to ultra-modern. Own workrooms. Poles/tracks fitted. Furniture restoration. Recommended.

Philips and Thornton   Unit 19, Sapcote Trading Centre, 374 High Road, Willesden NW10. *Tel*: 081-459 0569. *Open*: by appointment. Small, friendly, personal service mainly for designers. Curtain workshops established 50 years: all hand-sewn work.

Pickwick Papers and Fabrics
6 Nelson Road, Greenwich SE10 9JB. (10 mins Greenwich BR.) *Tel*: 081-858 1205. *Open*: Mon to Sat, 9.30am to 5.00pm. Early closing Thu, 3.30pm. Well-established. Well-trained staff who supervise orders in on-site workrooms. Numerous fabric/paper pattern books.

Royston Locke Curtains   19 Market Place, Hampstead Garden Suburb NW11 6JY. *Tel*: 081-455 7977. *Open*: Mon to Fri, 9.00am to 6.00pm. Curtains designed/made/ fitted. Also blinds, pelmets, bedcovers, bed-drapes. Fabrics, trimmings, poles.

Judy St Johnson   46 Markham Street, SW3 3NR. *Tel*: 071-352 2169. *Open*: by appointment. High-class, handmade designer curtains. Friendly, personal service. Excellent short courses on curtain-making.

Pauline K Taylor (Curtains of Distinction)   15 Gowan Avenue, Fulham, SW6. *Tel*: 071-736 6376. *Open*: by appointment. Individual service: work comes mainly from recommendation. All soft furnishings/blinds/tracks etc.

Woodward (Hampstead)
20 Heath Street, NW3 6TE. (1 min Hampstead tube.) *Tel*: 071-435 8876. *Open*: Mon to Fri, 9.00am to 5.30pm, Sat 9.30am to 5.30pm. Curtain/upholstery fabric specialist. Curtains made, tracks fitted. Reupholstery; upholstery made to order. Wallcoverings/paint. Interior design/refurbishment service.

Home Counties/ South East

Addingtons Furnishing Flair
448 Ewell Road, Tolworth, Surbiton. (A3, just off Kingston by-pass.) *Tel*: 081-399 1032/1445. *Open*: Mon to Fri, 9.30am to 5.00pm, Sat 9.00am to 5.00pm. Early closing Wed, 2.00pm. Browse peacefully amidst fabrics for curtains and covers, wallpapers and carpets. Making-up service for curtains and loose covers; reupholstery; carpet-laying.

BB Originals   Unit 5, Barwick Ford, near Ware, Herts SG11 1DA. *Tel*: (0279) 842511/842111. Sue Barker and Lynn Bendon are designer specialists. Friendly, personal service for custom-made soft furnishings: "we genuinely enjoy working with our clients."

Cascade   11 Western Parade, Great North Road, Barnet, Herts EN5 1AD. (10 mins High Barnet tube.) *Tel*: 081-449 9638. *Open*: Mon to Fri, 9.00am to 5.00pm, Sat 10.00am to 4.00pm. Pretty, welcoming shop; personal friendly service. Lots of samples fabrics/

wallcoverings. On-premises workroom for curtains, pelmets, blinds, quilts, loose covers, upholstery.

Curtain Concerns   219 Leigh Road, Leigh-on-Sea, Essex SS9 1JA. (1 mile Leigh-on-Sea BR.) *Tel*: (0702) 715520. *Open*: Mon to Sat, 9.30am to 5.30pm. Handmade curtains, reupholstery. Pelmets, blinds, bedspreads. Lampshades, tablecloths, loose covers. Fitting; interior design advice, home visits.

The Curtain Gallery   10/11 Thurlow Street, Greyfriars, Bedford MK40 1JT. *Tel*: (0234) 271104/57989. *Open*: Mon to Sat, 9.00am to 5.30pm. All soft furnishings from a friendly family business: "we know our products inside out." Wallpaper, fabrics, carpets. "Going to town can be such a drag: we've got all the samples here in Bedford."

Hammond Furnishings   1 Hadley Parade, High Street, Barnet, Herts EN5 5SX. (10 mins High Barnet tube.) *Tel*: 081-441 4424. *Open*: Mon to Sat, 9.00am to 5.00pm. Early closing Thu, 1.00pm. They reckon on being "one of best fabric selections in Hertfordshire". Friendly family business; well-trained staff. DIY advice or full making-up service, including fitting curtain rods/tracks.

E T Horne   3 Kings Court, 141 Uxbridge Road, Hampton Hill, Middx TW12 1BJ. (2 miles Hampton BR.) *Tel*: 081-979 2744. *Open*: Mon to Thu, 9.00am to 5.30pm, Fri until 5.00pm. Closed for lunch, 1.00pm to 2.00pm. Open Sat until 12.45pm. Established for 35 years, this shop is crammed with samples for fabrics to order (no stock). Curtain-making, loose covers. Blinds, bedspreads, reupholstery.

Interior Motives   151 Shirley Road, Croydon, Surrey CR0 8SS. (Easy parking.) *Tel*: 081-654 2776. *Open*: Mon to Sat, 9.30am to 5.00pm. Retail outlet for Barbara Collins Design Associates. Quality curtain-making. Home visits with samples. DIY advice, plus loan of cutting-room facilities.

Materialistic Curtain Studio, 60 Hampton Road, Twickenham TW2 5QB. (5 mins Strawberry Hill BR.) *Tel*: 081-898 2212. *Open*: Mon to Sat, 9.30am to 5.30pm. Closed Wed. Evenings by appointment. Around 100 rolls of furnishing fabrics, with masses more to order. Plus all tapes, tracks, etc. for DIY.

Rossdine Interiors 236 Balgores Lane, Romford, Essex RM2 6BS. (Park in side streets.) *Tel*: (0402) 458256. *Open*: Mon to Sat, 9.30am to 5.00pm. Double shop unit, established over 20 years, packed with fabric/wallpaper samples. Helpful, friendly service for all sorts of furnishings. Designer gifts.

Wonham Reid Retail PO Box 40, Farnham, GU10 4LZ. *Tel*: (0252) 734977. *Open*: please telephone for times. Interior design centre: Ian

Bunce advises on curtain design/colour co-ordination. All soft furnishings. In-house interior design service.

Mail Order

When ordering soft furnishings by post, do take extra care to measure accurately. Seek maker's advice, use a steel tape, write everything down, and then double-check! It's worth all the hassle to avoid (your own) expensive mistakes!

Coward Designs Church Street, Windemere, Cumbria LA23 1AQ. *Tel*: (0539) 444686. Small workshop makes up all soft furnishings. Curtains, lined or interlined, tailored to your measurements/styles.

Pelmets, accessories. Supply your fabric, or buy theirs.

Darnadelle Cobden Mill, Gower Street, Farnworth, Bolton, G. Manchester BL4 7YZ. *Tel*: (0204) 794534. Free brochures/colour samples. Cotton velvet made-to-measure curtains handfinished with mitred corners. Fully lined with polycotton, or thermal-coated polycotton for greater insulation. Co-ordinating cushion covers, tie-backs, pelmets and fabric by the yard. Plain satin also available.

Draperite Ltd Metroplex, Unit 120, Broadway, Salford, Manchester M5 2UW. *Tel*: 061-848 9922. Brochures/samples. Made-to-measure lined cotton velvet curtains at factory prices. Also silk-look Dupion, and cheaper velours. Orders take 14 days.

---

4. TRIMMINGS

Create today's ornate furnishing styles with braids, tassels, fringes and borders. An original trimming adds dash to cheap fabrics. Find trimmings at **Interior Design** shops, and **Soft furnishing** stores; also at **Department Stores**. The specialists listed below can advise on their most effective use.

London Postal Districts

Borderline 1 Munro Terrace, SW10 0DL. *Tel*: 071-823 3567. *Open*: Mon to Fri, 10.00am to 5.00pm. Closed for lunch, 1.00pm to 2.00pm. Fabric borders from 4 to 8in wide to stitch by hand/machine: instant cheer for plain curtains, cushions etc. Screen-printed/hand-blocked onto twill, linen, satinized cotton, cotton velvet. Sophisticated intricate florals/rich classic colourways based on antique textiles. Matching fabrics (striped designs with repeating borders). Silk taffeta striped ribbons.

Colefax and Fowler See **Decorating Materials 2. Co-ordinated Collections**. Fan/fringe edgings, bullions, tie-backs, tassels, button tufts, ropes etc.

Wendy Cushing 253 Fulham Road, SW6 6HY. (10 mins South Kensington tube.) *Tel*: 071-739 5909. *Open*: Mon to Fri, 9.30am to 5.30pm. On Sat, ring to check. Exclusive natural fibre trimmings ("passementerie") downstairs in Pierre Frey fabric showroom. Natural creamy wool, which can also be dyed to order. Linen (fine/silky) in stock colours, including gold/green/red. Handsome tartans, plus Gothic range.

Designers' Guild See **Decorating Materials 2. Co-ordinated Collections**. Cotton braids/fringes in famous brilliant DG colours, to go with their razzle-dazzle fabrics. Upholstery/cushions/curtains.

Distinctive Trimmings 17a Kensington Church Street, W8

4LF. (5 mins High Street Kensington tube.) *Tel*: 071-937 6174. *Open*: Mon to Fri, 9.30am to 5.30pm, Sat 9.30am to 1.00pm. This company pioneered accessible trimmings for the DIY decorator around 25 years ago. They were previously a "trade only" preserve. The company has been going strong ever since. Cords/braids/borders/fringing for curtains, upholstery, lampshades, cushions. Special colours dyed to order. Made-to-measure curtain tie-backs/staircase ropes.

John Lewis See **Department Stores**. Good selections. Braids, tassels, fringes, gimps, cords.

Osborne and Little See **Decorating Materials 2. Co-ordinated Collections**. Sumptuous trimmings range.

V V Rouleaux 201 New Kings Road, SW6 4SR. (5 mins Parsons Green tube.) *Tel*: 071-371 5929. *Open*: Mon to Sat, 9.30am to

6.00pm. Britain's first exclusive ribbon shop. "Ribbons aren't just for tying hair," says Annabel Lewis. Over 4,000 designs from all over the world, neatly displayed in elegant metal troughs. Paper/organdies/silk/grosgrain. Wire-edged ribbons for magnificent sculpted bows. Furnishing trimmings/upholstery braids. "The most extensive collection in Europe."
Also at: 23 Kings Road, SW3 4RP. (5 mins Sloane Square tube.) *Tel*: 071-730 4413. *Open*: Mon to Sat, 10.00am to 6.30pm.

---

5. BLINDS

"Mr Pritchard: I must dust the blinds and then I must raise them.
Mrs Pritchard: And before you let the sun in, mind it wipes its shoes."
Under Milk Wood, Dylan Thomas (1914–53)

Blinds are often a neater window-covering solution than curtains, and simple versions can be bought off the shelf. For made-to-measure styles, see **3. Made-to-Measure**, above, or visit shops listed under **Interior Design. Department and Chain Stores** are also good sources of supply. Listed below are blind specialists (some may also have curtains and other soft furnishings). Many will visit your home and may well be cheaper than furnishing stores, so compare prices. Some companies offer this service over a wide area, so also read entries under **Home Counties/South East**.

London Postal Districts

Austin Contracts and Design
Rookery Way, The Hyde, West Hendon NW9. *Tel*: 081-958 1602/205 0061. *Open*: by appointment. Home visits with samples. Venetian/festoon/roller. Customer's own fabric. Measure/fit. Cleaning.

City Blinds   273 Hackney Road, E2. (10 mins Bethnal Green tube.) *Tel*: 071-739 6206. *Open*: Mon to Fri, 9.30am to 5.30pm, Sat 10.00am to 5.00pm, Sun 10.00am to 2.00pm. Small family firm. Readymades/made-to-measure. Fitting/maintenance. Rollers, Venetians, micros. Wood venetians. Awnings. Vertical blinds. Festoons/Austrians.

Deans Blinds and Awnings
Haslemere Industrial Estate, Ravensbury Terrace, SW18 4SE. (3 mins Earlsfield BR.) *Tel*: 081-947 8931. *Open*: Mon to Fri, 9.00am to 5.00pm. Specialist manufacturers for nearly 100 years. Design/make/install. Scotchgarded Dralon awnings: fade-resistant. Also window/conservatory blinds.
See also **Home Counties/South East** below.

Eatons See **Floors 4. Mattings**. The original suppliers for cane stick roll-up blinds, standard sizes, or made-to-measure. Samples available. Send sae.

Flamingo Blinds and Fabrics
2 Chaseville Park Parade, Winchmore Hill N21 1PG. (15 mins Oakwood tube.) *Tel*: 081-364 1902. *Open*: Mon to Fri, 9.00am to 5.15pm, Sat 9.30am to 4.45pm. Blinds/curtains custom-made, fitted. Good range of fabrics/wallpapers. Specialists in canopies, awnings and conservatory blinds.
See also **Home Counties/South East** below.

▶ Bargains!

Ikea See **Furniture 1. General**. Possibly the cheapest roll-up cane blinds.

Jaygee Interiors   126 Hoxton Street, N1 6SH. *Tel*: 071-739 0035. *Open*: by appointment. Home visits with samples. Full range styles/fabrics. Also curtains, tracks, awnings, canopies. Repair/maintenance.

Morco (Tarpaulins and Blinds)
Riverside, Lombard Wall, SE7. *Tel*: 081-858 0156/2083/5785. *Open*: by appointment. Home visits with samples. All outside blinds/awnings. Venetians, verticals, rollers, festoons. Micro blinds/blackouts. Customer's own fabric. Cleaning.

Putney Blinds   4 Thornsett Road, SW18 4EN. (2 mins Earlsfield BR.) *Tel*: 081-874 6001/870 3127. *Open*: Mon to Fri, 7.00am to 4.30pm. Traditional specialist manufacturers of all types of awnings/exterior blinds/canopies. Also rollers/Venetians/vertical louvres/blackouts. Factory prices.

Rainbow Blinds   339 Regent's Park Road, Finchley N3 1DP. (2 mins Finchley Central tube.) *Tel*: 081-346 1679. *Open*: Mon to Fri, 9.30am to 5.15pm, Sat 10.00am to 2.00pm. All blind types: roller, Venetian, vertical, pleated, conservatory, exterior. Re-covering service for exterior blinds. Prices from budget to luxury. Experienced, friendly advice. Can make up your own fabric; handpainting service. Telephone quotes, or within 24 hours. Complementary nets, cushions, bedcovers, headboards.

Shades   2B Chingford Road, Bell Corner, Walthamstow E17 4PJ. (Blackhorse Road tube, plus bus.) *Tel*: 081-527 3991. *Open*: Mon to Sat, 9.30am to 5.00pm. All window coverings, including curtains. Roller blinds (including lace), Venetian blinds (including wood). Verticals. Festoon/Roman/Austrian. Cane blinds. Pelmets. Conservatory and outside awnings/canopies made-to-measure.

Tidmarsh and Sons   1 Laycock Street, N1 1SW. *Tel*: 071-226 2261. *Open*: by appointment. Old-established makers of wood Venetians and rollers: the place to go. "Timbershade" has 17 colour/grain effects. "Chain lath" blinds fit outside skylights/ conservatories. Sophisticated electrical controls. Measure/make/ install. Phone for leaflet/samples. Mail order.

Valley Blinds and Tiles   46 Manor Road, Ealing W13 0JA. (West Ealing BR.) Open: Mon to Fri, 9.00am to 5.30pm. Specialists in wooden slatted Venetians. Awnings/canopies. Tracks/poles. Home visits. Fitting.

C B Wright   23 Wimbledon Hill Road, SW19. (2 mins Wimbledon tube/BR.) Tel: 081-879 1313. Awnings/rollers/Venetian/ conservatory. All made to measure. Specialists in cleaning/repairing Venetian blinds.

Home Counties/ South East

A1 County Blinds   109 World's End Lane, Green Street Green, Orpington, Kent. (4 mins M25, junction 4.) Tel: (0689) 851093. Open: Mon to Sat, 9.00am to 5.30pm. Closed Thu. Huge range: 7,000 samples, all types. Friendly staff. Measure/fit. Kits for making own blinds. In-home repairs.

Amity Blinds   Solar House, Church Hill, Orpington, Kent BR6 0HE. Tel: (0689) 78418. Open: Mon to Fri, 9.00am to 5.30pm, Sat 9.00am to 5.00pm. Showroom/factory. "Everything for covering windows." All types of curtains. Fabric blinds. Venetians/verticals/wood. Conservatory/insulation/black-out blinds. Awnings/canopies. Security shutters/grilles. Electric controls. Design/install in London/South East.

Appeal Blinds   Unit 16, Barnack Trading Estate, Novers Hill,

Bedminster, Bristol, Avon BS3 5QE. Tel: (0272) 6377734. Conservatory blind specialists. Nationwide service: measure/make/install. Modern/traditional styles. From reeded wood-edged with tape, to fibreglass. Controls: from traditional winch/cord to thermostatically controlled "intelligent" motors.

Blinds Direct   12/14 Whitehorse Drive, Emerson Valley, Milton Keynes, Bucks MK4 2AS. Tel: (0908) 501880. Open: Mon to Fri, 9.00am to 5.30pm, Sat 10.00am to 5.00pm, Sun 10.00am to 1.00pm. Blinds galore. Also swags/tails, co-ordinating fabrics/papers. Measure/fit. Showroom adjacent to factory.

Deans Blinds and Awnings   427 London Road, Boxmoor, Hemel Hempstead, Herts HP3 9BD. Tel: (0442) 234334. Open: by appointment.
Also at: 2c Pipers Lane Industrial Estate, Thatcham, Newbury, Berks RG13 4NA. Tel: (0635) 61322. Open: by appointment.
See also **London Postal Districts** above.

Express Blinds   15/17 Church Street, Staines, Middx TW18 4EN. (Hatton Cross tube/Staines BR.) Tel: (0784) 463320. Open: Mon to Sat, 9.00am to 5.30pm. All types exterior/interior window blinds made to measure. Wallcoverings, fabrics by the metre, curtains made to measure. Advice, measuring. Brochure available.

Flamingo Blinds   Factory showroom, Unit 6, Garden Court Business Centre, Tewin Road, Welwyn Garden City, Herts. Tel: (0707) 331055.
See also **London Postal Districts** above.

E Hilburn (Blinds)   F5/B5 The Seedbed Centre, off Coldharbour

Road, Pinnacles, Harlow, Essex CM19 5AF. Tel: (0279) 453653. Open: by appointment. Home visits. Family blind business: one of oldest in country. Most types interior/ exterior blinds. Customer's own fabric. Wooden box traditional blinds. Laminated louvre drapes. Pinoleum conservatory blinds.

London Blind Co   205A Long Lane, Bexleyheath, Kent DA7 5AF. (Off A2.) Tel: 081-303 7964. Open: Mon to Sat, 9.30am to 5.00pm. "Smaller, cheaper, faster!" Five-day turnaround. Roller/vertical/Venetian. Conservatories/awnings. Measure/fit in London/South East.

Romford Blinds   105 Brentwood Road, Romford, Essex. Tel: (0708) 744603/741395. Specialist blind manufacturers. Awnings/security grilles. Full range of internal blinds. Home visits with samples. Customer's own fabric.

Mail Order

Do take care on measuring up. Seek the maker's advice.

Dainty Designs   68 Church Road, Tiptree, Colchester, Essex CO5 0HB. Tel: (0621) 819194. Open to personal callers: Mon to Sat, 9.00am to 5.00pm. Early closing Wed 1.00pm. Free catalogue. Broderie anglaise/chintz Austrian blind specialists. Also co-ordinating frilled curtains, lampshades, cushions, wastepaper bins, dressing-table sets. Full soft furnishings/linens service from shop.

Sunvene   7 Greenhays Lane, Manchester M15 6NQ. Tel: 061-226 4636. Colour brochure, slat and fabric samples. Venetian blinds, stove-enamelled slats, three widths. Six colours in same blind at no extra cost. Bottom rail locks for extra security. Plus rollers/verticals.

6. ARCHIVE FABRICS

Some people leap ahead with futuristic interiors. Others look back, and seek to restore their property to its former glories. For them, or those who simply yearn for rich tradition, numerous firms carefully guard a hoard of archives, reproducing treasured designs of the past as beautiful fabrics for today. See also **Decorating Materials 4. Period Papers**: many of these suppliers offer matching/co-ordinating fabrics. See also **Decorating Materials 2. Co-ordinated Collections**.

London Postal Districts

Alexander Beauchamp See **Decorating Materials 4. Period Papers**. Fabrics to match any paper in range.

Beaumont and Fletcher 134 Lots Road, SW10 0RJ. (15 mins Fulham Broadway tube.) *Tel*: 071-351 4333. *Open*: Mon to Fri, 9.30am to 5.30pm, Sat 10.00am to 3.00pm. Original designs from all over Europe: pastoral/classical themes. Curtains/upholstery. Reproduction furniture.

Bennison Fabrics 16 Holbein Place, SW1W 8NL. (5 mins Sloane Square tube.) *Tel*: 071-730 8076. *Open*: Mon to Fri, 10.30am to 5.30pm. 18th-/19th-century designs printed on cottons/linens. Order with fresh colours, or specify the degree of "fading" required (up to a quarter strength).

Rupert Cavendish Designs See **Furniture 4. 20th-Century Classics**. Splendid fabrics/papers for Empire settings. Archetypal neo-classic motifs: laurel wreaths, stars, urns and Napoleonic bees. Strong rich colours. Definitely grand; often gradiose.

Hodsoll McKenzie Cloths 52 Pimlico Road, SW1W 8LP. (3 mins Sloane Square tube.) *Tel*: 071-730 2877. *Open*: Mon to Fri, 10.00am to 6.00pm, Sat 11.00am to 4.00pm. Prints/weaves in pure cotton/wool/linen. 18th-/19th-century reproductions. Trimmings to match. Wallpapers.

Les Olivades See **1. Fabrics** above. Authentic Provençal archive fabrics.

Stothert and Miles 8 Holbein Place, SW1W 8NL. (3 mins Sloane Square tube.) *Tel*: 071-730 1957. *Open*: Mon to Fri, 9.30am to 5.30pm. Closed for lunch, 1.00pm to 2.00pm. Copies of original antique English Country House fabrics for curtains/upholstery. Mostly cotton/some linen. Colonial furniture.

7. TRACKS AND POLES

Curtain tops used to be so ugly that you had to hide them with a pelmet. Now smart tracks/poles are too good-looking to cover. (Although, in the perverse way of fashion, pelmets are also back in favour.) There are good displays of tracks/poles/pelmet kits at **Department Stores**, particularly John Lewis and Selfridges. Buy poles/tracks off the peg from **DIY Superstores**. **Interior Design** shops will explain your track options, arrange to have it fitted, and make the curtains, too. Many shops listed in **Soft Furnishings** stock tracks, and most have a fitting service, with or without curtain-making.

London Postal Districts

Artisan See **Accessories 1. General**. Exclusive, charming wrought-iron poles/finials.

Byron and Byron 4 Hanover Yard, off Noel Road, Islington N1 8BE. (10 mins Angel tube.) *Tel*: 071-704 9290. *Open*: (by appointment only) Mon to Fri, 9.00am to 6.00pm. Chunky poles with wonderful wooden finials: fleur-de-lys, arrow heads and tails, stately home designs. Plus Biedermeier collection.

Locks and Handles See **Doors 2. Door Furniture and Specialist Ironmongery**. Convenient selection of brass rods/brackets, including narrow diameters for nets. Traditional ball ends. Rod cut to size (they prefer a bit of notice, and you must pay first)!

McKinney Kidston 1 Wandon Road, SW6 2J7. (5 mins Fulham Broadway tube. Just off King's Road.) *Tel*: 071-384 1377/736 1196. *Open*: Mon to Fri, 9.30am to 5.30pm, Sat 11.00am to 4.00pm. One of London's most original shops, crammed with antique curtain poles/finials/pelmets/coronas/tiebacks. Also reproduction poles/curtain accessories. Plus slender modern steel supports from Merchants design partnership. Carved curtain tassels. Handpainted pelmets. Simple, chunky wooden/plain brass rings in large sizes. Special finishes/wood shades to order. Go there.

The Study see **Interior Design**. Modern design meets rod, rings and brackets with sensational effect. Elegant abstract patterns in gunmetal, antique and verdigris finishes. Finials, too, are ingeniously modern.

Tempus Stet See **Lighting 2. Traditional**.   Splendid curtain finials from moulded resins in various finishes. Every possible pineapple, plus laurel leaves. Also tiebacks, including lion's head and coronas. Over the top?

---

8. READY-MADES

For an instant room-lift, take home ready-made curtains and hang them up straight away. But make sure they are what you really want, because they are not necessarily cheap.

London Postal Districts

The Curtain Exchange
133 Stephendale Road, SW6 2PG. (15 mins Parsons Green tube.) *Tel:* 071-731 8316. *Open:* Mon to Sat, 10.00am to 6.00pm. Good quality, clean, secondhand curtains. Can recommend local alterers. *Also at:* 54 Abbey Gardens, NW8 9AT. *Tel:* 071-372 1044.

Interiors by Greens See **3. Made-to-Measure**, above.   Cash-and-Carry ready-mades. Prints/plains/velvets. Pencil pleating. Five drops: 54in, 72in, 90in, 108in.

K and K Fabrics See **3. Made-to-Measure** above.   Good choice of ready-mades.

Home Counties/ South East

Allied Maples See **Floors 3. Carpets**.   40 ranges: florals/plains/ abstracts/velvets. Sizes from 46 by 54in to 90 by 108in. Pencil-pleat headings. Co-ordinating valances/ tiebacks/Austrian blinds.

Separate linings available, including coloured/thermal. Some ranges are already lined. Designer ready-mades have frilled swags and arched/straight valances.

BhS See **Chain Stores**.   Always strong in ready-mades, with 3in pencil-pleat headings and three adjustable hook positions. Traditional printed satins/cotton velvets. Drops from 72in to 90in. Pelmets/tiebacks. Loose linings in white/cream/beige. Easycare polycottons, from 54in drop.

Marks and Spencer See **Chain Stores**.   Ready-made curtains in attractive but mostly middle-of-the-road designs are part of extensive co-ordinated ranges.

---

9. ANTIQUE TEXTILES

These are the most fragile of antiques, precious fragments of beautiful old fashions and rooms. Who knows who used or wore them once? As such, their power is potent.

London Postal Districts

Gallery of Antique Costume and Textiles   2 Church Street, NW8 8ED. (5 mins Marylebone tube/BR.) *Tel:* 071-723 9981. *Open:* Mon to Sat, 10.00am to 5.30pm. Friendly attitude towards browsing: walls are swathed in antique fabrics (mostly pre-1920) which can be taken on

approval. Cushions, curtains, pelmets, tapestries, hangings, quilts. Making-up service for cushions. Re-making service for curtains. Recommended.

Marilyn Garrow   6 The Broadway, White Hart Lane, Barnes SW13 0NY. (2 mins Barnes Bridge BR. Number 9 bus stops outside.) *Tel:* 081-392 1655. *Open:* Mon to Sat, 10.30am to 5.30pm. White walls and pine floors create a delightful gallery atmosphere for antique embroidered treasures: quilts/spreads/cloths/ shawls/linens. Framed embroideries/ ethnic costumes. Interior accessories.

Heraz See **Accessories 4. Cushions**. Cushions made from antique fabrics.

Paul Jones   569 King's Road, SW6. (Sloane Square tube plus bus. 12 mins, Fulham Broadway tube.) *Tel:* 071-351 2005. Famous for paisley shawls, some made into glorious cushions. Also antique curtains, tapestries, hangings, tiebacks. Some furniture upholstered with old fabrics.

Peta Smyth   42 Moreton Street, SW1V 2PB. (3 mins Pimlico tube.) *Tel:* 071-630 9898. *Open:* Mon to Fri, 10.00am to 5.30pm. Old velvets, tapestries, silks, damasks. Cushions/hangings/curtains/trimmings: "for that lived-in look."

10. COMMISSIONED FABRICS

A commissioned fabric turns a cushion, curtain or bedspread into a work of art. Designers will interpret your ideas and colour schemes, adding their talent, imagination, experience and training. Find them at your local art college, and visit end-of-course degree exhibitions, where work is often for sale and commissions are taken. You can also find textile designers in **British Crafts 1. Craft Centres and Workshops.**

London Postal Districts

Marie-Helene Bradley   321 Essex Road, N1 3PS. *Tel:* 071-354 9955. *Open:* by appointment. Studio with shop at front: visitors welcome. Screen-printed fabrics feature ethnic motifs and abstract patterns. Made-to-measure curtains, shower-curtains, blinds, bed covers. Lengths of fabric to order.

Demetra   3 Jonathan Street, SE11 5NH. *Tel:* 071-582 3600. *Open:* by appointment. Opulent Renaissance designs on shimmering velvets/cottons. Commissions.

Jay Edwards   c/o Handweavers' Studio, 29 Haroldstone Road, E17 78N. *Tel:* 081-521 2281. Working to commission, Jay produces wonderful weaves in spectacular, specially dyed natural fibres.

The Final Curtain Company   *Tel:* 081-699 3626. Susan McMullan can dye a wide range of natural fibre fabrics. Patch dying, plus painting produces rich theatrical effects.

Yumiko Inagaki   56 Ayres Street, SE1 1EU. *Tel:* 071-403 1216. *Open:* by appointment. Ikat and natural-fibre textiles dyed by Yumiko herself.

Home Counties/ South East

Sarah Collins   Home Farm, Delaport, Lamer Lane, Wheathampstead, Herts AL4 8RQ.

(M1, junction 4.) *Tel:* (0582) 833483. *Open:* by appointment. Wonderfully bright/simplistic, very domestic designs in sparkling colours reminiscent of children's paintings/ ethnic motifs. Sarah hand-prints onto cotton/silk, then uses the results to cover antique and traditional furniture—stunning. Also sells fabric by the metre: cushions, table-linen. Mail order tee shirts, scarves. Brochure available. Vividly unique.

Custom-Designed Prints
60 Wheatlands, Heston, Hounslow, Middx TW5 0SA. *Tel:* 081-570 3828. *Open:* by appointment. Irene Browning hand-prints her own designs onto natural fibres for curtains, cushions, decorative wall panels, placemats, table cloths and napkins. Bedlinens and duvets made to order.

14
TILES

Miles and miles of tiles . . . make sure you know what's on the market before making up your mind. More durable than paper and paint, your tiles will virtually never wear out. All the more reason for a well-considered choice. Happily, many tile specialists are delighted to advise. It's worth seeking them out, for ritzy tiles can add panache and flair to even low-budget kitchens and bathrooms.

"Gone are the drear, dead days of lavatorial tiling."

Tarquin Cole FRSA, tile designer.

Tile specialists have wall and floor displays to help you visualise tiles in situ. They will advise on suitability and design. Some have a fixing service; most can recommend local tilers. Others will help you to plan (and maybe even cut) tiles for DIY installation, and will sell you the necessary adhesive, grout, tools etc.

For genuine old tiles, prowl around **Markets** and **Architectural Salvage** merchants.

London Postal Districts

Acquisitions See **Heating 2. Fireplaces**. Reproduction Victorian fireplace tiles.

Caesar Ceramics 7 The Pavement, Popes Lane, Ealing W5 4NG. (10 mins South Ealing tube.) Tel: 081-840 3501. Open: Mon to Fri, 8.30am to 5.30pm, Sat 9.30am to 4.00pm. Over 2,000 Continental ceramic tiles. Fixing service. Design studio for commissions.

Castelnau Tiles 175 Church Road, Barnes SW13 9HR. (Hammersmith tube plus bus. Opposite Red Lion.) Tel: 081-741 2452/748 9042 Open: Mon to Sat, 8.30am to 5.30pm. Friendly service from efficient tile specialists. Fine handmade wall/ floor tiles: many from "undiscovered" factories overseas. Specialists in repro Victorian/Deco wall tiles. Handmade, hand-decorated wall tiles. Custom-designed panels/murals. Plan/ design/fix.

Ceramic Bathrooms 168 Old Brompton Road, SW5 0BA. (3 mins Gloucester Road tube.) Tel: 071-373 6890. Open: Mon to Sat, 9.00am to 5.30pm. (Or ring for appointment.)

Extensive/varied tile selections. Lots of samples on display; design/fixing service. Bathroom displays.

The Criterion Tile Shop
196 Wandsworth Bridge Road, SW6 2UF. (15 mins Parsons Green tube. Own parking.) Tel: 071-736 9610/731 3370. Open: Mon to Fri, 9.30am to 5.30pm, Sat 9.30am to 5.00pm. Attractive showroom, recently refurbished, with airy conservatory extension for daylight viewing. Specialists in British tiles/decorative techniques. Many displays of exclusive/bespoke designs. Owner Tom Sedgwick is no tile tyro: witness his impressive file of past commissions . . . "a lot of the work here is one-offs." Small, flexible British ceramicists can speedily alter designs/colours. Dados/borders/painted panels. Customers benefit from endless, enthusiastic service.

Danielle See **Decorating Materials 2. Co-ordinated Collections**. Tiles to match own ranges wallcoverings/ fabrics/borders/bedlinens: ideal for the en suite bathroom.

Elon Tiles 66 Fulham Road, SW3 6HH. (5 mins South Kensington tube.) Tel: 071-584 8966. Open: Mon to Sat, 9.30am to 5.30pm. Stunning, hand-decorated floor/wall tiles from Mexico/France. Naïve motifs in rich colours that never date. Delicate flower tiles and murals from Provence. Hand-stencilled tiles from Normandy. Catalogue available. Recommended.

Melissa Ferguson Ceramics
116 Chatham Road, SW11 6HH. (Clapham South tube.) Tel: 071-223 9097. Open: Mon to Fri, 9.30am to 5.30pm, Sat 11.00am to 5.00pm. Light, airy showroom for unusual ceramic imports. Also terracotta. Hand-painting service takes about three weeks.

Fired Earth 102 Portland Road,

W11 4LX. (5 mins Holland Park tube.) Tel: 071-221 4825. Open: Mon to Sat, 9.30am to 5.30pm (all branches). Nicholas Kneale is passionate about tiles and travels constantly to find them: in less than 10 years, he has built Fired Earth into a successful national chain. Emphasis is on handmade wall/floor tiles from all over the world. Over 45 lines/1,000 individual tiles. Over 60 per cent floorings: very strong in terracottas . . . they started with these in 1984. Wall tiles: dazzling rainbow of 100 glazed colours on handmade squares from Provence. Delft (superb blue-and-whites; separate fascinating catalogue). New vivid Islamics. Continuous innovations from British craft potters. Design/technical help. Superb catalogue. Essential viewing. Also at: 37/41 Battersea High Street, SW11 3JF. Tel: 071-924 2272. 2,000 sq ft of tiles, including room settings. See also **Home Counties/South East** below.

Langley London The Tile Centre, 161/167 Borough High Street, SE1 1HU. (5 mins London Bridge tube/ BR.) Tel: 071-407 4444. Open: Mon to Fri, 9.00am to 5.15pm. Importers of exclusive decorative tiles for kitchens/bathrooms. Design service for mosaics.

Laura Ashley See **Decorating Materials 2. Co-ordinated Collections**. Good choice of tiles integrated with wallcovering/ fabric/border collections.

The Merchant Tiler 187 New King's Road, SW6 4SW. (5 mins Parsons Green tube.) Tel: 071-736 5987. Open: Tue to Sat, 9.30am to 5.30pm. Cheaper offshoot of Fired Earth (see above). Dark polished wood, shiny brass and antique glass create a rich traditional atmosphere. Mainly machine-made floor/wall tiles from workshops around the world: India, China, Brazil, Mexico, Thailand, Portugal . . . even Norway.

Play around with lay-out ideas on large tabletops. Helpful staff. Can recommend tilers.
See also **Home Counties/South East** below.

▶ Bargains!

The Reject Tile Shop
178 Wandsworth Bridge Road, SW6 2UQ. (10 mins Fulham Broadway tube. Park behind shop.) *Tel*: 071-731 6098. *Open*: Mon to Fri, 9.30am to 5.30pm, Sat 9.30am to 5.00pm. Ceramic tile seconds (usually only sold from factory shops). Minute faults. Up to one-third original prices. Plains/patterns/borders/dados. Victorian reproductions. Floor quarries. Offshot of The Criterion Tile Shop (see above) down the road.

Roman Tiles   London House, 380 Lea Bridge Road, E10 7HU. (Walthamstow tube, plus bus.) *Tel*: 081-556 0904. *Open*: Mon to Sat, 8.30am to 6.00pm. Late night Wed, 8.30pm. Vast stocks at good prices.

Star Ceramics   75 Lower Sloane Street, SW1W 8DA. (3 mins Sloane Square tube.) *Tel*: 071-259 9300. *Open*: Mon to Fri, 9.30am to 6.00pm, Sat 10.00am to 1.00pm. New tile showcase is like an art gallery with curved glass doors and tiled panels on the walls. Wonderfully original floor designs: nine panels in situ, regularly changed. Slide-out panels of well over 1,000 wall tiles. Devon Delft. Naif pictorials. Encaustic tiles for decorative floor insets.

▶ Bargains!

The Tile Bin   20 Battersea Square, SW11 3JF. *Tel*: 071-924 6026. New venture of Fired Earth (see above), with seconds/ends of lines of their exclusive ranges. Everything for the DIY tiler.

Tile City   Ace Corner, North Circular Road, NW10 7UD (5 mins Hanger Lane tube. Own parking.)

Tel: 081-965 8062. *Open*: Mon to Fri, 9.00am to 6.00pm, Sun 10.00am to 4.00pm. Conveniently and prominently situated; spacious premises. Good selections floor/wall tiles at budget prices, especially Spanish (up to 16 in sq). Also quarries/terracotta/marble. Bathroom/kitchen displays.

Tile Collection of West Hampstead
60 Fortune Green Road, NW6 1DT. (10 mins West Hampstead tube.) *Tel*: 071-431 0900. *Open*: Mon to Sat, 9.30am to 5.00pm. Extensive ranges/all types. Traditional/modern: from Victorian reproductions to modern handmade reliefs. Continental/Moorish designs for wall/floor. Marble/terracotta. Handpainted murals to order.

Tile With Style   270 Kentish Town Road, NW5 2AA. (Adjacent Kentish Town tube.) *Tel*: 071-485 9455/267 6835. *Open*: Mon to Sat, 9.30am to 5.30pm. Wide range imported wall/border tiles in good choice colours/designs. Or your designs/colours to order. "Art Tiles" (Victorian reproductions in printed and plain majolica colours). Importers of handmade Chinese tiles/Spanish terracotta. Technical information/samples service.

Tiles and Flooring   175 Muswell Hill Broadway, N10 3RS. (Highgate tube, plus bus.) *Tel*: 081-883 8879. *Open*: Mon to Sat, 9.30am to 5.00pm. Extensive selections ceramic tiles. Fixing service from their own tiler.

West London Tiles   15 Portobello Road, W11 3DA. (5 mins Notting Hill Gate tube.) *Tel*: 071-221 0033/7280. *Open*: Mon to Fri, 8.30am to 5.00pm, Sat 9.00am to 4.00pm. Elaine Bailey and brother Richard give this business a friendly family enthusiasm. Tip-top designs, keen prices. Display over 4,000 tiles, mostly available 24 hours. Courteous, knowledgeable service. Help plan/estimate. Cutters for hire. Reliable port in any storm.
Also at: 119 Northfield Avenue, W13 9QR. (5 mins Northfields tube.) *Tel*: 081-567 1640/2930. *Open*: Mon to

Fri, 8.30am to 5.00pm, Sat 9.00am to 4.00pm.

World's End Tiles   British Rail Yard, Silverthorne Road, Battersea SW8 3HE. (5 mins Queenstown Road BR.) *Tel*: 071-720 8358. *Open*: Mon to Fri, 9.00am to 5.00pm. Closed for lunch, 1.00pm to 2.00pm. Open Sat, 9.30am to 1.00pm. Zingy, up-to-date exclusive own designs for wall/floor ceramic tiles; well displayed on large panels and in settings. Definitely inspiring. One of the largest selections in London, they claim. Speedy deliveries: all tiles made in London. Special colours to order. Traditional patterns/marbles are also a feature. Worth a special journey.
Also at: 9 Langton Street, World's End, Chelsea SW10 0JL. *Tel*: 071-351 0279.

▶ Bargains!

WW Just Tiles   46/48 Willesden Lane, Kilburn NW6 7ST. (5 mins Kilburn tube.) *Tel*: 071-328 6161. *Also at*: 134 King Street, Hammersmith W6 9JJ. (5 mins Hammersmith tube.) *Tel*: 081-741 5396.
See also **Home Counties/South East** below.

Home Counties/ South East

DR Betts (Ceramics)   The Barn, Church Road, Noak Hill, Romford, Essex. *Tel*: (04023) 81349/(0708) 747106. (Easy parking.) *Open*: Mon to Sat, 8.00am to 5.00pm. Or ring for appointment. Helpful and friendly family business. Selections British/continental wall/floor tiles, including borders/marble effects. Adhesives, grout, trim. Supply only, or supply/fix.

Color 1 Ceramics   412 Richmond Road, Twickenham, Middx. (5 mins Richmond tube.) *Tel*: 081-891 0691. *Open*: Mon to Sat, 9.30am to 5.30pm. Over 2,000 floor/wall tiles on display. Glazed ceramics, handmade floors. Terracotta, slate, stoneware. Marble wall/floor tiles. Victorian/Edwardian reproductions. Large range plaster ceiling centres/cornices. Fixing services.

▶ Bargains!

Decor Tiles   1/3 Euston Avenue, Watford, Herts WD1 8LZ. (15 mins Watford tube.) *Tel:* (0923) 248531. *Open:* Mon to Sat, 9.00am to 5.30pm. Large selections at discount prices. Also carpet/vinyl/cork tiles. Importers of European ceramic tiles.

Fired Earth   Twyford Mill, Oxford Road, Adderbury, Oxon OX17 3HP. *Tel:* (0295) 812088.
Also at: 69 Calverley Road, Tunbridge Wells, Kent TN1 2UY. *Tel:* (0892) 540220. *Open:* Tue to Sat, 9.30am to 5.30pm.
See also **London Postal Districts** above.

Interior Ceramics   3 Cork Street, Twickenham, Middx TW1 3JZ. (5 mins Twickenham BR.) *Tel:* 081-892 9002. *Open:* Mon to Fri, 9.30am to 5.30pm, Sat 10.00am to 5.00pm. Selections ceramics wall/floor tiles. Marble, terracotta, handpainting. Etruscan marble cobbles.

The Merchant Tiler   60 Holywell Hill, St Albans, Herts AL1 1BX. (5 mins town centre.) *Tel:* (0727) 55407. *Open:* Tue to Sat, 9.30am to 5.30pm (all branches).
Also at: 57 Moulsham Street, Chelmsford, Essex CM2 0JA. (10 mins town centre.) *Tel:* (0245) 494684.
And at: 2 Chapel Street, Guildford, Surrey GU1 3UH. (2 mins town centre.) *Tel:* (0483) 300052.
And at: 15 Burgate, Canterbury, Kent KT1 2HG. (2 mins town centre.) *Tel:* (0227) 464628.
See also **London Postal Districts** above.

Tile and Wall Finds   46 Enborne Road, Newbury, Berks. (M4 from London. 10 mins town centre.) *Tel:* (0635) 49779. *Open:* Mon to Sat, 9.00am to 5.30pm. Over 3,000 tiles, from budget to exotic. Samples loan service. Professional tilers recommended. Grouts/adhesives/tools.

Tilebase   141 Stanley Road, Teddington, Middx TW11 8UF. (Main road, south of Teddington High Street.) *Tel:* 081-943 0251. *Open:* Mon to Fri, 9.00am to 5.30pm. Early closing Wed 12.30pm. Open Sat 9.00am to 5.00pm. Looks small but

has extensive stocks of ceramic wall/floor tiles. Specialist selections and advice. Tile planning/cutting/fixing. Bathroom displays.

Tileplace   Bagshot Road, Bracknell, Berks RG12 3SE. (Bracknell bypass.) *Tel:* (0344) 420585. *Open:* Mon to Fri, 9.00am to 5.30pm, Sat 9.00am to 5.00pm, Sun 10.00am to 4.00pm. Largest tile store in the south, they say. Vast selections, unusual designs. Tile planning/cutting/fixing.

▶ Bargains!

WW Just Tiles   142/144 Kenton Road, Harrow, Middx HA3 8BL. (Kenton/Northwick Park tubes.) *Tel:* 081-907 3020/3088. *Open:* Mon to Sat, 8.00am to 5.30pm (all branches). Wholesale prices for trade/public. All ceramics, including mosaics/quarries/frost-proof. Own kiln for special colours/patterns to order. Paint mixing service.
Also at: 714/722 London Road, Hounslow, Middx. (Hounslow East tube.) *Tel:* 081-577 5592.
See also **London Postal Districts** above.

---

2. TERRACOTTA AND QUARRIES

The fashion for solid wooden kitchens has revived interest in imported terracottas—rich red, brown, and buff natural clays. Many of these tiles are suitable for conservatories and patios, but always check for frost resistance if you intend them for outdoor use. Some tiles need sealing when they are laid: check with the supplier. Specialist laying is usually advisable. Home-grown quarries are tougher and easier to lay: **DIY Superstores** have selections.

London Postal Districts

Castelnau Tiles See **1. Specialists** above.   Specialists in terracotta, including frost-resistant qualities.

Corres Mexican Tiles   15 Ewer Street, SE1 0NR. (5 mins Waterloo/Blackfriars tube.) *Tel:* 071-261 0941. *Open:* Mon to Fri, 9.00am to 5.30pm. Terracotta floor/wall tile specialists: huge selections. Variety shapes/sizes. Over 100 different coloured/decorated glazed tiles, cut/painted by hand. Brochure available.

Fired Earth See **1. Specialists** above.   This company has built its reputation on terracottas, from the cheapest extruded types to antique reclaimed tiles from France. Plus glazed terracottas, quarry and encaustic (inlaid) tiles.

▶ Bargains!

Leslux See **Decorating Materials 1. Paints and Papers.**   Discounted prices for quarries.

The Reject Tile Shop See **1. Specialists** above.   Reasonably priced terracottas/quarries (first quality).

Star Ceramics See **1. Specialists** above.   Wonderful floor inset, with original designs featuring several types of terracotta.

Terra Firma Tiles   70 Chalk Farm Road, NW1 4AN. (3 mins Chalk Farm tube.) *Tel:* 071-485 7227. *Open:* Mon to Fri, 9.00am to 6.00pm, Sat 11.00am to 5.00pm, or by appointment. Specialists in natural materials. Handmade/glazed terracottas. Slate from India/China/Africa. Encaustic (inlaid) patterned

tiles. Mosaic borders. Selected wall tiles. Free local deliveries. Recommended tilers.

Home Counties/ South East

▶ Bargains!

Decor Tiles See **1. Specialists** above.   Large stocks quarries,

discounted prices. Brown/red/sand/non-slip from stock.

Mail Order

The York Handmade Brick Co. Forest Lane, Alne, N. Yorks YO6 2LU. *Tel:* (0347) 38881. Colour brochure available. Traditional terracotta floor tiles of Vale of York clay. Natural orange/pink: touches of whites, yellows, browns, reds. Direct deliveries nationwide.

---

3. MARBLE, SLATE AND STONE

The charm of natural materials (these are a little grander than the terracottas in the previous section) is infinite: each tile is unique, with subtle variations in surface colouring and texture. In most cases professional fixing is advisable. See also **Floors 5. Marble, Slate and Stone**.

London Postal Districts

Castelnau Tiles See **1. Specialists** above.   Specialists in limestone, plus natural stone slabs/slates/marbles.

Marble and Granite Trading See **Kitchens 6. Worktops**.   Over 140 types of granite/marble wall/floor tiles in stock, from Greece, Italy,

Portugal, Spain. Colours span the delicate white Calacatta Oro to the rich black drama of Nero Marquina.

Paris Ceramics Shop   583 Kings Road, SW6 2EH. (5 mins Fulham Broadway tube.) *Tel:* 071-228 5785. *Open:* Mon to Fri, 9.30am to 5.30pm, Sat 10.00am to 4.00pm, or by appointment. Very top end of the trade for exclusivity/price/design. Steve Charles works tirelessly to give floor tiles a high design profile. For floors: terracottas, limestones, slate, mosaics (can be antiqued for extra effect). Special designs combine materials. Antique French tiles from grand houses. For walls: handpainted panels/murals. Any design can be produced to commission by The Annexe, their new "one-off" department. Restoration/matching service, plus patented protective sealers.

Quality Marble   Unit 1, Fountayne House, Fountayne Road, Tottenham N15 4QL. (5 mins Seven Sisters tube.) *Tel:* 081-808 1110. *Open:* Mon to Fri, 8.00am to 5.30pm, Sat 8.30am to 4.00pm. Polished marble tiles for walls and floors. Also granite/terrazzo. Fixing service.

Star Ceramics See **1. Specialists** above.   Good selections of stone and marble tiles. Weathered and aged marbles/stones. Stunning floor designs of mixed materials created to suit specific areas. See samples in showroom.

World's End Tiles See **1. Specialists** above.   Good selections marble wall/floor tiles in spacious settings.

Zarka Marble See **Kitchens 6. Worktops**.   Marble/granite specialists. Limestone tiles/riven slate. Supply/install.

---

4. COMMISSIONED

Artists abound to create individual tiles or panels: contact them through **1. Specialists** above, or use the entries in this section to discuss commissions with them direct.

London Postal Districts

Art on Tiles   Unit 230, Wandsworth

Workshops, 86/96 Garratt Lane, SW18 4DJ. *Tel:* 081-871 3965. *Open:* by appointment. Handpainted, hand-glazed tiles in traditional/modern styles. Originals/copies/reproductions. From single tiles to repeat patterns/complicated borders. Panels, murals.

Eleanor Greeves 12 Newton Grove, Bedford Park W4 1LB. (5 mins Turnham Green tube.) *Tel*: 081-994 6523. *Open*: strictly by appointment. Wall tiles in delightful graceful repeating foliage patterns. Handprinted/fired in small studio at bottom of inspirational garden; 10 standard colours, or any colour to order; around 30 exclusive designs. Colour brochure available.

Richard Henriques 25 Sumner Workshops, 80 Sumner Road, SE15 6LA. *Tel*: 071-263 5123. *Open*: by appointment. Hand-decorated ceramic wall tiles, exclusively designed in colourful underglazes or striking enamels and precious metal lustres. Murals, furniture, mirror surrounds, architectural inserts, kitchens, bathrooms. Commissions.

Reptile 494 Archway Road, Highgate N6 4NA. *Tel*: 081-341 4908. *Open*: by appointment. Carlo Briscoe/Eddie Dunn, brilliant ceramic artists, have an original vibrant style. Majolica/tin glazes for handmade, handpainted ceramics/tiles produce a singing clarity of colour. Ships, flowers, animals, birds, fish. Panels/reliefs. Decorative insets for terracotta floors. A delicious discovery.

Rye Tiles 12 Connaught Street, W2 2AS. (5 mins Marble Arch tube.) *Tel*: 071-723 7278. *Open*: Mon to Fri, 9.30am to 5.00pm. London showroom for celebrated Sussex tile specialists. Tarquin Cole (ex-RCA) put art into British tiles in early sixties. Exciting screen prints, geometrics/abstracts. Infinitely charming, handpainted images of English birds, flowers, boats, landscapes. You'll never tire of these miniature works of art.
See also **Home Counties/South East** below.

Joanna Veevers 8a Peacock Yard, Iliffe Street, SE17 3LH. (3 mins Kennington tube.) *Tel*: 071-701 3302. *Open*: by appointment. Designer/maker with studio workshop. Tiles, porcelain friezes, commemorative ceramic wall plaques and panels.

Home Counties/South East

Sally Anderson Tiles Parndon Mill, Harlow, Essex CM20 2HP. *Tel*: (0279) 420982. *Open*: by appointment. Sally popularised tile murals. Her clever tile designs build up into a choice of panels. See samples at specialist tile shops: phone for stockists. Or visit showroom. Wide choice of frieze/mural options (traditional, florals, classical, naturalistic, Islamic etc). Over 50 colours. Famous for translucent, glowing "real" glazes from oxides of copper, cobalt, iron, and manganese. Individual colour/design problems discussed.

Kenneth Clark Ceramics Southover Grange, Southover Road, Lewes, E. Sussx BN7 1TP. (Lewes BR. Map available. Limited parking.) *Tel*: (0273) 47676. *Open*: Mon to Fri, 10.00am to 6.00pm, Sat by appointment. Ann and Kenneth Clark have pioneered tile "specials" over 40 years. 16th-century studio, in historic county town. Decorated tiles and/or borders team with plains to cut costs. Also repeat designs/splendid decorative panels. Commissions. Blue-and-white numbers (square or round)/letters for signs. Free catalogue available.

Rye Tiles The Old Brewery, Wishward, Rye, E. Sussx TN31 7DH. *Tel*: (0797) 223038. *Open*: Mon to Fri, 9.00am to 5.00pm, Sat 10.30am to 4.30pm. Closed for lunch Sat, 1.00pm to 2.15pm). Seconds (as and when) from handpainted ranges. See also **London Postal Districts** above.

Jennifer Scott Coach Hill House, Coach Hill Lane, Burley Street, Ringwood, Hants BH24 4HN. *Tel*: (04253) 3361. *Open*: by appointment. Authentic, Oriental techniques/brushes for delicate trailing designs on pastel grounds. Individual tiles/murals.

15

Upholstery

Specialist firms offering a welcome return to traditional methods abound. Check delivery dates: these can range from immediate to 14 weeks. British anti-fire regulations for new upholstery are now the most stringent in the world. Don't be seduced by the lure of a pretty shape, or buy upholstery for looks alone. And remember—anything will feel comfortable when you are tired and fed up with shopping around.

1. CHAIRS, SOFAS AND SUITES

"I do most of my work sitting down; that's where I shine."

Robert Charles Benchley, US humorist/drama critic (1889–1945)

"Wedlock—the deep, deep peace of the double bed after the hurly-burly of the chaise longue."

Mrs Patrick Campbell, actress friend of George Bernard Shaw.

Shop also for upholstery at large **Interior Design** firms, and at many of the larger stores listed under **Furniture 1. General** and **Department Stores**.

London Postal Districts

Delcor Furniture   65 Tottenham Court Road, W1P 8PA. (2 mins Goodge Street tube.) *Tel:* 071-580 7900. *Open:* 9.30am to 6.00pm. Late night Thu, 7.30pm. Sofas/chairs; classic designs to order from the firm's workshops (allow six to eight weeks). Assembly on site available for deliveries where access is difficult. Standard sizes can be altered to meet individual needs. Huge choice of fabrics/accessories/ prints. Colour brochure/fabric swatches available, *tel:* 091-237 1303.
Also at: 279 King's Road, Chelsea, SW3 5EW. (10 mins Sloane Square tube.) *Tel:* 071-352 5551. *Open:* Mon to Sat, 9.30am to 6.00pm. Late night Wed, 7.00pm.
See also **Home Counties/South East** below.

Peter Dudgeon   Brompton Place, Knightsbridge, SW3 1QE. (2 mins Knightsbridge tube.) *Tel:* 071-589 0322. *Open:* Mon to Sat, 9.30am to 5.30pm. Trading since 1947. Top-quality handmade upholstery, over 30 styles. No foam: hand-tied springs/horsehair/cane seat edges. Beech frames, dowelled joints. Wonderful classic/traditional

designs, e.g. wing/leather club chairs. Plus simple modern shapes. Colour catalogue available.

▶ Bargains!

Foamplan   164 Holloway Road, N7 8DD. (2 mins Holloway Road tube.) *Tel:* 071-609 8569/2700. *Open:* Mon to Sat, 9.30am to 5.30pm. Invaluable service for cut to size, fire-retardant combustion-modified foam; covered in your fabric or theirs.

Highly Sprung   549 Battersea Park Road, SW11 3BL. (10 mins Clapham Junction BR.) *Tel:* 071-924 1124. *Open:* Mon to Fri, 10.00am to 7.00pm, Sat 10.00am to 6.00pm. Keenly priced classic upholstery designs, including Knole settee, chesterfield. Supply your own fabric or choose from a wide selection in the shop. Orders take two to three weeks. Bedheads, cushions, accessories. Loose covers, reupholstery.

Kingcome Sofas   305 Fulham Road, SW10 9EP. (10 mins Fulham Broadway/Earls Court tubes.) *Tel:* 071-351 3998. *Open:* Mon to Fri, 9.30am to 5.30pm, Sat 10.00am to 4.00pm. Twenty years ago, Brian and Lesley Kingcome pioneered made-to-measure upholstery. Over 40 designs made in firm's own workshops. Settees, sofabeds, chaises longues, corner units, chairs. Choose from a host of practical/ stylish variations: self-piping, kick- or box-pleats, fabric-covered plinths or legs, castors, ball feet, gathered skirts or fringes. Cushions: Dacron-wrapped fire-retardant foam or feathers and down. On-site assembly where access is tricky.

Multiyork   25/28 Thurloe Place, SW7 2HQ. (5 mins South Kensington tube.) *Tel:* 071-589 2303. *Open:* Mon to Sat, 9.30am to 5.30pm, Sun 10.00am to 5.00pm. Traditionally

made upholstery with a 10-year guarantee; classic designs; natural fillings. Removable covers. Co-ordinated soft furnishings/ accessories.
Also at: 309 Green Lanes, Palmers Green N13. *Tel:* 081-886 7514.
And at: 13 Harben Parade, Finchley Road, Swiss Cottage NW3 6JP. *Tel:* 071-722 7810.
See also **Home Counties/South East** below.

Norfolk Furniture   715 Fulham Road, SW6 5UL. (5 mins Parsons Green tube.) *Tel:* 071-371 9147. *Open:* Mon to Fri, 9.30am to 6.00pm, Sat 10.00am to 5.30pm. Upholstery made to order in firm's workshops. Commissions for any fabric/style.

George Smith   587 King's Road, SW6 2EH. (10 mins Fulham Broadway tube.) *Tel:* 071-384 1004. *Open:* Mon to Sat, 9.30am to 6.00pm. Stunning handmade British furniture from own workshops covered in antique Turkish kelims: a fashion they pioneered. Pricey but high quality.

Sofa So Good   2/10 Jerdan Place, Fulham SW6 1BH. (2 mins Fulham Broadway tube.) *Tel:* 071-385 4719. *Open:* Mon to Fri, 10.00am to 6.00pm, Sat 9.30am to 6.00pm, Sun 12.00 noon to 5.00pm (all branches). Largest independent supplier of sofas/sofabeds in the UK, they say. 220 stock designs, many available immediately; or made-to-measure in four weeks. 15,000 fabrics. Stain-and soil-proof treatments. Curtains/cushions to order. Exclusive cane furniture. Brochure available. Mail order.
Also at: 32/38 Battersea Rise, South Circular, SW11 1EE. (3 mins Clapham Junction BR.) *Tel:* 071-228 4546.
And at: 147 Chiswick High Road, Chiswick W4 4DT. (5 mins Turnham Green tube.) *Tel:* 081-994 9399. Late night Thu, 7.30pm.

Sofa Workshop Ealing Broadway Centre, 8 High Street, W5 5DB. (5 mins Ealing Broadway tube/BR.) *Tel:* 081-579 0693. *Open:* Mon to Sat, 9.30am to 6.00pm (all branches). Sun (East Sheen and Notting Hill only): 12.00 noon to 5.00pm. Large choice sofas/convertibles, wide fabric range. Furniture can be covered in customers' own choice of fabric. Exclusive fire-retardant treatment for any fabric.
Also at: 419/423 Upper Richmond Road West, East Sheen SW14 7PJ. *Tel:* 081-876 8254.
And at: 130 Notting Hill Gate, W11 3QC. (5 mins Notting Hill Gate tube.) *Tel:* 071-229 4988.
And at: 84 Tottenham Court Road, W1P 9HD. *Tel:* 071-580 6839.
See also **Home Counties/South East** below.

The Sofabed Factory 258/260 Lavender Hill, SW11 1LJ. (2 mins Clapham Junction BR.) *Tel:* 071-228 4588. *Open:* Mon to Sat, 10.00am to 6.00pm (all branches). Late night Thu 7.30pm. Open Sun, 11.00am to 5.00pm.
Also at: 461/465 North End Road, Fulham SW6 1NX. (5 mins Fulham Broadway tube.) *Tel:* 071-381 6425.
And at: 334/340 Caledonian Road, N1 1BB. (1 min Barnsbury/Caledonian Road BR.) *Tel:* 071-607 3096.
And at: Unit 2/6, Tariff Road (off Northumberland Park Road), N17 0DY. (5 mins White Hart Lane BR.) *Tel:* 081-885 4949. *Open* (factory and showroom): Mon to Sat, 9.00am to 5.30pm.
See also **Home Counties/South East** below.

Sofas and Sofabeds
219 Tottenham Court Road, W1P 9AF. (Opposite Goodge Street tube.) *Tel:* 071-580 4287. *Open:* Mon to Sat, 10.00am to 6.30pm. Late night Thu, 7.00pm. Sun viewing 12.00 noon to 5.00pm. Over 60 models sofas/sofabeds/chairs. Available immediately or made to measure. Top name fabrics. Reasonable prices.
Also at: 3 Fulham Broadway, SW6 1AA. (Opposite tube.) *Tel:* 071-381

3708. *Open:* Mon to Sat, 10.00am to 5.30pm. Sun viewing 12.00 noon to 5.00pm.
And at: 296/298 Upper Richmond Road, Putney SW15 6TH. (10 mins East Putney tube.) *Tel:* 081-789 8108. *Open:* Mon to Sat, 10.00am to 6.30pm. Late night Mon 7.00pm. Sun viewing 12.00 noon to 5.00pm.
And at: 3b Standard Industrial Estate, Henley Road, Docklands E16 2JJ. (Off Pier Road.) *Tel:* 071-511 1431. *Open:* Mon to Fri, 9.00am to 5.30pm, Sat 9.00am to 1.00pm.
See also **Home Counties/South East** below.

Tulleys of Chelsea 289/297 Fulham Road, SW10 9PZ. (20 mins South Kensington tube.) *Tel:* 071-352 1078. *Open:* Mon to Sat, 9.00am to 5.30pm. Over 20 classic designs of sofas/chairs made to traditional standards in the firm's workshops. Trading for over 100 years. Over 8,000 covering fabrics. "In the white" (unbleached calico) for your own loose covers. Upholstery/calico available for some models immediately. Promotional fabrics (50% discount) take six to eight weeks. Other fabrics and tight upholstery require 10 to 12 weeks, loose covers 12 to 14 weeks.
See also **Home Counties/South East** below.

Wesley-Barrell 60 Berners Street, W1P 3AE. (3 mins Oxford Circus tube.) *Tel:* 071-580 6979. *Open:* Mon to Sat, 9.30am to 6.00pm. Oxfordshire family business, trading for close on 100 years. Custom-made handcrafted upholstered/occasional furniture. Interior design/colour schemes. Co-ordinating cushions, curtains and upholstery. Handpainting for furniture and accessories. Free colour catalogue available, *tel:* (0608) 810481.
Also at: 409 Upper Richmond Road West, East Sheen SW14 4NX. (10 mins Richmond tube/BR.) *Tel:* 081-878 4001. *Open:* Mon to Sat, 9.00am to 5.30pm.
See also **Home Counties/South East** below.

Home Counties/ South East

Core Upholstery 15 Brookhill Close, East Barnet, Herts EN4 8SH. (High Barnet/Cockfosters tubes, plus bus.) *Tel:* 081-440 2708. *Open:* by appointment. Sofas/armchairs. To order: upholstery in white calico for loose covers. They supply patterns/instructions. Brochure available.

Delcor Furniture 50 High Street, Tunbridge Wells, Kent TN1 1XF. *Tel:* (0892) 47233. *Open:* Mon to Sat, 9.30am to 5.30pm (both branches).
Also at: 10/12 Market Street, Guildford, Surrey GU1 4LB. *Tel:* (0483) 570171.
See also **London Postal Districts** above.

Multiyork 16 St Christopher Place, St Albans, Herts AL3 5DG. *Tel:* (0727) 38588.
Also at: Unit 2, Safeway Complex, Grove Road, Sutton, Surrey. *Tel:* 081-643 3242.
And at: 66/68 Church Street, Weybridge, Surrey. *Tel:* (0932) 859390.
And at: Wickes Development, Weldale Street, Reading, Berks. *Tel:* (0734) 583052.
And at: 1 Villa Road, Stanway, Colchester, Essex CO3 5RH. *Tel:* (0206) 42007.
And at: High Street, Bromley, Kent. *Tel:* 081-464 2253.
And at: 38/40 Eden Street, Kingston-upon-Thames, Surrey KT1 1EP. *Tel:* 081-546 5040.
See also **Home Counties/South East** below.

The Old Bakery Furnishing Company Punnetts Town, near Heathfield, E. Sussex TN21 9DS. (About 2 miles from Heathfield on B2096.) *Tel:* (0435) 830608. *Open:* Mon to Fri, 9.00am to 5.00pm, Sat 9.00am to 1.00pm. Converted Victorian showrooms. Antique chairs/sofas restored or ready for restoration by traditional methods. Handbuilt English sofas/adaptable sizes/styles. Friendly professional design advice. Fabrics, wallpapers.

Made-to-measure soft furnishings. Also a large collection of fine decorative interior/exterior lighting.

Omega Furniture   Delamare Road, Cheshunt, Herts EN8 9TF. *Tel:* (0992) 26686. *Open:* Mon to Sat, 10.00am to 5.30pm (both branches). Made-to-measure sofas/sofabeds/armchairs/corner units at readymade prices. Expert advice, thousands of fabrics. *Tel* (24 hrs): (0992) 37820 for colour brochure.
Also at: 21 High Street, Old Town, Stevenage, Herts. *Tel:* (0438) 722412.

R and C Design Company
The Garden House, Brocket Park, Welwyn, Herts AL8 7XH. *Tel:* (0707) 334181. *Open:* by appointment. Friendly, involved service from husband-and-wife team. Speciality is kelim-covered furniture at reasonable prices, handmade in own workshops. Club sofas, chairs, pouffes, footstools, ottomans. Kelim re-covering service.

Sofa Workshop   The Great Hall, Mount Pleasant Road, Tunbridge Wells, Kent TN1 1RB. (Opposite Tunbridge Wells BR. Park at rear.) *Tel:* (0892) 34381. *Open:* Mon to Sat, 9.00am to 5.30pm. Open bank holidays.
See also **London Postal Districts** above.

The Sofabed Factory
159 Clarence Street, Kingston-upon-Thames, Surrey KT1 1TQ. (1 min Kingston BR.) *Tel:* 081-549 8383. *Open:* Mon to Sat, 10.00am to 6.00pm. Late night Thu, 7.30pm. Sun viewing 11.00am to 5.00pm. Sofas, armchairs, sofabeds, over two floors, with section for leather. Attractive settings with soft furnishings/accessories. Reasonable prices. Stock lines immediate delivery. Orders take from two

weeks. Brochures available. Mail order.
See also **London Postal Districts** above.

Sofas and Sofabeds   13/14 Norfolk House, Wellesley Road, Croydon, Surrey CR0 1LH. (5 mins East Croydon BR.) *Tel:* 081-667 1101. *Open:* Mon to Sat, 10.00am to 5.30pm.
And at: 29 Oxford Road, Reading, Berks RG1 7QG. (Opposite Waring and Gillow.) *Tel:* (0734) 566524.
And at: 58 Western Road, Hove, E. Sussx BN3 1JD. *Tel:* (0273) 736003. *Open:* Mon to Sat, 10.00am to 5.00pm. Sun viewing 12.00 noon to 5.00pm (phone first).
See also **London Postal Districts** above.

Spadesbourne   59 High Street, Ruislip, Middx HA4 7BD. (3 mins Ruislip tube.) *Tel:* (0895) 630577. *Open:* Mon to Sat, 10.00am to 5.30pm. Made-to-measure upholstery from firm's Leamington Spa workshops. Sofas, chairs, sofabeds, corner units, six to eight weeks. 8,000 fabrics. Some showroom models available off the floor. For brochures/enquiries, *tel:* (0926) 882881.
Also at: 26/30 London Road, Twickenham, Middx TW1 3RR. (2 mins Twickenham BR.) *Tel:* 081-891 5344. *Open:* Mon to Sat, 10.00am to 5.00pm, Sun 11.00am to 5.00pm.
Also at: Wheatsheaf House, Tunsgate, Guildford, Surrey GU1 3QT. *Tel:* (0483) 506445. *Open:* Mon to Sat, 10.00am to 5.30pm.
And at: The Bishop Centre, Bath Road, Taplow, Maidenhead, Berks SL6 0NY. *Tel:* (0628) 667530. *Open:* Mon to Sat, 10.00am to 5.00pm, Sun 10.00am to 5.00pm.

Tulleys of Chelsea   4 London Road, Guildford, Surrey GU1 2AF. *Tel:* (0483) 64643. *Open:* Mon to Sat,

9.00am to 5.30pm. Closed from 1.00pm to 2.00pm.
See also **London Postal Districts** above.

Wesley-Barrell   33 High Street, Tunbridge Wells, Kent TN1 1XL. *Tel:* (0892) 36286. No late night.
Also at: 73 North Street, Guildford, Surrey GU1 4AW. *Tel:* (0483) 37717.
And at: 3/11 Bridge Street, Witney, Oxon OX8 6BY. *Tel:* (0993) 776682.
And at: 2 Market Street, Watford, Herts WD1 7AD. *Tel:* (0923) 229825.
See also **London Postal Districts** above.

Mail Order

Chesterfields   Unit 1, 139a London Road, Shardlow, Derbyshire DE7 2HA *Tel:* (0332) 792575. Handmade chesterfields, wing/club chairs, suites, traditional deep-button styles, using whole skin leathers, not "stitched-up" pieces. Plain/antiqued finishes. Hardwood frames, fully sprung seat platforms/arms. Also full range of modern suites. Colour brochure available.

► Worth a Trip

A Barn Full of Sofas and Chairs
Furnace Mill, Lamberhurst, Kent. *Tel:* (0892) 890285. *Open:* Thu to Sat, 10.00am to 5.00pm. Sun viewing 10.00am to 12.30pm, or by appointment. Trading over 15 years. Sally Symons packs this old, three-storey mill with antique, period and good secondhand furniture. Original Victorian/Edwardian selections. Three-piece suites, two- and three-seater sofas, chaises longues, spoon-back/iron-frame chairs, dining/wing/easy chairs. Good range fabrics for reupholstery/loose cover service. Or buy them as they are, for reupholstering yourself.

2. SOFABEDS

"See home for rest
For home is best".

Thomas Tusser (1524–80), *Five Hundred Points of Good Husbandry*

Many upholstery firms listed above also offer sofabeds. Sofabeds for regular use must provide a proper sleeping surface. Check converting mechanisms for ease of use/ durability. Think where you will store bedding. See also **1. Chairs, Sofas and Suites** above, and **Bedrooms 10. Futons**. Shop also at firms listed in **Furniture 1. General**, and at **Department Stores**.

London Postal Districts

Estia   5/7 Tottenham Street, W1P 9PB. (2 mins Goodge Street tube.) *Tel:* 071-636 5957 (24 hours). *Open:* Mon to Sat, 10.00am to 6.00pm. Late night Thu, 7.30pm. Ingenious designs for fire-retardant chairs/sofabeds. Also trestles, trolleys, tables, desks, shelving cabinets and drawing boards. Catalogue available. Mail order.

London Sofa-Bed Centre
185 Tottenham Court Road, W1P 9LE. (5 mins Warren Street tube.) *Tel:* 071-631 1424. *Open:* Mon to Sat, 9.30am to 6.00pm. Late night Thu, 7.30pm. Over 300 designs for immediate delivery, or made-to-order (six to eight weeks). Durable, comfortable wooden slats to support mattress.

Also at: 236 Fulham Road, SW10 9NB. (South Kensington tube, plus bus.) *Tel:* 071-352 1358. *Open:* Mon to Sat, 10.00am to 6.00pm.

The Sofabed Shop   43a Colney Hatch Lane, Muswell Hill N10 1LJ. (Highgate tube, plus bus.) *Tel:* 081-444 7463. *Open:* Mon to Sat, 10.00am to 6.00pm (all branches). Late nights Thu and Fri, 8.00pm. Sun viewing 11.00am to 6.00pm. Over 100 models, many for immediate delivery. Special shapes/sizes to order (six to eight weeks). Well-arranged showrooms.
Also at: 93/97 Hampstead Road, NW1 3EL. (3 mins Warren Street tube/Euston BR.) *Tel:* 071-388 7689. See also **Home Counties/South East** below.

Home Counties/ South East

Dreams Superstore   156/158 Cowley Road, Oxford. (Opposite Boots and Tesco.) *Tel:* (0865) 792555. *Open:* 7 days, Mon to Sat 9.00am to 5.30pm. Sun viewing, 11.00am to 4.30pm. Phone individual branches for late nights. *Head office/enquiries tel:* (0494) 461146. "The largest selection of sofabeds in the country." Huge choice of styles for occasional/regular use. "Guaranteed lowest prices." Interest-free credit. Nationwide deliveries.
Also at: 73 Park Street, Aylesbury, Bucks HP20 1DU. (Corner of Stocklade Road.) *Tel:* (0296) 393355.
And at: 20 Hosier Street, Reading, Berks RG1 7JL. (By market, opposite Tesco.) *Tel:* (0734) 393555.
And at: 24 Watling Street, Bletchley, Milton Keynes, Bucks MK2 2DL. (On old A5 at Fenny Stratford.) *Tel:* (0908) 378557.
And at: 14/15 New Broadway, Uxbridge Road, Hillingdon, Middx UB10 0LJ. *Tel:* (0895) 253666.
And at: Halifax Road, Cressex Industrial Estate, High Wycombe, Bucks HP12 3SD. ($\frac{1}{4}$ mile from M40, junction 4.) *Tel:* (0494) 461146. Warehouse.
And at: 229/231 London Road, Croydon, Surrey CR9 2RL. (Near Cannon cinema.) *Tel:* 081-665 0551.
And at: 303 High Street, Slough, Berks SL1 1BD. (East end of Slough, opposite Comet.) *Tel:* (0753) 516416.
And at: 68 Market Street, Watford, Herts WD1 7AX. (Near Cannon cinema.) *Tel:* (0923) 223110.
And at: 22 High Street, Weybridge, Surrey. *Tel:* (0932) 829090.
And at: 9/10 South Bar, Banbury, Oxon. *Tel:* (0295) 258892.

The Sofabed Shop
182 Hornchurch Road, Hornchurch, Essex RN11 1QL. (5 mins Hornchurch tube.) *Tel:* (04024) 45555.
See also **London Postal Districts** above.

The Sofabed Shop   100 Tolworth Broadway, Tolworth, Surrey KT6 7JD. (5 mins Tolworth BR.) *Tel:* 081-390 0775.
See also **London Postal Districts** above.

16

FURNITURE

Britain has a poor furniture-buying record compared with the rest of Europe. The amount we spend on new furniture per year is right at the bottom of the league table. Perhaps this chapter will seduce you into changing the statistics.

1. GENERAL

"If beautiful things please thee, if exquisite furniture is all that thou mayest desire, our shop contains it."

Maples furniture shop inscription, Tottenham Court Road, 1929

Before shopping for furniture, always measure spaces carefully, and take tape with you to check sizes. Remember to allow enough space to use furniture comfortably: dining chairs must pull in and out, drawers and doors must open, and so on.

London Postal Districts

▶ Bargains!

Aero   96 Westbourne Grove, W2 5RT. (5 mins Bayswater tube. Whiteleys car park.) *Tel:* 071-221 1950. *Open:* Mon to Sat, 10.00am to 6.30pm. Huge, bright corner shop. Sculptural, witty, elegant. Inspired storage for bedsits/flats. Good-looking, stand-alone castored hanging rails with optional trays/baskets. Inexpensive wire frame systems with pull-out baskets: cool white/chic black. Storage racks to beat clutter. Dining chairs/tables. Beds/bed-sofas. Lighting/desks/accessories. Don't miss it.

Allied Maples See **Floors 3. Carpets.**

Authentics   42 Shelton Street, WC2H 9HZ. (3 mins Covent Garden tube.) *Tel:* 071-240 9845. *Open:* Mon to Sat, 10.30am to 6.00pm. Terry Jonas has created a spacious, elegant setting for 20th-century classics, plus newest designs from leading international designers/architects. Also lighting, ceramics, glassware, desk/office accessories. Tableware, mirrors, photo/picture frames, and more. Unique service: will hunt worldwide/import all possible products.

Coexistence   288 Upper Street, N1 2TZ. (10 mins Angel tube.) *Tel:* 071-354 8817. *Open:* Mon to Fri, 9.00am to 6.00pm. Telephone first to discuss requirements. Contemporary furniture/lighting.

The Conran Shop   81 Fulham Road, SW3 6RD. (8 mins South Kensington tube.) *Tel:* 071-589 7401. *Open:* Mon to Sat, 9.30am to 6.00pm. Open Tue, 10.00am. Internationally celebrated entrepreneur Sir Terence Conran has done more to bring well-designed furnishings to the British mass market than any other single force in British retailing. His chosen vehicle was Habitat, which he founded and controlled for 26 years. Now he has let Habitat go its own way. The Conran Shop is a splendid store in the exuberantly restored Michelin building. The 22,000 sq ft space vibrates with the force of its founder's creative approach to homemaking. It has a good range of furniture, from expensive international classics to simple, affordable shapes in china/glass. Plus exciting, exclusive fabrics/soft furnishing services. Carpets/rugs/bedlinens. Food shop with utensils/ingredients for every cuisine. Go there.

The Dining Room Shop See **14. Antiques** below.   Large, pleasant shop specialising in everything for the dining room, from furniture to candles.

Geoffrey Drayton Interiors 4 Porters' Walk, E1 9SF. (5 mins Wapping tube.) *Tel:* 071-702 1899. *Open:* 7 days, Mon to Sat, 10.00am to 6.00pm, Sun 12.00 noon to 6.00pm. Independent family business established for 30 years, specialising in the best contemporary furniture/accessories from all over Europe, including work by new designers. Sophisticated fitted furniture. Full interiors/soft furnishings service. See also **Home Counties/South East** below.

Estia See **Upholstery and Suites 2. Sofabeds.**   Metal tube in black, white, green, red or yellow is curved into a myriad of stylish furnishing solutions for tables, desks, shelving, trollies, etc. Clever, well-conceived designs at affordable prices. Well worth a special visit.

Habitat   196 Tottenham Court Road, W1P 9LD. (Opposite Goodge Street tube.) *Tel:* 071-631 3880. *Open:* Mon to Sat, 9.00am to 6.00pm. Late night Thu, 7.30pm. A new, streamlined Habitat has emerged for the nineties. Furniture is exclusive, mostly designed in-house and made in various workshops. Much more stylish/sophisticated than in the old days of pine/black stains/chrome, with strong emphasis on natural timbers/materials. Plus a wide range of fashion-conscious home accessories, in changing collections. The ads said Habitat was "revolting". Actually, it's very nice, but not exactly revolutionary. Cafés and Sunday openings at some stores.
Also at: 191/217 Finchley Road, Swiss Cottage, NW3 6NW. (1 min Finchley Road tube.) *Tel:* 071-328 3444. *Open:* Mon to Fri, 9.30am to 6.00pm, Tue 10.00am to 6.00pm. Late nights Thu and Fri, 7.00pm. Open Sat, 9.00am to 6.00pm, Sun 12.00 noon to 5.00pm.
And at: King's Mall, W6 0PZ. (5 mins Hammersmith tube.) *Tel:* 081-741 7111. *Open:* Mon to Thu, 9.00am to 5.30pm, Fri 9.00am to 7.00pm, Sat 9.00am to 6.00pm.
And at: 208 King's Road, SW3 5XP. (10 mins Sloane Square tube.) *Tel:* 071-351 1211. *Open:* Mon to Fri, 9.30am to 6.00pm, Tue 10.00am to 6.00pm, Sat 9.00am to 6.00pm, Sun 12.00 noon to 6.00pm.
And at: Brighton, Bromley, Canterbury, Chelmsford, Croydon, Guildford, Kingston, Maidenhead, Milton Keynes, Oxford, Tunbridge Wells, Wallingford.

Harrison Gibson   145 Tottenham

Court Road, W1P 9LL. (Opposite Warren Street tube.) Tel: 071-387 7000. *Open:* Mon to Fri, 9.30am to 6.00pm. Late night Thu, 7.00pm. This is where Maples was. Traditional, middle-market British furniture store.

Heal's   196 Tottenham Court Road, W1P 9LD. (Opposite Goodge Street tube.) *Tel:* 071-636 1666. *Open:* Mon 10.00am to 6.00pm, Tue to Sat, 9.30am to 6.00pm. Late night Thu, 7.30pm. Open Sat, 9.00am to 6.00pm. This large, beautiful store is part of London's aesthetic history, a bedrock of good design since the turn of the century. It lost its way a bit when it was controlled by the Storehouse Group, but is now independently managed and "pursuing a more adventurous, less bland policy." The emphasis, as ever, is on good design. The shop is particularly famous for its handmade beds (second floor, near the linens/bath shop). Latest international furniture (ground floor), along with lighting, china/glass, carpets/rugs, fabrics, accessories and kitchen shop. Interior design, fitted furniture, Humpherson kitchens/bathrooms (first floor). Full range of carpet/soft furnishing services. The new, stylish Mansard Café has replaced the restaurant.
See also **Home Counties/South East** below.

Ikea   Drury Way, North Circular Road, NW10 0JQ. (10 mins Neasden tube. Free car park.) Tel: 081-451 5611. *Open:* Mon to Fri, 10.00am to 8.00pm, Sat 9.00am to 6.00pm, Sun 12.00 noon to 6.00pm. Swedish megastore: over half its goods come from Sweden. Good value, self-assembly furniture. High design standards: all exclusive lines. Also beds/linens, lighting, floorings (including wood strip), china/tableware, cookware. Bathroom fittings, including fitted furniture. Kitchens. All furniture carries "mobelfakta" information (furniture facts), and is tested to conform to the rigorous standards of the Swedish Furniture Institute. Free catalogue. Café (with famous Swedish meatballs). Children's play areas (inside and out). Don't furnish until

you've been here! A new branch is opening in Croydon, end of 1992.

Ligne Roset   132 Shaftesbury Avenue, W1N 7DN. (5 mins Leicester Square tube.) *Tel:* 071-434 20712. *Open:* Mon to Sat, 10.00am to 6.00pm. Ligne Roset of France hosts this large, central showcase for modern European interiors. Storage systems for homes/offices. Beds, desks, dining furniture, occasional tables, rugs, modern lighting. Interior design advice. Free colour brochure.

Maison   917/919 Fulham Road, SW6 5HU. (10 mins Parsons Green tube.) *Tel:* 071-736 3121. *Open:* Mon to Sat, 9.30am to 6.00pm. Beautiful, colourful, stylish store with personal service from enthusiastic and energetic Smith brothers. Wide selections of modern living/dining/bedroom furniture from Britain, Italy, Spain. Wood, lacquers, glass. Also modern lighting/accessories. Table/cookware. Innovative, bright, bold, original: go and see.

New Venture Furniture   15/17 Colindale Avenue, NW9 5DR. (5 mins Colindale tube.) *Tel:* 081-205 7547. *Open:* Mon to Fri, 9.00am to 6.00pm, Sat 9.00am to 6.00pm, Sun 10.00am to 5.00pm. 14,000 sq ft of well-known brands. Beds/living room furniture, keen prices.

Charles Page   61 Fairfax Road, Swiss Cottage NW6 4EE. (5 mins Swiss Cottage tube.) *Tel:* 071-328 9851. *Open:* Mon to Sat, 9.30am to 5.30pm. Latest international furniture, selected for good design/value/quality. Bedrooms, dining rooms, living rooms, including beds, fitted furniture. International design/installation anywhere in world. Designers for 60 years.

▶ **Bargains!**

The Reject Shop   *Tel:* 071-736 7474 for details of nearest branch. *Star Store:* The Plaza, 116/128 Oxford Street, W1N 9DP. *Tel:* 071-255 2240. *Open:* Mon to Sat, 10.00am to 7.00pm. Late night Thu, 8.00pm. Misleading title: smart merchandise,

low prices. Good selections, mostly from stock. Now that Habitat has moved upmarket, this is the place for stylish, modern furniture at budget prices. Pine/black/chrome/glass. Tables/ chairs/storage/upholstery. Excellent space-savers. Definitely on the ball.
Also at: 209 Tottenham Court Road, W1P 9AF. *Tel:* 071-580 2895.
And at: 234 King's Road, SW3 5UA. *Tel:* 071-352 0307.
And at: Whiteley's, 141/165 Queensway, W2 4YH. *Tel:* 071-229 4449.
And at: Brighton, Bromley, Kingston, Wood Green, Guildford, Croydon, Hatfield, Watford.

The Treske Shop   5 Barmouth Road, SW18 2DT. (Vauxhall tube, plus bus.) *Tel:* 081-874 0050. *Open:* Tue to Fri, 10.30am to 6.00pm. Sat 10.00am to 5.00pm. Full range timber/fabric samples.
See also **Mail Order** below.

Waldorf See **Floors 3. Carpets**. Exciting modern furniture from all over Europe, in glitzy surroundings.

Oscar Woollens Interiors   81/85 Hampstead Road, NW1 2PL. (3 mins Warren Street tube.) *Tel:* 071-387 5840. *Open:* Mon to Sat, 9.30am to 5.30pm. Stylish modern European furniture, plus the best of British designs. Living/dining/fitted bedroom furniture. Rugs, lighting, upholstery. Interior design service, free delivery within M25 area.

Home Counties/ South East

Beadle and Crome   32 Oxford Street, High Wycombe, Bucks HP11 2DJ. (Car park at rear.) *Tel:* (0494) 23249. *Open:* Mon to Sat, 9.00am to 5.00pm. Personal service from family business trading for 65 years. Quality furniture: Danish/German fitted wardrobes; rosewood/teak dining furniture. Classic upholstery. *Also at:* 53 Broad Street Mall, Reading, Berks RG1 7QE. (Car park over store.) *Tel:* (0734) 581356.

Bennett and Brown 181/183 Windmill Street, Gravesend, Kent DA12 1AJ. (2 mins Gravesend Central BR.) *Tel:* (0474) 352235. *Open:* Mon to Sat, 9.00am to 5.30pm. Room sets over four floors, displaying upholstery, cabinet furniture, curtains and carpets.

Browns of Henley 37/39 Duke Street, Henley-on-Thames, Oxon RG9 1UR. (Only 3 mins from several car parks.) *Tel:* (0491) 410408. *Open:* Mon to Sat, 9.30am to 5.30pm. Peter and Catherine Brown opened this shop four years ago after many years in the furniture trade. Attractive, 2,500 sq ft showroom just a few minutes from the river. Top quality. Upholstery/ reproduction cabinetry/bedroom furniture/beds. Exclusive French solid cherrywood *Louis Philippe* and *Directoire* designs.

Clement Joscelyne Market Square, Bishop's Stortford, Herts CM23 3XA. (Town centre, adjacent car parks.) *Tel:* (0279) 506731. *Open:* Mon to Sat, 9.00am to 5.30pm (both branches). Captivating atmosphere. Family firm established in 1879, dedicated to quality and good design. Collection of old buildings, some dating back to Elizabethan times. Floor space now around 12,000 sq ft. International furniture selections. Hulsta, Grange, Titchmarsh and Goodwin. Interior design service. Own workroom for curtain making.
Also at: 9/11 High Street, Brentwood, Essex CM14 4RG. *Tel:* (0277) 225420.

Geoffrey Drayton Interiors 104 High Street, Epping, Essex CM16 4AF. *Tel:* (0878) 73929. *Open:* Mon to Sat, 9.00am to 5.30pm.
See also **London Postal Districts** above.

Fishpools 115 High Street, Waltham Cross, Herts EN8 7AL. (10 mins Waltham Cross/Theobalds BRs. Car park.) *Tel:* (0992) 31911. *Open:* Mon to Fri, 9.00am to 5.30pm. Closed Thu. Open Sat, 9.00am to 6.00pm. Family firm, founded 1899. Friendly, personal service, with

experienced staff. 42,000 sq ft, plus offices/warehouses. Complete furnishers: furniture, lighting, china/ glass. Interior design department: linen, bedding, carpets, soft furnishings. G-Plan, Ercol, and international furniture. Free delivery within 50 miles. Coffee shop.
Also at: 24/26 Market Street, Watford, Herts WD1 7AD. (On ring road.) *Tel:* (0923) 221844. *Open:* as above, but closed Wed.

Heals Tunsgate, Guildford, Surrey GU1 3QU. (5 mins Guildford BR.) *Tel:* (0483) 576715. *Open:* as London branch.
See also **London Postal Districts** above.

Holmes Interiors Chatham Street, Reading, Berks RG1 7JX. (Own car park. Adjacent multi-storey car park.) *Tel:* (0734) 586421. *Open:* Tue to Sat, 9.00am to 5.30pm. Late night Thu, 9.30am to 8.00pm. Founded 1815: present family management took over in 1920. 13,000 sq ft over two floors. 8,500 sq ft of furniture displays. Flexible/versatile Hulsta German wall furniture, in elegant wood/coloured finishes. Design/ install. French country house, American Shaker, Scandinavian classics, in solid woods, Italian dining ranges. Finishing touches department: cushions, rugs, mirrors, plants. Coffee shop.

Peter Knight 45 London End, Beaconsfield, Bucks HP9 2HP. (A40 from London.) *Tel:* (0494) 675561. *Open:* Mon to Sat, 9.00am to 5.30pm. Closed all day Wed. Complete interior furnishers. Merchandise/service reflects enthusiasm of delightful owner, who founded store 27 years ago. Attractive showrooms created from three Victorian houses. Classic furniture/upholstery, fabrics, Oriental rugs, lighting, china, glass, gifts. Full interior design service.

Lucas World of Furniture Robans Lane, Aylesbury, Bucks HP19 3RE. (Off A41.) *Tel:* (0296) 86255. *Open:* 7 days, Mon to Fri, 9.00am to 5.30pm, Sat 9.30am to 6.00pm, Sun 10.00am to 4.00pm. Traditional/

modern room settings over two floors. Beds, lamps, pictures. Amusements for children. Wine on special days. "Britain's most beautiful furniture store: we make sure you have a memorable day."

Maples 38 The Parade, High Street, Watford, Herts. *Tel:* (0923) 31348. *Open:* Mon to Sat, 9.00am to 5.30pm. Late night Thu, 8.00pm. A fine name in furniture retailing, going back 150 years, and now getting fresh impetus from the Allied Maples Group. 20 stores nationwide. Most well-known brands sold, including Ercol and G-Plan. Upholstered furniture, beds, cabinets, dining and occasional furniture, fitted bedrooms. Custom-made curtains/lighting. Free interior design advice from home consultants. Free delivery on most large items. Free fitting for all carpets over £9.99 sq yd.
Also at: Bishop's Palace House, Clarence Street, Kingston-on-Thames, Surrey KT1 1PB. *Tel:* 081-546 4506.

MFI *Tel:* 081-200 0200 for details of nearest branch. *Star stores:* Plough Lane, Wimbledon SW17 2PT. (Wimbledon Park tube/Haydon's Road BR.) *Tel:* 081-879 0606. *Open:* Mon to Fri, 9.00am to 6.00pm, Sat 9.00am to 6.00pm (all branches). Late nights Mon, Thu and Fri, 8.00pm. It's been an uphill struggle for MFI to shed their cheap/cheerful and often nasty image, but they show good signs of succeeding. Quality/display/service are all vastly improved. Go and wander round— you may be pleasantly surprised. Croydon and High Wycombe stores have had major refits.
Also at: Ely Industrial Estate, Angel Road, N18 3BH. (Angel Road BR.) *Tel:* 081-884 2626.
175 other stores nationwide.

Perrings Home Furnishing
Tel: 081-330 2621 for details of nearest branch. Well-established family firm, still with Perrings in charge. Quality furniture brands in middle/upper price range. Dining/ living/bedrooms. Imaginative room layouts. Attractive displays of soft

furnishings, with full making-up service. Good for carpets. Coffee shops in larger stores.
Also at: Basingstoke, Bedford, Crawley, Guildford, Kingston, Oxford, Reading, Southend, Staines, Watford, Woking, Worthing.
And at: Debenhams in Brighton, Bristol, Bromley, Chelmsford, Croydon, Gloucester, Guildford, Harrow, Romford, Southsea.

Stockwell and Oxford
16 Katharine Street, Croydon, Surrey CR9 1JY. (5 mins East Croydon BR.) *Tel*: 081-688 5521. *Open*: Mon to Sat, 9.00am to 5.30pm. Family firm founded in 1891. Friendly, personal service. Wide range of modern

furniture, living rooms, dining rooms, bedrooms. Carpets, soft furnishings. *Also at*: 1 Lower Square, Civic Centre, Sutton, Surrey SM1 3JW. *Tel*: 081-643 7424.

Trend Interiors   8 Richmond Hill, Richmond, Surrey TW10 6QX. (10 mins Richmond tube/BR.) *Tel*: 081-940 7261. *Open*: Tue to Sat, 9.30am to 6.00pm. Owner/buyer Mrs Pat Street promotes quality modern furniture from Germany, Italy, Scandinavia and England. Full interior design service: lots of fabric/paper samples, all top makes. Well established with countrywide reputation for service/design flair.

Mail Order

The Treske Shop   Station Works, Thirsk, N. Yorks YO7 4NY. *Tel*: (0845) 522770. Excellent, informative catalogue. Furniture in homegrown hardwoods (oak, ash, beech) commissioned from many famous designers. Beautiful simple shapes that will never date; customers can often dictate details. Small, private family firm catering for every room. Everything guaranteed; maintenance service. Visitors welcome.

2. PINE AND COUNTRY

Pine furniture lasts and doesn't date. But new pieces will go darker. Stripped pine is usually Victorian and was probably once painted. Pine made from old wood is romantic, but new pine with an antique finish can look almost the same. Colour stains include an attractive burgundy shade; some ranges are painted.

London Postal Districts

Adams Antiques   47 Chalk Farm Road, NW1 8AJ. (5 mins Chalk Farm tube.) *Tel*: 071-267 9241. *Open*: 7 days, 10.00am to 6.00pm. Large stock of antique pine furniture, plus original painted pieces. Also quality reproductions in oak/pine. Knowledgeable, friendly staff.

I and J L Brown   632/636 King's Road, SW6 2DU. (10 mins Fulham Broadway tube.) *Tel*: 071-736 4141. *Open*: Mon to Sat, 9.00am to 5.30pm. Specialists in English country/French provincial furniture. Reproductions of all the most popular styles. 30,000 sq ft warehouse in Hereford. Search service.

Chest of Drawers   281 Upper Street, Islington N1 2TZ. (7 mins Highbury and Islington tube.) *Tel*: 071-359 5909. *Open*: 7 days, 10.00am to 6.00pm. Antique/repro pine/country furniture. Farmhouse, refectory, wake, square leg, oval, round, gateleg, dropleaf tables. Irish, Welsh, Lancs, Lincs dressers. Very large stock, or made to any size.

Chiswick Country Pine   158 Chiswick High Road, W4 1PR. (5 mins Turnham Green tube.) *Tel*: 081-747 0734. *Open*: Mon to Sat, 10.00am to 6.00pm, Sun 12.00 noon to 5.00pm. Varied stock old/new pine furniture; special sizes, details, finishes to order.

Danta Pine   88 The Broadway, Mill Hill Circus, NW7 3LN. (5 mins Mill Hill BR. Mill Hill East tube, plus bus.) *Tel*: 081-959 4292. *Open*: Mon to Sat, 9.30am to 5.00pm. Early closing Thu, 1.00pm. Well-made solid pine furniture from own Luton workshops. Unfinished/varnished/antique finished. Special sizes to order (allow four to six weeks). Budget bedroom range. Price lists/drawings. See also **Home Counties/South East** below.

Icor Interiors   195 Upper Richmond Road, Putney, SW15 6SG. (4 mins East Putney tube.) *Tel*: 081-788 0982. *Open*: Mon to Sat, 10.00am to 5.30pm. Closed Thu. Reliable direct-selling workshop. Ultra-simple modern designs in solid pine, natural or 20 wood stains. Shelving, bookcases, chests, wardrobes, desks, sideboards, wall units. From stock (many showroom models are reduced) or within 14 days—even special sizes/colours. Futon sofabeds: pine/black lacquer, easily converted without futon removal. Catalogue/price list available.

Jasco Antiques   134 Upper Richmond Road, Putney SW15 2SP. (5 mins East Putney tube.) *Tel*: 081-789 0060. *Open*: 7 days, Mon to Sat 10.00am to 6.00pm, Sun 2.00pm to 6.00pm. Antique/reproduction pine. Old/new wood refectory/farmhouse tables. Bedroom furniture. Bookcases made to measure.
Also at: Furniture Cave, 533 King's Road, SW10. *Tel*: 071-351 9160. *Open*: Mon to Sat, 10.00am to 6.00pm.

John Lewis of Hungerford See **Kitchens 5. Luxury and Bespoke Kitchens**.

Living room furniture, in colour-washed, authentic country styles. Furniture to fall in love with. Dressers, settles, tables etc.

Kilburn Pine   266 Belsize Road, NW6 4BT. (2 mins Kilburn Park tube.) *Tel:* 071-328 7274. *Open:* Mon to Sat, 10.00am to 5.30pm. Traditional designs. Solid pine bedroom/dining furniture. Solid beech chairs. Wide range of solid pine bookcases.

Pine Collection   195 Upper Richmond Road West, SW14 8QT. (15 mins Mortlake BR/Richmond tube plus bus.) *Tel:* 081-876 4053. *Open:* 7 days, 9.30am to 6.00pm. Two floors solid pine furniture: new/restored.

Pine Grove   186 Wandsworth Bridge Road, Fulham SW6 2UF. (15 mins Fulham Broadway tube.) *Tel:* 071-731 7673/736 5802. *Open:* 7 days, 10.00am to 6.00pm. Sturdy pine furniture from 20 small country workshops. Good stock, or will make to order in special sizes. Reasonable prices. Painstaking, personal, friendly service.

Pine Interiors   49 Montpelier Vale, SE3 0TJ. (3 mins Blackheath BR.) *Tel:* 081-318 0477. *Open:* Mon to Sat, 10.00am to 6.00pm. Late nights Tue and Fri, 8.00pm. Good choice reproduction furniture for living/bedrooms. Three main makes: Ducal, Younger, Lovelace. Brochures available.

The Pine Market   3/4 Varley Parade, Edgware Road, Colindale NW9 6RR. (5 mins Colindale tube.) *Tel:* 081-205 5150. *Open:* Mon to Sat, 10.00am to 6.00pm, Sun 11.00am to 2.00pm. Large shop: vast selection of pine furniture, from spice racks to fitted wardrobes. Quick deliveries: sometimes same day.

Pine Mine   100 Wandsworth Bridge Road, SW6 2TF. (15 mins Fulham Broadway tube.) *Tel:* 071-736 1092. *Open:* Mon to Sat, 9.00am to 5.45pm. Victorian/Georgian old pine. Large stocks. Restoration

service. Make up furniture in old woods. Limited range of new pieces.

The Pine Shop   176/184 West End Lane, West Hampstead NW6 1SG. (5 mins West Hampstead tube/BR.) *Tel:* 071-435 4462/1044. *Open:* 7 days, Mon to Sat, 9.00am to 6.00pm, Sun 10.00am to 1.30pm. "London's largest specialist in new pine." Well-established. Handwaxed solid pine/dovetailed joints. Living/dining/bedroom furniture. Mostly from stock, or delivered within three/four days. Made-to-measure service. Telephone for brochures.
Also at: 311/323 Muswell Hill Broadway, N10 1BY. (Highgate tube, plus bus.) *Tel:* 081-444 6055/9856. *Open:* Mon to Sat, 9.00am to 6.00pm, Sun 10.00am to 1.30pm.
And at: 256/258 Chiswick High Road, W4 1PD. (5 mins Turnham Green tube.) *Tel:* 081-747 8999. *Open:* Mon to Sat, 9.00am to 6.00pm, Sun 11.00am to 2.30pm.
See also **Home Counties/South East** below.

Pine Warehouse   86 Wandsworth Bridge Road, SW6 2TD. (15 mins Fulham Broadway tube.) *Tel:* 071-371 8476. Richard Clifton, the friendly owner of Pine Grove, has opened a second shop for old pine. Good prices/service.

Rhode Design   86 Stoke Newington Church Street, N16 0AP. (Manor House tube. Stoke Newington BR.) *Tel:* 071-275 8261. *Open:* Mon to Sat, 10.00am to 5.00pm, or by appointment. New England-style freestanding storage, inspired by simple early 19th-century American craft designs. Cupboards/drawer units/dresser tops/chests/bookcases. Colours/ finishes: authentic early American shades/materials. Colour rubbed, antiqued, stippled, crackled, glazed, dragged. Or "in the wood" for DIY finishing: paint kits available. Reasonable prices. Fitted/unfitted kitchen furniture.

The Shaker Shop   25 Harcourt Street, W1H 1DT. (5 mins Edgware Road tube.) *Tel:* 071-724 7672. *Open:* Mon to Fri, 10.00am to

6.00pm, Sat 9.30am to 6.00pm. "Put your hands to work and your hearts to God," said the Shakers (an American religious sect). Genuine Shaker sewing/coffee tables. Benches/steps. Classic rocking chairs: Shakers believe an angel might sit on them. Famous Shaker "pegged" wall-rail takes small hanging cupboard, shelves, mirrors, and even chairs. Trestle tables in solid American cherry—elegant, practical classics. Colour catalogue: £3. Not so much a furniture shop as a religious experience.

Sophisto-Cat   192 Wandsworth Bridge Road, SW6 2UF. (Fulham Broadway tube, plus bus, or 15 mins Parsons Green tube.) *Tel:* 071-731 2221. *Open:* Mon to Fri, 10.00am to 6.00pm, Sat 10.00am to 5.00pm. Explore three adjoining shops filled with traditional repro pine furniture, some in old wood. Furniture in old wood made to order, including wardrobes/chests.

This and That   50/51 Chalk Farm Road, NW1 8AN. (5 mins Chalk Farm tube.) *Tel:* 071-267 5433. *Open:* 7 days, 10.30am to 6.00pm. Mix of old and new pine; bedrooms, living rooms, kitchens. Bookcases made to order. Also handstripped 1920s/30s oak tables, chairs, sideboards.

Village Collection   19 Chalk Farm Road, NW1 8AG. (3 mins Camden Town tube.) *Tel:* 071-485 4034. *Open:* 7 days, Mon to Sat 9.30am to 6.00pm, Sun 10.00am to 6.00pm. Extensive range traditional solid pine furniture for home/office. Mirrors/prints/lighting. Pleasant helpful service. Large showrooms on four floors; busy Camden atmosphere. Good selections of restored furniture.
See also **Home Counties/South East** below.

Vogue Pine Superstore 12 Springbridge Road, Ealing Broadway W5 2AA. (5 mins Ealing Broadway tube.) *Tel:* 081-579 4414. *Open:* Mon to Sat, 9.00am to 5.30pm, Sun 10.00am to 4.00pm. 4,500 sq ft modern/traditional pine

furniture from top makes. Ducal/ Jaycee/Craftsman/Orchard/ Harvest. Plus own Vogue Collection. Living rooms/bedrooms/kitchens. Discounted prices. Art gallery/one-hour picture framing. Exclusive sofabeds.
See also **Home Counties/South East** below.

Home Counties/ South East

Burgess Farm Antiques
Morestead, Winchester, Hants SO21 1LZ. *Tel:* (0962) 777546. *Open:* Mon to Sat, 9.00am to 5.00pm. 15,000 sq ft warehouse. Antique/pine/country furniture. Panelling/doors/fireplaces. Stripping service.

Danta Pine 96 Leagrave Road, Luton, Beds LU8 8HZ. *Tel:* (0582) 36236.
Also at: 17 High Street, Hemel Hempstead HP1 3AA. *Tel:* (0442) 214040.
See also **London Postal Districts** above.

Stewart Linford Kitchener Works, Kitchener Road, High Wycombe, Bucks HP11 2SJ. (1 mile High Wycombe BR.) *Tel:* (0494) 443657. *Open:* Mon to Fri, 9.00am to 5.00pm. Closed for lunch, 1.00pm to 1.30pm. Open Sat, 9.00am to 1.00pm. Other times by appointment. Specialists in Windsor and other English hardwood chairs; made to order. Loving craftsmanship of the highest order.

Pew Corner The Dairy Workshop, Trelawney House, Binscombe Village, Godalming, Surrey GU7 3QJ. *Tel:* (0483) 426485. *Open:* Fri and Sat, 10.00am to 5.00pm. Most bank holidays. Or by appointment. Wide selection of reclaimed pews. Brochure available.

The Pine Cellars 39 Jewry Street, Winchester, Hants SO23 8RY. *Tel:* (0962) 867014. *Open:* Mon to Sat, 9.00am to 5.00pm. 20,000 sq ft warehouse/showroom. Antique/ country/repro pine furniture.

Pine Productions 12/16 Whytecliffe Road South, Purley, Surrey CR8 2AU. (Next to Purley BR.) *Tel:* 081-660 1000. *Open:* Mon to Thu, 9.00am to 5.30pm, Fri to 7.00pm. Closed Sat. Pine furniture (bedroom, dining room, kitchen) with workshop behind for fitted kitchens in pine/oak. Immediate delivery.

The Pine Shop 2/3 St Onge Parade, Southbury Road, Enfield, Middx EN1 1YU. (Enfield Town BR. Large car park nearby.) *Tel:* 081-366 6339. *Open:* Mon to Sat, 9.00am to 6.00pm.
See also **London Postal Districts** above.

Pineapple Addison Court, 15 Heath Road, Twickenham, Middx TW1 4AG. (10 mins Twickenham BR.) *Tel:* 081-744 0444. *Open:* Mon to Sat, 9.30am to 6.00pm (both branches). Claims to have the largest range of traditional pine furniture in the country. Very reasonable prices. Furniture is made from old wood. Delightful room settings and wide choice of accessories.
Also at: 23/25 Bell Street, Reigate, Surrey RH2 7AD. (Car park at rear.) *Tel:* (0737) 222180.

Sussex Windsors Dormers Farmhouse, Windmill Hill, Herstmonceux, Hailsham, E. Sussx BN27 4RY. *Tel:* (0323) 832388. In a village workshop, Barry and Mary Murphy handmake 11 designs of traditional Windsor chair. Seats are handshaped with an adze from solid elm. Steam-bent ash bows, arms, stretchers. English hardwood tables, dressers, hunt boards. Commissions. Brochures 50p. Mail order.

Village Collection Old Greys Brewery Yard, 5 The Maltings, Springfield Road, Chelmsford, Essex CM2 6QR. (10 mins Chelmsford BR.) *Tel:* (0245) 266865. *Open:* Mon to Sat, 9.30am to 6.00pm, Sun 2.00pm to 5.00pm. Handy central location; three floors, good stocks, friendly staff.
Also at: 93 South Street, Romford RM1 1NX. (2 mins Romford BR. Multi-storey parking by BR.) *Tel:* (0708) 723111. *Open:* Mon to Sat,

9.30am to 6.00pm, Sun by appointment. Friendly shop; two floors of solid pine furniture.
And at: 51 High Street, Tunbridge Wells, Kent TN1 1XU. (10 mins Tunbridge Wells BR. Safeways car park.) *Tel:* (0892) 526512. *Open:* Mon to Sat, 9.30am to 6.00pm, Sun 10.00am to 6.00pm. Recently refurbished; friendly atmosphere. Three floors, good selection of old restored pine.
And at: 38/40 High Street, Guildford, Surrey GU1 3EL. (10 mins Guildford BR. Sainsbury's car park.) *Tel:* (0483) 67005. *Open:* Mon to Sat, 9.30am to 6.00pm, Sun 10.00am to 6.00pm. Large two-floor showroom. Good selection of solid pine furniture.
And at: 15 Chequer Street, St Albans, Herts AL1 3YJ. (5 mins St Albans BR. Central NCP car park.) *Tel:* (0727) 41599. *Open:* Mon to Sat, 9.30am to 6.00pm, Sun 10.00am to 6.00pm. Solid pine furniture in a period setting. Good selections of restored furniture.
And at: (Star Store) 42/3 Peascod Street, Windsor, Berks, SL4 1DE. (10 mins Riverside BR. 7 mins Eton and Windsor BR.) *Tel:* (0753) 855730. *Open:* 7 days, Mon to Sat 9.30am to 6.00pm, Sun 11.00am to 5.00pm. Main showroom; two floors; extensive selections. Mirrors/prints. Also restored furniture.
See also **London Postal Districts** above.

Vogue Pine Superstore 63 Station Road, North Harrow, Middx HA2 7SR. (1 min North Harrow tube.) *Tel:* 081-861 5665.
See also **London Postal Districts** above.

▶ Worth a Trip

Adams Antiques The Old Post Office, Brampton Road, Huntingdon. (2 mins Huntingdon BR.) *Tel:* (0480) 300455. *Open:* Mon to Sat, 9.00am to 5.00pm, Sun 11.00am to 5.00pm. Two vast warehouses, one for old pine, one for new. Restoration/ finishing. Pine-stripping service.

Chancery Antiques 8/10 Barrington Street, Tiverton, Devon EX16 6PU. (M5 to Tiverton Link Road.) *Tel*: (0884) 252416/253190. *Open*: Mon to Sat, 9.00am to 5.00pm. Closed Thu. Family business established 25 years in 3,800 sq ft space. Stripped pine/country furniture. Also craftsman-made reproduction pine furniture. Wardrobes, chests, farmhouse tables, desks, dressers, cupboards. Beautifully hand-finished. Weekly deliveries in London/South East.

---

3. SCANDINAVIAN

The simple shapes pioneered by the Scandinavian countries in the fifties and sixties have a classic and enduring appeal. Quality is usually good, with lots of solid wood. Teak only needs occasional oiling.

London Postal Districts

Ikea See **1. General** above.

Scandinavian World 72-94 Park Road, Crouch End N8 8JP. (Finsbury Park tube, plus bus. W7 stops outside.) *Tel*: 081-348 1854. *Open*: Mon to Fri, 9.00am to 5.00pm, Sat 10.00am to 4.00pm. Classic undating Danish designs. UK outlet for Dyrlund, manufacturers of quality furniture in teak/rosewood. Living/dining rooms. Lights. Leather recliners. Beautifully constructed and finished, to stand the test of time. Free colour brochure available.

Wharfside Danish Furniture 66 Buttesland Street, N1 6BY. (5 mins Old Street tube.) *Tel*: 071-253 3206. *Open*: 7 days, Mon to Sat 9.00am to 5.00pm. Early closing, Fri 1.00pm. Open Sun, 10.00am to 2.00pm. Family business trading 30 years. Rambling warehouse with vast selection dining/living room/home office furniture, imported directly from Scandinavia at very good prices.
See also **Home Counties/South East** below.

Home Counties/ South East

Distinctive Designs 87 Hillingdon Hill, Hillingdon Village, Uxbridge, Middx UB10 0JQ. (10 mins Uxbridge tube.) *Tel*: (0895) 236288. *Open*: Mon to Sat, 9.00am to 5.30pm. Closed Wed. Classic Finnish solid pine tables, chairs, drawing boards. Sizes compact to Jumbo (eg a table for 12 people, unextended). Attractive, self-assembly Swedish solid pine: bunk beds, storage, seating, ideal for young people. Fabrics. Full interior design service (free).

Wharfside Danish Furniture 11 North Street, Leatherhead, Surrey KT22 7AX. (5 mins Leatherhead BR.) *Tel*: (0372) 379810. *Open*: Mon to Sat, 9.00am to 5.00pm. Early closing Fri 1.00pm. Open Sun, 10.00am to 2.00pm.
See also **London Postal Districts** above.

---

4. 20TH-CENTURY CLASSICS: ORIGINALS AND COPIES

Now we've reached the very last decade, we can look back and admire those designs still considered desirable by homemakers and collectors alike.

London Postal Districts

Aram Designs 63/67 Heath Street, Hampstead NW3 6UQ. (2 mins Hampstead tube.) *Tel*: 071-431 4008. *Open*: Tue to Sat, 10.00am to 6.00pm, Mon 12.00 noon to 6.00pm. New retail showroom for the cream of 20th-century classic furniture: Alvar Aalto (simple curves in Finnish silky birch ply), Le Corbusier (tubular steel), Thonet (curly bentwood). Plus the lesser known steel/leather elegance of Eileen Gray.
Also at (trade showroom): 3 Kean Street, WC2B 4AT. (5 mins Covent Garden tube.) *Tel*: 071-240 3933.

Art Furniture 158 Camden Street, NW1 9PA. (5 mins Camden tube.) *Tel*: 071-267 4324. *Open*: 7 days, Mon to Sat, 10.00am to 6.00pm, Sun 12.00 noon to 6.00pm. Trade showroom with trade prices. Public welcome. Extensive Art Deco, Art Nouveau, Arts and Crafts and other furniture/furnishings from the 1860s to the 1960s. Newly converted warehouse. Good quality stock. Search service.

Atrium 22/24 St Giles High Street, WC2H 8LN. (2 mins Tottenham Court

Road tube.) *Tel*: 071-379 7288. *Open*: Mon to Sat, 9.00am to 6.00pm. Other times by appointment. Spacious well-arranged modern designs, highlighted by own French halogen lighting range. Le Corbusier Petit Confort/Chaise Longue designed in France, 1928. A little later, Gerrit Rietveld emulated Mondrian with The Red and Blue chair; sharp sloping uncomfortable angles have sculptural impact. Also desks/tables with sharp, modern styling, Italian/French/German. Full interior design service.

Authentics See **1. General** above. In stock: Le Corbusier chaise longue in steel/black leather plus club chair/matching coffee table. Famous Marcel Breuer Wassily (1925) named after Wassily Kandinsky, and made for his Bauhaus home: black strip of leather for seat/sides/back intersect in different planes around the tubular chromed steel frame. Two ultra-elegant Mies van der Rohe cantilevers: the MR, with sweeping chromed curves and one-piece seat/back of woven cane; and the Brno (1930). Probably best known is the M van der R Barcelona with scimitar curved chromed frame and buttoned black leather seat/back cushions, designed for the Barcelona International Exhibition of 1929. The brief from the German Government Pavilion was to design a chair fit to receive a king!

Rupert Cavendish Designs 98 Waterford Road, SW6 2HA. (10 mins Fulham Broadway tube.) *Tel*: 071-384 2642. *Open*: Mon to Sat, 10.00am to 6.00pm. Genuine Art Deco pieces, plus copies to order. Neo-classical/period fabrics/wallpapers.

Fiell 181/183 King's Road, SW3 5EB. (10 mins Sloane Square tube.) *Tel*: 071-351 7172. *Open*: Mon to Sat, 10.00am to 6.00pm. Designer furniture from 1945 to present day, but especially 1950s/60s. Licensed re-editions of Race Furniture's Antelope and BA chairs.

Freud 198 Shaftesbury Avenue, WC2 8JL. (10 mins Covent Garden

tube.) *Tel*: 071-831 1071. *Open*: Mon to Fri, 10.30am to 6.30pm, Sat 11.00am to 6.00pm. At last (after exorbitant Italian copies): the striking geometric designs of Glasgow architect Charles Rennie Mackintosh at affordable prices. Immaculate reproductions, made in England. Colour brochure available.

Luke Hughes 182 Drury Lane, WC2B 5QF. (3 mins Holborn/Covent Garden tubes.) *Tel*: 071-404 5995. *Open*: Mon to Fri, 9.00am to 6.00pm. Evenings/Sat by appointment. Youthful, enthusiastic designer-maker of timeless natural oak/modern furniture in deceptively simple styles. In the best tradition of the Arts and Crafts movement. Solidly satisfying and exquisitely made, to suit interiors, old or new. Highly recommended. Personal service. Commissions.

Jazzy Art Deco 67 Camden Road, NW1 9EU. (5 mins Camden tube. Next to Camden BR.) *Tel*: 071-267 3342. *Open*: Mon to Sat, 10.00am to 6.00pm, Sun by appointment. Over 1,300 sq ft original fine Art Deco furniture (1920s/30s). Plus ceramics, glass, bronzes. Good investments/reasonable prices. Reupholstery, French polishing.

Libra Designs Unit 47, Alfies Antique Market, Church Street, Marylebone NW8. (5 mins Edgware Road tube.) *Tel*: 071-402 1976. *Open*: Tue and Thu, 10.30am to 5.00pm, Fri and Sat 12.00 noon to 5.00pm. Or by appointment. Closed Sun, Mon, Wed. Marie Gottlieb scours the country for original Art Deco furniture. Substantial three-piece suites with e.g. cloud- or shell-shaped backs. Original coverings, or reupholstered to order in appropriate fabrics. Also wardrobes, cupboards, dressing tables, occasional furniture, much in burr walnut, with typical swirly graining, or flecked yellow birds' eye maple. 1930s accessories, too. Glass by Lalique; china by Clarice Cliff. Search/find service.

Lutyens Design Associates 11 Redcliffe Place, SW10 9DB. *Tel*:

071-352 4579. *Open*: by appointment. Candia Lutyens, granddaughter of the great Edwardian architect Edward Lutyens (1869–1944) offers handmade copies of his distinctive furniture designs.

Metropolis 3 D'Arblay Street, W1V 3FD. (5 mins Oxford Circus tube.) *Tel*: 071-494 2531. *Open*: Mon to Fri 10.00am to 6.30pm. Late night Thu 7.00pm. Open Sat, 10.00am to 6.30pm. Original pieces of furniture, lamps, etc. from 1920s right through to the present. This small shop on two levels salvages the best of the 1930s, 1940s and 1950s. Free gift-wrapping.

Jill Saunders 46 White Hart Lane, SW13 0PZ. (5 mins Barnes Bridge BR.) *Tel*: 081-878 0400. *Open*: Mon to Sat, 9.30am to 6.00pm. Original Lloyd Loom furniture. Sofas, chairs, tables, linen baskets. Steel framework woven with coiled paper strips. Repairs with original materials. Authentic colours; or can be resprayed to any colour. Replacement cushions feather-filled/foam wrapped with Dacron wadding kept in stock; covers to order. Also Victorian/Edwardian sofas/chairs plus reproduction upholstery. Pleasant, efficient service from knowledgeable proprietor.

SCP 135/139 Curtain Road, EC2A 3BX. (10 mins Old Street tube.) *Tel*: 071-739 1869. *Open*: Mon to Fri, 9.00am to 6.00pm, Sat 10.00am to 5.00pm. Minimalist modern furniture in chrome, glass, wood. Chairs, tables, shelving, trolleys and so on. Copies of 1930s classics, plus the very best of latest design. A visit is essential for lovers of modern style.

Themes and Variations 231 Westbourne Grove, W11 2SE. (6 mins Notting Hill Gate tube.) *Tel*: 071-727 5531. *Open*: Mon to Fri, 10.00am to 6.00pm. Closed for lunch 1.00pm to 2.00pm. Open Sat, 10.00am to 6.00pm. Specialists in original 1940s to 1960s Italian furniture/Venetian glass. Plus contemporary avant-garde designs.

The Treske Shop See **1. General** above. Modern British classics in solid wood from the past 15 years, by Dinah Casson/Robert Heritage.

Viaduct Furniture See **13. Avant-Garde** below. Classics by Le Corbusier and Mies van der Rohe.

Vitra 13 Grosvenor Street, W1X 9FB. (5 mins Bond Street tube.) *Tel*: 071-408 1122. *Open*: Mon to Fri, 9.00am to 5.30pm. Close 5.00pm Fri. Specialists in seating, particularly for offices. Exclusive re-editions of Charles Eames' designs.

Sasha Waddell 47 Anselm Road, SW6 1LH. (10 mins Fulham

Broadway tube.) *Tel*: 071-385 6430. *Open*: by appointment. Exclusive designs inspired by turn-of-century Swedish artist, Carl Larsson. Oak/ash/painted finishes. Elegant, well-proportioned, similar to Arts/Crafts Movement styles. Cot-sofa, tables, chairs, plate rack etc. All to order. Also on view at **Barker's**, see **Department Stores**.

Home Counties/ South East

Graham Mancha Springlands,

Wendover Road, Weston Turville, Aylesbury, Bucks HP22 5TG. *Tel*: (0296) 615121. *Open*: by appointment. Fine, reasonably priced copies of Gerrit Rietveld's designs, such as the famous "Red-Blue Chair", "End Table", and "Berlin Chair". Work is based on original pieces. Also restoration service for Lloyd Loom furniture, plus original Lloyd Loom/1930s classics.

5. LEATHER

Today's upholstery leathers are soft and supple, in furnishing fashion colours that go right through the thickness of the hide. It is the one upholstery covering that doesn't noticeably deteriorate with age.

London Postal Districts

Kingdom of Leather Unit 3, Gallions Road, Charlton SE7 7SA. *Tel*: 081-305 0101. *Open*: 7 days, 10.00am to 6.00pm. Late night Fri, 8.00pm.
Also at: Dorford Wharf, Angel Road, Edmonton N18. *Tel*: 081-807 1642.
And at: Sealand House, North Circular Road, Stonebridge Park, NW10 7QS. *Tel*: 081-961 4933. See also **Home Counties/South East** below.

World of Leather North Circular Road, NW10 7SX. (10 mins Hanger Lane tube. Free parking.) *Tel*: 081-961 4949. *Open*: 7 days, Mon to Fri, 10.00am to 7.00pm, Sat and Sun, 10.00am to 6.00pm. Huge choice of modern leather sofas/chairs, in fashion colours.
Also at: 156 Tottenham Court Road, W1P 9LJ. (2 mins Warren Street

tube.) *Tel*: 071-388 6084. *Open*: 7 days, Mon to Sat, 9.30am to 5.30pm. Late night Thu, 7.30pm. Open Sun, 10.00am to 5.00pm.
And at: Morden Road, Merton SW19 3BL. (10 mins South Wimbledon tube. Free parking.) *Tel*: 081-542 1571. *Open*: Mon to Fri, 10.00am to 7.00pm, Sat 10.00am to 5.00pm.
And at: Clifton's Roundabout, Sidcup Road, SE9 5LT. (Eltham BR, plus bus. Free parking.) *Tel*: 081-850 6483. *Open*: 7 days, Mon 10.00am to 8.00pm, Tue to Sat 10.00am to 6.00pm, Sun 10.00am to 5.00pm. See also **Home Counties/South East** below.

Home Counties/ South East

Kingdom of Leather Thurrock Lakeside Retail Park, Western Avenue, West Thurrock Grays, Essex RM16 1ZB. (Grays BR, plus bus to retail park. Free parking.) *Tel*: (0708) 864162. *Open*: 7 days, 10.00am to 6.00pm. Late night Fri, 8.00pm. 15,000 sq ft of fine leather upholstery, mainly from Italy. Largest collection of leather under one roof, they tell me. Over 100 designs/many colours. High quality, good value.

Free delivery.
Also at: Oaks Retail Park, Harlow, Essex CM20 2AB. *Tel*: (0279) 450066. *Open*: 7 days, 10.00am to 6.00pm. Late night Fri, 8.00pm.
And at: 69 Caversham Road, Reading, Berkshire RG1 8AD. *Tel*: (0734) 560756. *Open*: 7 days, 10.00am to 6.00pm. Late night Thu, 8.00pm.
See also **London Postal Districts** above.

World of Leather Jubilee Square, London Road, Reading, Berks RG1 2TA. (10 mins Reading BR. Free parking.) *Tel*: (0734) 861481. *Open*: Mon to Sat, 10.00am to 6.00pm. Late night Thu, 8.00pm. Open Sun, 10.00am to 5.00pm.
Also at: Lakeside Retail Park, West Thurrock, Essex RM16 1NN. (Off M25; Grays BR plus bus. Free parking.) *Tel*: (0708) 863865. *Open*: Mon to Sat, 10.00am to 6.00pm. Late nights Thu and Fri, 8.00pm. Open Sun, 10.00am to 5.00pm.
And at: 643 Eastern Avenue, Ilford, Essex IG2 6BW. (5 mins Newbury Park tube. Free parking.) *Tel*: 081-554 6721. *Open*: Mon to Sat, 10.00am to 6.00pm. Late night Mon, 8.00pm. Open Sun, 10.00am to 5.00pm. See **London Postal Districts** above.

6. STORAGE AND SHELVING

"Comes Simpson the joyner and he and I with great pains contriving presses to put my books upon, they now growing numerous."

Samuel Pepys, 23 July 1666

The cheapest shelving you make yourself: find materials at **DIY Superstores** and timber merchants. Furniture shops (see **1. General**) offer more sophisticated ideas. Firms listed under **12. Made-to-Measure and Commissioned** can also help.

London Postal Districts

Alcove Designs   103 Lavender Hill, Battersea SW11 5QL. (10 mins Clapham Junction BR.) *Tel:* 071-585 1481. *Open:* Mon to Sat, 9.30am to 5.30pm. Built-in alcove cupboards/shelving. Wardrobes, studies, replacement kitchen doors. Choice of styles and finishes. Fitted in one day. Design/install.

CubeStore   58 Pembroke Road, W8 6NX. (5 mins Earls Court tube.) *Tel:* 081-994 6016 (24 hours). *Open:* Tue, Wed and Fri, 10.00am to 4.00pm, Thu 10.00am to 7.00pm, Sat 10.00am to 5.00pm. Inventor/designer Donald Maxwell has done the country a big service with his flexible/versatile/low-cost storage. Comprehensive range of cupboards, cubes, drawer units, wardrobes, record storage, etc. For home,

office, studio. Finishes include plain chipboard, white/grey melamine, real beech veneer. Colour brochure available. Mail order.

Estia See **Upholstery and Suites 2. Sofabeds**.   Adjustable wall shelving with tubular frames and melamine-faced shelves. Wide range of sizes. "Leaning" shelves that do not need wall fixing.

Charles Hurst Workshop   Unit 21, Bow Triangle Business Centre, Eleanor Street, E3 4NP. (5 mins Bow Road tube.) *Tel:* 081-981 8562. *Open:* by appointment. Bespoke cabinetry: fitted/freestanding. Designed/made/installed.

Ikea See **1. General** above. Check out their shelving: some costs less than the British price of timber.

Marks and Spencer See **Chain Stores**.   Excellent selection of well-finished, tall, attractive bookcases with planked backs. White/natural rattan bookcases.

Pine Grove See **2. Pine and Country** above.   Attractive pine bookcases made-to-measure.

Shelfstore   160 Finchley Road, NW3 5HH. (2 mins Finchley Road tube.) *Tel:* 071-794 0313. *Open:* Mon to Sat, 10.00am to 6.00pm. Ingenious Swedish storage, built from solid pine components; add-on system established for over 12 years. Shelves, cabinets, wardrobes, bunk-

beds, desks, tables and more. Free design service.

Themesetter   164 Bows Road, N11 2JG. (5 mins Arnos Grove tube.) *Tel:* 081-881 9868. *Open for viewing:* Mon to Fri, 9.30am to 5.00pm, Sat 10.00am to 4.00pm, Sun 10.30am to 1.00pm. Fitted storage for living/dining/bedrooms, studies to order. Mahogany, teak, oak, lacquers any colour. Brochures available.
Also at: 733 Sidcup Road, SE9 3SA. *Tel:* 081-880 5944.
See also **Home Counties/South East** below.

Home Counties/South East

Hyperion Fitted Furniture 166 Oatlands Drive, Weybridge, Surrey KT13 9ET. *Tel:* (0932) 884783. *Open:* Mon to Sat, 9.30am to 5.30pm. Freestanding bookcases.

Themesetter   126 Western Road, Brighton, E. Sussx BN1 1DA. *Tel:* (0273) 771915.
Also at: The Mall, Eastbourne, E. Sussx BN21 3NW. *Tel:* (0323) 21029.
And at: 8 Newlands Place, Hartfield Road, Forest Row, East Grinstead, W. Sussx RH19 5DQ. *Tel:* (0342) 824841.
And at: 2 Westgate House, Spital Street, Dartford, Kent DA1 2EH. *Tel:* (0322) 278444.
See also **London Postal Districts** above.

7. CANE

"Cane" describes various materials. Bamboo (now less popular) is hollow with decorative rings and knots. Cane (sometimes called rattan) is solid, and its natural rings and blotches can be enhanced with

clear lacquer. Peeled cane can be stained and lacquered, or lacquered in vast range of colours, though white is most usual. Woven willow or wicker is lightweight; often lacquered white. Cane quality varies

according to method and country of manufacture. Buy from a reputable supplier who can advise on durability: some designs, like the famous Peacock chair (made from very fine cane), are predominantly decorative.

London Postal Districts

Cane Connection   57 Wimbledon Hill Road, SW19 7QW. (2 mins Wimbledon tube/BR.) Tel: 081-947 9152. Open: Mon to Sat, 9.30am to 5.30pm. Large stock of top-quality cane furniture for conservatory/ lounge/bedroom. Natural/coloured cane. Customers' designs made to order.

The Cane Furniture Centre   1/3 and 10 Chingford Road, E17 4PW. (5 to 10 mins Walthamstow Central tube.) Tel: 081-531 8369. Open: 7 days, Mon to Fri, 9.30am to 5.30pm, Sat 9.00am to 5.30pm, Sun 10.00am to 1.30pm. Three stores: vast selections for every room. Instant credit. Deliveries. Exceptionally good prices. Friendly service from well-established family specialists.

The Cane Store See **British Crafts 4. Craft Supplies**.   Cane furniture, plus materials for re-caning.

Chicane   40 Turnham Green Terrace, Chiswick W4 1QP. (3 mins Turnham Green tube.) Tel: 081-995 1229. Open: Mon to Sat, 9.30am to 6.00pm. Small shop conceals two floors of cane/willow furniture, basketware, gifts. Personal service.

Home Time   159/161 Green Lane, Palmers Green N13 4SP. (Wood Green or Arnos Grove tubes, plus bus.) Tel: 081-888 4220. Open: Mon to Sat, 9.30am to 5.30pm. Family business, established in 1972, makes/imports cane/basketware, sprayed white or to your colour choice. Stocks for immediate delivery.

Staks   24 Waterglade Shopping Centre, Ealing Broadway W5. (4 mins Ealing Broadway tube. Waterglade Centre car park.) Tel: 081-566 2245. Direct importers of good quality rattan furniture at marvellous prices. Attractive styles in natural/dark/white cane. Sofas/ armchairs/tables/rockers/storage. Cushions in attractive fabrics. "Staks" of pretty home accessories at bargain prices: well worth a visit, particularly for presents. Delightful in-store coffee shop.
See also **Home Counties/South East** below.

Home Counties/ South East

Cane and Things   55 King Street Parade, Cross Deep, Twickenham, Middx TW1 3SG. (20 yds from corner of King's Street and Cross Deep.) Tel: 081-892 7647. Open: Mon to Sat, 10.00am to 5.30pm. Family business with large warehouse and quick deliveries of cane furniture. Accessories/gifts including pottery, beanbags, cushions; dried/silk flowers.
Also at: 7 Odeon Parade, Isleworth, Middx TW7. (2 mins Isleworth BR.) Tel: 081-568 8113.
And at: 50 The Centre, Feltham, Middx TW13 4AU. (5 mins Feltham BR.) Tel: 081-890 0634.

Cane Direct   New Town Garden Rooms, Burnt Mills Road, Basildon, Essex SS13 1DY. (Off A127, close to M25.) Tel: (0268) 590779. Open: Mon to Sun, 10.00am to 4.00pm. Cane furniture/basketware for every room. Good prices: sold direct by importers. Choice of fabrics for cushion covers/curtains.

Settings   4 Fife Road, Kingston-on-Thames, Surrey KT1 1SZ. (2 mins Kingston BR.) Tel: 081-549 2123. Open: Mon to Sat, 9.30am to 5.30pm (all branches). Lots of pretty cane/pine furniture with fabrics, cushions, lamps, vases. Worth a browse.
Also at: 4/6 Pump Corner, South Street, Dorking, Surrey. (20 mins Dorking BR.) Tel: (0306) 885871.
And at: Designscene, 63 Portsmouth Road, Cobham, Surrey KT11 1JQ. (2 mins off A3.) Tel: (0932) 863650.

Staks   27/29 The Broadway, Old Amersham, Bucks HP7 0HL. (Large car park at rear.) Tel: (0494) 721733. Open: Mon to Fri, 9.00am to 5.30pm, Sat 9.00am to 6.00pm, Sun 1.00pm to 5.30pm. Particularly pretty setting: ideal for a weekend excursion. Fripps Restaurant above store.
And at: 40 Station Arcade, Vicarage Fields, Barking, Essex 1G11 8DQ. (2 mins Barking BR. Park in shopping centre.) Tel: 081-591 1800. Open: Mon to Sat, 9.00am to 6.00pm. Late night Thu, 8.00pm.
And at: 6 The Royals Shopping Centre, High Street, Southend-on-Sea SS1 1DQ. (6 mins Southend Central BR. Park in shopping centre.) Tel: (0702) 612897. Open: Mon to Fri, 9.00am to 5.30pm, Sat 9.00am to 6.00pm.
And at: 34 Market Place, Olney, Bucks MK46 4AJ. (Free parking in Market Square.) Tel: (0234) 711938. Open: Mon to Sat, 9.00am to 5.30pm, Sun 12.00 noon to 5.30pm. In-store coffee shop.
And at: 8 The Quadrant Centre, Old Christchurch Road, Bournemouth, Dorset BH1 2AB. (10 mins Bournemouth BR. Good parking in town centre.) Tel: (0202) 299428. Open: Mon to Sat, 9.00am to 5.30pm.
See also **London Postal Districts** above.

Trumps   9 The Hersham Centre, Hersham, Walton-on-Thames, Surrey KT12 4HL. (M25, junction 10. Large, free car park.) Tel: (0932) 246951. Open: Mon to Sat, 10.00am to 5.30pm. Rattan furniture that's definitely different. Stylish shapes by British designer Arthur Edwards. Bed/dining/living room ranges available in over 30 colour finishes. Upholstered in your fabric choice. Also artificial trees, plants, decorative lamps, baskets, accessories. Good quality. Brochure available.
Also at: 57/59 Poole Road, Westbourne, Bournemouth BH4 9BA. Tel: (0202) 763822.

8. GLASS, MARBLE AND METAL

Smooth and hard, furniture from more unusual materials adds a sophisticated touch to any room.

London Postal Districts

David Davies   10 Great Newport Street, WC2H 7JA. (5 mins Leicester Square tube.) *Tel:* 071-240 2223. *Open:* Mon to Fri, 10.30am to 7.00pm, Sat 10.30am to 6.00pm. This trendy fashion boutique has equally stylish furniture: a delightful discovery and well worth visiting when you are next in the West End. Gracious, modern wrought-iron sofas/tables/chairs etc., hand-forged by Davies' Northumberland blacksmith. Plus elegant cherrywood modern classics. Glass/ceramic/metal accessories.

Diametric Modern Furniture 18 Odhams Walk, Long Acre, Covent Garden WC2E 9SA. (2 mins Covent Garden tube.) *Tel:* 071-240 7493. *Open:* Mon to Sat, 10.00am to 6.00pm. Inventive, witty, minimalist metal shapes designed by Stephen Povey and made in his own factory. Beds, shelving, dining tables and chairs. Plus amazingly original office/domestic interiors.

Glass Distinction   196 New King's Road, SW6 4NF. (3 mins Putney Bridge tube.) *Tel:* 071-731 3460. *Open:* Mon to Fri, 9.30am to 5.30pm, Sat 11.00am to 3.00pm. Mark Elliot designs/makes inventive, all-glass designs for dining/coffee/console tables. Also clocks, mirrors, shelving, bathroom accessories. Special sizes/shapes to order. Also lacquered sideboards, chairs. Plus bedroom furniture sprayed in speckled or satin lacquer to any colour. Colour brochure available.

Iron Age   25 North End Parade,

North End Road, W14 0SJ. (5 mins West Kensington tube.) *Tel:* 071-381 4235. *Open:* Mon to Fri, 9.00am to 5.30pm, Sat 9.00am to 1.00pm. Dave Townsend of Capricorn at the Tasso Forge is one of London's last remaining smiths. Small decorative pieces: chairs and other furniture, candlesticks, firescreens.

McCloud and Co   269 Wandsworth Bridge Road, SW6 2TX. (20 mins Parsons Green tube.) *Tel:* 071-371 7151. *Open:* Mon to Fri, 9.00am to 6.00pm, Sat 9.00am to 1.00pm. The inspirational *Kevin McCloud Decorating Book* revealed its gifted author's formidable flair for decorative effects. His shop sells baroque, finely wrought metalwork for furniture/accessories.

Metalhouse   c/o Oblique Workshops, Stamford Works, Gillette Street N16 8JH. (2 mins Dalston Junction BR.) *Tel:* 071-923 4732. *Open:* by appointment. Steel furniture/lighting inspired by organic forms. Aluminium furniture for large interiors. Chrome-plated/stove-enamelled lights/accessories. Urban-inspired concrete/metal outdoor furniture. Making-up service for clients' own designs.

Monica Pitman   1 Elystan Place, SW3 3LA. (5 mins Sloane Square tube.) *Tel:* 071-581 1404. *Open:* Mon to Fri, 10.00am to 5.00pm. Elegant modern/classical intricate chairs, benches, tables. Plus lighting, mirrors.

Quality Marble See **Tiles 3. Marble, Slate and Stone**.   Table/desk tops cut to size in granite or superb choice of marble colours.

Suzanne Ruggles   90 Fulham Road, SW3 6HR. (7 mins South Kensington tube.) *Tel:* 071-584 3329. *Open:* Mon to Fri, 10.00am to 5.30pm, Sat 10.00am to 5.00pm. This determined

young designer uses the skills of British blacksmiths to produce fine, elegant furniture in an original modern idiom.

Soho Design   535 King's Road, SW10 0SZ. (10 mins Fulham Broadway tube.) *Tel:* 071-376 5855. *Open:* Mon to Sat, 10.00am to 6.00pm. Late night Wed, 7.00pm. New shop reflects new "right" image for "wrong" end of King's Road. Peter Leonard's tubular/wrought-iron designs have become modern classics: particularly Gothic range.

The Steel Studio   206b Bedford Hill, SW12 9HJ. (10 mins Balham tube/BR.) *Tel:* 081-673 5492. *Open:* by appointment. One-off/limited edition contemporary metalwork with classical features. Furniture, gates, chandeliers, candlesticks.

Stone Age   231 Sandycombe Road, Kew TW9 2EW. (7 mins Kew Gardens tube.) *Tel:* 081-940 4511. *Open:* Mon to Fri, 9.00am to 5.00pm, Sat 10.00am to 4.00pm. Well-established stonemasons, offering specialist selections of reasonably priced British/Continental metal furniture.

Townhouse Interiors   25g Lowndes Street, Belgravia SW1X 9JF. (5 mins Knightsbridge tube.) *Tel:* 071-235 3180/9. *Open:* Mon to Fri, 9.30am to 5.45pm, Sat 10.00am to 5.00pm. Closed Sat from 1.00pm to 2.30pm. Unusual furniture in clear Perspex acrylic sheet: largest collection in London. Imported Italian top makes, including Fabian of Rome. Every size of table. Upholstered furniture. Interior design service.

8×4   A Block, East Cross Centre, Waterden Road, E15 2HN. (5 mins Hackney Wick BR.) *Tel:* 081-985 6001. *Open:* by appointment. Design/make modern furniture in metal/timber/glass/marble to order.

9. PAINTED

The current fashion for painted finishes includes dragging, marbling, stippling and the like: ideal, in pastel shades, for bulky pieces to minimise size. Decoration can be painted free-hand, or stencilled. Why not try out your own skills on furniture that's secondhand?

London Postal Districts

Bella Figura See **Lighting 2. Traditional and Antique.** Wide range of delicate painted furniture.

Robert and Colleen Bery Designs 157 St John's Hill, SW11 1TQ. (5 mins Clapham Junction BR.) *Tel:* 071-924 2197. *Open:* Mon to Sat, 10.00am to 6.00pm. Exclusive handpainted chests, tables, bedheads by leading stencil artists.

Chalon UK The Plaza, 535 King's Road, SW10 0SZ. (Sloane Square tube, plus bus.) *Tel:* 071-351 0008. *Open:* Mon to Sat, 10.00am to 6.00pm. Kitchen room settings. Handmade country/classical furniture.
See also **Worth a Trip** below.

Dragons See **Children's Rooms.** Specialists in handpainted furniture. Made by craftsmen in firm's own workshops, and decorated by Rosie Fisher's team of artists, based largely in Sussex. Chests, bedside tables, storage boxes, etc. with stippled/marbled/sponged backgrounds for handpainted motifs.

Tom Faulkener Hand-Painted Furniture 13 Petley Road, W6 9SU.

Tel: 071-610 0615. *Open:* by appointment. Wonderful, colourful, flamboyant designs for tabletops.

Hayloft See **12. Made-to-Measure and Commissioned** below. Experts in painted furniture.

Hutson Designs Unit 208a Belgravia Workshops, Marlborough Road, N19 4NF. (10 mins Archway tube.) *Tel:* 071-281 9986/4175. *Open:* Mon to Fri, 9.30am to 5.30pm. Exquisite furniture: handmade in Sussex and handpainted in Islington by a team of 20 trained artists: "No stencils." Some pieces for immediate delivery. Serpentine bedside cabinets: real satinwood, handpainted classical motifs. Small "tip-top" tables which fold flat to show pretty paintwork. Tray tables. Dining tables/chests/ corner cupboards. TV cabinets/ headboards. Special designs/colours to order: eg commemorative pieces/ special presents.

Meaker and Son See **Children's Rooms.** Victorian/period-style furniture designed/painted to order.

Old Pine and Painted Furniture 594 King's Road, SW6 2DX. (10 mins Fulham Broadway tube.) *Tel:* 071-736 5999. *Open:* Mon to Sat, 10.00am to 5.30pm. Antique country styles (all originals) painted by hand in the prettiest of colours, then decorated with flowers/fruits/birds/ garlands by artists. But quite expensive. Tables/chairs/dressers/ cupboards/wardrobes. Each piece is carefully aged with rubbed/faded colours. Bookcases to order.

Home Counties/ South East

Duskminster Monk's Hill, Smarden, Kent TN27 8QJ. *Tel:* (0233) 77541. *Open:* Mon to Fri, 9.30am to 5.00pm (phone first). Extensive range of pretty furniture painted to match your wallpaper/ fabric. Also available through stockists.

George Robertson Prospect Cottage, Three Leg Cross, Ticehurst, E. Sussx TN5 7HL. *Tel:* (0860) 821921. *Open:* by appointment. George Robertson designs/makes/ paints furniture/decorative items. Murals, paint effects and other decorative work.

▶ Worth a Trip

Chalon UK Old Hambridge Mill, Hambridge, near Langport, Somerset TA10 0BP. (Taunton BR. Customer collection service.) *Tel:* (0458) 252374. *Open:* by appointment. Around 2,000 sq ft interlinking showrooms in old mill. Antique country furniture, handpainted in old-look finishes.

Palladian Plum 100 Whiteladies Road, Clifton, Bristol, Avon BS8 2QY. *Tel:* (0272) 741133. *Open:* Mon to Sat, 9.30am to 5.30pm. Handpainted furniture made to order. Wrought-iron candelabra, lamps, furniture. Picture-framing, mirrors, fabrics, cushions, beds, stencils. Mail order.

10. DESKS

The cheapest desks are secondhand, and several shops specialise in used office equipment, which may include filing cabinets, plan chests and so on for that authentic, high-tech touch!

London Postal Districts

▶ Bargains!

Andrews Office Equipment   48 Shepherd's Bush Road, W6 7PT. (5 mins Shepherd's Bush tube.) Tel: 071-602 6767. Open: Mon to Fri, 9.00am to 5.00pm, Sat 9.00am to 2.00pm. Large selections new/used office furniture.

The Desk Depot   274 Queenstown Road, SW8 3ND. (2 mins Queenstown Road/Battersea Park BR.) Tel: 071-627 3897. Open: Mon to Sat, 9.00am to 5.30pm, Sun by appointment. Reconditioned/reproduction desks. Filing cabinets/tables. Made to order bookcase/alcove units. Releathering service.

Estia See **Upholstery and Suites 2. Sofabeds.**   Smart, modern desks in tubular steel/melamine. Filing drawers, including trolleys. Plan chests.

▶ Bargains!

Ron Harris Business Equipment Unit 3B, Juno Way, Elizabeth Industrial Estate, New Cross, SE14 5RW. (20 mins New Cross Gate tube.) Tel: 081-469 2442. Open: Mon to Fri, 9.00am to 5.30pm. Office furniture, reasonable prices.

Just Desks   20 Church Street, NW8 8EP. (Close to M40. Edgware Road tube.) Tel: 071-723 7976. Open: Mon to Sat, 9.30am to 6.00pm. Three floors of showrooms in 150-year-old building. Antique/repro desks, chairs, filing cabinets, writing tables, bookcases. Home computer desk with "wire management". Good quality, keen prices, quick deliveries. Commissions. Restoration. Releathering including DIY postal kit with full instructions.
Also at: 6 Erskine Road, NW3 3AJ. (Chalk Farm tube.) Tel: 071-722 4902. Open: Mon to Sat, 9.30am to 5.30pm. Large, open showroom, 6,000 sq ft. Full range.

▶ Bargains!

Office System Services   Stirling Works, Canning Road, Abbey Lane Junction, Stratford E15 3NO. (5 mins West Ham tube.) Tel: 081-534 4191. Open: Mon to Fri, 8.30am to 5.30pm, Sat 10.00am to 1.00pm. Closed for lunch, 1.00pm to 2.00pm. Huge, secondhand stocks. Desks/filing cabinets/screens. Substantial discounts on new furniture.

▶ Bargains!

Wagstaff Office Equipment   46/68 De Beauvoir Crescent, N1 5AU. (10 mins Old Street tube.) Tel: 071-923 1212. Open: Mon to Fri, 9.00am to 5.00pm. Over 10,000 sq ft new/used reconditioned office furniture.

Quality ex-hire executive desks/filing cabinets/swivel chairs. Plan chests. Drawing-boards.
Also at: 10 Fulham High Street SW6 3LQ. (5 mins Putney Bridge tube.) Tel: 071-736 6360/3624. Open: Mon to Fri, 9.00am to 5.00pm.

Home Counties/ South East

The Dorking Desk Shop   41 West Street, Dorking, Surrey RH4 1BU. (Own parking.) Tel: (0306) 883327. Open: Mon to Fri, 8.00am to 5.30pm, Sat 10.30am to 5.30pm (closed for lunch on Sat, 1.00pm to 2.00pm). This narrow shop opens into a large warehouse. "The best selection of antique desks and writing furniture in the country," says owner Jan Elias, who has been collecting/restoring for over 20 years. Rolltops/secretaires/bureaux. Knee-hole desks. Over 30 partners' desks. Local/international deliveries. "Finding service" for odd sizes or rare types.

▶ Worth a Trip

David Burkinshaw   Sugworth Farmhouse, Borde Hill Lane, Haywards Heath, W. Sussx RH16 1XP. (1 mile Haywards Heath BR. 47 mins Victoria BR.) Tel: (0444) 459747. Open: Mon to Sat, 9.00am to 5.00pm (appointments advisable). Expert antique restorer works in 500-year-old farmhouse on around 20 genuine 18th/19th-century desks, all for sale. Excellent investments. Send £5 and desk top size required for photos of appropriate stock.

11. REPRODUCTION

"I love it I love it, and who shall
    dare
To chide me for loving that old arm
    chair,
I've treasured it long as a holy prize,
I've bedewed it with tears, and
    embalmed it with sighs;
Tis bound by a thousand bands to
    my heart;
Not a tie will break it, not a link will
    start.
Would ye learn the spell, a mother
    sat there,
And a sacred thing is that old arm
    chair."

Eliza Cook, 1836

London Postal Districts

Heritage   154/156 Upper
Richmond Road West, East Sheen,
London SW14 8AG. (Richmond
tube/BR plus bus.) *Tel:* 081-876 3886.
Open: Mon to Sat, 10.00am to
6.00pm, Sun 11.00am to 4.00pm (1st
in month only). Mahogany/yew
desks, bureaux, occasional tables,
bookcases, TV/video cabinets,
stereo units, sideboards, chests in
18th-century styles. Dining chairs in
14 designs, Regency drum edge and
standard dining tables from 6ft
upwards.

Lexterten   289/293 Neasden Lane,
Neasden Shopping Centre, NW10
1QR. (6 mins Neasden tube.
Shopping centre car park.) *Tel:* 081-
450 9922.
See also **Home Counties/South East**
below.

Parsons Green Reproductions
151 Lower Richmond Road, Putney
SW15 1EZ. (20 mins Putney Bridge
tube.) *Tel:* 081-788 7477. *Open:* Mon
to Sat, 9.30am to 5.30pm. Late night
Wed, 8.00pm. Six large showrooms
with quality reproductions in
mahogany/yew. Mostly ex-stock.
Catalogues available.

Simon Pugh   79 Walton Street,
SW3 2HP. (5 mins South Kensington
tube.) *Tel:* 071-823 9311. *Open:* Mon
to Fri, 9.30am to 6.00pm, Sat
10.30am to 5.00pm. Now trading
under his own name (formerly
Antique Designs) and from bigger
premises, Simon Pugh stocks
decorative Italian reproduction
furniture; Biedermeier/Empire.
"Papa" Biedermeier was an early
19th-century cartoon character. His
name (from *bieder*, plain, and *Meier*,
a common German surname) was
applied to the solid, simple furniture
style that originated in Vienna
between 1815–30. Reproductions suit
new or old schemes. Lighter
hardwoods (cherry, maple, walnut)
with fruitwood/ebony ornamentation.
Simon Pugh discovered Italian
craftsmen making this style 5 years
ago. Also Art Deco, Georgian,
Colonial Indian and Dutch Colonial.
Also exhibitions of contemporary
artists/sculptors/designers.

Youngs Reproduction Furniture
570/574 Commercial Road, Stepney
E14 7JD. (Next to Docklands Light
Railway—Limehouse.) *Tel:* 071-790
4474/4691. *Open:* Mon to Sat,
9.30am to 6.30pm. Closed all day
Thu. Open Sun, 10.00am to 2.00pm.
Mahogany veneers with some yew.
Large selection, warehouse cash-
and-carry prices. Delivery service
available. Storage for TV/video/hi-fi.
Also dining room ranges, nests of
coffee tables, corner cabinets,
library bookcases. Plus full range
office furniture. French polishing,
renovations, colour matching in own
workshops.

Home Counties/ South East

Brights of Nettlebed   Kingston
House, Nettlebed, near Henley-on-
Thames, Oxon RG9 5DD. (Henley
BR, plus coach.) *Tel:* (0491) 641115.
Open: Tue to Sat, 9.00am to 5.30pm.

Probably the largest collection of
reproduction furniture under one
roof in the UK, if not in Europe:
8,000 sq ft of handmade 17th/18th-
century styles. Oak/walnut/
mahogany/yew from 40 cabinet
makers, including own Exeter
workshops. Immediate deliveries, or
to order: 10 to 12 weeks. Tailor-
made upholstery. Furniture on
approval.
Also at: Topsham, Torquay, Devon.

British Antique Replicas   School
Close, Queen Elizabeth Avenue,
Burgess Hill, near Brighton, E. Sussx.
(5 mins Burgess Hill BR.) *Tel:* (0444)
245577. *Open:* Mon to Sat, 9.00am
to 5.30pm. Closed for lunch, 1.00pm
to 2.00pm. Antique/reproduction
dining furniture: 18th, 19th, 20th
centuries.

Lexterten   16/20 The Causeway,
Teddington, Middx TW11 0HE. (2
mins Teddington BR.) *Tel:* 081-977
9244/8080. *Open:* Mon to Sat,
9.30am to 5.30pm (all branches).
Substantial manufacturer (own Kent
workshops)/retailer reproduction
furniture. Founded in 1971:
management buy-out in 1990. 53
showrooms/in-store concessions
nationwide. Furniture for dining
room/lounge/office/ occasional use.
Regency/Victorian copies plus
period styles for TV/hi-fi etc.
Mahogany/yew finishes, with
inlays/marquetry. Competitive
prices/good quality. Free deliveries.
For free brochure, tel: 081-977
9244/8080.
Also at: 38 London Road, Bromley,
Kent BR1 3QR. (10 mins Bromley
North BR. Hill car park.) *Tel:* 081-
460 1515.
And at: 3/6 Savoy Parade, Southbury
Road, Enfield, Middx EN1 1RT. (5
mins Enfield Town BR. Shopping
centre car park.) *Tel:* 081-363 6456.
And at: 186/190 High Road, Ilford,
Essex. (5 mins Ilford BR. Car parks
nearby.) *Tel:* 081-478 2434.
And at: 12/14 Madrid Road,
Guildford, Surrey GU2 5NT. (Near

cathedral. 5 mins Guildford BR. Park outside.) *Tel:* (0483) 576010. *And at:* 39 High Street, Tunbridge Wells, Kent TN1 1XL. (2 mins Tunbridge Wells BR. Car park behind station.) *Tel:* (0892) 38858. See also **London Postal Districts** above.

Stuart Interiors Barrington Court, Ilminster, Somerset TA19 0NQ. (Taunton BR. Company will collect. M3, junction 7.) *Tel:* (0460) 40349.

Open: Mon to Fri, 9.00am to 5.00pm, Sat 10.00am to 5.00pm. Or by appointment. Magnificent National Trust lichen-encrusted Elizabethan manor house: the most beautiful "shop" I have ever visited. Fabulous showcase for Tudor/Stuart furnishings. Green labels: antiques. Red labels: faithful, loving reproductions. Complete design/furnishing service for early houses, or lovers of earlier English interiors. Particularly attractive: authentic-

looking repro dining chairs, upholstered with authentic fabrics. *Also at:* Seechem Manor, off Rowney Green Lane, Alvechurch, Worcs B48 7EL. (Close to M42.) *Tel:* 021-445 2240. *Open:* Mon, Wed, Fri and Sat, 9.00am to 5.30pm. Please write/ring for appointment. Well-restored medieval hall house with 17th/18th-century adaptions. Period interiors by Stuart Interiors. Handmade furniture, antiques, fabrics, lighting. Tapestries, pottery, treen, brass, tiles.

12. MADE-TO-MEASURE AND COMMISSIONED

Many of the architectural joinery firms listed under **Walls 3. Wooden Mouldings** and **4. Panelling** can supply bespoke furniture. As can many of the joinery firms listed under **Staircases.** Specialists in made-to-measure furniture are also listed in **Bedrooms** and **Kitchens.**

London Postal Districts

John Coleman A–Z Studios, Hardwidge Street, SE1 3SY. *Tel:* 071-403 0016. *Open:* by appointment. Furniture to commission in beautiful woods by leading designer-maker. Tables, chairs, mirrors, occasional pieces.

Contemporary Applied Arts See **British Crafts 3. Craft Shops and Galleries.** Commissioning service for best of British modern art/crafts/furniture. See slides/portfolios, discuss requirements.

The Crafts Council 44a Pentonville Road, Islington N1 9BY. (2 mins Angel tube.) *Tel:* 071-278 7700. *Open:* Tue to Sat, 11.00am to 6.00pm, Sun 2.00pm to 6.00pm. Expert, friendly commissioning advice. Slides/portfolios etc.

Hayloft Woodwork 3 Bond Street, Chiswick W4 1QZ. (5 mins Turnham Green tube.) *Tel:* 081-747 3510.

Open: Mon to Fri, 10.00am to 3.00pm, or by appointment. Late night Thu, 7.30pm. Cole Manson is an inspired woodworker with a theatrical background. He and his team can make virtually anything in wood: sympathetic/professional.

Timothy Hine Kingsgate Workshops, 110/116 Kingsgate Road, NW6 2JG. (10 mins Brondesbury BR.) *Tel:* 071-328 2824. *Open:* by appointment. Simple modern furniture in solid timber, made to order.

Charles Hurst Workshop Unit 21, Bow Triangle Business Centre, Eleanor Street, E3 4NP. *Tel:* 081-981 8562. *Open:* by appointment. Bespoke cabinetry: fitted/freestanding. Designed/made/installed.

The David Linley Co 1 New King's Road, SW6 4SB. (10 mins Fulham Broadway tube.) *Tel:* 071-736 6886. *Open:* Mon to Fri, 10.00am to 6.00pm, Sat 10.00am to 5.00pm. David Linley, Parnham trained, expresses his love affair with wood in sensitive, careful, commissioned cabinetry enriched with exotic veneers and marquetry . . . The ultimate in aristocratic elegance, at aristocratic prices. But you can buy a royal candlestick for £20.

Oblique Stamford Works, Gillette St, N16 8JH. (2 mins Dalston

Junction BR.) *Tel:* 071-249 7363. *Open:* by appointment. Distinctive, practical, beautifully constructed furniture. Limited editions of own designs; one-off commissions.

Stemmer and Sharp Furniture 2 Wren Street, WC1X 0HA. (10 mins King's Cross tube/BR.) *Tel:* 071-837 1627. *Open:* by appointment. Simple designs of folding furniture for small living spaces, in sustainable hardwoods.

James Summers 1a Fawe Street, E14 6PD. (5 mins Devon's Road BR.) *Tel:* 071-987 8145. *Open:* by appointment. One-off beds, cupboards, dressers, tables etc. in solid timber, veneers, laminates, coloured finishes. Designed/made to order.

Workshop 43 Bow Triangle Business Centre, Eleanor Street, E3 4NP. *Tel:* 081-980 1583. *Open:* by appointment. Andrew Cabrelli makes purpose-built furniture. Wardrobes/bookcases/hardwood kitchens. Modern designs.

Home Counties/ South East

Nicholas Dyson Unit 2, Home Farm, Ardington, Wantage, Oxon OX12 8PN. *Tel:* (0235) 634311. *Open:* by appointment. Distinctive modern furniture designed/made to commission.

Robin Evans The Furniture Workshop, Warlies, Upshire, Waltham Abbey, Essex EN9 3SL. *Tel:* (0992) 767403. *Open:* Mon to Sat, 8.30am to 6.00pm. Telephone first for an appointment. Contemporary furniture in sustainable hardwoods.

Exquisite Interiors Bagshot Road, Chobham Village, Surrey GU24 8BP. (M25/M3 intersection.) *Tel:* (0276) 858885. *Open:* Mon to Sat, 9.00am to 1.00pm. Custom-made fitted furniture.

FB Design David James Forrest, 14 Hazel Road, Four Marks, Alton, Hants GU34 5EY. (Alton BR, plus bus.) *Tel:* (0420) 64470 and (0962) 733432. *Open:* by appointment. Skilled/imaginative furniture designers/makers. Solid hardwood/ veneers, fibreboard/laminates. Contemporary/traditional commissions.

Fowler and Brace Castle Ditch Lane, Lewes, E. Sussx BN7 1YZ. *Tel:* (0273) 479680. *Open:* by appointment. Fine contemporary furniture in hardwoods. Designed/ handmade to order.

Keith Gray and Co Great Priory Farm, Panfield, Braintree, Essex CM7 5BQ. (2 miles Braintree BR.) *Tel:* (0376) 24590. *Open:* 7 days, 9.00am to 9.00pm, but telephone first for appointment. High quality, made-to-measure furniture/joinery for every room: tables/chairs/doors/ architraves. Very personal service.

Neil Griffin 1 Primrose Hill, Waterloo Lane, Holwell, Herts SG5 3SS. *Tel:* (0462) 712655. *Open:* by appointment. Custom-built, traditional furniture.

Lucinda Leech Furniture King Street, Jericho, Oxford OX2 6DF. *Tel:* (0865) 56376. *Open:* by appointment. Custom-made tables,

chairs, desks, cabinets in British/ American/tropical hardwoods.

John Presswood Rooks Farm, Rotherwick, Hook, Hants RH27 9BG. *Tel:* (0256) 768400. *Open:* by appointment. Beautiful bespoke furniture, jewel chests, small items in solid hardwoods. Personal design service. Lovely to use/touch, functional/long-lasting. Repairs.

Wales and Wales The Longbarn Workshop, Muddles Green, Chiddingly, E. Sussx BN8 6HW. (20 mins Lewes BR.) *Tel:* (0825) 872764. *Open:* by appointment. Husband and wife partnership, specialising in commissioned furniture in English hardwoods. Also light-duty ash/bent birch screens in stock/to order.

Richard Williams 5 The Maltings, School Lane, Old Amersham, Bucks HP7 0ES. *Tel:* (0494) 729026. *Open:* by appointment. Traditional woodworking techniques for contemporary design in finest timbers/veneers.

13. AVANT-GARDE

"You can't invent a design. You recognise it, in the fourth dimension. That is with your blood and your bones as well as with your eyes."

D H Lawrence (1885–1930)

See also **8. Glass, Marble and Metal** above.

London Postal Districts

Aero See **1. General** above. Designer Paul Newman puts the avant-garde into mass production.

AKA 70 Rivington Street, EC2 3AY. (3 mins Old Street tube.) *Tel:* 071-729 0820. *Open:* by appointment. Five designers make one-off pieces with "1950s American Deco feel", in wood/metal/glass/concrete.

Atrium See **4. 20th-Century Classics: Original and Copies** above. A showcase for the finest modern Italian designers: classics of the future, alongside classics of the past.

James Codrington Unit 5, Sullivan Enterprise Centre, Sullivan Road, SW6 3DJ. *Tel:* 071-371 0618. *Open:* by appointment. One of the most exciting new furniture designers. Sculptured, free-flowing forms combining wood, glass and metal in sumptuous synthesis. Furniture becomes art, which inevitably is reflected in high prices.

Jakki Dehn A–Z Studios, 3 Hardwidge Street, SE1 3SY. *Tel:* 071-378 0512. *Open:* by appointment. Furniture/accessories to commission: creative artist offers exceptionally

fine craftsmanship. Here elegant, often fanciful shapes combine with metal/rare woods/inlays. Sensitive interpretations of clients' requests. Highly recommended.

Dirc Products 155 Ferme Park Road, Crouch End N8 9BP. *Tel:* 081-348 5490. *Open:* by appointment. Unusual shapes in wood/stainless steel/copper. Individually made to commission.

Tom Dixon Furniture 12 Dolland Street, SE11 5LN. (5 mins Vauxhall tube/BR.) *Tel:* 071-820 0288. *Open:* by appointment. A rising reputation is reflected in the rising prices of these charismatic chairs. Unquestionably unique.

DMK Designs 1/5 Chance Street, E1 6JT. *Tel:* 071-739 4253. *Open:* by appointment. *New showroom:* 70

Mornington Road, NW1. (1 min Mornington Crescent tube.) *Tel:* 071-383 5131. *Open:* Mon to Sat, 10.30am to 5.00pm. Beautiful, bow-fronted cabinets with curved doors, elegant upright glazed panels, bun feet. Marvellous range of finishes: stain black with red; natural mahogany with crossbanding; red/blue/green crackle over black.

Julienne Dolphin-Wilding   34 Cecil Rhodes House, Goldington Street, NW1 1UG. *Tel:* 071-380 0950. *Open:* by appointment. Unique, over-sized chairs by this young artist are already collectors' pieces. For indoor/outdoor use. Raw materials include Thames driftwood, rope, boat chandlery and telegraph poles.

David Gill Furniture   60 Fulham Road, SW3. (5 mins South Kensington tube.) *Tel:* 071-589 5946. *Open:* Mon to Sat, 10.00am to 6.00pm. This delightful gallery elevates modern artefacts to art status. Watch out for trend-setting special exhibitions.

Graham and Green See **Accessories 1. General**.   Antonia Graham has a keen eye for the very new.

Gerald Moran Interiors   Goulding House, 85 Heath Street, NW3 6UG. (1 min Hampstead tube.) *Tel:* 071-435 4098/431 3665. *Open:* Mon to Sat, 9.30am to 5.30pm. Sun viewing 1.00pm to 5.00pm. Highly individual, modern Italian/German pieces in an exquisite art gallery atmosphere: hardwoods, aluminium, marble, glass. Reproduction classics of Charles Rennie Mackintosh, Frank Lloyd Wright. Handmade English rugs: modern abstract patterns, unusual shapes. Decorative antiques. Go there.

One Off   62 Chalk Farm Road, NW1 8AN. (5 mins Chalk Farm tube. Opposite Roundhouse.) *Tel:* 071-379 7796. *Open:* Mon to Fri, 10.00am to 6.00pm, Sat by appointment. Ron Arad, original *enfant terrible* of 1980s British furniture design, is still ''terrible'' although (like all of us) no longer an *enfant*. Essential viewing for serious design buffs. But steel/

concrete chairs are not so very cosy . . . and dreadfully expensive.

Pearce Pieces   31 Appach Road, SW2 2LD. *Tel:* 081-674 2074. *Open:* by appointment. Would you welcome a hippo in your livingroom? Many do. Carved in limewood with a glass top, he is one of Derek Pearce's far-fetched but fetching tables. Other natty numbers include seals, duckponds and reclining nudes . . . not for the faint-hearted.

Pearl Dot   2 Roman Way, N7 8XG. (5 mins Caledonian Road tube.) *Tel:* 071-609 3169. *Open:* Mon to Fri, 9.00am to 6.00pm. Please ring first. Open Sat and Sun by appointment. Patiently, and through sheer merit over 15 years, Robert Williams has built this modern furniture craftshop into an international centre of excellence for batch production. His distinctive designs in solid hardwoods are in regular demand: particularly the Plank dining chair, with its tall, curved back. Look for the hallmark . . . a little inlaid mother-of-pearl dot, of course.

Sharon Plant   *Tel:* 071-354 3073. *Open:* by appointment. This energetic, charismatic champion of modern art/crafts runs a modern art/crafts commissioning service from her Highbury home, which she calls The Applied Arts Showhouse. She can put you in touch with 400 craftspeople through a 5,000 slide index, plus displays. Mainly furniture, also glass, ceramics. Friendly, approachable.

SCP See **Furniture 4. 20th-Century Classics: Originals and Copies** above.   Founded in a Shoreditch converted factory in 1985 by Sheridan Coakley, who has brought formidable energy and entrepreneurial skills to the cause of modern furniture design. He presents architects Nigel Coates, Matthew Hilton and Jasper Morrison. A visit is well worth any effort involved.

Something Wild   17 Monmouth Street, WC2H 9DD. (3 mins Covent Garden tube.) *Tel:* 071-497 0398. *Open:* Mon to Wed, 10.30am to

5.30pm, Thu to Sat, 11.30am to 6.30pm. Gina Newman proffers a warm welcome: she is a fervent style enthusiast and fifties fan. Zany, original furniture, some with a dash of Deco, some fifties style, some firmly nineties. Plus affordable, fake fur cushions—zebra, leopard, tiger. And crazy zebra/dotty china. Wow!

Tribeca Designs   16 Lena Gardens, W6 7PZ. (5 mins Hammersmith tube.) *Tel:* 071-371 1532. One-off/limited batch modern ''aero dynamic'' furniture in steel/leather by Swiss-born designer Stephan Preisig. Exciting, curvy, tapered shapes in chrome, glass, wood and leather.

Robert Troke Furniture   Unit 11, Summerstown, SW17 0BQ. *Tel:* 081-879 3230. *Open:* by appointment. Exquisite bow-fronted chests and other high-class joinery gems. Worth investigating.

Viaduct Furniture   Spring House, 10 Spring Place, NW5 3BH. (5 mins Kentish Town tube.) *Tel:* 071-284 0156. *Open:* Mon to Sat, 9.30am to 6.00pm, Sat by appointment. Large showroom for innovatory British contemporary designs, marketed throughout Britain and abroad. Martin Ryan's work is simple, subtle and sparse. Nicholas Kary balances traditional/modern materials for a timeless quality. Plus avant-garde Italian imports. Worth a visit.

Home Counties/ South East

Nigel Lofthouse   The Old Church, Rishangles, Suffolk IP23 7JZ. *Tel:* (0379) 71715. *Open:* by appointment. This unpretentious, friendly designer (a firm family man) handmakes unique, one-off chairs/tables/lamps of astounding originality. Handpainted leather and stained wood is embellished with horn, parchment, pewter, copper, and rich braids/tassels. Style is heavily decorative, in rich, dark colours. Pieces have all the exuberance of tribal art and make fine focal points for modern rooms. See them.

Stephen Owen   The Studio, Whipley Manor Farm, Bramley, near Guildford, Surrey GU5 0LL. (A281, 6 miles south of Guildford.) *Tel:* (0483) 278309. *Open:* Mon to Fri, 9.00am to 5.00pm, Sat by appointment. Works closely with clients on imaginative, distinctive, individualistic pieces: he has made,

for example, a cutlery canteen as a scale model of Charterhouse School Chapel! Much of his wood has been recycled from recent storms.

Nicholas Tatt Furniture   The Furniture Workshop, Warlies, Upshire, Waltham Abbey, Essex EN9 3SL. (2 mins M25, junction 26.) *Tel:* (0992) 767403. *Open:* by appointment. Distinctive, contemporary furniture from timber/

glass/metal. One-off pieces/small batches.

Rupert Williamson   5 New Bradwell Workspace, St James' Street, Milton Keynes MK13 0BW. *Tel:* (0908) 221885. *Open:* by appointment. One-off pieces are already established as antiques of the future, and have been sold through Sotheby's.

14. ANTIQUES

Antique shops flourish in London and the South East. Good areas to explore include the Fulham and King's Roads, Westbourne Grove/Portobello Road, Camden Town, Kensington Church Street and Pimlico Road. Go and admire the treasures on show in Bond Street. There are also many antique markets, which give small traders an under-cover permanent base. They are well worth browsing through, and often surprisingly affordable.

London Postal Districts

Adam Rooms   18/20 The Ridgeway, SW19 4LN. (10 mins Wimbledon tube/BR.) *Tel:* 081-946 7047. *Open:* Mon to Sat, 10.00am to 5.30pm. Good selections of domestic 18th- and 19th-century antique furniture: dining tables/chairs/ sideboards. Very reasonable prices: "much cheaper than Bond Street!" Full interior design service. Own workshops for repairs/restorations.

Alfies Antique Market   13/25 Church Street, NW8 8DT. (5 mins Marylebone/Baker Street tubes.) *Tel:* 071-723 6066. *Open:* Tue to Sat, 10.00am to 6.00pm. This is the largest covered antique market in the UK: 200 dealers with 370 stands sell a huge range of antiques and collectables, from £5 to £15,000.

Antiquarius   135/141 King's Road, SW3. (Sloane Square tube.) *Tel:* 071-351 5353. *Open:* Mon to Sat, 10.00am to 6.00pm. Over 120 dealers, with a wide range of antiques from all periods: clocks, watches, silver, glass, jewellery, antiquarian books, boxes, paintings, prints, porcelain and collectors' items.

Bermondsey Antique Market   Long Lane, SE1. *Tel:* 071-351 5353. *Open:* Fri, 7.00am to 2.00pm. Dealers are here from 5.00am or earlier.

Bond Street Antiques Centre 124 New Bond Street, W1. (Bond Street/Green Park tubes.) *Tel:* 071-351 5353. *Open:* Mon to Fri, 10.00am to 5.45pm, Sat 10.00am to 4.00pm. Top traders sell antique jewellery, silver, watches, porcelain, glass, Oriental antiques and paintings.

Chenil Galleries   181/183 King's Road, SW3. (Sloane Square tube.) *Tel:* 071-351 5353. *Open:* Mon to Sat, 10.00am to 6.00pm. Reputable for Art Deco/Art Nouveau and fine art, as well as being specialist dealers in 18th- and 19th-century paintings, textiles, period clothing, books, prints, silver and toys.

Cutler Street Antique Market Goulston Street, E1. *Tel:* 071-351 5353. *Open:* Sun, 7.00am to 2.00pm.

The Dining Room Shop   62/64 White Hart Lane, Barnes SW13. (Hammersmith tube, plus bus.) *Tel:* 081-878 1020. *Open:* Mon to Sat, 10.00am to 5.30pm. Unique service: the only shop in the country to specialise in everything for the dining room. Around 75% is antique, such as furniture, glass, china, linens. Services: furniture finding, repro and modern, furniture made to measure; dinner services to customer's designs.

Duke's Yard Antiques Market   1a Duke Street, Richmond. *Tel:* 081-332 1051. *Open:* Tue to Sat, 10.00am to 6.00pm. 70 dealers. Roof-top café.

Eldridge of London   99/101 Farringdon Road, EC1R 3BT. (1 min Farringdon tube.) *Tel:* 071-837 0379. *Open:* Mon to Fri, 10.00am to 5.00pm, Sat 10.00am to 1.00pm. Original 18th-/19th-century furniture, not restored/repolished. 500 items always on display.

The Furniture Cave   533 King's Road, SW10 0TZ. (10 mins Fulham Broadway tube.) *Tel:* 071-352 4229. *Open:* Mon to Sat, 10.00am to 6.00pm, Sun 11.00am to 4.00pm. One of the largest collections of antique furniture in London. 17 individual galleries: 17th- to 19th-century English/Continental furniture/furnishings, architectural salvage, garden ornaments, Oriental furniture, paintings, Art Deco, antique pine.

Grays Antique Market   58 Davies Street, W1Y 1LB. (1 min Bond Street tube.) *Tel:* 071-629 7034. *Open:* Mon to Fri, 10.00am to 6.00pm. Over 100 dealers. Large variety of antiques. Cafeteria.

Grays in the Mews   1/7 Davies Mews, W1Y 1AR. (2 mins Bond Street.) *Tel:* 071-629 7034. *Open:* Mon to Fri, 10.00am to 6.00pm. Over 100 dealers and a large variety of antiques. Cafeteria, bureau de change.

HRW Antiques   4a Kings Avenue, SW4 8BD. (5 mins Clapham Common tube.) *Tel:* 071-978 1026. *Open:* Mon to Fri, 10.00am to 5.00pm, Sat 10.00am to 1.00pm, or by appointment. Converted warehouse with lavish displays of antiques in room settings.

Old English Antiques   190 Westbourne Grove, W11. (Off Portobello Road.) *Tel:* 071-727 2699. *Open:* Mon to Sat, 9.30am to 6.00pm. Large shop on three levels with good selections of cherry and oak reproduction country furniture. Also furniture made to individual requirements.

Phelps   133/5 St Margaret's Road, East Twickenham, Middx TW1 1RG. (Next to St Margaret's BR.) *Tel:* 081-892 1778/7129. *Open:* Mon to Fri, 9.00am to 5.30pm, closed for lunch, 1.00pm to 2.00pm. Open Sat, 9.00am to 5.00pm. Established 1870: antique/reproduction Victorian/ Edwardian furniture modified into video cabinets/bookcases. Restorations, reupholstery. Fabrics, wallpapers, full interior design service.

17

HEATING

Warmth is an invisible furnishing. You can't see it, you don't exactly use it, but you certainly feel its absence and life is miserable without it. What gives out the warmth in your home should be attractive, economical, easy to control and maintain, and safe. Bear this in mind when you discuss your heating needs with the specialists in this chapter.

1. RADIATORS

There are now radiators available in many materials, colours, shapes and sizes for "designer" central heating. So allow time to make a careful choice. For genuine, period cast-iron radiators (ideal for restoration work), try the suppliers listed under **Architectural Salvage.**

London Postal Districts

Bisque   244 Belsize Road, NW6 4BT. (5 mins Kilburn Park tube.) *Tel:* 071-328 2225. *Open:* Mon to Fri, 9.00am to 5.30pm, Sat 10.00am to 1.00pm. Geoffrey Ward pioneered the designer radiator: his shop is "more like an art gallery than a plumber's merchant". There is a huge choice of sizes/colours/styles, from old-fashioned pillar to ultra-modern sculptural wall panels, long and low or tall and thin. Towel/skirting radiators. UK agents for stunning Arbonia series from Switzerland. Any colour from Dulux Colour Dimensions 1650 shades, or metallic gold/bronze/chrome/nickel. "Heatcalc" computer programme instantly estimates radiators required for any room size. Site visits from engineers.

Diamond Merchants   43/45 Acre Lane, SW2 5TN. (10 mins Brixton tube/BR.) *Tel:* 071-274 6624/5. *Open:* Mon to Fri, 8.00am to 5.30pm, Sat 9.00am to 5.00pm. Plumbing/heating supplies. Large, independent, service-conscious. Combination boiler specialists. *Also at:* 371 Lewisham High Street, SE13 6NZ. *Tel:* 081-690 8445.

The Gas Shop   122/126 Kilburn High Road, NW6 4HY. (5 mins Kilburn tube.) *Open:* Mon to Sat, 9.00am to 5.00pm. Stylish new version of traditional gas showrooms. Explore over two floors: the Heat Shop, the Shower Shop, and the Money Shop.

Monogram Cabinets
291 Cricklewood Lane, NW2 2JL. *Tel:* 081-455 9962. *Open:* Mon to Fri, 9.30am to 6.00pm. Cabinets individually made to any size. Wide choice of styles/grille patterns. Easy access to valves.

▶ **Bargains!**

Priority Plumbing Supplies
80b Uxbridge Road, W13 8RA. (10 mins Ealing Broadway tube.) *Tel:* 081-579 2288. *Open:* Mon to Fri, 7.30am to 5.00pm, Sat 8.00am to 2.00pm (all branches). Discount prices for large range boilers/radiators/copper tube. Press steel baths/lagged cylinders. Watch out for "bargain buys": sometimes a bottle of Scotch is thrown in! Services: radiator angling/curving; white/gold plating.
Also at: 86 Askew Road, W12 9BJ. *Tel:* 081-749 2966.
And at: 175 Uxbridge Road, W12 9RA. *Tel:* 081-740 5952.

Radiating Style   194 New King's Road, SW6 4NF. (5 mins Putney Bridge tube.) *Tel:* 071-736 0600. *Open:* Mon to Fri, 9.30am to 5.30pm, Sat 9.30am to 1.30pm. Every conceivable radiator shape/colour. Column radiators to almost any length: sections in tubular steel/steel fins/pressed steel. Zehnder Multicolumn made-to-order in thousands of sizes/1,600 colours, plus chromed/metallic finishes. Traditional cast-iron radiators. Narrow tubular radiators for room dividers. Wanplan skirting system. Trough heating. Low surface-temperature radiators for children/old people. Well-designed valves in chrome/bronze/gold. Paint-spraying service for old/new radiators.

The Radiator Cover Company
167 Lower Richmond Road, SW14 7HX. (5 mins Mortlake BR.) *Tel:* 081-392 2058. *Open:* Mon to Fri, 10.00am to 5.00pm, Sat 10.00am to

4.00pm. Established 5 years; initiators of the cover-up craze. All covers made to order: measuring/fitting included in price. Service within M25 area. Choice of fronts includes Screenlite, wooden lattice, rattan, and brass grilles. Orders take about four weeks.

Rainbow Fairweather   555 King's Road, SW6 2EB. (10 mins Fulham Broadway tube.) *Tel:* 071-736 8693. *Open:* Mon to Sat, 9.30am to 5.30pm. Tailor-made Cover Charm radiator covers. Variety of grilles in hardwood and brass. Colour brochure available. Also bespoke hardwood panelling specialists.

A Touch of Brass See **Doors 2. Door Furniture and Specialist Ironmongery.**   Service for boxing-in radiators, with a wide choice of decorative grilles.

Home Counties/ South East

▶ **Bargains!**

Ashford Heating Supplies
193 London Road (A30), Staines, Middx TW18 4HR. *Tel:* (0784) 459432. *Open:* Mon to Fri, 8.00am to 5.30pm. Large stocks of top heating brands; substantial discounts. Sanitaryware/shower equipment.

Gas Works   Lakeside Retail Park, West Thurrock, Essex RM16. (M25, junction 30/31.) *Tel:* (0708) 863366. *Open:* 7 days, Mon to Thu, 10.00am to 6.00pm, Fri and Sat, 9.00am to 6.00pm, Sun 10.00am to 5.00pm. Late night Thu, 8.00pm. British Gas Superstore. Relaxed, spacious. Central-heating systems, fires, cookers. Fitted kitchens/bathrooms. Power showers. Accessories. Installations.

2. FIREPLACES

"'A clear fire, a clean hearth and the rigour of the game.' This was the celebrated wish of old Sarah Battle (now with God), who, next to her devotions, loved a good game at whist."

Charles Lamb (1775–1834), *Essays of Elia*

The past 20 years have seen a major revival of the Great British Fireplace. The firms below will help you take part. Make sure installers are properly trained and experienced. Mistakes can be not only expensive, but dangerous. For genuine old fireplaces, see also **Architectural Salvage**.

London Postal Districts

Acquisitions 269 Camden High Street, NW1 7BX. (3 mins Camden Town tube.) *Tel:* 071-485 4955. *Open:* Mon to Sat, 9.00am to 5.00pm. Specialists in reproduction Georgian/Edwardian/Victorian cast-iron fireplaces (available also from 150 stockists nationwide). Victorian reproduction tiles. Log/coal gas fires. Installations. Brochure £2 (refundable).

The Antique Fireplace Warehouse 194/196 Battersea Park Road, SW11 4ND. (5 mins Queenstown Road/ Battersea Park BR.) *Tel:* 071-627 1410. *Open:* Mon to Sat, 9.00am to 6.00pm. Original antique English fireplaces: "the largest stock in London". 1,600 sq ft display space, 4,000 sq ft warehousing. Marble, pine, cast-iron fireplaces, plus gas coal-effect fires. Expert period advice; experienced fitters. Brochures available.

Elegance 570 Romford Road, Manor Park E12 5AS. (2 mins Manor Park BR.) *Tel:* 081-553 1066. *Open:* Mon to Sat, 10.00am to 5.00pm. Late night Mon, 8.00pm. Ornate classical

plaster fire surrounds. Also cornices/ ceiling decorations/wall panels at keen prices. Fitting service.

The Fire Place 257 High Street, Eltham SE9 1TY. (5 mins New Eltham BR.) *Tel:* 081-850 4887. *Open:* Mon to Sat, 9.00am to 5.30pm. Family business, "quality service". Victorian/Edwardian original fireplaces plus handmade marble reproductions, made-to-measure if necessary. Log/coal gas fires. Over 50 fireplaces on display. Service/ advice. Installations, own fitters. Brochure available.
Also at: 1 Burnt Ash Hill, Lee SE12. (1 min Lee BR.) *Tel:* 081-857 2229.

Firecraft 188 Northfield Avenue, Ealing W13 9SJ. (7 mins Northfields tube.) *Tel:* 081-840 4077. *Open:* Mon to Sat, 9.00am to 5.00pm. Original Victorian cast-iron fireplaces, pine and mahogany mantels, coal-effect gas fires. Model marble works for surrounds, hearths etc. at keen prices. Fenders/fireguards. Installations. Brochure available.

Fireplace Designers 157c Great Portland Street, W1N 5FB. (5 mins Great Portland Street tube.) *Tel:* 071-580 9893/4. *Open:* Mon to Fri 9.30am to 5.30pm, Sat 9.30am to 4.00pm. Hand-carved/handfinished traditional mantelpieces, classical fire grates. Individual orders made-to-measure.

H and D Fireplace Company 70 Mountgrove Road, Highbury N5 2LT. (10 mins Arsenal/Finsbury Park tubes.) *Tel:* 071-359 8179. *Open:* Mon to Sat, 9.00am to 6.00pm, Sun by appointment. Antique/ reproduction fireplaces. Other architectural items include leaded lights. 5,000 sq ft of showroom, workshops, warehouse. Restorations, installations. Search service. Brochure available.

Hallidays Carved Pine Mantelpieces 28 Beauchamp Place, SW3 1NJ. (10

mins Knightsbridge tube.) *Tel:* 071-589 5534. *Open:* Mon to Fri, 10.00am to 6.00pm. Carved pine mantelpieces.
See also **Home Counties/ South East** below.

C Kent (Fireplaces) 14 Greyhound Road, W6 8NX. (10 mins Hammersmith/Fulham Broadway tubes.) *Tel:* 071-385 1494. *Open:* Tue to Fri, 10.00am to 5.00pm, Sat 9.00am to 4.00pm. Clinton Kent sells restored antique iron fireplaces. Antique tiles are also available. No reproductions. John Gregory makes pine surrounds. "We deliberately remain small (no staff!) to keep prices down."

La Belle Cheminee 81/85 Albany Street, NW1 4BT. (3 mins Great Portland Street tube.) *Tel:* 071-486 7486. *Open:* Mon to Fri, 10.00am to 5.00pm, Sat 10.00am to 1.00pm. Showroom filled with unique decorator designs by Robert Hamilton, the great fireplace innovator. See the Obelisk, and the Deco Arc de Triomphe. Exotic materials: lapis lazuli/gold/smoked glass/stainless steel . . . it's more like a jeweller's. Marble/fossil stone. Free-standing metal designs; Provençal limestone fireplaces. Plus semi-assembled kits from leading European manufacturers. Also cash-and-carry warehouse.

Old Flames 22 Battersea Rise, SW11 1EE. (5 mins Clapham Junction BR. Parking opposite.) *Tel:* 071-228 7594. *Open:* Mon to Fri, 9.30am to 5.30pm, Sat 9.30am to 5.00pm. Everything for marble, cast-iron and pine mantels. Shotblasting, cleaning, welding, taking out, installing. Gas log/coal fires fitted. Friendly advice.

Realistic Fires 133/135 Kingston Road, Wimbledon SW19 1LT. (10 mins Wimbledon tube/BR.) *Tel:* 081-543 2170. *Open:* Mon to Sat, 9.30am to 5.30pm. Closed Fri (Jun to Aug). Antique cast-iron/marble fireplaces. Gas coal fires. Installations.

Thornhill Galleries   rear of 78 Deodar Road, Putney SW15 2NJ. (5 mins East Putney tube.) Tel: 081-874 2101/5669. Open: Mon to Fri, 8.30am to 5.00pm, Sat 9.00am to 12.00 noon. Family firm. English/French period chimney pieces. Period panelling, architectural items. Garden statuary. Also at: 76 New King's Road, Fulham SW6 4LT. (8 mins Parsons Green tube.) Tel: 071-736 5830. Open: Mon to Fri, 10.00am to 5.00pm, Sat 9.00am to 2.30pm.

Home Counties/ South East

Galleon Claygate   216/230 Red Lion Road, Tolworth, Surbiton, Surrey KT6 7RB. (Tolworth/Surbiton BR. Own car park.) Tel: 081-397 3456. Open: Mon to Fri, 9.00am to 5.00pm, Sat 9.00am to 4.00pm. Largest fireplace showroom in the South (they claim). Gas coal-effect fires, DIY kits, fireside accessories. Over 100 fireplaces: ceramic, period, stone, slate, marble, cast-iron, briquette. Traditional and contemporary hole-in-the-wall designs. Installations within a 50-mile radius. Free colour brochure available.

Hallidays Carved Pine Mantelpieces The Old College, High Street, Dorchester-on-Thames, Oxon OX10 7HL. (Off A423.) Tel: (0865) 340028. Open: Mon to Fri, 9.00am to 5.15pm, Sat 10.00am to 5.00pm. Period showroom for pine mantelpieces carved on the premises in traditional Georgian styles. Marble slips, infills, hearths. Grates, accessories. Also period pine panelling. Designs to customers' specifications.
See also **London Postal Districts** above.

Marble Hill Fireplaces   70/72 Richmond Road, Twickenham, Middx TW1 3BE. (5 mins Twickenham BR.) Tel: 081-892 1488. Open: Mon to Sat, 10.00am to 5.30pm. Expert, personal service. Quality fireplaces handcrafted in own workshops. Waxed pine, white, limed and painted finishes. Adam-style firebaskets for open fires or log/coal-effect gas fires. Also electric fires and mahogany or oak mantelpieces. Large selection antique French marble mantels. Old-style fenders (made-to-measure service for three designs); fire irons, fire screens, tile surrounds. Over 30 colours marble slips and hearths. Sixteen-page colour brochure.

Petit Roque   5a New Road, Croxley Green, Rickmansworth, Herts WD3 3EJ. (Rickmansworth/Croxley tubes.) Tel: (0923) 779291/720968. Open: Mon to Fri, 9.00am to 5.30pm, Sat 9.00am to 4.00pm. Early closing Wed, 1.00pm. Late night Fri to 8.00pm. Extensive showrooms, established nearly 30 years. Particularly caters for DIY enthusiasts. Exclusive fireplace designs, each with installation instructions. Individual design and installation within 50-mile radius. French stone wall cladding. Exclusive hand-carved mantel surrounds in yew, cherry, lime, mahogany, oak etc. Copper, brass, stainless steel canopies. Chimney extraction fans. Advisory service on problem chimneys. Marble, panelling, beams, fireplace accessories.

M A Pope (Fireplaces)   14 Western Parade, Great North Road, Barnet, Herts EN5 1AD. (5 mins High Barnet tube.) Tel: 081-449 5893. Open: Mon to Sat, 10.00am to 5.30pm. Closed Thu. Established 28 years. Large displays fireplace designs, made in their Potters Bar factory. Marble, mahogany, pine, briquettes. Hole-in-the-wall kits. Helpful colour leaflet available. Also marble vanity units.

3. STOVES

Nick Hills (0865) 748-652

Stoves (enclosed heaters which burn coal, smokeless fuel or wood) are romantic and practical, bringing the heat out into a room. They provide a decorative and emotional focal point. Get advice from a specialist supplier on the types best suited to your needs and chimney. Homes without a chimney can be provided with one: some stoves even come with their own.

London Postal Districts

The Ceramic Stove Company (London Showcase)   Chesil Court Studios, Chelsea Manor Street, SW3 5QP. Tel: 071-351 2481. Open: by appointment.
See also **Home Counties/South East** below.

Gallery La Cornue   62 Westbourne Grove, W2 5SH. (10 mins Queensway tube.) Tel: 071-792 0991. Open: Mon to Fri, 9.00am to 5.00pm. New, larger showroom for exclusive French stoves based on traditional kitchen range. Made from stainless steel/nickel-plated steel/ bronze. Hand-built to order, with clients' choice of features. Built-in ovens/rotisseries. Bespoke hardwood kitchen furniture accommodates stoves/hobs. Extraction systems. "Five-star" service plan. Twice-monthly cooking demos by top chefs. Installations.

Home Counties/ South East

The Ceramic Stove Company
387 Cowley Road, Oxford OX4 2BS. *Tel*: (0865) 748652. Swedish 18th-century wood-burning stoves, hand-built to order, covered with plain/decorated tiles, standard/bespoke. Heights from 180 to 360cm.
See also **London Postal Districts** above.

Country Stoves Lower Road, Cookham, Berks SL6 9EH. (5 mins Cookham BR. A4094.) *Tel*: (06285) 28262. *Open*: Mon to Sat, 9.00am to 5.30pm. Closed for lunch Sat 1.00 to 2.00pm. (Close Sat 1.00pm, Apr to Aug.) 25 wood/multifuel/gas-fired stoves on display. Rayburn cookers. Pine surrounds, cast-iron inserts, gas log- and coal-effect fires. Selkirk chimney systems. Full installation service. Log baskets/accessories. Fire care products: marble polishes/black spray. Cooking demonstrations every six weeks in winter.

Cranleigh Heating Supplies
Littlemead Industrial Estate, Cranleigh, Surrey GU6 8ND. *Tel*: (0483) 277173. *Open*: Mon to Fri, 8.00am to 5.30pm. Closed for lunch, 1.00pm to 2.00pm. Open Sat, 9.00am to 12.00 noon. Discount prices for Rayburn cookers. Central heating/plumbing supplies. Boilers/flues/radiators. Sanitaryware/showers.

The Morley Stove Shop •
Coronation Hall, Coronation Road, Ware, Herts SG12 9DX. (A10. Easy parking.) *Tel*: (0920) 468001. *Open*: Tue to Fri, 9.00am to 5.00pm, Sat 9.00am to 4.00pm. Around 25 stoves on display, many installed and working. Solid fuel/gas/wood. From Britain, America, France, Belgium, Scandinavia. Rayburn Nouvelle, gas-fired Vermont Burlington, Godwin, Morley. Chimney linings. Installations.

The Stove Shop The Street, Hatfield, Peveral, Chelmsford, Essex CM3 2DY. (Just off A12. 10 mins Chelmsford BR.) *Tel*: (0245) 380471. *Open*: 7 days, Mon to Fri, 9.00am to 5.30pm, Sat 10.00am to 5.00pm, Sun 11.00am to 4.00pm. Woodburning stove specialist John Opie has purpose-built premises for Jotul/Coalbrookdale/Rayburn stoves and cookers burning wood/coal/gas/oil. Full fitting service. Fireside accessories/brassware. Chinese ceramics, cast iron, bronzes and more.

Mail Order

Chase Heating and Plumbing Merchants Pickersleigh Road, Malvern, Worcs WR14 2QP. *Tel*: (0684) 892224. Nationwide deliveries. Solid-/multi-fuel stoves/cookers. Discounts on radiators/controls/boilers. National distributors of Rayburn cookers. Showroom at Head Street, Pershore, Worcs WR10 1DA.

The Hot Spot 53/55 High Street, Uttoxeter, Staffs ST14 7JQ. *Tel*: (0889) 565411. Robust woodburning stoves at low prices. Plain no-nonsense designs, in six sizes. Popular for homes, caravans, boats, workshops.

The Graham Wright Stove Company 303 Bolton Road, Edgworth, Bolton BL7 0AW. *Tel*: (0204) 852076 (24 hours). Nationwide deliveries/discount prices on leading makes/models gas and multi-fuel stoves in cast iron/steel. Around half are British, half imported from Europe. Brochures available.

▶ Worth a Trip

Country Cookers 5 Sherford Street, Bromyard, Here and Worcs HR7 4DL. *Tel*: (0885) 483633. *Open*: Mon to Fri, 9.30am to 5.00pm. Closed for lunch, 1.00pm to 2.00pm. Open Sat, 9.30am to 4.30pm. Family business. Rebuilt/reconditioned Agas/Rayburn cookers: good savings. Wide range of cookers and stoves. Also own designs of new wood burning stoves. Nationwide deliveries.

4. FIRESIDE ACCESSORIES

Keep your fire burning smoothly and add style to your hearth. Most specialists (see **2. Fireplaces** above) offer a good choice of coal buckets, firescreens, tongs and so on. A hunt among **Architectural Salvage** shops may also be profitable. Handmade items are often offered by craft shops (see **British Crafts**).

London Postal Districts

La Belle Cheminee See **2. Fireplaces** above. Firebaskets, firegrates. Tinted glass firescreens. Leather fenders. Tools; mesh spark curtains.

Locks and Handles See **Doors 2. Door Furniture and Specialist Ironmongery.** Eight brass fender styles, from simple ball-and-rail to majestic club. Some adjustable, some made to order. Iron firebacks/spark screens, including classic nursery guard, and Gothic arch. Pokers/log rollers/bellows.

Fire dogs/companion sets. Grates, including Adam/chestnut styles.

David Mellor See **Kitchens 9. Kitchenware.** Good selection of handmade English log baskets: deep with two handles for carrying. Various shades, from pale stripped to red/brown barks.

Home Counties/ South East

Acres Farm Fenders Acres Farm, Bradfield, Berks RG7 6JH. *Tel:* (0734) 744305. *Open:* by appointment. Club fenders, handmade by craftsmen in any size/design. Copies can be made from photographs. Brass, steel, copper, wood or any combination.

Fire and Iron Gallery See **British Crafts 7. Metalwork.** Modern grates, fire irons, screens etc. by designer blacksmiths. In stock/to commission.

Marble Hill Fireplaces See **2. Fireplaces.** Made-to-measure brass fenders, brass coal buckets, hanging fire irons. Antique/brass firescreens.

Mail Order

Erme Wood Forge Woodlands, Ivybridge, Devon PL21 9HF. *Tel:* (0752) 892343. *Open to personal callers:* Mon to Fri, 9.00am to 4.00pm. Firebaskets, spark-proof firescreens, firedogs, from their designs or yours. Made-to-measure service. Excellent leaflet on the history of the great British grate. Send two 1st-class stamps. Also ornamental gates, balustrades, weather vanes etc. Suppliers/ restorers to the National Trust.

Luscombe Bellows Luscombe Farm, Buckfastleigh, Devon TQ11 0JD. *Tel:* (0364) 42373. Fine handmade bellows in elm, oak or beech. Bellow/restoration. Mail order catalogue.

---

5. LOG AND COAL-EFFECT GAS FIRES

Even people who hate fakes admit that gas coal- and log-effect fires are incredibly realistic. Coals are usually more convincing than logs. But although they look cheery, they are not, on the whole, very fuel-efficient.

London Postal Districts

Gas Coal Fires 50 Honor Oak Park, Forest Hill SE23 1DY. (2 mins Honor Oak BR.) *Tel:* 081-291 1748. *Open:* Mon to Sat, 10.00am to 5.00pm. Closed all day Wed. Dedicated personal service from experienced gas fitter and wife.

Coal-effect gas fires a speciality. Victorian/marble fireplaces. Customers journey from all over the country.

The Gas Log Fire Centre 232 Fulham Road, SW10 9NB. (15 mins Gloucester Road tube.) *Tel:* 071-352 2560/351 5298. *Open:* Mon to Sat, 10.00am to 6.30pm. Extensive range of gas log-/coal-effect fires. Working displays of gas log fires. Installations.

La Belle Cheminee See **2. Fireplaces** above. Robert Hamilton introduced coal-/log-effect gas fires into Britain in 1974. See them burning now complete with pine cones (true or false?). Colour crystals for multi-coloured flames; twigs for real-life aromatic incense; woodland moss-effect embers; flame gas lighters.

Real Flame 80 New King's Road, SW6 4LT. (8 mins Parsons Green tube.) *Tel:* 071-731 3056/2704. *Open:* Mon to Sat, 9.30am to 5.30pm (both branches). Largest manufacturer in Europe (they claim) of decorative log-/coal-effect gas fires. Fireplace designers. Supply/fit complete fireplaces in timber/marble from their huge range, or to your own design. Qualified builders/ fitters. Courteous, painstaking, personal service. New: decorative gas fire that needs no chimney. *Also at:* 26 Sydenham Road, SE26. *Tel:* 081-659 5899.

18

LIGHTING

Lighting possibilities range from the shimmering central chandelier, the tried-and-tested table lamp and the ubiquitous spotlight, to the modern mysteries of halogen and low-voltage systems. London's specialists will, of course, illuminate the matter.

"I'm not frightened of the darkness outside. It's the darkness inside the house I don't like."

Shelagh Delaney, British dramatist

A whole range of light fittings is available from the stores below, which can offer specialist advice.

London Postal Districts

After Dark Lighting
229 Kensington High Street, W8 6SA. (5 mins Kensington High Street tube.) Tel: 071-937 6314. Open: Mon to Sat, 9.00am to 6.30pm, Thu 10.00am to 7.00pm. Modern, traditional, classic fittings arranged in groups: bedroom, livingroom, garden, kitchen, bathroom, hi-tech. Friendly, helpful staff. Design advice.

BhS See **Chain Stores**. Buy nothing until you've seen what's on offer at BhS. Their stylish selections, modern and traditional, remain unrivalled for price.

Chelsea Lighting Design Unit 1, 23a Smith Street, Chelsea SW3 4EJ. (10 mins Sloane Square tube.) Tel: 071-824 8144. Open: Mon to Fri, 9.30am to 5.30pm, Sat 10.00am to 4.00pm. Interior designers Sandra Newton and Tom Oates have created a new showroom to demonstrate lighting effects. Low-voltage fittings. Miniature track systems. Concealed cornice lighting. Mini-recessed wall/step lights. Fibre optics. Display lighting. In-home consultancy or full lighting design service (chargeable).

John Cullen Lighting 216 Fulham Palace Road, W6 9NT. Tel: 071-381 8944. Open: Mon to Fri, 9.30am to 5.30pm, Sat 11.00am to 4.00pm. Emphasis here is on lighting effects. Magical displays show light distribution of fittings (many of which are exclusive): up-lighters/down-lighters/tracks/spots. Plus the potential of new, low-voltage halogen lighting. Specialist garden section. Consultancy service for lighting design.

Home-Lights 98 Berwick Street, W1V 3PP. (10 mins Piccadilly Circus tube.) Tel: 071-437 3443. Open: Mon to Fri, 10.00am to 6.00pm, Sat 10.00am to 5.00pm. Traditional/modern lighting; statues, busts, columns, mirrors. Lampshades made to order.
Also at: Umaka Lampshade Co, 5a Walkers Court, Brewer Street, W1R 3FQ. Tel: 071-437 5193.
And at: Helen Lane Antiques, 212 Camden High Street, NW1. (1 min Camden Town tube.) Tel: 071-267 6588. Open: Wed to Sun, 11.00am to 6.00pm, ring first.

Into Lighting Design 49 High Street, SW19 5AX. (5 mins Wimbledon tube/BR.) Tel: 081-946 8533. Open: Mon to Fri, 9.30am to 5.30pm, Sat 9.30am to 1.30pm. Good source for modern European lighting, with many exclusive lines. Low-voltage designs, plus "intelligent" controls. Design/supply/install for single call-out fee.

Lightworks 94 Tottenham Court Road, W1P 9HE. (5 mins Tottenham Court Road tube.) Tel: 071-637 4858/071-436 2250. Open: Mon to Sat, 9.30am to 6.00pm. Modern lighting specialists. Schemes/layouts. Expert advice, installations.

London Lighting Company
135 Fulham Road, SW3 6RT. (5 mins South Kensington tube.) Tel: 071-589 3612. Open: Mon to Sat, 9.30am to 6.00pm. Large, modern showroom, with high quality Continental/English fittings. Expert advice.

Menos 225/227 High Street, Acton W3 9BY. (15 mins Acton Town tube.) Tel: 081-993 7013. Open: 7 days. Mon to Fri, 9.30am to 6.00pm. Late night Thu, 7.00pm. Open Sat, 9.30am to 6.30pm, Sun 10.30am to 5.00pm. Large showroom selling from stock/to order. Modern/traditional designs. Crystal chandeliers; brass, spots, wall lights, table and floor lamps. Friendly advice. Workshop carries out alterations.

Millet Lighting 118/120 Brompton Road, Knightsbridge SW3 1JJ. (1 min Knightsbridge tube.) Tel: 071-581 5555. Open: Mon to Fri, 9.00am to 6.00pm, Sat 9.00am to 5.30pm. Exclusive light fittings from all over the world. Chandelier cleaning. Catalogue available, nationwide delivery, installations.

Mr Light 275 Fulham Road, SW10 9PZ. (5 mins South Kensington tube.) Tel: 071-352 7525. Open: Mon to Sat, 9.30am to 6.00pm (both branches). Mike Piercy is Mr Light. He's been trading since 1975, with a wide choice of well-priced modern/traditional British/Continental designs. Downlights, track systems, low-voltage spots, wall/floor halogen uplighters. Brochures available. International mail order.
Also at: 279 King's Road, SW3 5EW. (10 mins Sloane Square tube.) Tel: 071-352 8398.

Quip 243 Westbourne Grove, W11 2SE. (5 mins Notting Hill Gate tube.) Tel: 071-727 5377. Open: Tue 2.30 to 6.00pm, Wed to Sat, 10.00am to 6.00pm. Architectural lighting consultants, with stylish indoor/outdoor light fittings in stock/to order.

Ryness 34/41 White Lion Street, N1 9PQ. (3 mins Angel tube.) Tel: 071-278 8993. Open: Mon to Sat, 9.00am to 6.00pm (all branches). Over 3,000 electrical lines for DIY enthusiasts/electrical contractors. Light fittings: interior, exterior, garden. Tracks, spots, down-lighters, recessed etc. Cables, 1,500 light bulbs, sockets, switches, telephones,

small appliances. Ceiling fittings turned on for demonstrations. Expert, friendly approach has led to rapid expansion.
Also at: 326 Edgware Road, W2. *Tel*: 071-723 5376.
And at: 54 Fleet Street, EC4. *Tel*: 071-353 0575. Closed Sat.
And at: 67 Camden High Street, NW1. *Tel*: 071-387 4594.
And at: 84 Victoria Street, SW1. *Tel*: 071-828 8377. Closed 5.30pm Sat.
And at: 211 Kensington High Street, W8. *Tel*: 071-937 9830.
And at: 103 King Street, Hammersmith W6. *Tel*: 081-741 4398.
And at: 37 Goodge Street, W1. *Tel*: 071-636 9681.
And at: 45 Old Compton Street, W1. *Tel*: 071-437 8833.
See also **Home Counties/South East** below.

Christopher Wray's Lighting Emporium See **2. Traditional and**

Antique below.   CW is best known for period lighting. But at its massive new showrooms you will find modern fittings, including low-voltage halogen track. Uplighters, downlighters, wall floods, pin spots available. Bulb Boutique: every type of lamp. Cast-iron, 19th-century spiral leads to Lighting Laboratory: experiment with different lighting, using cut-away ceiling, chimney breast and kitchen.

Home Counties/ South East

Caz Systems   19 Church Street, Brighton, E. Sussx BN1 1RB. (5 mins Brighton BR.) *Tel*: (0273) 26471. *Open*: Mon to Sat, 10.00am to 6.00pm. Sleek Italian modern designs. Affordable, low-voltage halogen. Design service. Installations.

Private Lives See **Interior Design**.   Decorator lighting demonstrated in a beautiful converted barn. Low-voltage halogen for minimal elegance. Ceramic bases/handmade silk shades, any style. Glass/marble column lamps. Handpainted bases. Hall lanterns. Wall sconces.

Ryness   184 High Street, Sutton, Surrey. *Tel*: 081-643 8339. See also **London Postal Districts** above.

28 Lighting   28 East Street, Saffron Walden, Essex CB10 1LS. (M11, junction 8/9.) *Tel*: (0799) 522133. *Open*: Mon to Sat, 9.00am to 5.30pm. Lighting designer/engineer John Collins can design/supply/ install any scheme. Modern/classic stock.

---

2. TRADITIONAL AND ANTIQUE

London Postal Districts

Ann's Lighting   34a/b Kensington Church Street, W8 4HA. (8 mins Kensington High Street tube.) *Tel*: 071-937 5033. *Open*: Mon to Fri, 9.00am to 6.00pm, Sat 9.00am to 5.30pm. Good range traditional lighting. Handmade lampshades to order. Conversions/repairs.

Tulissio de Beaumont   277 Lillie Road, SW6 7PN. (15 mins Fulham Broadway tube.) *Tel*: 071-385 0156. *Open*: Mon to Sat, 10.00am to 6.00pm. Genuine period lighting, mostly 1850 onwards. Chandeliers, lamps, wall-brackets. Restoration of small chandeliers. Bronzes/ decorative pieces.

Bella Figura   715 Fulham Road, SW6 5UL. (2 mins Parsons Green tube.) *Tel*: 071-371 9147. *Open*: Mon

to Fri, 9.30am to 6.00pm, Sat 10.00am to 5.30pm. Classic fittings, lamps, shades. Copies of Florentine, 18th-century chandeliers/wall lights; gilded or painted metal. Handmade silk lampshades to order in clients' fabrics/card/parchment. Distinctive lampbases: ceramic/wood/glass. Repairs, conversions, rewires.

Besselink and Jones   99 Walton Street, SW3 2HH. (5 mins South Kensington tube.) *Tel*: 071-584 0343. *Open*: Tue to Fri, 10.00am to 5.30pm, Sat 10.00am to 4.00pm. High quality repro/antique lighting. Lamp conversions/repairs.

Fergus Cochrane   570 King's Road, SW6 2DY. (10 mins Fulham Broadway tube.) *Tel*: 071-736 9166. Lighting antiques from Regency to Deco. Lampbases, lanterns, chandeliers, table lamps.

Dernier and Hamlyn   47/48 Berners Street, W1P 3AD. (10 mins

Tottenham Court Road/Oxford Circus tubes.) *Tel*: 071-636 0122. *Open*: Mon to Fri, 9.00am to 5.00pm. More than 200 styles of repro, 18th-/19th-century light fittings; eight different finishes. Catalogue available.

* **The End of Day Lighting Co** 54 Parkway, NW1 7AH. (2 mins Camden Town tube.) *Tel*: 071-485 6846. *Open*: Tue to Sat, 9.00am to 5.30pm. Handmade copies of Victorian/Edwardian/Deco styles. Brochures available.

* **Jones (Antique Lighting)** 194 Westbourne Grove, W11 2RH. (5 mins Notting Hill Gate tube.) *Tel*: 071-229 6866. *Open*: Mon to Sat, 9.30am to 6.00pm. Largest selection of original lighting in Europe: Victorian, Edwardian, Art Nouveau, Art Deco, 1860–1960.

* **The Lamp Gallery** 355 New King's Road, Fulham SW6 4RJ. (5 mins

Putney Bridge/Parsons Green tubes.) *Tel*: 071-736 6188. *Open*: Mon to Sat, 10.00am to 6.00pm. Authentic decorative lighting from around 1815–1950. Good displays, competitive prices.

Oddiquities   61 Waldram Park Road, Forest Hill SE23 2PW. (2 mins Forest Hill BR.) *Tel*: 081-699 9574. *Open*: Mon to Fri, 10.00am to 5.00pm. Closed all day Thu and Sat. Established 27 years. Genuine, pre-1930s lighting, including converted gas models, all rewired. Fire/furniture/general antiques.

Tempus Stet   Trinity Business Centre, 305/309 Rotherhithe Street, SE16 1EY. (5 mins Surrey Quays tube. Ample parking.) *Tel*: 071-231 0955. *Open*: strictly by appointment. "Let time stand still." Or roll gently backwards. Unique collection of decorator lighting, moulded from resins into wonderful wall-lights, chandeliers, lamp bases. Nine finishes: three burnished gilts; dull French grey, verdigris, and Chinese red; and three woods: limed oak, medium oak and grained mahogany. Colour catalogue £3.50.

Tindle   168 Wandsworth Bridge Road, SW6 2UQ. (10 mins Fulham Broadway tube.) *Tel*: 071-384 1485. *Open*: Mon to Fri, 9.30am to 5.30pm, Sat 10.00am to 5.30pm. Large displays repro/antique/decorative lighting. Wall and ceiling lights; chandeliers. Lamp conversions. Shades to order.

Turn On Lighting   116/118 Islington High Street, Camden Passage N1 8EG. (5 mins Angel tube.) *Tel*: 071-359 7616. *Open*: Tue to Sat, 10.30am to 5.00pm. Genuine antique lighting, 1840–1940. Wall lamps, chandeliers, table/standard lamps. Original shades, varying designs/colours. Fittings converted for North Sea Gas!

Christopher Wray's Lighting Emporium   600 King's Road, SW6 2DX. *Tel*: 071-736 8434. *Open*: Mon to Sat, 9.30am to 6.00pm. Approaching 25 years ago, ex-actor Christopher Wray started the Victorian light fittings craze, and mopped up the market. Now he has the largest traditional lighting centre in the UK, possibly in Europe. Opened early in 1989, the 10,000 sq ft showrooms blaze with 10,000 light fittings. Bohemian/Georgian crystal

chandeliers, sconces, pendants. Sconces in carved, pickled pine. Downstairs are ships' lanterns, blue-and-white Chinese vase lamps, simple shaded candle lamps, lights in pâte de verre art glass (including famous serpent lamp). Antique fittings, painstakingly restored by CW's full-time craftsmen. Antique oil/gas/early electric lights: all restored, cleaned, polished; brasswork rebrazed, broken/missing parts replaced; new parts may be made specially. 500 different types of replacement shades available from stock. Bulb Boutique: all bulb types, plus spare parts for oil/gas lamps.

Home Counties/South East

Temple Lighting   Stockwell House, 1 Stockwell Lane, Wavedon, Milton Keynes, Bucks MK17 8LS. *Tel*: (0908) 583597. *Open*: Mon to Sat, 10.00am to 5.00pm. 19th-/early 20th-century interior lighting specialists. Original shades; good selections of Victorian oil lamps. Gas lamp conversions; early fittings can be rewired for safe, modern electrical supply.

3. CHANDELIERS

See also **British Crafts 7. Metalwork.**

London Postal Districts

A and H Brass See **Doors 2. Door Furniture and Specialist Ironmongery.**   Brass/crystal chandeliers.

Bella Figura See **Lighting 2. Traditional and Antique** above.

Mrs M E Crick Chandeliers 166 Kensington Church Street, W8 4BN. (5 mins Notting Hill Gate tube.)

Tel: 071-229 1338. *Open*: Mon to Fri, 9.30am to 5.30pm (appointments advisable). Chandeliers, wall-lights, candelabra.

Hooper and Purchase   303/305 King's Road, SW3 5EP. (12 mins Sloane Square tube.) *Tel*: 071-351 3985. *Open*: Mon to Fri, 10.30am to 5.30pm. Evenings by appointment. Antique 18th-/early 19th-century chandeliers. Period dining tables.

Kensington Lighting Company   59 Kensington Church Street, W8 4HA. (7 mins Kensington High Street tube.) *Tel*: 071-938 2405. *Open*: Mon to Fri, 9.30am to 6.00pm, Sat 9.30am to

5.30pm. Crystal/metal chandeliers, wall fittings, lampbases. Full lighting consultancy service.

Period Brass Lights   9a Thurloe Place, Brompton Road, Knightsbridge SW7 2RZ. (10 mins South Kensington/Knightsbridge tube.) *Tel*: 071-589 8305. *Open*: Mon to Fri, 9.30am to 5.30pm, Sat 9.30am to 6.00pm. Family business, established over 30 years ago. Glorious chandeliers/period lighting over three floors. Austrian glass drops reflect brilliant rainbows; Czech styles are duller and more gracious. Assemblies to your specifications. Expert fixing/advice.

Over 100 different wall brackets in stock. Handmade period brass wall candle brackets can burn real candles or convincing imitations, complete with fake wax drip. Repairs/restorations.

Home Counties/ South East

Elite Lighting   18 Bromley Hill, Bromley, Kent BR1 4JX. (A21. Bromley South BR.) *Tel:* 081-290 0371. *Open:* Mon to Sat, 9.30am to 5.30pm. Chandelier specialists. Importers/manufacturers. High quality/low prices. Vast stock for all rooms, from domestic livingrooms to banqueting halls. Matching wallbrackets. Commissions. Individual attention. Mail order.

▶ Worth a Trip

Delomosne and Son   Court Close, North Wraxall, Chippenham, Wilts SN14 7AD. (Trains to Chippenham met by appointment; M4, junction 17/18.) *Tel:* (0225) 891505. *Open:* Mon to Sat, 9.30am to 5.30pm, and by appointment. Antique English glass chandeliers, candelabra.

4. TABLE LAMPS AND SHADES

London Postal Districts

Bella Figura See **Lighting 2. Traditional and Antique** above.

Clare House   35 Elizabeth Street, SW1W 9RP. (10 mins Victoria tube/BR.) *Tel:* 071-730 8480. *Open:* Mon to Fri, 9.30am to 6.30pm. Specialise in lamp conversions/ restorations and shades. Chinese vases, Italian columns, turned wood designs. All shades made to order in silk, card or clients' fabric.

Green and Stone See **Accessories 3. Frames.**   Hand-marbled lampshades.

Lion, Witch and Lampshade   35 St Barnabas Street, Pimlico Road, SW1W 8QB *Tel:* 071-730 1774. *Open:* Mon 10.30am to 7.00pm, Tue, Thu and Fri, 10.30am to 5.30pm, Wed 12.30pm to 7.00pm, or by arrangement. Lamp "converters": can turn, for example, a ceramic vase into a lamp base. Also service for handmaking/restoring lampshades. Pretty wallbrackets/ chandeliers (can be made to order).

Audrey Scannell   14 Wilton Crescent, SW1X 8RN. *Tel:* 071-235 6237. *Open:* by appointment. Exclusive silk/pleated decorator shades made to order. Old shades recovered. Selection of lampbases, including a fabulous ceramic unicorn.

Home Counties/ South East

Ideas Unlimited See **Interior Design**. Shades made to order, in customers' own fabric.

Mail Order

Suzie Clayton   PO Box 78, Twickenham TW1 1TB. *Tel:* 081-892 2300. Charming mail-order selection of candlestick lamps.

Silk Shades   12 Market Place, Lavenham, Suffolk CO10 9QZ. *Tel:* (0787) 247029. Silks: beautiful colours, patterned/plains/textured. Samples: £2 refundable.

5. STAINED GLASS

Light behind stained glass fittings produces a magical glow. The companies listed in **Windows 2. Stained and Decorative Glass** can also make up light fittings.

London Postal Districts

Lead and Light See **Windows 2. Stained and Decorative** Glass.   Tiffany-style pendants, wall-lights and elegant up-lighters.

James Preece Stained Glass Studio Unit 11, Portobello Green, 218 Portobello Road, W10 5TD. (3 mins Ladbroke Grove tube.) *Tel:* 081-968

8807. *Open:* Tue to Sat, 9.30am to 6.00pm. Selections of stained-glass lamps, including black and white and shades. Lamps, windows, screens etc. to commission.

Tiffany Art Studio 12e Bracknell Gardens, NW3 7EB. *Tel:* 071-794 7053. *Open:* strictly by appointment. Alexander Daszewski imports/sells direct at reasonable prices superb Tiffany/Art Nouveau reproduction lights by Edward Magdziarz. I have seen them meticulously crafted in Warsaw. Dragonflies, clematis, wisteria and other favourite Tiffany motifs. Over 100 different designs; made to order: special colours/designs (allow three to four weeks). Choice of solid brass lamp bases, cast by hand. Finish: high sheen, or antique patina. Colour catalogue available.

Christopher Wray's Lighting Emporium See **2. Traditional and Antique** above. Splendid reproduction Tiffany/stained-glass table/pendant lamps. Louis Comfort Tiffany, son of the famous jeweller, a painter turned interior decorator, produced colourful, imaginative Art Nouveau lamps around turn of the century. CW has an impressive repertoire of original Tiffany designs. Intricate pieces of handmade, opalescent glass all match for continuity, and are banded together. Bases are individually bronzed, burnished and lacquered.

6. ACCESSORIES

London Postal Districts

Forbes and Lomax 205b St John's Hill, SW11 1TH. (5 mins Clapham Junction BR.) *Tel:* 071-738 0202. *Open:* Mon to Sat, 9.30am to 5.30pm. Perspex light switches with brass dollies. Unlacquered brass switches, circular switches. Switches/sockets prepared for painting.

Christopher Wray's Lighting Emporium See **2. Traditional and Antique** above.

Mail Order

Classicana The Old Oak Tree Unit, West Heathly, W. Sussx RH19 4QF. *Tel:* (0342) 811029. Light switches/ceiling roses in polished brass, silver plate, or antique bronze, mounted onto solid oak. They blend well into traditional homes. Brochure available.

House of Brass See **Doors 2. Door Furniture and Specialist Ironmongery**. Solid brass switches, sockets, dimmers.

Woods Electrical Accessories 3/4 Simmons Place, Kingsmill Industrial Estate, Cullompton, Devon EX15 1BH. *Tel:* (0884) 34247. Switches and sockets in eight hardwoods.

7. AVANT-GARDE AND DESIGNER LIGHTING

London Postal Districts

Artemide 17/19 Neal Street, WC2H 9PU. (2 mins Covent Garden tube.) *Tel:* 071-836 6753. *Open:* Mon to Fri, 9.30am to 6.30pm, Sat 10.00am to 5.00pm. Top-of-the-range Italian designer lighting. Plus new hi-tech, low-price range.

Atrium See **Furniture 4. 20th-century Classics: Originals and Copies**. In the van with classy, modern Italian styles.

John Cullen Lighting See **1. General** above. John Cullen was a lighting designer *par excellence* and has created fittings for designing with light. They are excellently demonstrated in the shop.

Diametric Modern Furniture See **Furniture 8. Glass, Marble and Metal**. The slenderest halogen lamps you ever saw, on etiolated stalks.

Emporium 34/38 Turnham Green Terrace, W4 4PL. (3 mins Turnham Green tube.) *Tel:* 081-747 8385. *Open:* Mon to Fri, 10.00am to 6.00pm, Sat 9.00am to 6.00pm. Work with local artists to produce distinctive, one-off designs. Definitely different.

Formula 376 St John Street, EC1V 4NN. *Tel:* 071-837 8369. *Open:* by appointment. Ryan Solomon and Maerisna Adnan design/produce lights/bowls/clocks patinated in a variety of colours.

Ligne Roset See **Furniture 1. General**. Nouveau neon notions . . . strips of brilliant coloured tubes, for impact rather than function. Plus a variety of adventurous fittings.

Metal House   Oblique Workshops, Stamford Works, Gillette Street, N16 8JH. *Tel*: 071-923 4732. *Open*: by appointment. Caroline Vivian makes slender, metal structures for low-voltage halogen bulbs. Davey Boyall's work is often humorous: like his skeletal metal "frogdogs" climbing up the wall.

SKK Lighting   34 Lexington Street, W1R 3HR. (5 mins Oxford Circus/ Piccadilly Circus tubes.) *Tel*: 071-434 4095. *Open*: Mon to Fri, 9.00am to 6.30pm, Sat 12.00 noon to 6.00pm. Original modern fittings; lighting advice/consultancy. Shu Kay Kan is endlessly innovative and unfailingly courteous.

Home Counties/ South East

Margaret O'Rorke   Corpus Christi Farm House, Sandford Road, Littlemore, Oxford OX4 4PX. *Tel*: (0865) 771653. *Open*: by appointment. Fine, translucent high-fired porcelain lights, thrown on a potter's wheel create a calm, restful atmosphere.

Clare Thatcher   Unit 14, Harold's Road, The Pinnacles, Harlow, Essex CM13 5BJ. *Tel*: 081-524 0912. *Open*: by appointment. Slender sculptural shapes in metal and glass, which can be sandblasted and kiln-formed. Commissions.

19
CHILDREN'S ROOMS

Children! Delinquent or docile, lively or listless, bright or bored, they all need their own space. So do you, so make theirs as nice as possible.

"I have a big house—and I hide a lot".

Mary Ure, British actress (1933–1975) explaining how she coped with her family of large children.

The problem with furnishing for children is their rapid rate of growth. Small babies are probably very much less aware of decor than their fond parents. Toddlers and young children however are very appreciative of furnishings chosen specially for them: but change their mind very rapidly about what they prefer. I don't think there are any universal answers to these problems: every family finds their own solutions, according to the needs/demands of their children, and the overall budget.

London Postal Districts

Baby B's   779/781 Fulham Road, Fulham SW6 5HA. (2 mins Parsons Green tube.) *Tel*: 071-731 7348. *Open*: Mon to Fri, 9.30am to 5.30pm, Sat 10.00am to 5.00pm. "The most civilised place to shop for a baby in London." Advice from experienced staff. For 0 to 5 years, with clothing from the top end of the British market.

▶ **Bargains!**

Babycare   74 High Street, Acton, W3 6LE. (15 mins Acton Town tube. Opposite Town Hall.) *Tel*: 081-993 8542. *Open*: Mon to Sat, 10.00am to 5.30pm. Discount prices for leading makes of cots, prams, pushchairs, high chairs. Everything for babies/toddlers, from the premature to 5 years old, including cot bedding, clothes and toys.

Bellevue Interiors See **Decorating Materials 1. Paints and Papers**. Good choice of children's speciality wallcoverings/fabrics.

Children's World   Unit 3, Angel Road, Edmonton N18 3HD. (Seven Sisters tube plus bus. 5 mins Angel

Road BR.) *Tel*: 081-807 5518. *Open*: 7 days, Mon to Fri, 10.00am to 8.00pm, Sat 9.00am to 6.00pm, Sun 10.00am to 5.00pm. Wide selections of all types baby/children's equipment, including good choice safety products.
Also at: 317 Cricklewood Broadway, NW2 6PH. (Kilburn Park tube, plus bus.) *Tel*: 081-208 1088.

Dragons   23 Walton Street, SW3 2HX. (10 mins South Kensington tube.) *Tel*: 071-589 0548. *Open*: Mon to Fri, 9.30am to 5.30pm. Late night Wed, 7.00pm. Open Sat, 10.00am to 5.00pm. Rosie Fisher started making charming handpainted children's furniture over 10 years ago, because there were no suitable designs for her own children. Now her range includes chests, tables, miniature chairs with rush seats (names to order), toy chests, etc. Also scaled-down upholstery for nurseries. Beatrix Potter fabrics/papers, plus filmy voiles. Catalogue £2.50.

Ikea See **Furniture 1. General**. Wide selection of bright ideas for children's furnishing, at sensible prices.

Meaker and Son   166 Wandsworth Bridge Road SW6 2UQ. (15 mins Fulham Broadway tube.) *Tel*: 071-731 7416. *Open*: Mon to Sat, 10.00am to 6.00pm. Victorian/period style children's furniture, designed and painted to order.

Moriarti's Workshop See **Bedrooms 3. Pine Beds**.   Sturdy bunk beds in pine or hardwood.

Mothercare   *Tel*: (0923) 210210 for details of nearest branch. This high street regular is always worth a visit for its wide selection of baby/children's equipment. *Star Store*: 461 Oxford Street, W1R 1DB. (5 mins Bond Street tube.) *Tel*: 071-629 6621. *Open*: Mon to Fri, 9.30am to 6.00pm. Late nights Thu, 7.30pm, Fri 7.00pm. Open Sat, 9.00am to 6.00pm. Over 250 stores nationwide, 100 in London and the South East. Branch opening hours vary. Attractive cribs/cots. Own-brand linens in bright colours/pastels.

Lamps/shades. Children's co-ordinates: ready-made curtains plus accessories. Shopping service: orders assembled for later collection. Mother-and-baby rooms at larger branches. Mail order services. Catalogue 40p.

Naturally British See **British Crafts 3. Craft Shops and Galleries**. Good selection handpainted, old and new children's furniture.

The Nursery   103 Bishop's Road, SW6 7AX. (5 mins Parsons Green tube.) *Tel*: 071-731 6637. *Open*: Mon to Sat, 10.00am to 6.00pm. Traditional-style children's shop, now selling mainly gifts. Toys, clothes, china, books, handpainted boxes.

The Nursery Window   83 Walton Street, SW3 2HP. (10 mins Sloane Square tube.) *Tel*: 071-581 3358. *Open*: Mon to Sat, 10.00am to 5.30pm. Exclusive co-ordinates; patterns range from chic tartans to rabbits/teddies. Fabrics, friezes, papers with accessories made to match.

Paper Moon See **Decorating Materials 2. Co-ordinated Collections**.   Wide selection of stylish children's wallpapers/fabrics/borders.

Peeking Hippo See **Ethnic Crafts and Furnishings**.   Children's co-ordinated fabrics/wallpapers/borders. Rainbows, animals, targets, aeroplanes . . . even embracing hippos, aptly called Hippo Love. Alphabet letters entwined with decorative animals adhere magnetically to a background board: instantly assemble personal gift/wall decoration . . . or stick on fridge.

▶ **Bargains!**

Pillow Talk See **Bedrooms 11. Bed Linen**.   Good stocks/keen prices. Duvet/pillowcase sets featuring comic cuts: Beano/Garfield. Also Mickey and Goofy, Batman, The

Flintstones, Winnie the Pooh. Plus Gazza, Mutant Hero Turtles, Ed the Duck, American Football, Ghostbusters. More extensive co-ordinates are Teddytime, Zoo, Kids Kapers. Bed linens, ready-made curtains, fabrics by the metre. Also lampshades/waste bins, made up specially.

Potty People   302 Bethnal Green Road, E2 0AG. (5 mins Bethnal Green tube.) Tel: 071-729 2217. *Open:* Mon to Sat, 9.30am to 5.30pm. Closed all day Thu. Good prices for baby equipment.

Sophisto-Cat See **Furniture 2. Pine and Country**.   Complete range painted pine furniture, with appealing decoration.

Swallows and Amazons   40 Webbs Road, Battersea, SW11 6SF. (10 mins Clapham South BR.) Tel: 071-228 6909. *Open:* Mon to Fri, 10.00am to 5.00pm, Sat 10.00am to 1.00pm. Sellers and buyers of "good-as-new" children's clothes/toys/equipment.

The Uncommon Touch
18 Northcote Road, SW11 3TF. (10 mins Clapham Junction BR.) Tel: 071-228 1487. *Open:* Mon to Sat,

10.00am to 5.30pm. Specialist collection of children's paper/fabrics, plus some furniture. Making-up service for all soft furnishings. Curtain-making courses.

Peter de Wit   21 Greenwich Church Street, Greenwich Village, SE10 9BJ. (In centre of Greenwich. 2 mins Cutty Sark.) *Tel:* 081-305 0048. *Open:* Mon to Fri, 2.00pm to 5.00pm (but phone first), Sat and Sun, 10.30am to 7.00pm. Tiny shop: exclusive, handpainted toys/furniture to order.

Home Counties/ South East

Children's World   Vastern Court, Caversham Road, Reading, Berks RG1 8BA. Tel: (0734) 503340. *Also at:* Trafalgar Way, Croydon, Surrey CR9 4PB. *Tel:* 081-760 0484. *And at:* Riverside Park, Victoria Road, Chelmsford, Essex CM1 1PG. *Tel:* (0245) 268425. *And at:* Rom Valley Way, Romford, Essex RM7 0AF. *Tel:* (0708) 730130. See also **London Postal Districts** above.

Miniwinks   Old School House,

High Street, Offord D'Arcy, Huntingdon, Cambs PE18 9RH. *Tel:* (0480) 810200. *Open:* by appointment. Handmade cribs/Moses baskets to order. Dressed in range of fabrics or clients' own, with canopy, mattress, drapes, quilt, sheets. Natural beech/painted white finishes. Repair/renovation old cribs/cradles.

Mail Order

Newcome Marketing   Freepost, Dronfield, Derbys S18 6LZ. Tel: (0246) 416306. Brochure available. Stackerjack plastic stacking storage boxes; six sizes, five colours, delivered flat. Lids available.

Poppy   44 High Street, Yarm, Cleveland TS15 9AE. *Tel:* (0642) 790000. Fabrics, wallpapers, borders, curtains, bedding especially for kids. Clowns, bears, moons, and the alphabet run riot. Primaries/pastels. Send an sae for colour catalogue.

Ulike UK   24 Lambourn Road, SW4 0LY. *Tel:* 071-627 5244. Wire storage cubes for toys/general clutter. Red/black/white.

20

ACCESSORIES

Every smart girl knows that shoes, bags, scarves, jewellery—and even a hat—make or mar an outfit. It's the same with rooms. They take their tone from cushions, rugs, pictures, mirrors and so on. Happily lots of shops specialise in takeaway taste to lift a tired old interior, or finish off a new one.

"To fight against the shoddy design of those goods by which our fellow men are surrounded becomes a moral duty."

Nikolaus Pevsner (1902–83)

London Postal Districts

Artisan 797 Wandsworth Road, SW8 3JT. (5 mins Clapham Junction BR. 137 bus from Sloane Square.) *Tel:* 071-498 6974. *Open:* Mon to Sat, 10.00am to 6.00pm. Karen Lansdown and Beverley Mills offer highly original artefacts. Furniture from old wood is colour-washed in wonderful clear shades. Plus pottery, glass, metal. Elegant, exclusive modern wrought-iron items include original curtain rails/four-poster beds.

Barclay and Bodie 7 Blenheim Terrace, St John's Wood NW8 0EH. (5 mins St John's Wood tube.) *Tel:* 071-328 7879. *Open:* Mon to Sat, 9.30am to 5.30pm. Ruth and Sherrie have established their spacious, two-unit shop as an essential source for original home accessories/presents. Trays, wastebins, cushions, embroidered towels, candlesticks, boxes, screens, antique furniture, kitchen accessories: all are exclusive and covetable.

The British Museum Shop Great Russell Street, WC1B 3DG. (5 mins Russell Square/Holborn tubes.) *Tel:* 071-323 8613. *Open:* Mon to Sat, 10.00am to 5.00pm, Sun 2.30pm to 6.00pm. Awesome replicas of internationally famous museum pieces. Striking Egyptian black cats; and copies of Greek marbles.

Casa Fina 9 Central Avenue, The Market, Covent Garden WC2E 8AH. (2 mins Covent Garden tube.) *Tel:* 071-836 0289. *Open:* Mon to Wed, 10.30am to 6.00pm, Thu, 10.30am to 7.30pm. Distinctive Casa Fina look, linking all shops: exclusive ceramics, rugs, lighting: pretty colours and occasional/conservatory furniture. Gift wrapping. Wedding lists. *Also at:* 132 Notting Hill Gate, W11 3OG. *Tel:* 071-221 9112.

The Conran Shop See **Furniture 1. General**. Chic, sharp accessories, often surprisingly affordable.

The Covent Garden General Store 111 Long Acre, WC2N 4BA. (Immediately opposite Covent Garden tube.) *Tel:* 071-240 0331. *Open:* 7 days. Mon to Wed, 10.00am to 11.00pm, Thu to Sat, 10.00am to 12.00 midnight, Sun 11.00am to 9.00pm. Note the late closing times—handy for emergency shopping. Three floors packed with fun ceramics, pictures, books, decorative tinware, prettily packed food/toiletries. Unfortunately this is also a tourist trap, with a rugger scrum atmosphere and heavies rather than assistants. Café at back: salad bar.
Also at: Sideshow, Victoria Place, SW1. (Above Victoria station.) *Tel:* 071-931 8827. *Open:* 7 days, Mon to Sat, 9.00am to 8.00pm, Sun 11.00am to 7.00pm.

Tessa Fantoni (Kids) 24 Abbeville Road, Clapham SW4 9NH. (6 mins Clapham South tube.) *Tel:* 081-673 5215. *Open:* Mon to Sat, 10.00am to 6.00pm. Packed with children's books, traditional toys/games. Rocking horse for children to play on.
Also at: 77 Abbeville Road, Clapham SW4 9JN. (8 mins Clapham South tube.) *Tel:* 081-673 1253. Hand-bound visitors' books, photograph albums, blank books made from marbled paper/leather. Cards, wrapping paper, fine pens, china, jewellery, pottery.

The Front Room 1 Windmill Row, Kennington SE11 5DW. (2 mins Kennington tube.) *Tel:* 071-582 1437. *Open:* Mon to Sat, 10.00am to 7.00pm. Julia O'Dowd brings colour to Kennington with this full interior decorating service. Furniture/reupholstery/loose covers. Bright, shiny pottery. Carved woodware. Cachepots, planters, vases, pots. Cushions/rugs a speciality. Candlesticks. Dried flowers.

The General Trading Company 144 Sloane Street, SW1X 9BL. (2 mins Sloane Square tube.) *Tel:* 071-730 0411. *Open:* Mon to Fri, 9.00am to 5.30pm, Sat 9.00am to 2.00pm. Late night Wed, 7.00pm. Difficult to classify this genteel and gracious store, which holds four Royal warrants. Charmingly crowded with all kinds of furnishings/gifts in eleven departments. Antiques, furniture, rugs, cookware, books, beautiful artificial and dried flowers. Catalogue £1.

Gore Booker 41 Bedford Street, WC2E 9HA. (5 mins Covent Garden tube.) *Tel:* 071-497 1254. *Open:* Mon to Fri, 10.30am to 6.00pm, Sat 10.00am to 6.00pm. Peter Gore and George Booker fill this spacious corner design site (on two floors) with old and new furniture/accessories. Many "one-offs". Table-, kitchen-, bathroomware. Original paintings/prints. Candleholders/candles. Rugs. Personal accessories: pens, stationery, lighters, soaps.

Graham and Green 4 and 7 Elgin Crescent, W11 2JA. (8 mins Notting Hill Gate tube.) *Tel:* 071-727 4594. *Open:* Mon to Sat, 10.00am to 6.00pm. Antonia Graham ceaselessly seeks unusual accessories/gifts. New/antique/wrought-iron furniture, bedspreads, rugs, cushions, china, kitchenware, lamps. Browsing is well rewarded.

The Green Parrot 2 Turnpin Lane, SE10 9JA. (Private lane, off Greenwich Church Street.) *Tel:* 081-

858 6690. *Open:* Tue to Sun, 10.30am to 5.30pm. Dedicated owner offers collector's items, antique and new. Pottery, handcrafted glass. Durries/kilims/throws/bedspreads/wall hangings/cushion covers from India/Burma. Antique pine chests, mirrors. Also mobiles, finger puppets and marble games.

Muji 26 Great Marlborough Street, W1V 1HB. (5 mins Oxford Circus tube.) *Tel:* 071-494 1197. *Open:* Mon to Sat, 10.00am to 6.30pm. Late night Thu, 7.00pm. New retail concept from Japan. Unadorned household basics in simple materials/natural colours based on "kanketsu": Japanese for simplicity. Kitchenware is mainly stainless steel. Thick bathroom towels; lots of brushes. Ultra-plain bedlinen. Popular storage boxes in plain cardboard/clear plastic/chic galvanised metal.

Ogetti 135 Fulham Road, SW3 6RT. (10 mins South Kensington tube.) *Tel:* 071-581 8088. *Open:* Mon to Sat, 9.30am to 6.00pm. Wide-ranging stock of well-designed furnishing accessories from around the world, including tableware, rugs, cushions. Sleek and chic, for design devotees.

Saville Edells 25 Walton Street, SW3 2HU. (5 mins Knightsbridge/South Kensington tubes.) *Tel:* 071-584 4398. *Open:* Mon to Sat, 9.30am to 6.00pm. Framed prints, mirrors and ceramics. Photo frames: burr walnut, glass, crystal, silver. Antiques. Vases, plant holders. Free mail order catalogue from shops, or £2.50 by phone (redeemable on first order). *Tel:* 071-584 4398.

Also at: Simpson, 203 Piccadilly, W1. *Tel:* 071-734 2002.

Verandah 15b Blenheim Crescent, W11 2EE. (5 mins Ladbroke Grove tube.) *Tel:* 071-792 9289. *Open:* Mon 1.00pm to 6.00pm, Tue to Sat, 10.00am to 6.00pm. Anne Jaye is committed to "beautiful things made by hand in real materials". Terracotta, glazed pots, planters, rustic glass, wooden bowls, trays, candlesticks, storm lamps, picnic baskets, hampers. Eucalyptus twig chairs from Kenya.

Victoria Waymouth Interiors 30 Old Church Street, SW3 5BY. (10 mins Sloane Square tube.) *Tel:* 071-376 5244. *Open:* Mon to Fri, 10.00am to 6.00pm, Sat 10.00am to 4.00pm. Good selection of accessories from leading London interior decorator.

Wimbles 39a High Street, Wimbledon Village SW19 5BY. (10 mins Wimbledon tube/BR.) *Tel:* 081-947 4899. *Open:* Mon to Sat, 9.30am to 5.30pm, Sun 12.00 noon to 5.00pm (both branches). Everything from pocket-money gifts and stocking fillers to substantial presents and home ideas.
Also at: 37 High Street, Wimbledon Village SW19 5BY. *Tel:* 081-946 5437.

Joanna Wood 48a Pimlico Road, SW1. (5 mins Sloane Square tube.) *Tel:* 071-730 5064. *Open:* Mon to Sat, 10.00am to 6.00pm. Chic decorating accessories from leading interior designer, culled from many buying trips abroad. China, lamps, candlesticks, mirrors, photo-frames, handpainted chairs/tables, cushions, pillboxes, bedlinen, *objets d'art*.

Home Counties/ South East

The Aspidistra 29 Sun Street, Hitchin, Herts SG5 1AH. (Opposite Sun Hotel.) *Tel:* (0462) 453817. *Open:* Mon to Sat, 9.30am to 5.30pm. British/ethnic crafts, satin, lace, nostalgic and unusual gifts.

Helios 1 Grace Reynolds Walk, Camberley, Surrey GU15 3SN. (10 mins Camberley BR.) *Tel:* (0276) 27076. *Open:* Mon to Sat, 9.00am to 5.30pm. Porcelain, crystal, glass and woodware, pottery, gifts, jewellery.

MacDonalds 71/73 High Street, Camberley, Surrey GU15 3RB. (10 mins Camberley BR.) *Tel:* (0276) 23005. *Open:* Mon to Sat, 9.00am to 5.30pm. Glass, lighting, pine/cane furniture, cushions, vases, rugs, terraria. Picture framing.

Quelque Chose 9 King Street, Richmond, Surrey TW9 1ND. (10 mins Richmond tube/BR.) *Tel:* 081-948 3036. *Open:* Mon to Sat, 10.00am to 5.00pm. Teddies, Beatrix Potter merchandise. Soft toys, books, furnishing fabrics, cards, children's clothes, mugs, china ornaments/sets. Run by Belinda and Ian McCarraher for 20 years.

Rainbow's End 126 High Street, Epsom, Surrey KT19 8BT. *Tel:* (03727) 723434. Gifts/home ideas.

Stoneleigh Galleries 9 The Broadway, Stoneleigh, Epsom, Surrey KT17 2JA. (2 mins Stoneleigh BR.) *Tel:* 081-393 0424. *Open:* Mon to Sat, 9.30am to 5.30pm, Wed to 1.00pm. Ceramics, lace/satins, glass, enamel. Gift wrapping service.

2. PAINTINGS, PRINTS AND POSTERS

"If you want to kill a picture, all you have to do is to hang it beautifully on a nail and soon you will see nothing of it but the frame."

Pablo Picasso (1881–1973)

London Postal Districts

Artbeat 703 Fulham Road, SW6 5UL. (5 mins Parsons Green tube.) *Tel:* 071-736 0337. *Open:* Mon to Sat, 10.00am to 6.00pm. Small shop, crammed with unusual prints/posters plus ready-made frames. Framing service on premises.

Flashbacks 6 Silver Place, W1R 3LJ. (5 mins Piccadilly Circus tube.) *Tel:* 071-437 8562. *Open:* Mon to Sat, 10.30am to 7.00pm. Specialists in movie posters, old and new.

Grosvenor Prints 28/32 Shelton Street, WC2H 9HP. (3 mins Covent Garden tube.) *Tel:* 071-836 1979. *Open:* Mon to Fri, 10.00am to 6.00pm, Sat 11.00am to 4.00pm. Antiquarian prints, many several centuries old: dogs, portraits, maps, architecturals.

London Transport Museum Shop The Piazza, Covent Garden WC2. (2 mins Covent Garden tube.) *Tel:* 071-379 6344. *Open:* 7 days, 10.00am to 5.45pm. Historic London Transport posters/contemporary London Underground art posters. Also a vast range of general travel/transport art. The Underground map is available in two sizes. Stationery, T-shirts, postcards.

The Picture Man 184 Chiswick High Road, Chiswick W4 1RP. (2 mins Turnham Green tube.) *Tel:* 081-995 6359. *Open:* Mon to Wed and Fri, 9.00am to 6.00pm, Thu 10.00am to 7.00pm, Sat 9.30am to 6.00pm. Limited edition prints/posters. Fine art cards. Framing, plus frame and picture restoration, artists' materials.

Pigeonhole Gallery 13 Langton Street, SW10 0JL. (15 mins Sloane Square tube.) *Tel:* 071-352 2677. *Open:* Mon to Fri, 10.00am to 6.00pm. Appointments preferred. Reproductions of great botanical engravings of the 18th-/19th-centuries by Redouté, Ehret, Thornton and others. Also full-sized Audubon "Birds of America" and birds by Lear and Gould. New portfolio of architecturals, by Piranesi and others. Ninety-page colour catalogue of complete range, £5. Decorative mounting/framing specialists, supplying prestigious interior designers.

The Poster Shop 1 Chalk Farm Road, Camden NW1 8AA. (2 mins Chalk Farm tube.) *Tel:* 071-267 6248. *Open:* Mon to Fri, 10.00am to 6.00pm, Sat and Sun, 10.30am to 6.30pm. Instant take-away art. Over 1,800 images from all over world; top 350 ready-framed. The rest can be framed in two weeks maximum. Art/photographic reproductions. Advertising. Full colour catalogue. Mail order. *Tel:* (0933) 400555. *Also at:* 168 Fulham Road, Chelsea SW10 9PR. (7 mins South Kensington tube.) *Tel:* 071-373 7294. *Open:* Mon to Fri 10.30am to 6.00pm, Sat 10.30am to 6.30pm. *And at:* 28 James Street, Covent Garden WC2 8PP. (3 mins Covent Garden tube.) *Tel:* 071-240 2526. *Open:* 7 days, Mon to Sat 10.00am to 8.00pm, Sun 12.00 noon to 6.00pm.

And at: 34 Great Marlborough Street, W1V 1HA. (5 mins Oxford Circus tube.) *Tel:* 071-434 0248. *Open:* Mon, Tue and Sat 10.00am to 6.00pm, Wed to Fri 10.00am to 7.00pm.
And at: 109 King's Road, Chelsea SW3 4PA. (8 mins Sloane Square tube.) *Tel:* 071-376 5569. *Open:* Mon to Sat, 10.00am to 7.00pm.
And at: Unit 106, Whiteley's Centre, Queensway W2 4YH. (2 mins Queensway tube.) *Tel:* 071-792 3825. *Open:* 7 days, Mon to Sat, 10.00am to 8.00pm, Sun 12.00 noon to 6.00pm.

The Tate Gallery Shop Millbank, SW1P 4RG. (5 mins Pimlico tube.) *Tel:* 071-821 5001. *Open:* Mon to Sat, 10.00am to 5.30pm, Sun 2.00pm to 5.30pm. Marvellous selections of prints: British painting, Turner, Pre-Raphaelites, Impressionists, modern favourites. Allow plenty of time for browsing.

The Victoria and Albert Museum Shop Cromwell Road, SW7 2RL. (2 mins South Kensington tube.) *Tel:* 071-938 8500. *Open:* 7 days, Mon to Sat, 10.00am to 5.00pm, Sun 2.00pm to 5.30pm. Exhibition posters, Constable, Turner, William Morris, fashion photography, Indian/Chinese prints. Jewellery, textiles, sewing kits.

Home Counties/ South East

The Antique Print Gallery Village Farmhouse, Little Barrington, Burford, Oxon OX18 4ZE. *Tel:* (04514) 643. *Open:* Mon to Sat, 9.00am to 5.30pm. Framed prints, reasonable prices. Mounts and framing take four or five days.

3. FRAMES

"When the war broke out she took down the signed photograph of the Kaiser and with some solemnity hung it in the menservants' lavatory; it was her one combative action."

Evelyn Waugh (1903–1966), *Vile Bodies*

Many of the firms in **Services 7. Framing and Frames/Picture Restoration** are specialist picture framers. Please also consult this section.

London Postal Districts

Fellowes and Saunderson
116 Blythe Road, Brook Green W14 0UH. (Behind Olympia.) *Tel:* 071-603 7475/0577. *Open:* Tue to Sat, 9.30am to 5.30pm. High-class bespoke framing. Unique frames/mounts. Handfinished frames: painted, stained, gilded. Picture restoration for oils, paper, frames. Prints, framed/unframed. Reliable, friendly expert service.

Fix-a-Frame   280 Old Brompton Road, SW5 9HR. (10 mins Earls Court tube.) *Tel:* 071-370 4189. *Open:* Tue to Fri, 11.30am to 8.00pm, Sat 10.00am to 6.30pm. Make instant frames yourself on the premises, guided by experts! Bespoke framing also available.

Frame Express   82 Charing Cross Road, WC2H 0BA. *Tel:* 071-836 2943. *Open:* Mon to Sat, 9.30am to 6.00pm (all branches). Speedy framing, while you wait, or within 24 hours. Good choice frames/mounts, traditional or modern. Clear sample displays with prices. Clip and photo frames, cards, posters.
Also at: 81 Baker Street, W1M 1AJ. *Tel:* 071-935 7794.
And at: 172 Queensway, Bayswater W2 6LY. *Tel:* 071-243 0219.
And at: 137 Strand, WC2R 1HH. *Tel:* 071-497 2607.

And at: 266 Kensington High Street, W8 6ND. *Tel:* 071-602 2277.
And at: 111 Old Brompton Road, South Kensington SW7 3HZ. *Tel:* 071-589 7635.
And at: 376 King's Road, Chelsea SW3 5UZ. *Tel:* 071-351 5975.
And at: 658 Fulham Road, SW6 5RX. *Tel:* 071-731 2394.
And at: 1 Queens Road, Wimbledon, SW19 9NG. *Tel:* 081-947 7838.
And at: 845 High Road, North Finchley, N12 8PT. *Tel:* 081-445 2477.
See also **Home Counties/South East** below.

Frame Factory   20 Cross Street, Islington N1 2BQ. (10 mins Angel/Highbury and Islington tubes.) *Tel:* 071-226 6266/071-354 3134. *Open:* Mon to Sat, 9.30am to 6.00pm. Bespoke framing in wood/metal. Clip frames, black lacquer/varnished pine stock frames. Box/display framing, conservation framing, posters dry-mounted. Mirrors.
Also at: 172 Chiswick High Road, Chiswick W4 1PR. (5 mins Turnham Green tube.) *Tel:* 081-742 1764. Reproduction/antique frames. Cards, local artists' work.
And at: 159 Haverstock Hill, NW3 4QT. (2 mins Belsize Park tube.) *Tel:* 071-483 2050.
And at: 92 Stoke Newington Church Street, N16 0AP. (5 mins Stoke Newington BR.) *Tel:* 071-254 0066.
And at: 18 Hornsey High Street, N8 7PD. (5 mins Hornsey BR.) *Tel:* 081-341 4385.
And at: 296 Streatham High Road, SW16 6GH. (5 mins Streatham BR.) *Tel:* 081-677 1882.
And at: 14 Jordan Place, SW6 1BH. (1 min Fulham Broadway tube.) *Tel:* 071-381 9583.
See also **Home Counties/South East** below.

Green and Stone   259 King's Road, Chelsea SW3 5EL. (Sloane Square tube, plus bus.) *Tel:* 071-352 0837. *Open:* Mon to Fri, 9.00am to 5.30pm, Sat 9.30am to 6.00pm.

Picture framing/restoration. Restoration materials for china, paper, paintings. Antique artists' materials for sale/hire. Handmade papers, photograph albums, frames. Decorative paint finishes: glazes, brushes, stencils, books. Catalogue available.
See also **Home Counties/South East** below.

Harris Fine Art   712 High Road, North Finchley N12 9QD. (10 mins Woodside Park tube.) *Tel:* 081-445 2804/446 5579. *Open:* Mon to Sat, 9.00am to 5.30pm. Thousands of ready-made picture frames in stock. Or framing to order. Artists'/graphic materials. Prints gallery.

Ikea See **Furniture 1. General**. Remarkably wide selection of instant frames, most supplied with a squared mount; buy their cheap, passe-partout knife and cut it to size. Glass/clips. Silver/aluminium. White/black epoxy lacquered metal frames, plus synthetic glass mini-frames. Also sophisticated strip picture lighting.

The Picture Factory   44/48 Birkbeck Road, North Finchley N12 8DZ. *Tel:* 081-446 3164. *Open:* Mon to Sat, 9.00am to 6.00pm, Sun 10.00am to 2.00pm. This saleroom is not much like a factory. It has converted stables with a cobbled yard, and ivy up the walls. Established for over 25 years. Skilled craftsmen. Over 500 wood/metal mouldings available. Rag-rolling/staining/gilding are specialities. Tapestries/embroideries stretched/framed. Ready-made frames. Picture restoration (to museum standards) for oils, watercolours, prints.

Home Counties/ South East

Frame Express   12 High Street, Epsom, Surrey KT19 8DA. *Tel:* (03727) 45861.

Also at: 224 High Street, Bromley, Kent BR1 1PG. *Tel:* 081-466 5955. *And at:* 44 High Street, Croydon, Surrey CR0 1YB. *Tel:* 081-681 3168. *And at:* 9 Queen Street, Maidenhead, Berks SL6 1NB. *Tel:* (0628) 21732.
See also **London Postal Districts** above.

Frame Factory   45 Gloucester Street, Brighton, E. Sussex BN1 4EW.

Tel: (0273) 609207. *Open:* Mon to Sat, 10.00am to 6.00pm.
See also **London Postal Districts** above.

Green and Stone   1 North House, North Street, Chichester, W. Sussex PO19 5LR. *Tel:* (0243) 533953. *Open:* Mon to Sat, 9.00am to 5.30pm.
See also **London Postal Districts** above.

Masterframes   857 Honeypot Lane, Stanmore, Middx HA7 1AR. *Tel:* 081-952 2664. *Open:* Mon to Fri, 9.00am to 6.00pm. Closed 1.00pm Thu. Open Sat, 9.00am to 5.00pm. Bespoke framing service, own workshop. Prints, watercolours, tapestry, embroidery, mirrors, etc. Own handfinished frames/decorated mounts. Speciality: frames with your own fabrics, wallpapers. Customers journey from all over the country.

4. CUSHIONS

Cushions add comfort, style and colour to a home—you really cannot have too many.

London Postal Districts

▶ Bargains!

Alexander Furnishings See **Soft Furnishings 1. Fabrics**.   Plain/patterned cushions made from fabric remnants, sold complete with pads at prices that really hit rock bottom.

Claridge and Co   154 Wandsworth Bridge Road, SW6 2UH. (15 mins Fulham Broadway tube.) *Tel:* 071-384 1265. *Open:* Mon to Fri, 10.00am to 6.00pm, Sat 10.00am to 5.00pm. Cushion specialist. Point/kelim covers. New embroidery/appliqué. Plus stripes, checks, frills. Covers sold separately from pads. Most 15/18in square. Also quilts, bedcovers, throws.

Cushions and Covers   The Design and Decoration Building, 107a Pimlico Road, SW1W 8PH. (5 mins Sloane Square tube.) *Tel:* 071-373

1631. *Open:* by appointment. Ready made, covetable cushions with an interior designer touch. Feather pads. Frilled/piped/quilted. Plain/stripes/tartans. Cottons/silks. High quality, superb colours. All-cotton tablelinens/bedcovers. Matching napkins/place mats. A delightful discovery.

Graham and Green See **Accessories 1. General** above.   Wonderful cushion selections include Kashmiri intricate crewelwool work, designed in Britain by Veronica Marsh. Good range of sizes/designs. Also Ikat fabrics from India: characteristic blurred designs, with a plain weft through a shaded warp. Square cushions from old kelims. And exquisite square, old cotton lace pillowcases; Dutch/German, with cushions to fill. Tapestry cushion kits.

Heraz   25 Motcomb Street, SW1X 8JU. (5 mins Knightsbridge tube.) *Tel:* 071-245 9497. *Open:* Mon to Fri, 10.00am to 6.00pm. Closed for lunch, 1.00pm to 2.00pm. Very special cushions from antique textiles, in glorious fabric mix: velvet/silk/brocade. Antique trimmings (fringes/braids). From tiny headrests to floor sizes. Also old tapestries/curtains.

▶ Bargains!

Nice Irma's See **Ethnic Crafts and Furnishings**.   Standard cushion sizes: 18/21/36 in sq, made up in virtually all their exclusive fabrics. Piped/zipped. Subtle ikats; textured natural cottons. Intricate Kashmiri embroidered crewel work. Plus exotics: rich brocades, and zari work, which sparkles with colours/metallic sequins/threads.

Petit and Chestnut   47 Leamington Road Villas, W11 1HT. *Tel:* 071-221 0320. *Open:* by appointment. Log cabin patchwork to commission, from old fabrics.

Sussex House   63 New King's Road, SW6 4SE. (7 mins Fulham Broadway/Parsons Green tubes.) *Tel:* 071-371 5455. *Open:* Mon to Fri, 10.00am to 6.00pm, Sat 10.00am to 4.00pm. Cushions covered with fragments of genuine Oriental carpets. Effect is superb. Carpet and kelim cushions/stools. Belts/purses/curtain tie-backs. Kelim-covered fender stools. Kelim-covered home filing box.

5. CANDLES AND CANDLESTICKS

Candles create atmosphere and intimacy in any setting. Don't wait for a power cut!

London Postal Districts

The Candle Shop (London)   30 The Market, Covent Garden, WC2E 8RE. (2 mins Covent Garden tube.) *Tel:* 071-836 9815. *Open:* Mon to Sat, 10.00am to 8.00pm. (Closed at 7.00pm in summer.) Established for 20 years, this shop claims the largest selection of candles in Britain. Good value church/dinner/pure beeswax candles. Variety of sizes/colours. Novelty candles, from politicians to floating lotus flowers. Ceramic/wrought-iron candlesticks/chandeliers.

McCloud and Co See **Furniture 8. Glass, Marble and Metal**. Exquisite, distinctive candlesticks in patinated metals.

Nice Irma's See **Ethnic Crafts and Furnishings**.   Good selections of reasonably priced candlesticks.

Price's Candles   110 York Road, Battersea SW11 3RU. (10 mins Clapham Junction BR.) *Tel:* 071-228 3345. *Open:* Mon to Sat, 9.30am to 5.30pm. A fine selection of church/dinner candles, candle holders, candle lamps. Christmas candle decorations. Trading from this site for over 100 years.

The Shaker Shop See **Furniture 2. Pine and Country**.   Hand-rolled/dipped beeswax candles. Traditional tin candleholders: plain/decorated, single/double, wall/freestanding.

Soho Design See **Furniture 8. Glass, Marble and Metal**.   Classic, wrought-iron candlesticks, with candles to suit.

Home Counties/South East

Wax Lyrical   14 Hill Street, Richmond, Surrey TW9 1TN. (6 mins Richmond tube/BR.) *Tel:* 081-332 0362. *Open:* 7 days, Mon to Sat, 9.30am to 6.00pm, Sun 12.00 noon to 6.00pm. Original range, including scented candles/candles with pressed flowers in wax. Gothic candle holders, wrought-iron chandeliers, lanterns, oil lamps, water/garden candles.
Also at: 61 High Street, Hampstead NW3 1QH. *Tel:* 071-435 5105. *Open:* 7 days, Mon to Sat, 10.00am to 6.30pm, Sun 11.00am to 6.30pm.

6. FLOWERS, PLANTS, POTS AND STATUES

"Send two dozen roses to Room 424 and put 'Emily, I love you' on the back of the bill."

Groucho Marx (1895–1977), *A Night in Casablanca*

London Postal Districts

Barnes Flowers   77 Church Road, SW13 2HH. (10 mins Barnes BR.) *Tel:* 081-748 3759. *Open:* Mon to Thu, 8.30am to 6.30pm, Fri and Sat, 8.30am to 7.00pm, Sun 9.00am to 3.00pm. English country flowers, plus more unusual blooms. Lemon/olive trees. Indoor/outdoor plants. Window-boxes.

The Chelsea Gardener
125 Sydney Street, SW3 6NR. (10 mins Sloane Square tube.) *Tel:* 071-352 5656. *Open:* 7 days, 10.30am to 6.00pm. Inspirational garden centre with a good selection of exotic plants. Urns, statues, pots, conservatory furnishings. Interior landscaping. Essential port of call for all town gardeners.

Clifton Nurseries   5a Clifton Villas, Warwick Avenue, W9 2PH. (5 mins Warwick Avenue tube.) *Tel:* 071-289 6851. *Open:* 7 days, Mon to Sat, 8.30am to 6.00pm, Sun 9.30am to 4.00pm. High quality garden centre with trellis/decorative pots/furniture. Antique statues/ornaments a speciality.

The Conservatory and Within
162 Fortis Green Road, Muswell Hill, N10 3DU. (Highgate tube, plus bus.) *Tel:* 081-883 7700. *Open:* Mon to Sat, 10.00am to 6.00pm. Quality cane furniture, kilim rugs, candelabra and rustic candlesticks, plus Mediterranean terracotta marble-top tables for conservatories and outdoors.

The Dutch Blooms   34 Whiteleys Centre, 151 Queensway, W2 4YA. (5 mins Bayswater tube.) *Tel:* 071-792 2861. *Open:* 7 days, Mon to Thu, 10.00am to 8.00pm, Fri 10.00am to 9.00pm, Sat 10.00am to 8.00pm, Sun 10.00am to 6.00pm. Extensive range of imported Dutch flowers. House/outdoor plants. Bouquets a speciality (the charge is only for flowers).

The Flowershop   Heal and Son, 96 Tottenham Court Road, W1P 9LO. (1 min Goodge Street tube.) Tel: 071-636 1666. Open: Mon 10.00am to 6.00pm, Tue to Fri, 9.30am to 6.00pm. Late night Thu, 7.30pm. Open Sat, 9.00am to 6.00pm. Fragrant reception for design-conscious shoppers. Exotic blooms: "not boring old carnations". *Also at:* The Flower Van, Michelin Building, 81 Fulham Road, SW3 6RD. (3 mins South Kensington tube.) *Tel:* 071-589 1852. *Open:* Mon to Wed, 8.00am to 7.00pm, Thu and Fri, 8.00am to 8.00pm, Sat 9.00am to 6.30pm. Here the approach is pretty, rather than extreme.

Flowersmith   34 Shelton Street, WC2H 9HP. (5 mins Covent Garden tube.) *Tel:* 071-240 6688. *Open:* Mon to Fri, 10.00am to 6.00pm, Sat 12.00 noon to 8.00pm. "We're avant-garde and sophisticated." Imaginative to an extreme. Exotic blooms. Rare dried flowers/twigs/bark. Baskets filled with bulbs/plants. Vast selection of plain glass tanks.

Fulham Palace Garden Centre
Bishop's Avenue, SW6 6EE. (5 mins Putney Bridge tube.) *Tel:* 071-736 2640. *Open:* Mon to Thu, 9.30am to 5.30pm, Fri and Sat, 10.00am to 5.00pm. Enthusiastic team of previously unemployed gardeners provide first-class plant selections for outdoors/inside, on a previously derelict site.

The Garden Centre   Alexandra Palace, N22 4BB. (Alexandra Palace BR.) *Tel:* 081-444 2555. *Open:* 7 days, Mon to Sat, 9.30am to 6.00pm. Late night Thu, 8.00pm. Open Sun, 10.00am to 6.00pm. Extensive garden centre. Shop with imaginative house/conservatory plants, plus pots/tubs and conservatory/garden furniture.

Harper and Toms   13 Elgin Crescent, W11 2JA. (10 mins Notting Hill Gate tube.) *Tel:* 071-792 8510. *Open:* Mon to Sat, 9.00am to 7.00pm. Tom kept a stall round the corner from Mr Harper, from whom he bought the shop. He still goes to market at 3.00am every day.

Laurel's Florist   61b Judd Street, WC1H 9QT. (5 mins Russell Square tube.) *Tel:* 071-387 6200. *Open:* Mon to Fri, 9.00am to 6.00pm, Sat 9.00am to 4.00pm. Country-style flowers; lilies/roses.

Manic Botanic   2 Silver Place, W1R 3LL. (5 mins Picadilly Circus.) *Tel:* 071-287 9856. *Open:* Mon to Fri, 10.00am to 6.00pm, Sat 12.00 noon to 5.00pm. Lilies/country garden flowers. Cacti a speciality . . . and insect-eating plants!

Outside Inside   68 Fortune Green Road, West Hampstead NW6 1DS. *Tel:* 071-431 3527. *Open:* Tue to Sat, 10.00am to 6.00pm. Everything for the conservatory, including displays of "designer" trellis from Trellisworks.

Jane Packer Floral Design
56 James Street, W1M 5HS. (3 mins Bond Street tube.) *Tel:* 071-935 2673. *Open:* Mon to Sat, 9.00am to 6.00pm. "Natural and uncontrived, in middle of the city." Summer flowers all year round. Dried flowers/windowboxes. Unusual flowering plants. Video: "Living with Flowers". Fragrant candles. Flower-arranging classes/courses.

Home Counties/ South East

Crowther of Syon Lodge   London Road, Isleworth, Middx TW7 5BH.

(Behind Syon Park. M4, junction 2.) *Tel:* 081-560 7978. *Open:* Mon to Fri, 9.00am to 5.00pm, Sat and Sun, 11.00am to 4.00pm. Garden crammed with splendid antique sculptures, fountains, urns and benches. World famous.

Garden Crafts   Sissinghurst Road, Biddenden, Kent TN27 8EJ. (5 mins Sissinghurst Castle.) *Tel:* (0580) 292070. *Open:* 7 days, Tue to Fri 9.00am to 5.00pm, Sat 10.00am to 5.00pm, Sun 10.00am to 4.30pm. Garden ornaments/furniture. Arresting outdoor displays of classical reproductions. Specialists for over 65 years.

Hannah Peschar Gallery   Black and White Cottage, Standon Lane, Ockley, Surrey RH5 5QR. *Tel:* (0306) 79269. *Open:* May to Oct, Fri and Sat, 11.00am to 6.00pm, Sun 2.00pm to 5.00pm. Other times by appointment for group visits/buyers. Modern sculptures/ceramics for gardens/exteriors, displayed in wonderfully landscaped garden, where the wilderness is carefully ordered to create visionary vistas. Essential viewing for garden/fine art lovers. Admission £3, children £1.50.

Pots and Pithoi   Grange Farm, Turner's Hill Road, Crawley Down, W. Sussx. *Enquiries to:* Bankton Cottage, Turner's Hill Road, Crawley Down, W. Sussx RH10 4EY. (M23/A264. Turn right at Duke's Head pub, onto B2028.) *Tel:* (0342) 714793. *Open:* Mon to Fri, 2.00pm to 6.00pm, Sat and Sun, 10.00am to 6.00pm. Terracotta pots, up to 115cm tall, made by hand in Crete and imported. Free leaflet available.

7. TELEPHONES

"Mr Watson, come here; I want you."

The first telephone conversation of Alexander Graham Bell (1847–1922), who patented the telephone in 1876.

Time was, you had any colour, so long as it was black with a dial. Time present, anything rings.

London Postal Districts

Alternative Telephones
1 Shepherds Bush Shopping Centre, W12 8PP. (2 mins Shepherds Bush tube.) *Tel*: 081-740 7733. *Open*: Mon to Fri, 10.00am to 6.00pm, Sat 10.00am to 2.00pm. Good range of telephones, sophisticated call-logging/answering machines, pay phones, speaker phones. Novelty piano, phone box phones.

British Telecom Shop   Ealing Broadway Centre, W5 5JY. (3 mins Ealing Broadway tube/BR.) *Tel*: 081-456 8222. *Open*: Mon to Sat, 9.00am to 5.30pm (all branches). Full range of BT telephones, answering machines, faxes, pagers, cellular phones. DIY extension kits, phonecards, bill payment facility. BT approved novelty phones.
Also at: 21–23 Worple Road,

Wimbledon SW19 4BA. *Tel*: 081-666 2929.
See also **Home Counties/South East** below.

Echo Communications
80 Brompton Road, SW7 3LQ. (5 mins South Kensington tube.) *Tel*: 071-581 8011. *Open*: Mon to Fri, 9.00am to 6.00pm, Sat 10.00am to 5.00pm. Complete range of telephone/communication equipment, including hand-portable phones. Plus duck/piano/car-shaped phones on the frivolous side.

The Telephone Store   48 Blythe Road, W14 0HA. (5 mins Olympia tube.) *Tel*: 071-602 6880. *Open*: Mon to Fri, 9.30am to 6.00pm, Sat 9.30am to 1.30pm. Dealers for all major telephone manufacturers. Supply everything to do with telephones; "all the latest technology".
Also at: 97–99 Praed Street, W2 1NT. *Tel*: 071-258 0234. *Open*: Mon to Fri, 9.00am to 6.00pm, Sat 10.00am to 5.00pm.
And at: 26 Queen's Parade, Friern Barnet Road, N11 3DA. *Tel*: 081-361 2926. *Open*: Mon to Sat, 9.30am to 6.00pm. Early closing Wed, 1.30pm.
And at: 33 Railway Approach, London Bridge, SE1 9SR. *Tel*: 071-378 6625. *Open*: Mon to Fri, 9.00am to 6.00pm, Sat 11.00am to 2.00pm.
See also **Home Counties/South East** below.

Home Counties/ South East

British Telecom Shop   Allders Mall, North End, Croydon, Surrey CR9 1SB. *Tel*: 081-681 3394.
Also at: 3 High Street, Bromley, Kent BR1 1LF. *Tel*: 081-460 6777.
And at: 199 High Street, Lewisham SR13 6JT. *Tel*: 081-852 7400.
And at: 336/338 Station Road, Harrow HA1 2DR. *Tel*: 081-863 6262.
And at: 82 High Street, Watford, Herts WD1 2BP. *Tel*: (0923) 33444.
And at: 189 High Street, Hounslow TW3 1BL. *Tel*: 081-577 6777.
And at: 33 Market Square, Uxbridge, UB8 1LH. *Tel*: (0895) 55755.
And at: 2 Eden Walk, Kingston KT1 1BP. *Tel*: 081-547 3232.
See also **London Postal Districts** above.

The Telephone Store   120 Sheen Road, Richmond, Surrey TW9 1UR. *Tel*: 081-948 1300. *Open*: Mon to Sat, 9.30am to 6.00pm.
Also at: 206 High Road, Woodford Green, Essex IG8 9EF. *Tel*: 081-504 4805. *Open*: Mon to Sat, 9.30am to 6.00pm. Early closing Wed 1.30pm.
See also **London Postal Districts** above.

8. RUGS

Add flair to a floor that's seen better times, or has a humdrum budget aura. Use rugs to cushion wear, add softness to hard surfaces, or even to conceal stains and other imperfections.

London Postal Districts

Robert and Colleen Bery Designs
See **Furniture 9. Painted**.
Handpainted canvas floorcloths, continuing an 18th-century tradition. Heavy-duty canvas, strengthened

with waterproof sealer, colour-washed, handpainted, varnished.

David Black Oriental Carpets
96 Portland Road, Holland Park W11 4LM. (5 mins Holland Park tube.) *Tel*: 071-727 2566. Embroideries, knotted carpets, flat weaves and tapestries.

Casa Pupo See **Ethnic Crafts and Furnishings**. Classic, Spanish, heavy woven wool rugs, with deep fringing. Circular, oval, square, rectangles. Vivid colour combinations, or woven to order in any colours.

Duval Carpet Co Duval House, 1/2 Glebe Road, E8 4BD. (Liverpool Street tube, plus bus.) *Tel*: 071-739 7596/071-249 9635. *Open*: Mon to Fri, 9.30am to 5.00pm. Closed Sat. Open Sun, 9.30am to 1.30pm. Three floors packed with thousands of beguiling rugs/carpets from Persia, Pakistan, China, Turkey, Afghanistan, Romania, Russia. Three-generation family business, founded in 1927 by Mr Hajioff. Friendly atmosphere: "We take the mystique out of Orientals." They buy direct, in order to sell at best prices. Take rugs on approval to check out colour schemes.

Gallery Zadah 29 Conduit Street, W1R 9TA. (5 mins Oxford Circus tube.) *Tel*: 071-493 2622. *Open*: Mon to Fri, 10.00am to 5.30pm, Sat by appointment. Stock of around 1,000 fine old carpets for decoration or investment. Family business: Lida and her brother, Alex Zadah, are the second generation.

Daphne Graham 1 Elystan Street, SW3 3NT. (10 mins South Kensington tube.) *Tel*: 071-584 8724. *Open*: Mon to Fri, 9.30am to 5.30pm, Sat 10.00am to 1.00pm. Fine antique kelims, and kelim-upholstered furniture. Also exclusive floral kelim-style flat-woven rugs, made to 19th-century designs. Antique Persian carpets. Occasional antique French Verdure tapestries.

Graham and Green See **Accessories 1. General** above. Antonia Graham visits Turkey annually to buy kelims in a variety of sizes; "attractive, usable rugs, rather than collectors' pieces". Turkey/Iran/Afghanistan.

Sally Hampson 45 Charlotte Road, EC2A 3PD. (5 mins Old Street tube.) *Tel*: 071-739 4988. *Open*: by appointment. Woven rugs/blankets to commission.

Kelim and Nomadic Rug Gallery 5 Shepherds Walk, Hampstead NW3 5UE. (5 mins Hampstead tube.) *Tel*: 071-435 8972. *Open*: Tue to Sat, 10.30am to 5.30pm. Del Blacker hunts down kelims, from the antique to the merely secondhand. Kelim-covered cushions. Rug repairs/restorations on the premises.

The Kilim Warehouse 28a Pickets Street, SW12 8QB. (5 mins Clapham South BR.) *Tel*: 081-675 3122. *Open*: Mon to Fri, 10.00am to 6.00pm, Sat 10.00am to 4.00pm. Flat woven kelims, old/new. Variety sizes, designs, colours from Turkey, Afghanistan, Yugoslavia, Persia, Romania, Poland, Egypt. Informative staff, cleaning/restoration service. *Also at*: The Kilim House, 951/953 Fulham Road, SW6 5HY. *Tel*: 071-731 4912.

▶ **Bargains!**

Nice Irma's See **Ethnic Crafts and Furnishings**. Top value rag rugs from 2 by 3ft upwards, in bright colours/pastels. Also Pokhran rugs. Simple, heavyweight natural shades in wool/cotton; they cover large areas at surprisingly low cost.

Orientalist 74 and 78 Highgate Road, NW5 1PB. (3 mins Kentish Town tube.) *Tel*: 071-482 0555. *Open*: Mon to Sat, 10.00am to 5.00pm. Ground floor displays, workrooms above. Oriental handmade rugs, carpets, textiles, tapestries. Expert repair of all antique rugs and textiles.

Annie Sherburne Waterside Workshops, 99 Rotherhithe Street, SE16 4NF. (Rotherhithe tube.) *Tel*: 071-237 0017. *Open*: by appointment. One-off, hand-tufted rugs, felt hangings. Commissions.

Something Wild See **Furniture 13. Avant-Garde**. Wild rugs in zebra stripes.

Surface Solutions Larnaca Works, Grange Walk, Bermondsey SE1 3EH. (10 mins Tower Hill tube.) *Tel*: 071-231 3009. *Open*: by appointment.

High quality hand-tufted rugs and wall hangings in stock/to commission.

David J Wilkins Oriental Rugs 27 Princess Road, Regent's Park NW1 8JR. (Close to London Zoo. Unrestricted parking.) *Tel*: 071-722 7608. *Open*: by appointment. Small showroom/office. Trading for over 20 years. Clients taken by appointment to bonded carpet warehouses—about 10 mins by car. Handmade new/antique rugs at reasonable prices. Excellent value/investments. Expert advice.

Home Counties/ South East

Lucy Clegg 42 Cross Tree Road, Wicken, Milton Keynes, Bucks MK19 6BT. *Tel*: (0908) 57318. *Open*: by appointment. Tufted rugs inspired by forms in nature.

Christopher Legge Oriental Carpets 25 Oakthorpe Road, Summertown, Oxford OX2 7BD. *Tel*: (0865) 57572. *Open*: Mon to Sat, 9.30am to 5.00pm. 19th- and early 20th-century Oriental carpets; DOBAG vegetable-dyed Turkish rugs. Expert advice. Cleaning/restoration. Talks/courses on rug conservation/repairs. Mailing list.

Karel Weijand Lion and Lamb Courtyard, Farnham, Surrey GU9 7LL. *Tel*: (0252) 726215. *Open*: Mon to Sat, 9.30am to 5.30pm, or by appointment. Fine selections of Oriental rugs, carpets, runners, kelims; over 35 years' experience. Valuations, restorations, cleaning. *Also at*: Odiham Gallery, 78 High Street, Odiham, Hants. *Tel*: (0256) 703415.

Mail Order

Standfast Filtec Developments Unit 1, Tower Road, Berinsfield, Oxon OX10 7LN. *Tel*: (0865) 341666. Anti-creep underlays for rugs on carpets/hard floors.

9. MIRRORS AND SCREENS

Mirror, mirror on the wall . . . where did you come from?

London Postal Districts

Robert and Colleen Bery Designs
See **Furniture 9. Painted**.
Intricately stencilled screens in wonderful colourings; stock or to order.

Chelsea Glass   650 Portslade Road, SW8 3HD. (1 min Wandsworth Road BR.) *Tel:* 071-720 6905. *Open:* Mon to Fri, 8.00am to 5.30pm, Sat 8.00am to 12.00 noon. Established for 100 years. "The biggest selection of mirrors in Europe!" Antique, tinted, Art Deco, Art Nouveau and more. Restorations, expert advice, deliveries.

▶ Bargains!

The Dormy House See
10. Occasional Furniture
below.   Super screens in elegant shapes to cover in your own fabrics.

Fellowes and Saunderson See
3. Frames above.   Unusual mirror frames to order: your ideas or theirs.

House of Mirrors   597 King's Road, SW6 2EL. (5 mins Fulham Broadway tube.) *Tel:* 071-736 5885. *Open:* Mon to Sat, 9.00am to 6.00pm. Genuine 19th-century mirrors; restorations.

Just Mirrors   675 Fulham Road, SW6 5PZ. (10 mins Fulham Broadway tube.) *Tel:* 071-736 1955. *Open:* Mon to Sat, 9.30am to 5.30pm. Well-established specialists in handmade, reproduction antique period frames. Gold leaf, bronze, Dutch gold, various veneers. Stained/marbled frames or made from your wallpaper/fabric. Made-to-measure service. Specials. Mail order catalogue.

Laura Ashley See **Decorating Materials 2. Co-ordinated Collections**.   Choice of screens in co-ordinated furnishing fabrics.

Lead and Light See **Windows 2. Stained and Decorative Glass**. Stained glass screens.

The Mosaic Studio   43 Vallance Road, N22. (Alexandra Palace BR. Bounds Green tube.) *Tel:* 081-889 0190. *Open:* by appointment. Yehudit (Judy) Morrell, born in Israel, creates glittering mosaic frames around bevelled geometric mirror shapes: diamonds, octagons, rectangles, squares. Commissions take about two weeks. Some in stock. Mirrors come ready to hang. Mosaic floors also undertaken.

Overmantels   66 Battersea Bridge Road, SW11 3AG. (Sloane Square/ South Kensington tubes.) *Tel:* 071-223 8151. *Open:* Mon to Sat, 9.30am to 5.30pm. Mirrors for chimney breasts. Traditional Victorian/ Regency styles. Triptychs (three sections) are particularly impressive.

Also upholstered fender stools in calico for covering, or your choice of fabric. Advise, deliver, fit.
Also at: 3 Highgate High Street, N6 5JR. (10 mins Hampstead/Archway tubes.) *Tel:* 081-348 8362. *Open:* Mon to Sat, 10.00am to 6.00pm.

Through the Looking Glass
563 King's Road, SW6 2EB. (10 mins Fulham Broadway tube.) *Tel:* 071-736 7799. *Open:* Mon to Sat, 10.00am to 5.30pm (both branches). 19th-century antique mirrors, mainly French/British. Varied styles/shapes/ sizes.
Also at: 137 Kensington Church Street, W8 7LP. (2 mins Notting Hill Gate tube.) *Tel:* 071-221 4026.

Home Counties/ South East

Screens Gallery   The Malt House, Bridgefoot Path, Emsworth, Hants PO10 7EB. *Tel:* (0243) 377334. *Open:* by appointment. Bev and Mark Houldings take commissions for hand-carved, painted interior screens. Textural, colourful, figurative, painted, printed, carved: these are international collectors' pieces.

Juliet Helen Walker
79a Southampton Road, Lymington, Hants SO41 9GH. *Tel:* (0590) 675135. *Open:* by appointment. Richly decorated, highly original interior screens.

10. OCCASIONAL FURNITURE

"No man . . . who has wrestled with a self-adjusting card table can ever quite be the man he once was."

James Thurber (1894–1961), *Let Your Mind Alone*

Finding all those extra pieces you need can be tricky . . . occasional tables, trollies, TV tables and so on. Firms listed in the **Furniture** chapter can help, so browse through it for some extra ideas: **1. Reproduction** will help with period designs, while **12. Made-to-Measure and Commissioned**, and **13. Avant-garde** may produce ideas for something more special. Many shops in the **Ethnic Crafts and Furnishings** chapter sell exotic small tables/stools etc.

London Postal Districts

Glass Distinction See **Furniture 8. Glass, Marble and Metal**. Glass coffee tables made to order in any size/shape.

Ikea See **Furniture 1. General**. Large choice of attractive, low-cost, useful designs. Wood/steel/glass. Brightly coloured lacquers. Hi-fi storage. A good hunting-ground.

Kassis   77 Hamilton Terrace, NW8 9QX. *Tel:* 071-266 3455. *Open:* by appointment. Interior designer coffee table collection. Variety of styles: classic/contemporary. Craftsmen include joiners, painters, gilders, masons, metalworkers. Tops in "scagliola", an ancient technique simulating rare marbles, using pressed marble powder. Elegant Perspex "collector's" tables. Deco designs in birds' eye maple. Antiques from India/China. Plus side/console tables.

Marks and Spencer See **Chain Stores**. Comprehensive choice of coffee tables in pine/repro/cane. Plus video units.

The Reject Shop See **Furniture 1. General**.   Excellent source for no-frills coffee tables, TV/hi-fi storage, trollies etc.

The Treske Shop See **Furniture 1. General**.   Simple, well-made classic modern designs for trollies, small tables etc. in native hardwoods.

Mail order

The Dormy House   Stirling Park, East Portway, Andover, Hants SP10 3TZ. *Tel:* (0264) 365808. *Showroom open:* Mon to Fri, 10.30am to 3.30pm, Sat (by appointment), 9.00am to 1.00pm. Slot-together "instant" tables in chipboard/MDF to paint yourself, or supplied lacquered. Round/semi-circular. Conceal with pretty cloths, also supplied. Use for sofa/bedside tables, wall tables, display/occasional tables. Special oval designs take TV/video. Brilliant ideas, well thought out and conscientiously marketed by imaginative, friendly family firm. Free colour catalogue.

11. TABLEWARE AND TABLE LINEN

"It is interesting to reflect that the cost of four servings of smoked salmon will buy you a beautiful bone china plate, and a crystal glass costs only the same as two or three bottles of modest wine."

David, Marquess of Queensberry, former Professor of Ceramics and Glass, Royal College of Art, and a partner of Queensberry Hunt design group.

Large china stores, with their comprehensive selections, are well known. **Department Stores** are also fruitful sources and many have "concessions" with stock/service

controlled by big-name manufacturers. Below you will find extra inspiration. See also **British Crafts** and **Kitchens 9. Kitchenware**.

London Postal Districts

Anta See **Soft Furnishings 1. Fabrics**. Wonderful tartan ceramics, functional and decorative.

Aria Tableart   10/11 Upper Kingswell, Heath Street, Hampstead NW3 1EN. (5 mins Hampstead tube.)

Tel: 071-433 3453. *Open:* 7 days, Mon to Fri, 10.00am to 6.00pm, Sat 10.30am to 6.00pm, Sun 12.30pm to 6.00pm. Functional/decorative pottery/glass/metalware, plus production pieces "to set alight any room or table".
Also at: 133 Upper Street, Islington N1 1QP. (5 mins Angel tube.) *Tel:* 071-226 1021. *Open:* Mon to Sat, 10.00am to 7.00pm.

At Home In The Village   2 High Street, Wimbledon Village SW19 5DX. (5 mins Wimbledon tube/BR.) *Tel:* 081-946 4559. *Open:* Mon to Sat, 9.30am to 5.30pm. Mrs Khan (ex-Royal Doulton/Chinacraft) promises "traditional personal service, sadly lacking in modern-day shopping," for quality crystal/bone china. Lalique, Baccarat, Royal Worcester, Boehm, Moorcroft, Royal Crown Derby.

Emma Bridgewater   739 Fulham Road, SW6 5UL. (5 mins Parsons Green tube.) *Tel*: 071-371 9033. *Open*: Mon to Fri, 9.30am to 5.00pm, Sat 10.00am to 5.00pm. Chez Chelsea, everyone has a bit of that fashionable sponged tableware. The lady that started the craze now has her own large corner shop. Chunky shapes/pretty patterns. Also vivid, shiny plain glazes. Plus unusual furniture/accessories for kitchen/diningroom, dating from the thirties backwards. Dollies' teasets, which grown-ups love. Charming children's plates/mugs.

Ceramica Blue   10 Blenheim Crescent, W11. (10 mins Holland Park/Ladbroke Grove tubes.) *Tel*: 071-727 0288. *Open*: Tue to Sat, 10.30am to 6.30pm. Modern Italian ceramics. Handmade, handpainted English plates, vases, tiles etc. Practical/decorative; unusual, bold colours. Commissions.

Chinacraft (House of)   198 Regent Street, W1R 4DF. (5 mins Piccadilly Circus tube.) *Tel*: 071-437 2332. *Open*: Mon to Sat, 9.00am to 6.00pm. Late night Thu, 8.00pm. Flagship store for UK's largest independent china retailer. Most famous names, most popular patterns. All fairly run-of-the-mill, but nonetheless splendid for that. Ground floor: tableware; lower ground: gifts; first: crystal/cutlery; second: limited editions. Monogramming/special designs: you can even put your dog on a plate . . .
Also at: 71 Regent Street, W1R 7HG. (3 mins Piccadilly tube.) *Tel*: 071-734 4915. *Open*: Mon to Sat, 9.00am to 6.00pm. Late night Thu, 7.30pm.
And at: 566 Oxford Street, W1N 9HJ. (5 mins Marble Arch tube.) *Tel*: 071-724 8493. *Open*: Mon to Sat, 9.00am to 6.00pm. Late night Thu, 8.00pm. Open Sun, 10.00am to 5.00pm.

And at: 1 Beauchamp Place, SW3 1NG. (5 mins Knightsbridge tube.) *Tel*: 071-584 8981. Late night Wed, 7.00pm.
And at: 7 Burlington Arcade, Piccadilly W1V 9AB. (5 mins Green Park tube.) *Tel*: 071-491 7624. *Open*: Mon to Fri, 9.00am to 6.00pm, Sat 9.00am to 5.30pm.
And at: 121 Park Street, W1R 2BH. *Tel*: 071-499 9881. *Open*: Mon to Sat, 9.00am to 6.00pm. Late night Thu, 7.00pm.
And at: Unit V20, Brent Cross NW4 3FG. *Tel*: 081-202 6206. *Open*: Mon to Fri, 10.00am to 8.00pm, Sat 9.00am to 6.00pm.
And at: Whiteleys Shopping Centre, W2.
See also **Home Counties/South East** below.

Richard Dare   93 Regent's Park Road, NW1 8UR. (10 mins Chalk Farm tube.) *Tel*: 071-722 9428. *Open*: Mon to Fri, 9.30am to 6.00pm, Sat 10.00am to 4.00pm. A delightfully personal service for robustly patterned French tableware/cutlery: Luneville, Gien, de Quimper, Limoges. Chic and cheerful. Replacements readily available. Emphasis on design continuity . . . Richard's been in business since 1969.

Divertimenti See **Kitchens 9. Kitchenware**.   Wide range cutlery/tableware. Mainly Italian/French charming provincial patterns; hand-decorated modern/traditional designs. Good for large bowls/platters.

Thomas Goode and Co   19 South Audley Street, W1Y 6BN. (2 mins Bond Street tube.) *Tel*: 071-499 2823. *Open*: Mon to Sat, 9.30am to 5.30pm. Possibly the grandest of posh tableware shops in W1. Fine china, glass and silver-plated tableware. Browsing is inspirational. Antecedents are impeccable: wealthy Mayfair cognoscenti have been shopping here since 1827. Now an international and frequently royal clientele beat a path to the door, for their claim to be "the most famous china and glass retailer in the world" has great credibility. The

exotic pair of Minton elephants that grace the façade are tourist landmarks. Nevertheless, the atmosphere is not intimidating. This is still an independent family concern (fifth generation) with courteous, knowledgeable, friendly staff: "we call it service." Royal Doulton, Herend, Minton, Royal Crown Derby, Wedgwood, Royal Worcester, Spode, etc. From cosy willow pattern to finest, thinnest gilded bone. Plus crystal from Baccarat, Crystal de Sèvres, Royal Brierly, Waterford, Stuart, Goodewse Cumberland: superbly simple quality plain tumblers/wine glasses. Silverware: coffee/teapots, covered vegetable dishes, jugs, bowls, champagne buckets, coasters, hotplates, napkin rings, nutcrackers. Silver-plated cutlery holders, keeping 24 pieces easily accessible. Classic cutlery in sterling silver and silver plate. Accessories/gifts. Awash with royal warrants. Goode's execute commissions for crests/monograms. Antique/modern ornaments/plates/vases. Deliveries. Engraving service. Glass repairs.

Graham and Green See **Accessories 1. General**.   Good selections of attractive tableware at reasonable prices, including plain/decorated ranges from Poland.

Ikea See **Furniture 1. General**.   It is well worth braving the crowds (try and shop off-peak) for rock-bottom prices. Plain, no-nonsense shapes/patterns for chinaware: e.g. white-glazed chunky dishwasher/microwave safe stoneware. Stainless-steel, simple modern cutlery. Good choice of glasses, including excellent party packs. Glazed flintware plates/bowls in bright shades with a designer feel. Imaginative plastics.

Georg Jensen/Royal Copenhagen 15 New Bond Street, W1. (5 mins Green Park/Bond Street tubes.) *Tel*: 071-499 6541. *Open*: Mon to Fri, 9.15am to 5.30pm, Sat 10.00am to 5.00pm. Fine Scandinavian design, in newly refurbished showroom. For understated elegance: Arne Jacobsen's famous cutlery in silver plate/stainless steel. A softer note is struck by Royal Copenhagen's exquisite bone china, first requested in London by Queen Alexandra in 1897. Wedding lists/engraving.

Mappin and Webb   170 Regent Street, W1R 6BQ. (5 mins Piccadilly Circus tube.) *Tel:* 071-734 3801. *Open:* Mon to Sat, 9.00am to 5.30pm. Major name in London's table talk. Silver specialists with an international reputation. The company's history dates back to Jonathan Mappin's small Sheffield workshop. Mappin Plate classic designs are available, such as gadroon/capstan for bowls, dishes, cruets, condiment sets, candlesticks, grape scissors, sauce boats and sugar dredgers. Holloware sterling silver/Mappin Plate tea/coffee sets with elegant matching trays. Classic plated or solid silver cutlery individually or in seven-piece place settings; designs from simple Rattail to ultra-ornate Russell. Stag-horn meat carvers. Watches/clocks. Jewellery with custom design workshop. Repairs/cleaning/ restorations. Expert valuations. Special commissions for china/porcelain, silver, glass. Crystal engraving. Gift vouchers. Wedding service. New personal stationery service. Colour gift catalogue.
Also at: 65 Brompton Road, Knightsbridge, SW3 1DB. (5 mins Knightsbridge tube.) *Tel:* 071-584 9361.
And at: 2 Queen Victoria Street, EC4N 4TL. *Tel:* 071-248 6661.
And at: 125/6 Fenchurch Street, EC3 5DL. *Tel:* 071-626 3171.

Molino Coffee Shop   16 Leeland Road, West Ealing W13 9HH. (Just off Ealing Broadway.) *Tel:* 081-567 2853. *Open:* Mon to Sat, 9.00am to 5.00pm. Excellent coffee! Emilia Castro also stocks a wide range of Italian coffee machines (some at bargain prices) plus all sizes of French cafetières and Bistro green/ gold china.

Perfect Setting   151 Fulham Road, SW3 6SN. (5 mins South Kensington tube.) *Tel:* 071-581 6781. *Open:* Mon to Sat, 9.30am to 6.00pm. Lace

reigns supreme at very affordable prices (made in China). Cluny lace mats, cutwork, tape lace table linen. Also woven damask in fine patterns. White/cream. Mail order catalogue. For those who still love to set a pretty table.

Perfect Presents   5 Park Walk, SW10 0AJ. (10 mins Fulham Broadway tube.) *Tel:* 071-351 5342. *Open:* Mon to Sat, 10.00am to 6.00pm. Late night Wed, 7.00pm (open 11.00am). Incorporates "The Perfect Glass Shop". Small but perfectly formed . . . both shop and wares. Inspired selections: from everyday cheapos to finest crystal. Plain/ coloured/re-cycled. Etched/ engraved. Contemporary/antique. Individual pieces from premier craft workshops. Repairs/engraving. Wedding lists/gift wrapping. Mail order.
Also at: Chelsea Farmers' Market, Sydney Street, SW3 6NR. *Tel:* 071-376 8514. *Open:* as above, plus Sun, 11.00am to 5.00pm.

Portmeirion London Shop
4 Holland Street, W8 4LT. (5 mins High Street Kensington tube.) *Tel:* 071-938 1891. *Open:* Mon to Sat, 10.00am to 5.30pm. Complete range (lots of different shapes) of Susan Williams-Ellis' deservedly perennial Botanic Gardens, introduced in 1972: based on 32 flowering plants/butterflies taken from 19th-century, hand-coloured natural history books. The pattern romps over all table-/kitchenware/ crockery/rolling pins/cookware. Plus co-ordinating tiles/trays/mats; fabric accessories by the metre. The ultimate in kitchen/table set-and-match: wonderful for presents.

The Reject China Shop   134 Regent Street, W1R 4DF. *Tel:* 071-437 3576/434 2502. *Open:* Mon to Sat, 9.00am to 6.00pm. Late night Thu, 8.00pm. Caters for tighter budgets than its ritzier neighbours: what a relief. The goods are not actually "rejects" at all (the name lingers from earlier trading policies). Goods are mostly "firsts": practical and pretty. Continuous promotions/ discounts. "Rummage baskets",

however, offer seconds/special offers. For a real china binge, go to Knightsbridge, for the famous cluster of adjacent branches listed below.
Also at: 183 Brompton Road, SW3 1NF. (5 mins Knightsbridge tube.) *Tel:* 071-581 0739.
And at: 33/35 Beauchamp Place, SW3 1NF. (5 mins Knightsbridge tube.) *Tel:* 071-581 0737/8. Giftware/crystal.
Also at: 74 Southampton Row, WC1. (5 mins Knightsbridge tube.) *Tel:* 071-242 3271.
See also **Home Counties/South East** below.

▶ Bargains!

Reject Pot Shop   56 Chalk Farm Road, NW1 8AN. (5 mins Chalk Farm tube.) *Tel:* 071-485 2326. *Open:* Tue to Sun, 11.00am to 5.30pm. Crammed with plates/ teapots/cups/casseroles bought weekly by the enterprising owners direct from potteries. Undecorated factory "seconds" in earthenware/ china. Also many popular patterns.

Something Wild See **Furniture 13. Avant-garde.**   Polka dots/zebra stripes for exclusive zany bone china.

Table Matters   6 Harriet Street, SW1X 9JS. (5 mins Knightsbridge tube.) *Tel:* 071-245 9747. *Open:* Mon to Fri, 10.00am to 6.00pm, Sat 10.00am to 5.00pm. Mostly chic (but sometimes chi-chi) mix of old/new stock from antique dealer owners. Opulent settings on ground floor, plus pretty basement. Exclusive merchandise includes tableware/ candle sconces. Flamboyant table settings: worth viewing, but at a price.

The Tea House   15a Neal Street, WC2H 9PU. (3 mins Covent Garden tube.) *Tel:* 071-240 7539. *Open:* 7 days, Mon to Sat, 10.00am to 7.00pm, Sun, 11.00am to 6.00pm. Over 200 teapots from traditional/ antique to unusual or even bizarre. Trays, tea infusers, caddies, mugs, strainers, stirrers, cosies, milk jugs, jumbo cups and saucers. Many pots escape the tea table to become collector's items. 45 varieties of fine teas.

Villeroy and Boch Creation   203 Regent Street, W1R 7DE. (5 mins Oxford Circus tube.) *Tel:* 071-434 0249. *Open:* Mon to Sat, 9.30am to 6.00pm. Late night Thu, 7.00pm. New light, airy showrooms over two floors. Stunning modern designs. Bone china, porcelain, lead crystal, cutlery, gifts, accessories, linen from Europe's largest ceramics manufacturer, founded in 1748. Très snob: apparently the Pope chooses and uses goods from Villeroy and Boch! Its stable of classy European designers includes Paloma Picasso. Wedding lists/free gift-wrapping.

Waterford Wedgwood   158 Regent Street, W1R 5TA. (5 mins Piccadilly Circus.) *Tel:* 071-734 7262. *Open:* Mon to Sat, 9.30am to 6.00pm. Late night Thu, 7.00pm. Regent Street is the premier international promenade for top tableware: a suitable setting for this palatial store with wall-to-wall china (no bulls, please). Best British brands available for china/

crystal/boxed gifts. Bridal register. *Also at:* 270 Regent Street, W1R 6HA. (At Oxford Circus.) *Tel:* 071-734 5656. *Open as above.* *And at:* 173/174 Piccadilly, W1V 0PD. (5 mins Green Park tube.) *Tel:* 071-629 2614.

Wilson and Gill   137 Regent Street, W1R 8ND. (5 mins Oxford Circus tube.) *Tel:* 071-734 3076. *Open:* Mon to Sat, 9.00am to 6.00pm. Late night Thu, 7.00pm. Ultra-elegant, modern designs. Rosenthal/Thomas. Glass, china, boxed gifts, cutlery. Thomas is *the* brand for plain white porcelain classics. Plus flamboyant designer pieces. Wedding lists. Monograms/crests. Glass engraving. *Also at:* Rosenthal Studio House, 102 Brompton Road, SW3 1JJ. (5 mins Knightsbridge tube.) *Tel:* 071-584 0683/4.

Home Counties/ South East

Ashton House   181b High Street, Hampton Hill, Middx TW12 1NL. *Tel:*

081-979 0027. *Open:* Mon to Sat, 9.00am to 5.30pm. Pretty shop overflowing with china, glass, table linen, cookware. Also stationery/gifts. Helpful staff. Gift wrapping.

Chinacraft   149 High Street, Bromley, Kent BR1 1JD. *Tel:* 081-464 5954. *Also at:* 1/2 Dukes Lane, Brighton, E. Sussx BN1 1BG. *Tel:* (0273) 25408. *And at:* Army and Navy, Maidstone and Gravesend. See also **London Postal Districts** above.

Reject China Shop   1 Castle Hill, Windsor, Berks SL4 1PD. *Tel:* (0753) 850870. *Open:* 7 days, 9.00am to 6.00pm. *Also at:* 105 Cranbrook Road, Ilford Essex IG1 4PU. *Tel:* 081-478 5693. *And at:* 38 Burgate, Canterbury, Kent CT1 2JJ. *Tel:* (0227) 471834. See also **London Postal Districts** above.

21
BRITISH CRAFTS

The lure of the handmade is potent: for a relatively modest sum, which certainly compares favourably with factory-produced items, you can own/use something that is truly unique. Incidentally, many makers are unduly sensitive about the word "craft"; associations with corn dollies and baskets are often considered demeaning.

Glass and Ceramics artists can also be found in this section. For arts and crafts from other countries, please look under **Ethnic Crafts and Furnishings.**

Workshops with several craftsmen under one roof are worth exploring. Some are craft centres in attractive buildings with a café/restaurant, making a pleasant afternoon out.

London Postal Districts

Camden Lock Chalk Farm Road, NW1 8AF. (3 mins Chalk Farm/Camden Town tubes. Or by waterbus from Little Venice. *Tel:* 071-482 2550 for details.) *Tel:* 071-485 7963/3459. *Open:* Tue to Sun, 10.00am to 5.30pm. Rambling, recently redeveloped assortment of studio/shops: exploration is essential. Very crowded/touristy on weekend market days: a peaceful weekday visit is preferable. Lots of places to drink/eat. **Lead and Light** (see **Windows 2. Stained and Decorative Glass**): stained-glass workshop/supplies. *Tel:* 071-485 4568. **Antique and Modern**: antique clocks, watches, repairs. *Tel:* 071-267 5310. **Fabric and Flowers**: pots, vases, frames. *Tel:* 071-267 2435. **The Illustrated Potter** (see **5. Ceramics** below): decorated ceramics. *Tel:* 071-485 5116. **Cane and Able**: furniture/artefacts from India; kelims/rugs. *Tel:* 071-485 2350. **Camden Lock Balloon Company**: custom prints. *Tel:* 071-267 4885. **Victorian Fireplace Company**: original antiques. *Tel:* 071-482 2543. **Ashvale Oriental Carpets**: *Tel:* 071-482 5049. **Light Industry**: designer lighting. *Tel:* 071-267 6530/7876. **The Lock Shop**: best of British crafts. *Tel:* 071-485 3450.

Gabriel's Wharf 56 Upper Ground, SE1. (5 mins Waterloo tube/BR.) *Tel:* 071-485 4451. *Open:* Tue to Sun, 10.00am to 5.00pm. Charming complex of around 20 shops/studios, with cafés/bars, and pleasant river views. **Pieces**: Oriental rugs and kelims. *Tel:* 071-401 2335. **Indigo** (see **Ethnic Crafts and Furnishings**): antique Indian furniture restoration. *Tel:* 071-401 2597. **Sculpt**: ceramic sculpture. *Tel:* 071-928 0985. **Immaterial**: handpainted textiles. *Tel:* 071-401 2323. **Vivienne Legg**: ceramics. *Tel:* 071-401 2240. **The Glass Studio**: blown, engraved, stained glass. *Tel:* 071-620 0245.

Kingsgate Workshops 110/116 Kingsgate Road, NW6 2JG. (5 mins West Hampstead tube.) *Tel:* 071-328 7878. 60 artists/craftspeople, plus exhibition gallery for hire. **Alisoun Howie**: painted/stained glass. *Tel:* 071-625 8595. **Daphne Carnegy**: handmade, brightly coloured earthenware. *Tel:* 071-328 2051. **Philip Hughes**: ultra-stylish modern furniture; chairs/tables in unusual woods. *Tel:* 071-328 7496. **Chris Bramble**: large ceramics; urns, jardinières, sculpture. *Tel:* 071-624 0674. **Jonathan Knowles**: handprinted textiles for furnishings; curtains, covers. *Tel:* 071-625 9338. **Katy Reese**: handpainted silks for wallhangings, screens, cushion covers. *Tel:* 071-625 9338.

Merton Abbey Mills Watermill Way, SW19 2RD. (8 mins Colliers Wood tube. Free parking.) *Tel:* 081-543 9608. *Open:* Wed to Sun, 10.00am to 5.00pm. Shops/workshops; tearoom. **Kempcrafts**: hand-marbled papers, engraved glass, candles. *Tel:* 081-545 0185. **Festivals**: crafts. *Tel:* 081-545 0162. **Merton Abbey Mill Framing**. *Tel:* 081-543 9763. **Macondo**: South American Crafts. *Tel:* 081-947 5070. **Enchanted Wood**: framed mirrors, antiques, china. *Tel:* 081-545 0144. **Greencades**: herbs, spices, baskets, gifts. *Tel:* 081-543 0519. **Antique Mews**: pine furniture. *Tel:* 081-544 0863/(0737) 359097. **Merton Abbey Rugs**: *Tel:* 081-540 6009. **Ceramico**: landscape/interior design; ceramic pots. *Tel:* 081-544 1066.

Portobello Green 281 Portobello Road, W10 5TD. (Underneath motorway arches.) *Open:* Mon to Sat, 9.30am to 6.00pm. **James Preece Stained Glass** (see **Windows 2. Stained and Decorative Glass**). *Tel:* 081-968 8807. **Caroline Ceylon**: hand-painted textiles in bold, abstract patterns. *Tel:* 081-969 2448. **Hickmott Hodge**: huge, impressive vases/plates/urns in brilliant floral, heavy-relief patterns. *Tel:* 081-968 5800. **Deborah Windsor**: classic porcelain tableware, handpainted. Commemorative pieces, dinner services, mosaic panels, tile murals. *Tel:* 081-968 5800.

The South Bank Craft Centre Hungerford Arches, Royal Festival Hall, SE1 8XX. (5 mins Waterloo tube/BR.) *Tel:* 071-928 0681. *Open:* by appointment. Twenty studio spaces for designer/craftsmen.

401½ Workshops 401½ Wandsworth Road, SW8 2JP. *Tel:* 071-627 1523. *Open:* by appointment. Michael Haynes founded one of the first of London's group workshops, and attracts artists of the highest calibre. Ceramics/textiles/furniture.

Home Counties/ South East

Digswell Arts Trust Attimore Hall Barn Studios, The Ridgeway, Welwyn Garden City, Herts AL7 2AD. (Entrance by Attimore pub.) *Tel:* (0707) 334848. *Open:* by appointment. **Paul Fuller**: ceramics, especially coiled pots with textured surfaces. **Jeanette Appelton**: strongly coloured, textured hangings from raw fibres. **Raoma Budins**: handwoven textiles in traditional banded designs. Silk/wool/cotton pastel shades, for hangings/furniture covers.

Langston Priory Workshops Kingham, Oxon OX7 6UP. (Between Stow and Chipping Norton on B4450.) *Tel:* (0608) 658645. *Open:*

by appointment. **John Sparling**: wood turning; balustrades, four-poster beds, rush-seated Cotswold chairs, ladder- and spindle-backed chairs. **Graham White**: woodturning, dressers, bookcases, panelling. **Tiles of Stow (Sebastian and Odette John)**: hand-decorated/fired tiles for kitchen/bathroom; murals. **Richard Henshaw**: bronze casting; pots, small busts, handles.

Viables Craft Centre   Harrow Way, Basingstoke, Hants RG22 4BJ. (M3, junction 6: 20 mins Basingstoke BR.) *Tel*: (0256) 473634. *Open*: Tue to Fri, 1.00pm to 4.00pm, Sat and Sun, 2.00pm to 5.00pm. Old farm buildings, converted into craft workshops. Miniature railway. Tea room. **Ruth Wiseman**: handmade commissioned crackers for special celebrations. *Tel*: (0256) 21012. **Jeanette Moore**: hand/machine engraving. *Tel*: (0256) 474009. **Allwood (S J Hussey)**: high-quality garden furniture. *Tel*: (0256) 471431. **Framework (Gloria Thomas)**: picture framing. *Tel*: (0256) 844011.

Everlasting (Victoria Rubery): dried flowers. *Tel*: (0256) 817847. **Centric Studio (Brian Hannam)**: decorative wood turning; tuition available. *Tel*: (0256) 81191. **Cairncraft Pottery**: decorative/sculptural earthenware and stoneware; house signs; anniversary plates. *Tel*: (0256) 54663. **Mike Burrows Glass Engraving**: hand-engraving for birthdays, weddings etc.; over 100 different items of glass in stock. *Tel*: (0256) 50983.

▶ **Worth a Trip**

The Cirencester Workshop Brewery Court, Cirencester, Glos GL7 1JH. *Tel*: (0285) 657181. *Open*: Mon to Sat, 10.00am to 5.00pm. Contemporary arts/crafts centre in converted Victorian brewery. Coffee House/wholefood. Tuition/workshops. **Hugh and Sophie Blackwell**: print your own, brightly coloured designs on to cotton textiles. *Tel*: (0285) 656263. **Ruth**

Pringle: hand-printed silk furnishings; drapes, cushions. *Tel*: (0285) 656263. **Liz Lippiatt**: hand-printed silk textile artist. *Tel*: (0285) 656263. **Hilary Flexen**: terracotta/earthenware; planters; decorative vases/turned pots. *Tel*: (0285) 640403. **Elizabeth Taylor**: antique rug restorer (mainly Persian). *Tel*: (0285) 641177.

Wroxham Barns   Tunstead Road, Hoveton, Norwich, Norfolk NR12 8QU. (Free admission/car park.) *Tel*: (0603) 783762. *Open*: 7 days, Jan to Eas, Mon to Fri, 10.00am to 5.00pm, Sat and Sun, 10.00am to 6.00pm, Eas to Christmas daily, 10.00am to 6.00pm. Shop, tearooms, adventure playground with traditional fairground, in 10 acres of Norfolk parkland. **Tricia Francis**: potter. **Broadland Stained Glass**: terrariums, lampshades, clocks, mirrors. **Ron Lyons**: wood-turner. **Adde Ford**: folk artist; hand-painted mirrors, chests, spoons, kitchen scales. **George Albon**: decorative glass-making.

---

2. CRAFT MARKETS

Craft stalls are a particularly attractive feature of London's markets. Here you find handmade goods that never get into the shops, at prices which are often extremely reasonable. Admittedly there is a plethora of dried flowers and lumpy pottery, but the keen eye frequently finds treasures.

London Postal Districts

The Apple Market   The Piazza, Covent Garden WC2. (5 mins Covent Garden tube.) *Open*: Tue to Sat,

9.00am to 5.00pm. (Mon is antiques.) Pretty (and sometimes pretty pricey) stalls in a shopping arcade that is packed with tourists. But worth inspection. Lots of decorative accessories; particularly strong at Christmas.

Camden Lock See **Centres and Workshops** above.   Crafts, "alternative design", antiques, bric-à-brac.

The Courtyard   St Martin's Church Yard, St Martin's Place, WC2. (5 mins Charing Cross tube). *Open*: Mon to Sat, 11.00am to 6.30pm.

Packed with small stalls: pottery, toys, leather, prints, etc. Good café. Brass-rubbing centre in church. Good prices (for central London).

Greenwich Arts and Crafts Market Square, SE10. (Greenwich BR.) *Open*: Sat and Sun, 9.30am to 5.00pm. Covered outside market, with folksy stalls.

Merton Abbey Mills See **1. Centres and Workshops** above. *Open*: Sat and Sun, 10.00am to 5.00pm (market), Wed 8.00am to 2.00pm (antique market), Thu 12.00 noon to 5.00pm (flea market).

3. CRAFT SHOPS AND GALLERIES

"I have tried to produce goods which should be genuine as far as their mere substances are concerned, and should have on that account the primary beauty in them which belongs to naturally treated substances; I have tried for instance to make woollen substances as woollen as possible, cotton as cotton as possible, and so on; I have only used the dyes which are natural and simple."

William Morris (1834–96)

London Postal Districts

Amalgam Gallery   3 Barnes High Street, Barnes SW13 9LB. (Barnes/ Barnes Bridge BR. Hammersmith tube, plus bus.) *Tel:* 081-878 1279. *Open:* Tue to Sat, 10.00am to 6.00pm. Closed for lunch, 1.30pm to 2.30pm. Tim Boon's gallery, established for nearly 20 years, deserves its excellent reputation. It has three rooms, with watercolours/ drawings/prints out in front. At the rear are pots/glassware (mostly functional) and some one-offs. Hand-thrown mugs/jugs. Vases, platters, storage jars, casseroles, bowls, dishes; mostly decorated.

Celia Colman Gallery   67 St John's Wood High Street, NW8 7NL. (5 mins St John's Wood tube.) *Tel:* 071-722 0686. One-off ceramics/glass. Carved/turned wood. Unusual jewellery.

Contemporary Applied Arts 43 Earlham Street, WC2H 9LD. (Corner Neal Street. 5 mins Covent Garden tube.) *Tel:* 071-836 6993. *Open:* Mon to Sat, 10.00am to 5.30pm. Formerly the British Crafts Centre: its newer title reflects its upgraded image. Lofty exhibition space on ground floor; large, well-lit selling area in basement. Glass, wood, ceramics, textiles and

jewellery are of the highest quality . . . prices to match.

The Crafts Council Shop   Victoria and Albert Museum, South Kensington SW7 2RL. (5 mins South Kensington tube.) *Tel:* 071-589 5070. *Open:* Mon to Sat, 10.00am to 5.30pm. The best of modern arts/ crafts at steepish prices, which reflect the top quality of the work by contemporary artists. Ceramics, glass, textiles, wood, jewellery. Commissions. Gift tokens.

Designers' Guild See **Decorating Materials 2. Co-ordinated Collections**.   (NB: crafts are at 271 King's Road; fabrics/papers at 277). Designer Tricia Guild's selections of innovative British arts/crafts include wrought iron, wirework, lead sconces, mirrors, glass and ceramics. A sparky spotlight on the very new.

Leigh Gallery   17 Leigh Street, WC1H 9EW. (5 mins Russell Square tube.) *Tel:* 071-242 5177. *Open:* Mon to Fri, 10.30am to 5.30pm. Pottery/ glass by new/established artists, with resident potter.

David Mellor See **Kitchens 9. Kitchenware**.   David has consistently encouraged the best of British traditional crafts: ceramics, baskets, wood. Nothing flashy: very satisfying to view/handle/use.

Naturally British   13 New Row, Covent Garden WC2N 4LF. (5 mins Leicester Square tube.) *Tel:* 071-240 0551. *Open:* Mon to Sat, 10.30am to 6.15pm. This delightful shop stretches well back from the pedestrianised street; explore its basement also. The endearing theme is old and new British handmade goods, from antique furniture to traditional clothes/Arran sweaters. Lots of small gift ideas: wooden spoons, egg cosies, fire screens, ceramic house names, pin cushions.

More craft than art, but none the less delightful for that.

Peepul Tree Trading   291 New King's Road, SW6 4RE. (5 mins Parsons Green tube.) *Tel:* 071-736 9132. *Open:* Mon to Sat, 10.00am to 6.00pm. Beautifully designed interior for British crafts: ceramics, furniture, glass, jewellery, metal. Unusual work at good prices. Very good for gifts.

The South Bank Craft Shop and Gallery   Royal Festival Hall, SE1 8XX. (5 mins Waterloo tube/BR. Or Charing Cross/Embankment, plus Hungerford Bridge.) *Tel:* 071-921 0930. *Open:* 7 days, 12.30pm to 7.30pm. Stocks a wide variety of contemporary crafts: textiles, metal, wood, ceramics, glass etc. Enjoy all the amenities of the Royal Festival Hall (while it's still there).

The Study See **Interior Design**. Designer Christopher Nevile expresses his declared "campaign against pot pourri" with a sharp collection of artefacts from avant-garde makers. Essential accessories for advanced interiors.

Sue Williams   320 Portobello Road, W10 5RU. (5 mins Ladbroke Grove/Westbourne Park tubes.) *Tel:* 081-960 6123. *Open:* Tue to Sat, 10.00am to 5.30pm. The imaginative and charming gallery owner has a small shop at the back, crammed with original, affordable British arts/crafts. Ceramics, glass, metal, wood. Come here for something different.

Wilson and Gough   106 Draycott Avenue, SW3 3EA. (5 mins South Kensington tube.) *Tel:* 071-823 7082. *Open:* Mon to Sat, 10.00am to 6.00pm. Elegant, minimalist interior displays crafts as serious collectors' art: exquisite glass, ceramics, pewter, wood, but stinging prices.

Home Counties/
South East

The Ashdown Gallery   70 Newton High Street, Uckfield, E. Sussx TN22 5DE. (A22 via Croydon/East Grinstead.) *Tel:* (0825) 767180. *Open:* Feb to Dec, Tue to Sat, 10.00am to 5.00pm. Converted Victorian pub with spacious, well-lit displays of studio glass, ceramics, furniture, metalwork, jewellery, prints. Regular exhibitions.

Hugo Barclay   7 East Street, Brighton, E. Sussx BN1 1HP. *Tel:* (0273) 21694. *Open:* Mon to Sat, 10.00am to 5.30pm. Closed for lunch, 1.00pm to 2.00pm. Pleasant gallery, reflecting the enthusiasm of the owner. Functional/decorative pieces, individual and original. Mostly one-offs from one-person workshops. Ceramics, glass, wood, jewellery, and work of original printmakers. Regular exhibitions.

Broughton Crafts   High Street, Stockbridge, Hants SO20 6HB. *Tel:* (0264) 810513. *Open:* Mon to Sat, 9.30am to 5.30pm. Closed for lunch, 1.00pm to 2.00pm. The best British contemporary craftwork; a mix of well-known makers plus newer discoveries.

Candover Gallery   22 West Street, New Alresford, Winchester, Hants SO24 9AE. (M3 junction 6.) *Tel:* (0962) 733200. *Open:* Mon to Sat 9.30am to 5.30pm, or by appointment. Potter Barbara Ling provides a friendly/knowledgeable service in a 200-year-old listed building on two floors. Studio glass, ceramics, watercolours. Commissions.

Charleston Shop Gallery Charleston Farmhouse, near Firle, Lewes, E. Sussx BN8 6LL. (A27. Lewes BR.) *Tel:* (0323) 811265/6. *Open:* Apr to Oct, Wed, Thu, Sat and Sun, 2.00pm to 6.00pm. The Bloomsbury style of Duncan Grant and Vanessa Bell continues in ceramics, textiles, decorated furniture and other applied arts.

The Craft Shop   Lamb Arcade, High Street, Wallingford, Oxon OX10 0BS. (Just off High Street.) *Tel:* (0491) 33800. *Open:* Mon to Fri, 9.30am to 5.30pm, Sat 9.30am to 5.30pm, Wed 10.00am to 4.00pm. Anne Brooker stocks her shop in a converted Georgian Hotel with a varied selection of British crafts. In the same building are 15 antique shops, a wine bar, and a coffee shop, making a pleasant day out.

The Craftsman Gallery   8 High Street, Ditchling, E. Sussx BN6 8TA. *Tel:* (0273) 845246. *Open:* Mon to Sat, 10.00am to 5.00pm. Closed for lunch, 1.00pm to 2.00pm. Closed all day Wed. Pottery workshop for thrown earthenware by Jill Pryke, including anniversary plates/named mugs. Other Sussex crafts: wallhangings, weaving, ceramics, frames, turned wood.

Fenny Lodge Gallery   Simpson Road, Fenny Stratford, Bletchley, Milton Keynes, Bucks MK1 1BD. (M1, junction 13. Bletchley BR, plus taxi. Or come by canal from Little Venice, moor outside.) *Tel:* (0908) 642207. *Open:* Mon to Fri, 9.00am to 5.00pm, Sat 9.00am to 4.00pm. Decorative/functional pottery, glass, patchwork, lamps, woodware. Wall-hangings etc.

The Gowan Gallery   3 Bell Street, Sawbridgeworth, Herts CM21 9AR. (Free car park nearby.) *Tel:* (0279) 600004. *Open:* Tue to Sat, 10.00am to 5.00pm. Renovated, 18th-century building with old display cabinets/ original pictures. Small gallery for contemporary arts/crafts. Ceramics, glass, wood, jewellery, fine art. Commissions. Exhibitions.

Heirlooms Upstairs   Fern Cottage, 28/30 High Street, Thames Ditton, Surrey KT7 0RY. *Tel:* 081-398 2856. *Open:* Mon to Sat, 10.00am to 5.30pm. Wide range of British handicrafts. Glass, pottery, pewter, handpainted silk, collage, kites, embroideries, cards.

Hitchcocks'   11 East Street, New Alresford, Hants SO24 9EQ. (East of Winchester.) *Tel:* (0962) 734762.

Open: Mon to Sat, 9.30am to 5.00pm. Closed for lunch, 1.00pm to 2.00pm. Friendly gallery in converted 19th-century building, run by mother-and-daughter partnership. British craftwork in glass, ceramics, treen, wooden toys, jewellery.

Lannards Gallery   Okehurst Lane, Billinghurst, W. Sussx RH14 9HR. (1 hour from London, A29. 25 mins from M25.) *Tel:* (0403) 782692. *Open:* Wed to Sun, 11.00am to 5.00pm. Octagonal pine-built country gallery. Sculpture, ceramics, watercolours, glass.

The Minories   74 High Street, Colchester, Essex CO1 1UE. (Opposite castle, next to multi-storey car park.) *Tel:* (0206) 577067. *Open:* Tue to Sat, 10.30am to 5.30pm. Design/craftwork: glass, ceramics, wood, toys.

Newson Gallery   1 Windmill Hill, Enfield, Middx EN2 5SE. (1 min Enfield Chase BR.) *Tel:* 081-363 3675. *Open:* Mon to Sat, 9.00am to 5.30pm. Closed all day Wed. Dolls' house specialists, plus miniatures, rocking-horses, toys. Fine craft pottery/ceramics.

Nexus   14 Broad Street, off St James Street, Brighton, E. Sussx BN2 1TJ. *Tel:* (0273) 684480. *Open:* Wed to Fri, 11.00am to 6.00pm. Phone for opening times on other days. A Georgian window fronts Cynthia Cousens' uncluttered displays of original contemporary crafts, much from local workshops. Willow baskets, porcelain tableware, saltglaze jugs, hand-blown glass, hand-printed silk cushions.

The Old Bull Arts Centre   68 High Street, Barnet, Herts EN5 5SJ. (5 mins High Barnet tube.) *Tel:* 081-449 0048. *Open:* Mon to Sat, 9.30am to 5.30pm. Witty modern ceramics. Vases, jewellery, glass, toys, cards, prints, pottery, pewter. Workshops/ courses.

Terrace Gallery   7 Liverpool Terrace, Worthing, W. Sussx BN11 1TA. (8 mins Worthing BR.) *Tel:* (0903) 212926. *Open:* Tue to Fri,

10.30am to 4.30pm, Sat 10.30am to 1.00pm. Closed Aug and Jan. Contemporary paintings, etchings, ceramics, studio glass, turned/carved wood, sculpture, textiles, shown in changing exhibitions. Commissions. Personal service/informal friendly atmosphere. Moderate prices.

Trading Place Art Galleries 11 New Road, Ware, Herts SG12 7BS. (Car park opposite.) *Tel:* (0920)

469620. *Open:* Tue to Sat, 11.30am to 4.30pm. Elegant gallery in 18th-century coaching inn. Contemporary British oil/watercolours, studio ceramics, glass, jewellery.

▶ Worth a Trip

Collection Gallery 13 The Southend, Ledbury, Hereford, Here and Worcs HR8 2EY. (M4, M5, M50;

or M4 and Severn Bridge.) *Tel:* (0531) 4641. *Open:* Mon to Sat, 9.30am to 5.30pm. A longish drive from London, but a pretty gallery in a half-timbered building, worth seeing. Refurbished with whitewashed walls, mellow original flooring, unobtrusive hi-tech lighting. Glass, blown/etched. Carved/turned wood. Baskets, framed prints. Clocks, brass desk accessories. Saltglaze ceramics, hand-thrown pottery.

4. CRAFT SUPPLIES

This section gives help and inspiration for your own craft furnishing projects.

London Postal Districts

Candle Makers' Supplies 28 Blythe Road, W14 0HA. (Just behind Olympia. 1 min Olympia tube. 10 mins Hammersmith tube.) *Tel:* 071-602 4031. *Open:* Mon to Fri, 10.00am to 6.00pm, Sat 10.30am to 5.00pm. Closed for lunch, 1.00pm to 2.00pm. All materials for candlemaking/silk painting, batik, mould-making, resin-casting. Courses.

The Cane Store 207 Blackstock Road, N5 2LL. (7 mins Arsenal tube.) *Tel:* 071-354 4210. *Open:* Mon to Sat, 10.00am to 7.00pm. Materials for cane/basketwork, including recaning. Books, expert advice. Attractive panels of woven cane, split bamboo, reed screening; grass/straw. Cane/rush repairs. Mail order.

Creativity Needlecrafts 45 New Oxford Street, WC1A 1BH. (4 mins Tottenham Court Road/Holborn tubes.) *Tel:* 071-240 2945. *Open:* Mon to Sat, 9.30am to 6.00pm. Late night Thu, 7.00pm. Large needlecraft specialists. Tapestry, knitting,

embroidery, rug-making, machine-knitting, haberdashery, crochet yarns. Wide selection of books. Mail order.

Eaton's See **Floors 4. Mattings**. Raffia/bamboo/rattan canes. Seagrass/cane for chair repairs.

Ehrman 14/16 Lancer Square, Kensington Church Street, W8 4EP. (4 mins High Street Kensington tube.) *Tel:* 071-937 8123. *Open:* Mon to Sat, 9.30am to 6.00pm. Kaffe Fasset's tapestry kits are stitched by thousands: you may prefer one of their lesser-known, but equally beautiful designs for cushions/rugs.

Fulham Pottery 8/10 Ingate Place, SW8 3NS. (1 min Queenstown Road BR. Sloane Square tube, plus 137 bus.) *Tel:* 071-720 0050. *Open:* Mon to Sat, 9.00am to 5.00pm. All basic materials for potters/artists/sculptors, including clays, paints, brushes, paints, pigments, glazes etc. Blank pottery to decorate at home (including unglazed bisque). Terracotta storage jars with wooden lids. Mugs. Books. Catalogue available. Mail order.

Glorafilia The Old Mill House, The Ridgeway, NW7 4EB. (Mill Hill/Edgware tubes, plus bus.) *Tel:* 081-906 0212. *Open:* Mon to Fri, 10.00am to 5.00pm, Sat 10.00am to 4.00pm. Exquisite samplers, cushion

covers, tapestries, footstools, chair seats, pictures. Special commissions undertaken. Colour catalogue £1, refundable. Mail order.

Handweavers' Studio and Gallery 29 Haroldstone Road, E17 7HN. (5 mins Blackhorse Road tube.) *Tel:* 081-521 2281. *Open:* Tue to Sat, 10.00am to 5.00pm. Late night Fri 9.00pm. Specialists in weaving/spinning/dyeing run by caring craftspeople. Yarns, fibres, fleece, looms, spinning wheels, books. Popular secondhand noticeboard. Commissions advisory service. Popular weekend courses. Mail order.

John Lewis See **Department Stores**. Good Oxford Street base for wide range of furnishing craft supplies: tapestry/rug kits and supplies. Felts. Lacemaking, patchwork templates, fabric paints/dyes, stool-making kits.

Liberty See **Department Stores**. Packets/bags of Liberty fabrics for patchwork.

Luxury Needlepoint 324 King Street, Hammersmith W6 0RR. (5 mins Stamford Brook tube.) *Tel:* 081-741 1314. *Open:* Mon to Sat, 9.00am to 5.00pm. Largest collection "traméed" tapestry designs (over 1,500) in the country. Tramé is a unique feature. Canvas is prepared with lengths of wool, which you then stitch over. Designs are therefore simple to work, and the results are hard-wearing. Also a good selection of tapestry cushions, rugs, wallhangings, bell-pulls, firescreens, footstools, pictures, waistcoats, etc.

Maple Textiles   188/190 Maple Road, Penge SE20 8HT. (1 min Penge East/West BRs. Adjacent parking.) *Tel:* 081-778 8049. *Open:* Mon to Fri, 9.00am to 5.30pm, Sat 9.00am to 5.00pm. Largest craft textile specialist in London/South East. Needlecraft centre. Daylight simulation bulbs. Haberdashery. American patchwork fabrics. Lampshade frames/fabrics/ trimmings.

Muraspec Wallcoverings See **Soft Furnishings 1. Fabrics**.   Extra-wide felts in glorious colours by the metre.

Anna Pearson's Needlepoint Network   25 Kildare Terrace, W2 5JT. *Tel:* 071-727 9696. Kits/books for cushions, chairs, rugs. Mail order. Small friendly classes in London/South East.

Pottery Crafts   2 Norbury Trading Estate, Craignish Avenue, Norbury SW16 4RW. (5 mins Norbury BR.) *Tel:* 081-679 7606. *Open:* Tue to Sat, 9.00am to 5.00pm (both branches). Ceramic and other raw materials; tools, wheels, kilns, glazes. For the hobbyist or professional. Kilns for hire (order a week in advance). Materials/tools only: no finished items. Catalogue. Mail order. *Also at:* 75 Silver Street, Edmonton N18 1RP. (Silver Street BR.) *Tel:* 081-803 7402.

Russell and Chapple See **Soft Furnishings 1. Fabrics**.   Inexpensive muslins, hessians, canvas, sailcloth, cotton duck.

Tapisserie   54 Walton Street, SW3 1RB. (7 mins Knightsbridge tube.) *Tel:* 071-581 2715. *Open:* Mon to Fri, 10.00am to 5.30pm, Sat 10.00am to 4.00pm. Exclusive handpainted tapestry canvasses. Wool, kits. Top-quality accessories, including needle safes, threaders, gold-/platinum-plated needles, bags. Completed tapestries blocked, stretched, made into cushions (customer must supply fabric).

Home Counties/ South East

Barbara of Windsor   85a Victoria Street, Windsor, Berks SL4 1EH. (M4, M25). *Tel:* (0753) 854151. *Open:* Mon to Sat, 9.30am to 5.00pm. Barbara Reid has been trading for eight years. Wool/needlecraft/lace-making. Speciality yarns; tapestry/ embroidery kits. Demonstrations/ problem-solving.

Coleshill Collection   The Griffin, The Broadway, Old Amersham, Bucks HP7 0HP. (Free parking opposite.) *Tel:* (0494) 727700. *Open:* Mon to Sat, 10.00am to 5.00pm. Unusual tapestry kits for cushions, stools (including low fender versions), fireplace screens, stitched pictures. Making-up service. Colour catalogue £1, refundable. Mail order.

In Stitches   48 King's Road, Brentwood, Essex CM14 4DW. (5 mins Brentwood BR.) *Tel:* (0277) 230448. *Open:* Tue to Sat, 9.30am to 5.00pm. Tue to Fri, closed for lunch 2.30pm to 3.30pm. Early closing Thu, 1.00pm. Specialist needlework shop; huge variety of materials. Established for 12 years. Books: especially counted cross stitch.

Reward Clayglaze   Talbot Road, Rickmansworth, Herts WD3 1HW. (5 mins Rickmansworth tube.) *Tel:* (0923) 770127. *Open:* Mon to Fri, 9.00am to 5.00pm, Sat 9.00am to 1.00pm. Full range of pottery materials available. Established for 15 years: lots of advice for amateurs, plus firing service. Ceramics moulds for slip-casting. Books. Catalogue available. Mail order.

Royal School of Needlework Apartment 12a, Hampton Court Palace, East Molesey, Surrey KT8 9AU. *Tel:* 081-943 1432. *Open:* by appointment. Designs for all embroidery/canvas projects. Designs painted onto canvas. Wool-matching service. Restoration of antique textiles. Stretching/mounting/ cushion-making. Commissions. Workroom visits once a month by arrangement.

Mail Order

Elizabeth Bradley Designs   1 West End, Beaumaris, Anglesey, Gwynedd LL58 8BD. *Tel:* (0248) 811055. Unique Victorian needlework, featuring animals/birds. Use as cushions; sew together for rugs.

The Enamel Shop   PO Box 43, London SE19 2PN. *Tel:* 081-653 8708. Enamelling is the fusion of kiln-fired glass to metal. Specialists for all supplies, run by enamellers for enamellers. 100 enamel colours.

J and J Designs   57 Lonesome Lane, Reigate, Surrey RH2 7QT. Delightful Elizabethan-style samplers. Send three 2nd-class stamps for colour leaflet.

Strawberry Fayre   Chagford, Devon TQ13 8EN. *Tel:* (06474) 33250. American cotton patchwork prints (150 designs); plus American/ English plains (100 colours). Threading/wadding/hoops. Send sae for catalogue, plus eight 1st-class stamps for samples.

5. CERAMICS

London Postal Districts

Amalgam Gallery See **3. Craft Shops and Galleries** above.

Astrig Akseralian   326 Liverpool Road (Basement), Islington N7. *Tel:* 081-366 8052. *Open:* by appointment. Brightly coloured handpainted tableware.

Idonia van der Bijl   122 Columbia Road, E2 7RG. *Tel:* 071-729 7976. *Open:* Sun, 8.00am to 2.00pm. One-off/short-run ceramics sold in small shop at Columbia Road's Sunday flower market. Handmade. Underglaze colours give the effect of drawings/watercolours on ceramics.

James Burnett-Stuart
70 Southerton Road, W6 0PH. *Tel:* 081-748 0335. *Open:* by appointment. Thrown/handbuilt earthenware. Striking colours, simple shapes.

Rachel Clark   25 Limehouse Cut, Colman's Court, Morris Road, E14 6NQ. *Tel:* 071-987 8776. *Open:* by appointment. Ceramics with many layers of decoration: energetic, bold, painterly, extensive colour range. Large oval platters, plates, vases, bowls, mirror frames. Very functional, very decorative.

Craftsmen Potters' Shop   William Blake House, 7 Marshall Street, W1V 1SD. (5 mins Oxford Circus tube.) *Tel:* 071-437 7605. *Open:* Mon to Sat, 10.00am to 5.30pm. Late night Thu, 7.00pm. Contemporary ceramics/gallery shop filled with excellent work of Craftsmen Potters' Association. Convenient West End location for collectors.

Isobel Dennis Clockwork Studios 38 Southwell Road, Camberwell, SE5 9PG. *Tel:* 071-326 1880. *Open:* by appointment. Bright, floral ceramic bowls with raised reliefs produced from individually carved moulds.

Sheila Dobson Decorative Ceramics Prior's Hatch Cottage, Prior's Hatch Lane, Godalming, Surrey GU7 2RJ. *Tel:* (0483) 810786. *Open:* by appointment. Decorative plates/bowls of individual design. Commissions.

Annie Doherty   Basement Studio, 7 New Cavendish Street, W1M 7KT. *Tel:* 071-935 4137. *Open:* by appointment. Handpainted china tableware. Floral/fruit designs in bold Mediterranean colours.

Jill Fanshawe Kato   58 Beechfield Road, N4 19E. *Tel:* 081-800 7101. *Open:* by appointment. Stoneware by artist trained in Japan, decorated with birds, fish, animals, and natural motifs. Functional/architectural/sculptural.

Galerie Besson   15 Royal Arcade, 28 Old Bond Street, W1X 3HD. (5 mins Green Park tube.) *Tel:* 071-491 1706. *Open:* Tue to Fri, 10.00am to 5.30pm, Sat 10.00am to 12.30pm. The very best of classic 20th-century potters: Leach, Cardew, Hans Coper, Lucie Rie. Also younger potters and international work.

Gallery Seven   7 Turnpin Lane, Greenwich SE10 9JA. (10 mins Greenwich BR. Or river launch from Charing Cross/Westminster piers.) *Tel:* 081-858 2290. *Open:* Tue to Sun, 11.00am to 5.00pm. Contemporary ceramics/fine art. *Also at:* 156 Westcombe Hill, Blackheath SE3 9DH. (5 mins Westcombe Park BR.) *Tel:* 081-293 4945. *Open:* Mon to Sat, 10.00am to 5.00pm.

J K Hill   89 Old Brompton Road, South Kensington SW7 3LD. (1 min South Kensington tube.) *Tel:* 071-584 7529. *Open:* Mon to Fri, 9.30am to 8.00pm, Sat 9.30am to 7.00pm. Janet Hill deserves her new, spacious gallery. Her professional yet unpretentious shop is a welcome showcase for British potters. Functional mugs, jugs, tableware, casseroles and so on, plus decorative one-offs. Huge variety, good prices. Basement café.

The Illustrated Potter   26 Camden Lock Place, Chalk Farm Road, NW1 8AF. (5 mins Camden Town/Chalk Farm tubes.) *Tel:* 071-485 5116. *Open:* Tue to Sun, 11.00am to 5.30pm. Mike Levy's joyful sunshine designs on simple thrown shapes are universally loved. Marmalade cats, cheeky toucans, beaming suns, naked sun-worshippers . . . orange, blue, green, black-and-white. Bowls, jugs, vases. Unique. Also colourful work from other potters.

Lisa Katzenstein   17 Belsize Park Gardens, NW3 4JG. *Tel:* 071-722 5795. *Open:* by appointment. Slipcast tableware for children/adults. Children's pottery, illustrated with fables such as the tortoise and the hare.

Mac Products   62 Allen Road, N16 8RZ. *Tel:* 071-254 5928. *Open:* by appointment. Marise Cumber and Roland Ward are among the most innovative ceramic artists in Britain today. Work is handpainted onto bone china. Also some transfer designs. The pretty "Fish" pattern is signed/dated. Nine colours. The Chagall-inspired "Lovers" pattern is popular for weddings. Plates, teapots, vases, mugs. Seasonal specials. Commissions.

North Street Potters   24 North Street, SW4 0HB. (7 mins Clapham Common tube.) *Tel:* 071-622 0681. *Open:* Tue to Sat, 11.00am to 6.00pm. Pottery workshop, plus shop. Finely thrown stoneware: tableware/decorative pieces. Traditional shapes and unusual pieces, with colourful glazes. Very reasonable prices. Pieces made to order.

Pot Workshop   Collins Street, Blackheath Village SE3 0BY. *Tel:* 081-852 4133/081-858 5875. *Open:* by appointment. Stylised fish/flowers/animals on dark grounds on bowls/platters. Modern, fine bone china tableware with black ground and brilliant coloured designs in handpainted enamels.

Rimmington Vian   5a Iliffe Yard, Crampton Street, SE17 3QA. (5 mins Kennington tube.) *Tel:* 071-708 0864. *Open:* by appointment. Brilliant ceramic workshop artists selling direct and through stockists. Classically inspired vases/bowls in fantasy shapes with modern decorations. Heirlooms.

Beryl Sedgwick   8 Fabyc House, Cumberland Road, Richmond, Surrey

TW9 3HH. (2 mins Kew Gardens tube.) *Tel:* 081-948 5804. *Open:* by appointment. Painted bowls/jugs/teapots in bolt bright under-glaze designs. Tea sets to order.

Rob Turner   The Celestial Studio, 17/19 Blackwater Street, East Dulwich SE22 8RS. (5 mins East Dulwich BR.) *Tel:* 081-693 7977. *Open:* Tue to Sat 10.00am to 5.00pm. Exquisite floral/marbled bone china tableware. Handpainted, brightly coloured lustres.

Home Counties/ South East

Bettles Gallery   80 Christchurch Road, Ringwood, Hants BH24 1DR.

Tel: (0425) 475353. *Open:* Tue to Sat, 10.00am to 5.00pm. Specialist gallery for studio ceramics.

Robert Goldsmith   Lower Neatham Mill, Holybourne, Alton, Hants GU34 4ET. *Tel:* (0420) 80915/87597. *Open:* 10.00am to 7.00pm. Highly decorated, handthrown domestic stoneware; rich blue/red glazes complemented by gold/platinum lustres.

Susan Mundy Ceramics 53 Anderson Avenue, Earley, Reading, Berks RG6 1HD. *Tel:* (0734) 265063. *Open:* by appointment. One-off sculptural vases made by handbuilding techniques in stoneware.

6. GLASS

London Postal Districts

Wenna Bishop Glass   18 Southwell Road, Camberwell SE5 9PG. *Tel:* 071-737 4066. *Open:* by appointment. Decorative/functional blown studio glass, using sandblasting/cutting techniques.

The Glasshouse   65 Long Acre, WC2E 9JH. (3 mins Covent Garden tube.) *Tel:* 071-836 9785. *Open:* Mon to Fri, 10.00am to 6.00pm, Sat 11.00am to 5.00pm. The furnace at the back is where the four celebrated glass artists work: Annette Meach, Fleur Tookey, David Taylor, and Christopher Williams. They create handblown studio glass for sale in the front gallery. Annette Meech's solid opaque fruit paperweights are classics, as are her heavy bobbin decanters. Goblets galore: buy singly or in sets.

London Glass-Blowing Workshop 109 Rotherhithe Street, SE16 4NF. (5 mins Rotherhithe tube.) *Tel:* 071-237

0394. *Open:* Mon to Fri, 11.00am to 6.00pm, Sat and Sun by appointment. Established in 1976 by Peter Layton. Now housed in a refurbished shipwright's shed overlooking the Thames, with a gallery/shop in adjacent building. Peter and his fellow artists free-blow innovative shapes in sumptuous colours/finishes. Bowls, vases, sculptures, ornaments. Decorative techniques include sandblasting, electro-forming, and acid-etching.

Opus 1   The Centre for Contemporary and Decorative Arts, 25a Maddox Street, W1R 9LE. (5 mins Bond Street tube.) *Tel:* 071-495 2570. *Open:* Mon to Fri, 9.30am to 5.30pm. Late night Thu, 7.00pm. Open Sat, 11.00am to 5.30pm. Delightful gallery with friendly atmosphere. One of the largest collections of studio glass in the UK, plus seasonal exhibitions. Other crafts, too, all at reasonable prices.

Anthony Stern   205 Avro House, Havelock Terrace, SW8 4AL. *Tel:* 071-622 9463. *Open:* by appointment. Fine modern studio glass.

Home Counties/ South East

Jonathan Andersson   Dean Farm Studios, Kingley, near Bordon, Hants. *Tel:* (0420) 87155. *Open:* by appointment. Exclusive interior design accessories from blown glass with electro-formed metals. Small runs of glassware, plus one-off pieces, including glass-and-metal furniture.

Sarah Broadhead   1 The Ridgway, Alton, Hants GU34 2RZ. *Tel:* (0420) 85083. *Open:* by appointment. Kiln-formed, laminated toughened glass for bowls, plates, screens, windows. Colours overlap and bubbles are trapped between two glass layers.

Michael Carman   41 Windmill Road, Brentford, Middx TW8 0QQ. *Tel:* 081-568 2543. *Open:* by appointment. Copper/silver foil, sandwiched between glass layers, plus fused chips of coloured glass, for sculptures/"stars" plates.

7. METALWORK

See also **Furniture 8. Glass, Marble and Metal**

London Postal Districts

Kevin Boys   54 Southwark Park Road, SE16 3RS. *Tel:* 071-277 5239. *Open:* by appointment. Sinuous, curvy, Gaudi-esque forms (handforged in mild steel) for candelabra, screens, architectural fixtures and fittings. Also chests, coffers, tables, chairs, chandeliers, mirrors.

Iron Age   25 North End Parade, North End Road, W14 4QJ. (5 mins West Kensington tube.) *Tel:* 071-603 1282. *Open:* Mon to Fri, 8.30am to 6.00pm, Sat 9.00am to 2.30pm. Candlesticks, furniture etc. in wrought iron from local forge.

Home Counties/ South East

Fire and Iron Gallery   Rowhurst Forge, Oxshott Road, Leatherhead, Surrey KT22 0EN. (M25, junction 9.) *Tel:* (0372) 375148. *Open:* Mon to Fri, 9.00am to 5.00pm. Closed for lunch, 1.00pm to 2.00pm. Open Sat, 9.00am to 1.00pm. Richard Quinnell's working forge is an exhibition centre for the work of leading designer blacksmiths. Sculptures, grates, fireirons, screens, grilles, hooks, bookends, candlesticks, lightfittings and so on.

Maurice Long   20 Buscot, Farringdon, Oxon SN7 8BZ. *Tel:* (0567) 52787. *Open:* by appointment. Handforged ironwork, distinctive designs.

Charles Normandale   Wheely Down Forge, Warnford, Hants SO3 1LG. *Tel:* (0730) 829300. *Open:* by appointment. Designer blacksmith for contemporary architectural/ domestic ironwork to commission. Impressive slender patterns for gates, screens, grilles etc.

8. WOOD, PAPER AND BASKETS

London Postal Districts

Marion Elliot Papier-Maché Design Unit 5, Cockpit Workshops, Cockpit Yard, Northington Street, WC1N 2NP. *Tel:* 071-831 6212. *Open:* by appointment. Vibrant, decorative/ functional papier-maché accessories. One-offs/limited editions.

John Galloway   72 Vicar's Hill, Ladywell SE13 7JL. (10 mins Ladywell/Lewisham BRs.) *Tel:* 081-690 3927. Individual dyed willow baskets using traditional techniques. Send fabric/wallpaper samples for baskets to match furnishings.

Peter Niczewski   164A Stroud Green Road, N4 3RS. *Tel:* 071-263 6775. *Open:* by appointment. Painted wood/marquetry. Mirrors, candlesticks: standard ranges/ one-offs.

Lois Walpole and Rapid Eye Baskets 100 Fairfoot Road, E3 4EH. *Tel:* 071-515 6014. *Open:* by appointment. Colourful baskets in interesting shapes, using traditional/non-traditional materials.

Home Counties/ South East

Bert Marsh   43 Wolverstone Drive, Brighton, E. Sussex BN1 7FB. *Tel:* (0273) 554587. *Open:* by appointment. Uniquely thin and very finely turned decorative wood, following the pattern of the grain. Exquisite bowls, platters, vases, boxes.

▶ Worth a Trip

Warmingham Mill   Sandbach, Ches CW11 9QW. *Tel:* (0270) 77337. *Open:* by appointment. Distinctive turned/carved wooden vessels/ "objets".

David Woodward   Studio 6, The Craft Centre, Oxford Road, Hay-on-Wye, Hereford HR3 1XX. *Tel:* (0497) 821355. *Open:* by appointment. Turned wooden bowls/platters/vases from British hardwoods. Finished in natural oils/beeswax.

22

ETHNIC CRAFTS AND FURNISHINGS

Ethnic crafts and furnishings are at last gaining the recognition they deserve.
Levels of craftsmanship which sadly have all but died out in Western Europe
exist plentifully in other lands. London is rich in shops that specialise in goods
from various parts of the world: decorative, functional, or both. Why fork out for
airline tickets and struggle back with heavy baggage when such treasures are
right here, on your doorstep?

"The meanest artisan contributes more to the accommodation of life than the profound scholar."

Samuel Johnson (1709–84)

London Postal Districts

Africraft   107a Fulham Palace Road, W6 8JA. (5 mins Hammersmith tube.) *Tel:* 081-746 3885. *Open:* Tue to Fri, 10.00am to 7.00pm, Sat 10.00am to 5.00pm. Authentic West African tribal art/craft. Expert advice/help. Importers selling fine quality handmade furniture/bronze/woodcarvings, direct to the public. Also traditional leather, native cloths, batik, jewellery. Sculpture/statues.

Anokhi   22 Wellington Street, WC2E 7DD. (5 mins Covent Garden tube.) *Tel:* 071-836 0663. *Open:* Mon to Sat, 10.00am to 6.00pm (both branches). Wholesalers/retailers of cotton furnishings/fashions. Designed in India by British designers. Handprinted in Rajasthan with handmade blocks; hand-dyed with natural dyes. Cushion covers/tablecloths/napkin sets. Reversible quilted bedspreads. Scarves/belts/bags.
See also **Home Counties/South East** below.

Art of Africa   158 Walton Street, SW3 2JZ. (5 mins South Kensington tube.) *Tel:* 071-584 2326. *Open:* Mon to Sat, 10.00am to 6.00pm. "An Anglo-Afro art/craft gallery," says Zimbabwean proprietor Deborah Norman. Everything here is handmade and natural: wood, stone, clay, cotton, wool. Furnishings/jewellery. Sculptures in solid teak, mukwa, wild olive. Fine stone Shona sculptures. Solid brass ornaments. Fruit in bright painted wood. Hand-printed fabric lengths, brightly coloured traditional designs: geometrics/animal patterns.

Casa Catalan   15 Chalk Farm Road, NW1. (10 mins Camden Town/Chalk Farm tubes.) *Tel:* 071-485 3975. *Open:* 7 days, 10.00am to 6.00pm. Casa means home in Spanish, and decorative accessories imported from Spain/Portugal spill from this pretty shop onto the pavement. Add a sunny Mediterranean touch to conservatories/patios with plain or fancy handmade terracotta vases, jardinières, pots/urns, rugs and wicker furniture. New patio section at back for plants/garden accessories.

Casa Pupo   56/60 Pimlico Road, SW1W 8LR. (10 mins Sloane Square tube.) *Tel:* 071-730 7111. *Open:* Mon to Sat, 9.00am to 6.00pm. Extensive, rather rambling premises for the shop that first introduced Londoners to Mediterranean accessories over 30 years ago. Particularly famous for the original Casa Pupo woven and heavily fringed rugs in bold, reversible patterns. Stock includes huge selections of Italian/Spanish/Portuguese ceramics. Ornate lampbases. Display columns, picture frames, plant pots, ornaments in shiny glazes from white/pastels to vivid lime/fuschia/cobalt/lemon. Decorative wicker/cane furniture in white/pastels.

Cebu   30 Artesian Road, W2 5DD. (7 mins Notting Hill Gate tube.) *Tel:* 071-221 1232. *Open:* Mon to Sat, 10.30am to 5.30pm. Dramatic furnishings from India, Indonesia, the Philippines, Thailand. Textiles, baskets, boxes, brassware, sculptures. Enthusiastic, friendly owners.

China Mainland   172 Kensington High Street, W8 7RG. (5 mins Kensington High Street tube.) *Tel:* 071-376 0304. *Open:* Mon to Sat, 9.00am to 6.00pm. Late night Thu, 7.00pm. Vast variety of goods from Chinese workers' co-operatives: very keen prices. Black lacquer furniture is spectacular. Also finely carved/inlaid rosewood. Porcelain/cloisonné table lamp bases/shades. China vases/lamps. Handmade cotton tablecloths. Silk kimonos/pictures. Jade carvings. Colour mail order catalogue for larger pieces (£1.95). *Also at:* Courts Mammoth, Ravenside Trading Estate, Angel Road, Edmonton N18 3HR. *Tel:* 081-345 5811.
See also **Home Counties/South East** below.

Eastern Accents   111 Walton Street, SW3 2HP. (5 mins South Kensington tube.) *Tel:* 071-581 3702. *Open:* Mon to Sat, 10.30am to 6.00pm. Neville and Linda Codling (she is Chinese, from Malaysia) worked for many years in the Far East. "We are a special mix of old/new, expensive/cheap, fun/serious. We buy direct from Asia, cutting out middlemen costs . . . and tastes!" New/antique furniture from Korea/India/Thailand. Also a wide range of wood carvings from Thailand/India/Bali: cats, ducks, frogs, owls, pigs, monkeys. Screens/mirrors/masks. Wooden table bases for glass coffee tables. Candlesticks/porcelain.

Filipina Store   5 Kensington Church Walk, W8 4NB. (4 mins Kensington High Street tube.) Behind St Mary Abbot's Church. *Tel:* 071-937 8332. *Open:* Mon to Fri, 11.30am to 6.00pm, Sat 11.30am to 4.30pm. This charming shop is in its ninth year. Handcrafts from the Philippines. Embroidered tablecloths, shell photo frames, mother-of-pearl butter dishes/knives, shell place mats/trays, salad bowls. Blouses/dresses. Shell flowers, lampshades, wood carvings.

Ganesha   6 Park Walk, Fulham Road, SW10 0AD. (15 mins South Kensington tube.) *Tel:* 071-352 8972. *Open:* 7 days, Mon to Sat, 12.00 noon to 7.00pm, Sun 1.00pm to 7.00pm. For over 15 years London's cognoscenti have sought out this fascinating little shop, lovingly packed by caring proprietors with home accessories/gifts/jewellery from Indonesia, Thailand and Nepal. Incense, wood carvings, baskets, cookware, and more. Exclusive, unique terracotta from the island of Lombok near Bali: classic garden pots, and casseroles with animal shapes. Down very steep stairs are more treasures: mostly Indian furniture.

Global Village 247/249 Fulham Road, SW3 6HY. (10 mins South Kensington tube.) *Tel:* 071-376 5363. *Open:* Mon to Fri, 10.00am to 7.00pm, Sat 10.00am to 6.00pm. Large double-unit, formerly occupied by top decorator. Handicrafts/artefacts from all over. Thrilling merchandise with a very high standard of design/art. Wonderful furniture in wood/metal/cane. Papier-mâché from the Philippines. Burmese lacquer. Colonial chests. Indonesian fabrics. Carvings/figures/pictures/lamps. "Few companies in the world import from so many countries." Friendly, involved staff. Go there.

The Greek Shop 6 Newburgh Street, W1V 1LH. (8 mins Oxford Street tube.) *Tel:* 071-437 1197. *Open:* Mon to Fri, 11.00am to 6.00pm, Sat 11.30am to 5.30pm. Memories of Grecian holidays permeate this pleasant shop. Hand-decorated, boldly coloured ceramics, very reasonably priced. Assorted handicrafts include icons, jewellery and leather.

Inca 45 Elizabeth Street, SW1W 9PP. (5 mins Victoria tube/BR.) *Tel:* 071-730 7941. *Open:* Mon to Fri, 10.00am to 6.00pm, Sat 10.00am to 2.00pm. For nearly 20 years Londoners have flocked to this little South American trading post, seeking brilliant colour, original artefacts and low, low prices. Largely South American fashion sweaters (with two new collections a year by British designers). Also rugs/hangings/accessories . . . and fabulous, inexpensive gifts. Do go and see.

Indigo 3 Gabriel's Wharf, 56 Upper Ground, SE1 9PP. (5 mins Waterloo tube/BR.) *Tel:* 071-401 2597. *Open:* Tue to Sun, 11.00am to 6.00pm. Two small shops, side-by-side, in a charming trading community by the river, with pleasant places to eat. Antique chests/boxes/unusual "collectables". Plus contemporary handicrafts from all over India. Exceptionally good prices.

Java Cotton Co 52 Lonsdale Road, W11 5BY. (10 mins Notting Hill Gate tube.) *Tel:* 071-229 3022. *Open:* Tue to Fri, 10.00am to 5.00pm, Sat 11.00am to 3.00pm. Judith Kennard imports wrap-around affordable colour from Indonesia. In stock: 3–5 metre lengths of genuine handprinted batiks: no screen prints. Large choice colours/designs. Fabrics also made into quilts, tablecloths, cushions, umbrellas, lampshades. Plus trays/sarongs/bags.

Kikapu 48 Porter's Walk, Tobacco Dock, Pennington Street, Wapping, E1 1AA. (Wapping tube. Docklands Light Railway—Shadwell. Tobacco Dock car park.) *Tel:* 071-702 4937. *Open:* Mon to Sat, 10.00am to 6.00pm, Sun 12.00 noon to 5.00pm. A *kikapu* is a traditional Kenyan woven sisal basket, dyed with root colours. Brick barrel vaults (built by Napoleonic prisoners of war) create a magical atmosphere for these African tribal arts/crafts. Wood/stone carvings: decorative animals/accessories/masks/chairs. Strings of Ethiopian silver/amber. Wedding necklaces from Masai tribe. One of my favourites.
Also at: The Africa Centre, 38 King Street, WC2 8JT. (5 mins Covent Garden tube.) *Tel:* 071-240 6098. *Open:* Mon to Sat, 10.00am to 7.00pm.
And at: 3 Gees Court, St Christopher's Place, W1M 5HQ. (5 mins Bond Street tube.) *Tel:* 071-355 3867. *Open:* Mon to Sat, 10.00am to 7.00pm. Late night Thu, 8.00pm.

Lotus and Frog 32 England's Lane, NW3 4UE. (5 mins Belsize Park tube.) *Tel:* 071-586 3931. *Open:* Mon to Fri, 9.30am to 5.30pm, Sat 10.30am to 5.30pm. Lalage Millns (established for over 7 years) personally buys from the Far East. Extensive collections of rosewood/inlaid black lacquer furniture: coffee/end tables, chests, dining tables, chairs. Rosewood special sizes/designs to order. Handpainted coromandel/silk screens. Chinese/Japanese porcelain and cloisonné. Rosewood jewellery boxes. Vases and temple jars.

Neal Street East 5 Neal Street, WC2H 9PU. (2 mins Covent Garden tube.) *Tel:* 071-240 0135. *Open:* Mon to Sat, 10.00am to 7.00pm. Christina Smith (Covent Garden suprema with shops/restaurant/gallery) trail-blazed accessible Oriental imports. Through countless buying trips to China/India (from 1972 onwards), she became London's leading source of Oriental furnishings/accessories/books/fashions, creating a spacious, enticing emporium, full of unexpected departments/treasures. Goods also from Burma, Thailand, Bali, Malaya, and West Africa. The welcoming foyer has cards/wrapping paper. Speciality textiles include lengths of fabric, cushion covers, dressing gowns, silk tee shirts. Block-printed Kalimkari bedspreads. Bookshop with huge array of titles on all aspects Oriental life: history/design/alternative medicines/philosophy/religion. Ikebana accessories, vases, and exquisite artificial flowers, such as exotic, double-silk poppies. In the basement are famous party toys/stocking-fillers—many less than £1 each. Also children's books/toys, kites, feather birds, lanterns, origami. The new, enlarged cookshop has Japanese/Chinese/Indian ironware, ceramics, woks, kebab sticks, trays, lacquerware, herbs and spices, plus screens, tatami mats, and futons. Hampers/baskets are a speciality. Bird cages/dog baskets. Frequent free talks/demonstrations/exhibitions. Eminently affordable. Do not miss.

Nice Irma's 46 Goodge Street, W1P 1FJ. (5 mins Goodge Street tube.) *Tel:* 071-580 6921. *Open:* Mon to Fri, 10.00am to 6.00pm. Late night Thu, 7.00pm. Dan and Della Hirsch have tirelessly imported Indian furnishings/accessories for nearly 20 years. In the beginning, Dan carried rugs from remote villages home on his back. Now he and his wife have transformed the image of Indian goods from hippy tat to high chic. Bedcovers, rugs, china, brassware, boxes, candlesticks, trays and more. Superb for cushions. Wonderful lengths of fabric. Elegant, spacious store covering two floors. Mail order catalogue £1.25. My very favourite people. My very favourite place.

Peeking Hippo   47 Palliser Road, W14 9EB. (Adjacent Baron's Court tube.) *Tel:* 071-381 4837. *Open:* Tue to Fri, 10.00am to 6.00pm. Close Sat, 5.00pm. Telephone first. Large stocks of high-quality, reasonably priced porcelain from the Chinese mainland. Predominantly larger decorative items: ginger jars, vases, tureens, fish bowls. Lamp conversions (very popular). Shades available. Elephant candlesticks. Chinese dogs. Sweet boxes: hearts/circular/rectangular.

Ravissant   157 Fulham Road, SW3 6SN. (5 mins South Kensington tube.) *Tel:* 071-584 3319. *Open:* Mon to Sat, 10.00am to 6.00pm. This shop cocoons you in sensual silk: rich textures/vibrant colours. Elegant, spacious showroom (3,000 sq ft). Tie-dyed sari lengths ("bandini") embroidered with real silver/gold—use them as exotic drapes. Heavy, fringed silk bedspreads. Plain/embroidered silk cushions/bolsters: many colours, intricate designs. Antique silk throws. Hand-embroidered cotton sheets/pillowcases. Silk fabrics, plain/embroidered, by the metre. Accessories. Natural fibres at their most sophisticated.

The Russian Shop   99 Strand, WC2R 0EW. (5 mins Charing Cross/Embankment tubes.) *Tel:* 071-497 9104. *Open:* Mon to Sat, 10.00am to 6.00pm. Nesting Matrioshka wooden dolls are international celebrities. Explore other Eastern European delights: carved soapstone, wooden boxes, lacquerwork, trays. Catalogue available. Mail order.

William Sheppee   77 Waterford Road, SW6 2DT. (5 mins Fulham Broadway tube.) *Tel:* 071-371 7432. *Open:* Mon to Sat, 10.00am to 6.00pm. Authentic Indian colonial furniture from late-19th/early 20th centuries. Superb "planter's" chairs with long, solid arms, beloved by tea-merchants. Goanese benches/sofas in romantic shapes. Chests,

sideboards, chaise longues, chairs. Accessories. Prints/glass paintings, bowls/jars, brass/lacquerware, wooden figures, sandstone reliefs. All furniture carefully restored. Reasonable prices.

Tapatl   659 Fulham Road, SW6 5RX. (7 mins Fulham Broadway tube. Safeway car park opposite.) *Tel:* 071-736 1898. *Open:* Mon to Sat, 10.00am to 8.00pm. Spacious corner shop for Mexican arts/crafts, with back annexe and basement. Pretty furnishings from small village workshops at very good prices. Textiles/ceramics/glass/accessories. Mexican oval, ornamental tin-framed mirrors. Cheap Mexican mouthblown glass. Handpainted functional pottery. Very jolly, and jolly cheap.

Tumi   23 Chalk Farm Road, Camden Town, NW1 8AG. (5 mins Camden Town/Chalk Farm tubes.) *Tel:* 071-485 4152. *Open:* 7 days, 10.00am to 6.00pm. Brilliantly coloured Latin American wood carvings: parrots/toucans. Handmade ceramics. Mobiles/toys. Gourd carvings: dishes/bowls. Furniture from Peru, hand-carved, with tooled leather. Mirrors/tapestries/bedcovers.
See also **Home Counties/South East** below.

Turkish Craft Centre   Unit 3, Blythe Mews, 186 Blythe Road, W14 0HW. (7 mins Hammersmith tube.) *Tel:* 071-371 1416. *Open:* Mon to Fri, 9.00am to 5.00pm. Silk carpets. Kelims. Kelim-upholstered chairs/stools/pouffes. Wonderful antique brass: samovars/ewers/bowls/braziers. Turkish brass coffee cups, lined with ceramic. Brilliant ceramic tiles.

Home Counties/South East

Anokhi   60 North Street, Guildford, Surrey GU1 4AH. *Tel:* (0483) 303829.
See also **London Postal Districts** above.

China Mainland   193/207 High

Road, Ilford, Essex IG1 1LZ. *Tel:* 081-478 9819.
Also at: Allders of Basildon, Eastgate Centre, Basildon, Essex. *Tel:* (0268) 533425.
And at: Allders of Croydon, 2 North End Road, Croydon CR9 1SB. *Tel:* 081-681 4014.
And at: Allders of Sutton, 71–79 High Street, Sutton, Surrey. *Tel:* 081-770 1934.
And at: Court's Mammoth, Heron Retail Park, Miles Gray Road, Basildon, Essex SS14 3AF. *Tel:* (0268) 287534.
And at: Courts Mammoth, 207 Kingston Road, New Malden, Surrey. *Tel:* 081-336 1441.
And at: Court's Mammoth, Lamarsh Road, Botley, Oxford OX2 0QP. *Tel:* (0865) 791405.
And at: Court's Mammoth, Lakeside Estate, West Thurrock, Essex RM16 1WP. *Tel:* (0708) 890100.
See also **London Postal Districts** above.

Hacienda   28 East Street, Brighton, E. Sussx BN1 1HL. (Opposite the Pavilion.) *Tel:* (0273) 777914. *Open:* Mon to Sat, 10.00am to 5.30pm. Handmade crafts from Spain, at very good prices: ceramics/baskets/woodware. Very pretty blue recycled glass.

Mah Jong   58 Church Street, Twickenham, Middx TW1 3NR. (5 mins Twickenham BR. One-hour parking at rear.) *Tel:* 081-744 2567. *Open:* Mon to Fri, 10.00am to 6.00pm, Sat 9.00am to 6.00pm. Pauline (Chinese, born in Mauritius) and husband David White offer countless Oriental attractions. Japanese/Chinese/Thai ceramics. Philippino pottery. Silk flowers. Embroidered cushion covers. Japanese lacquerware, wooden figures, silk photo frames. Extensive cloisonné. Lacquer screens. Black lacquer/rosewood furniture. Hand-embroidered silk kimonos.
Also at: 21 Commercial Way, Woking, Surrey GU21 1XR. *Tel:* (0483) 767800.

One Village   Charlbury, Oxford OX7 3SQ. (M40, then A34 northbound, off Oxford ring road.)

Tel: (0993) 812866. *Open*: Mon to Sat, 9.30am to 6.00pm, Sun 2.00pm to 5.30pm. Handmade goods from Africa/Asia/South America. Trust fund for craft co-operatives. Good-quality furnishings/accessories/gifts. Wool rugs/cotton dhurries. Coir carpets. Cotton batik quilt covers. Ikat bedcovers. Silk, handblocked cushion covers. Richly embroidered textiles. White cotton Glowbal lampshades on cane frames. Ornaments/sculptures in hand-carved wood/soapstone/brass. Decorative hanging sikas for storage. Thai lacquer/bamboo trays. Admirable aims. Splendid goods.

Orientation   48 Hill Rise, Richmond, Surrey TW10 6UB. (7 mins Richmond tube.) *Tel*: 081-940 7887. *Open*: Tue to Sat, 11.00am to 5.30pm, Sun 12.00 noon to 5.30pm. This dedicated team tours South-East Asia, bringing back vans of merchandise, new/old. Exquisite ikat/batik/patchwork. Furnishings/fashions. Bedspreads/cushions. Antique baskets.

Orientique   40 Oak End Way, Gerrards Cross, Bucks SL9 8BR. *Tel*: (0753) 888361. *Open*: Mon to Sat, 9.30am to 5.30pm. Large shop with selections of Oriental furniture/decorative arts. Coffee tables, Korean chests, Chinese lacquer, screens, ceramics, lamps.

Perusal   Wessex Place, 127 High Street, Hungerford, Berks. (Hungerford BR.) *Tel*: (0488) 84002. *Open*: Mon to Sat, 9.00am to 5.00pm. Family business, specialising in Peruvian knitwear, ethnic and fashion goods.

Tumi   1/2 Little Clarendon Street, Oxford OX1 2HJ. *Tel*: (0865) 512307.
See also **London Postal Districts** above.

▶ Worth a Trip

Alain Rouveure   Crossing Cottage Galleries, Todenham, near Moreton-in-Marsh, Gloucs GL56 9NU. *Tel*: (0608) 50418. *Open*: Fri, Sat, Sun and Bank Holidays, 10.00am to 5.00pm. Other times by appointment. Tibetan rugs and Himalayan textiles and tribal art are brought back by the gallery owner.

23
SECURITY

So nice to come home to . . . but not if the burglar gets there first. It's not just the loss of precious possessions that makes a break-in so distressing for the victim, but the disruption and vandalism, and the invasion of privacy. Why not foil all would-be thieves at base?

"'There's been an accident,' they
   said,
'Your servant's cut in half; he's
   dead!'
'Indeed!' said Mr Jones, 'and please
Send me the half that's got my
   keys.'"

Harry Graham (1874–1936), *Ruthless
Rhymes for Heartless Homes*.
See also chapter on **Doors**.

London Postal Districts

AKP Security Services   88 Wilton
Road, SW1V 1DN. (10 mins Victoria
tube.) *Tel:* 071-821 1991. *Open:* Mon
to Fri, 8.30am to 6.00pm. All security
products. Expert advice, installations.

The Alarm Shop   110 Balls Pond
Road, Islington N1 4AG. (10 mins
Highbury and Islington tube.) *Tel:*
071-241 5680. *Open:* Mon to Sat,
9.00am to 6.00pm.

Banham Patent Locks   233/235
Kensington High Street, W8 6SF. (5
mins High Street Kensington tube.)
Tel: 071-937 4311/938 3311. *Open:*
Mon to Fri, 9.00am to 5.30pm, Sat
9.00am to 12.30pm (both branches).
Full security services from this
famous name. Locks, alarms, grilles,
window bars, folding door gates.
24-hour emergency alarm service.
Also at: 11 Lillie Road, SW6 1TX. (1
min West Brompton tube.) *Tel:* 071-
385 3322.

Barrs Security   329 Fulham Palace
Road, SW6 6PE. (10 mins Putney
Bridge tube.) *Tel:* 071-736
7668/2918. *Open:* Mon to Fri,
9.00am to 5.30pm. In stock: most
makes locks/safes; workshop at rear
for special orders. Installations. 24-
hour emergency locksmith service.

Barry Bros   121/123 Praed Street,
W2 1RL. (5 mins Paddington tube.)
Tel: 071-734 1001. *Open:* Mon to
Fri, 8.00am to 12.00 midnight, Sat
9.00am to 12.00 midnight. Established
in 1945 and now run by the
founder's sons. Security here has a
human face. You can hire an in-

home security guard or use their
security patrol service for a periodic
check on your property. All security
devices: safes, fire extinguishers,
burglar alarms, fire escape
equipment, fireproof- and gun-
cabinets. Trained staff. Full fitting
service.

W D Bishop and Sons   9 Park
Road, Hornsey N8 8TE. (Finsbury
Park tube, plus bus.) *Tel:* 081-341
0859. *Open:* Mon to Sat, 9.00am to
5.30pm. All security products. Free
consultations. Installations.

A Buckenham (Locksmiths)   rear of
158 Blackstock Road, Highbury N5
1HA. (5 mins Arsenal tube.) *Tel:* 071-
226 8734. *Open:* Mon to Fri, 8.45am
to 5.00pm. Early closing Thu,
1.00pm. Family firm, trading for over
30 years. Speedy, friendly service.
High security locks. Advice, fitting.

Crown Security Locksmiths
6 Crown Passage, Pall Mall SW1Y
6PP. (5 mins Green Park/St James'
Park tubes.) *Tel:* 071-839 3253.
Open: Mon to Sat, 8.30am to
5.00pm (both branches). All security
products. Supply/install all locks.
Also at: 34 Station Approach,
London Bridge SE1 9RS. (1 min
London Bridge tube.) *Tel:* 071-403
3477.

Dennis Lock and Key Services   139
Wood Street, Walthamstow E17 3LX.
(20 mins Walthamstow Central
tube/2 mins Wood Street BR.) *Tel:*
081-520 7450/521 2444. After-hours
emergencies: 081-529 0223. *Open:*
Mon to Fri, 9.00am to 5.30pm, Sat
9.00am to 1.30pm.

FGW (City) Locksmiths
129 Whitecross Street, EC1 8JL. (5
mins Barbican/Moorgate/Old Street
tubes.) *Tel:* 071-253 9454/9721.
Open: Mon to Fri, 6.30am to
3.30pm. Family firm, trading for over
100 years. Locks, tools, alarms,
security bars. Trained staff.
Installations.

Finch DIY Stores   329/333 Regent's
Park Road, Finchley N3 1DP. (2 mins
Finchley Central tube.) *Tel:* 081-346
4417. *Open:* Mon to Fri, 8.15am to

6.00pm, Sat 8.30am to 6.00pm, Sun
9.30am to 1.30pm. Trading for over
25 years. Locks for doors, windows,
patio doors, etc. Security devices,
including security bars for windows,
property-marking kits. Lock-fitting,
key-cutting. Safe engineers, security
specialists. Friendly, knowledgeable
family firm.

Market Lock and Safe   251a East
India Dock Road, E14 0EG. (3 mins
Docklands Light Railway—All
Saints.) *Tel:* 071-515 2121/987 5757.
Open: Mon to Fri, 9.00am to
5.00pm, Sat 9.00am to 4.00pm.
Small, family locksmith. Advice,
outside repairs, 24-hour emergency
service. Safes, key cutting,
installations. Vehicle specialists.

R and R Security Services
169 South Ealing Road, W5 4QT. (1
min South Ealing tube.) *Tel:* 081-847
3129/847 4404. *Open:* Mon to Fri,
9.00am to 6.00pm, Sat 9.00am to
1.00pm. Locks, alarms, safes, grilles,
supplied and fitted. Key specialists.
Fire protection. Burglary prevention.

J Reeder Lock and Safe Co Ltd
587 Barking Road, Plaistow E13 9EZ.
(15 mins Plaistow tube.) *Tel:* 081-472
3431. *Open:* Mon to Fri, 8.00am to
5.30pm, Sat 8.00am to 1.00pm. Safe
engineer, specialist locksmith. Expert
advice. All locks supplied and fitted.

Saxon Security Locks   208c/d
Mitcham Road, Amen Corner SW17
9NN. (10 mins Tooting Broadway
tube/5 mins Tooting BR.) *Tel:* 081-
767 6281. *Open:* Mon to Fri, 8.30am
to 5.30pm, Sat 10.00am to 4.00pm.
Expert advice, speedy fitting, made-
to-measure sliding gates and grilles.
Safes. Registered key system.

Trafalgar Lock and Key Co
36 Kensington Road, SE1 7BL. (1 min
Lambeth North tube.) *Tel:* 071-928
0796. *Open:* Mon to Fri, 9.00am to
5.00pm (both branches). All aspects
of security. Locks/safes.
Also at: 110 Trafalgar Road,
Greenwich SE10 9UW. (3 mins Maze
Hill BR.) *Tel:* 081-853 3614.

Willet and Sons   87/89 Loampit
Vale, Lewisham SE13 7TF. (2 mins

Lewisham BR.) *Tel*: 081-692 1080. *Open*: Mon to Sat, 9.00am to 6.00pm. Supply/install all locks. Emergency locksmith service.

Young and Marten Grove Crescent Road, Stratford E15 1BT. (5 mins Stratford tube/BR.) *Tel*: 081-534 6630. *Open*: Mon to Fri, 8.00am to 5.00pm, Sat 9.00am to 4.00pm. Expert advice. All security supplies/services. Large builders' merchants with good kitchen/bathroom departments.
See also **Home Counties/South East** below.

Home Counties/ South East

Richardsons 6/7 Rochester Parade, High Street, Feltham, Middx TW13 4DX. (Hounslow West tube, plus bus. 15 mins Feltham BR.) *Tel*: 081-890 4399. *Open*: Mon to Sat, 9.00am to 5.30pm. Three partners: efficient, uniformed family business. All keys cut. Safes, boxes, locks. Chubb Lock Centre. Window grilles. Security surveys.

Young and Marten 634 Hanworth Road, Hounslow TW4 5NP. (Hounslow Central tube, plus bus.)

Tel: 081-755 4455. *Open*: Mon to Fri, 8.00am to 5.00pm, Sat 9.00am to 1.00pm. Closed for lunch, 1.00pm to 2.00pm.
Also at: 73 High Street, Clacton-on-Sea, Essex CO15 6PW. (5 mins Clacton-on-Sea BR.) *Tel*: (0225) 425241. *Open*: Mon to Fri, 8.00am to 5.00pm, Sat 8.30am to 12.00 noon. Closed for lunch, 1.00pm to 2.00pm.
And at: Greenstead Road, Essex CM5 9HQ. (15 mins Ongar tube.) *Tel*: (0277) 362231. *Open*: Mon to Fri, 8.00am to 5.00pm, Sat 8.00am to 12.00 noon. Closed for lunch, 12.30pm to 1.30pm.
See also **London Postal Districts** above.

24
DEPARTMENT STORES

London's department stores are legendary: a magnet for visitors from all over the world. As specialist shops multiply, the furnishing strengths of these giant emporiums are sometimes overlooked. But they are well worth getting to know. Enjoy the luxury of total service: variety, value, deliveries, credit, restaurants, cafés, toilets. Avoid visiting them, if possible, during peak, crowded periods, such as weekends, lunch hours and late nights.

"Wagered Mr Woodman Burbidge that within six years of the declaration of peace, we would overtake and pass Harrods Limited in annual returns. The stake is to be a silver miniature replica of the loser's store."

Bet placed by H Gordon Selfridge, 4 January 1917. He lost.

London Postal Districts

Debenhams   334/348 Oxford Street, W1A 1DF. (1 min Bond Street tube.) *Tel*: 071-408 3536. *Open*: Mon 9.30am to 6.00pm, Tues 10.00am to 6.00pm, Wed to Fri 9.30am to 8.00pm, Sat 9.30am to 7.00pm. Debenhams have worked hard to upgrade home merchandise: they now have many exclusive lines at keen prices. Very much a family store: pleasant attractive shopping environment, comfortable cafés. Departments include home interiors; casual dining; glass; cutlery; minor electricals; curtains; bathshop; lighting; nursery; cookshop; bedlinen. Home concessions nationwide include Perrings, Dorma, John Willman, Carpet Craft, Comet. LEB have Powerstore and Powerpoint shops in 13 stores. *Also at*: (glamorous new store) Lakeside Shopping Centre, West Thurrock RM16 1ZQ. *Tel*: (0708) 860066.
And at: Bedford, Bromley, Chelmsford, Colchester, Croydon, Eltham, Farnborough, Gravesend, Guildford, Harrow, Hounslow, Luton, Newbury, Reading, Romford, Southend, Staines, Winchester, Worthing.

Fenwick   Brent Cross Shopping Centre, Hendon NW4 3FN. (Hendon Central/Brent Cross tubes, plus bus.) *Tel*: 081-202 8200. *Open*: Mon to Fri, 10.00am to 8.00pm, Sat 9.00am to 6.00pm. Furniture, electrical appliances, soft furnishings, lighting, glass, cookshop, kitchenware, linens. *Also at*: 63 New Bond Street, W1A 3BS. *Tel*: 071-629 9161.

Harrods   87/135 Brompton Road, Knightsbridge SW1X 7XL. (5 mins Knightsbridge tube. Own car park.) *Tel*: 071-730 1234. *Open*: Mon to Sat, 10.00am to 6.00pm. Late night Wed 8.00pm. Food Halls open at 9.00am. Premier international tourist attraction, but don't be put off! Motto: *omnia omnibus ubique*: all things for all people everywhere. Ambience is unsurpassed. Six storeys, six selling floors, 72 window displays. Second floor: linens, with monogramming service; interior design; cookshop; Smallbone/Bosch kitchens with design service; radio/TV; glass engraving on the spot. Third floor: furniture, pianos, picture framing, dry-cleaning. Fourth floor: contemporary art/antique prints and maps. Eleven places to eat and drink.

Harvey Nichols   Knightsbridge SW1X 7RJ. (1 min Knightsbridge tube.) *Tel*: 071-235 5000. *Open*: Mon to Fri, 10.00am to 7.00pm, Sat 10.00am to 6.00pm. Modest beginnings as small linen store of 1813. Now it has seven floors of high-quality fashion/design. On-going programme of modernisation/innovation is now backed by capital from Hong Kong entrepreneur Dickson Poon. Reputation as the most elegant store in Europe. Two Royal warrants. Atmosphere of elegance and luxury. Exclusive new Mulberry and Ralph Lauren boutiques. Accessories (china, glass, silverware, linens, lighting, gifts, bathroom): fourth floor. Oriental carpets: fifth floor. Wedding lists and toilets: third floor. Baby changing/nurse: fourth floor. Meals, snacks, drinks: Harveys At The Top, fifth floor, or Joe's Café, basement.

House of Fraser   *Tel*: 071-834 1515 for details of nearest branch. Extensive refurbishment is taking place throughout House of Fraser, with ultimately all stores being revamped and given the H of F name.

D H Evans   Oxford Street, W1A 1DE. (5 mins Oxford Circus tube.) *Tel*: 071-629 8800. *Open*: Mon to Fri, 9.30am to 6.00pm, Sat 9.00am to

7.00pm. Late night Thu, 8.00pm. Extends over seven floors. You have to get to the third before you find furnishings, plus audio and TV; lighting and major electricals; haberdashery; The Bath Shop; soft furnishings, linens. Fourth floor: silverware; china/glass; gifts; housewares. Fifth floor: furniture; carpets; beds. Sixth floor: The River Restaurant: Coffee shop: lower ground floor. Toilets: fifth floor.
Also at: **Barkers**, Kensington High Street, W8 5SE. (3 mins Kensington High Street tube.) *Tel*: 071-937 5432. *Open*: Mon to Fri, 9.30am to 6.00pm, Sat 9.30am to 6.30pm. Late night Thu, 8.00pm. What many of us knew and loved as Barkers has shrunk to four floors (including basement), with newspaper offices above. Designer furniture department has avant-garde styles. Lower ground floor: carpets; soft furnishings; haberdashery; lighting; luggage; linens; Café Express. Second floor: silverware; gifts; radio/TV; electrical; china and glass. Restaurant: second floor.
And at: **Army and Navy**, Victoria Street, SW1E 6QX. (5 mins Victoria tube.) *Tel*: 071-834 1234. Currently under refurbishment.
And at: **Army and Navy**: Lewisham, Gravesend, Bromley, Guildford, Camberley, Basildon, Wood Green.
And at: **D H Evans**, Wood Green, and House of Fraser, Lakeside Shopping Centre, Thurrock.

The John Lewis Partnership
22 stores nationwide. Staff are "partners", sharing profits. Good value, keen prices. Jonelle own brand: good value/design. Jonelle fabrics: outstanding designs/colours, quality, price. Extensive making-up services for all soft furnishings (own workshops). Home service for carpets and loose covers. Kitchen planning: £30 refundable. Accept no credit cards except their own: lowest APR of all store groups.

John Lewis   Oxford Street, W1A 1EX. (5 mins Oxford Circus tube.) *Tel*: 071-629 7711. *Open*: Mon to Sat, 9.00am to 5.30pm, Thu 9.30am to 8.00pm. Flagship store. Furnishing fabrics, soft furnishings, carpets, flooring, linens: second floor. Furniture, wallcoverings, paints, paint mixing: third floor. China, glass, cutlery, lighting, kitchens, appliances, picture framing: basement. Coffee shop: fourth floor. Place to Eat (licensed): third floor. Ladies: basement, also first–fourth floors. Gents: second and third floors. New garden/leisure section: fifth floor.

Also at: **John Lewis**, Brent Cross Shopping Centre, NW4 3FL. *Tel:* 081-202 6535. *Open:* Mon to Fri, 10.00am to 8.00pm, Sat 9.00am to 4.30pm.

And at: **Peter Jones**, Sloane Square, SW1W 8EL. (2 mins Sloane Square tube.) *Tel:* 071-730 3434. *Open:* Mon to Sat, 9.00am to 5.30pm, Wed 9.30am to 7.00pm. Reputation particularly for soft furnishings, plus antique/repro furniture. Furnishing fabrics, soft furnishings, linens, pictures, picture framing, china, glass: ground floor. Carpets, flooring: fifth floor. Antiques/ reproduction furniture: fourth floor. Lighting, wallcoverings, paint: basement. Coffee shop: fifth floor. Restaurant (licensed): fourth floor. "Brides' book", third floor, *tel:* 071-730 0200.

And at: **John Lewis Furnishing and Leisure**, Holmers Farm Way, Cressex Centre, High Wycombe, Bucks HP12 4NW. (Easily accessible from M40. Parking for 765 cars.) *Tel:* (0494) 462666. *Open:* Tue to Fri, 10.00am to 8.00pm, Sat 9.00am to 6.00pm. Two floors of uncluttered furnishing displays in purpose-built premises. The fullest showing for most merchandise outside Oxford Street. Easy collection of purchases by car.

And at: **John Lewis Kingston**, Wood Street, Kingston-upon-Thames, Surrey KT1 1TE. (Own car park.) *Tel:* 081-547 3000. *Open:* Tue and Wed, 9.30am to 6.00pm, Thu and Fri, 9.30am to 8.00pm, Sat 9.00am to 6.00pm. Closed Mon. Large, newly opened purpose-built store with innovatory interior and extensive displays.

Liberty 210/220 Regent Street, W1R 6AH. (3 mins Oxford Circus tube.) *Tel:* 071-734 1234. *Open:* Mon to Sat, 9.30am to 6.00pm. Late night Thu, 7.30pm. Best known for its wonderful furnishing fabrics. Third floor: upholstery/curtain-making services, quilt commissions. Basement: wedding list, kitchen shop, The Bath House, coffee shop. John Hungerford custom-made kitchens/ bathrooms. Restaurant. Fourth floor: furniture, including Liberty Guild reproductions.

Selfridges 400 Oxford Street, W1A 1AB. (5 mins Marble Arch/ Bond Street tubes. Own car park.) *Tel:* 071-629 1234. *Open:* Mon to Fri, 9.30am to 6.00pm, Sat 9.00am to 6.00pm. Late night Thu, 8.00pm. Rivals Harrods in size, with its vast Art Deco edifice. Spacious/ comfortable. Basement: extensive fitted kitchen department. Fourth floor: furniture/ carpets. Exact match carpet service. Basement "service arcade" has dry-cleaner, shoe-mender/engraver, locksmith, building society, travel agent, four telephones, and a stamp machine. Computerised printer for instant stationery including cards/ notepaper. Inspirational DIY department (basement). Westminster cable TV customers can key in orders at home, for next day delivery. The fabled food hall recently had a £6 million refurbishment. Deliveries are free for orders over £25 (selected areas). Hampers. Nine restaurants.

Home Counties/ South East

Allders The Whitgift Centre, Croydon, Surrey CR9 1NN. (East Croydon BR. Dingwall Avenue multi-storey car park.) *Tel:* 081-681 2577. *Open:* Mon to Sat, 9.00am to 6.00pm, Tue 9.30am to 6.00pm. Late night Thu, 9.00pm. The third largest department store in the UK, after Harrods and Selfridges. Six floors; strong emphasis on home furnishings/own-brands. Basement: housewares; electrical (largest department of its kind in Europe).

Ground floor: carpets (free measuring/estimating); china/glass. First floor: soft furnishings, linens. Second floor: beds/furniture; interior design. Third floor: nursery furniture. Fourth floor: audio/TV. Tea/coffee/ snacks: basement, ground, first floor. Restaurants: third and fourth floors. Mother-and-baby room: third floor.

Also at: Arding and Hobbs, Clapham Junction SW11 1QL. *Tel:* 071-228 8877.

And at: Eastgate Centre, Basildon, Essex SS14 1HR. *Tel:* (0268) 27858.

And at: High Street, Bromley, Kent BR1 1HJ. *Tel:* 081-464 6533.

And at: High Street, Camberley, Surrey. *Tel:* (0276) 692122.

And at: High Street, Chatham, Kent. *Tel:* (0634) 407377.

And at: High Street, Eltham SE9 1TP. *Tel:* 081-850 9911.

And at: St Nicholas Centre, Sutton, Surrey SM1 1WA. *Tel:* 081-642 6000.

And at: The Peacocks Centre, Woking, Surrey GU21 1GE. *Tel:* (0483) 766488.

Bentalls Wood Street, Kingston-upon-Thames, Surrey KT1 1TX. (5 mins Kingston BR.) *Tel:* 081-546 1001. *Open:* Mon to Fri, 9.15am to 6.00pm. Late night Thu, 9.00pm. Open Sat, 8.30am to 6.00pm. New store, opened in July 1990. Four floors, dramatic central atrium, spectacular glass roof. Lower ground: china/glass, cutlery, table linen, electrical, housewares. Second: beds, linens, carpets, curtains, furniture, lighting, pictures, mirrors, TV/audio, brides' bureaux, furnishing advisory service. Brasseries. First: Atrium Café. Toilets: first, second, third floors. Mother-and-baby room, disabled facilities: third floor. Free deliveries within van area.

Also at: Ealing Broadway Centre, W5 5JY (3 mins Ealing Broadway tube/BR. Car park, 1,000 spaces.) *Tel:* 081-567 3040.

And at: High Street, Bracknell, Berks RG12 1DW. *Tel:* (0344) 424678.

And at: Angel Centre, Angel Lane, Tonbridge, Kent TN9 1SF. *Tel:* (0732) 771177.

And at: South Street, Worthing, W. Sussx BN11 3AM. *Tel:* (0903) 31801.

25
CHAIN STORES

Britain's "chain" stores are the very backbone of the High Street, under siege from newer ways of trading but striving with varying degrees of success to inject modern merchandise and selling methods into premises which may be old-fashioned, but score heavily on accessibility and convenience—unless you want to park your car.

BhS   *Tel:* 071-262 3288 for details of nearest branch. *Star store:* 252/258 Oxford Street, W1N 9DD. (2 mins Oxford Circus tube.) *Tel:* 071-629 2011. *Open:* Mon to Fri, 9.00am to 7.00pm. Late nights Thu 8.00pm, Fri 7.00pm. Open Sat, 9.00am to 6.00pm. BhS offers fairly stolid mid-market furnishing selections (which have become overly staid of late). Even the marvellous lighting has been reduced in range, to become very traditional. Pretty china and kitchenware, though. Very good for ready-made velvet curtains.
Also at: Bexley Heath, Bromley, Croydon, Gravesend, Harrow, Kensington, Maidstone, Thurrock, Wood Green.

Littlewoods   *Tel:* 051-235 2673 for details of nearest branch. *Star store:* 207 Oxford Street, W1N 9LA. (3 mins Oxford Circus tube.) *Tel:* 071-434 4301. *Open:* Mon to Sat, 9.00am to 6.00pm. Late nights Wed, Fri and Sat, 7.00pm, Thu 8.00pm. Open Wed, 9.30am. Inside Story is the name to look out for in Littlewoods branches. Stylish selections of French cookware, china and glass, with British furniture/linens.
Also at: Clarence Street, Kingston-upon-Thames KT1 1RF. (5 mins Kingston BR.) *Tel:* 081-549 8877.

Marks and Spencer   *Tel:* 071-935 4422 for details of nearest branch. *Star store:* 458 Oxford Street, W1N 0AP. (4 mins Marble Arch tube.) *Tel:* 071-935 7594. *Open:* Mon to Fri, 9.00am to 7.00pm. Late night Thu, 8.00pm. Open Sat, 9.00am to 6.00pm. Second floor: stylish quality furniture/soft furnishings, wall coverings, kitchenware, electrical items, tableware, fitted carpets, fitted bathrooms, lighting and furniture. M and S has worked hard on its furnishing ranges, which now appear in an annual, bulky colour catalogue (£1.75. *Tel:* (0925) 851100.) Fabric available by the metre/swatch service. The general tone is very traditional, but excellent quality/value. Well worth exploring for unexpected treasures: cane furniture, club/wing chairs, bathroom accessories, stripey linens. Major stores offer a custom-made furnishing service, plus customer advice desks.
Also at (major stores for furnishings): Guildford, High Wycombe, Kingston, Milton Keynes, Oxford, Slough, Thurrock, Watford.

Woolworth   *Tel:* 071-262 1222 for details of nearest branch. *Star store:* 168/176 Edgware Road, W2 2DX. (5 mins Edgware Road tube.) *Tel:* 071-723 2980. *Open:* 7 days, Mon to Fri 9.00am to 8.00pm, Sat 9.00am to 6.00pm, Sun 2.00pm to 5.30pm. With its merchandise range drastically pruned to achieve profitability, Woolworth's selections seem thin on the ground compared with the old days. However, it is still a useful port of call for kitchen and DIY basics.
Also at: 115/119 High Street, Camden Town NW1 7JS. (5 mins Camden Town tube.) *Tel:* 071-485 3932. *Open:* Mon to Thu, 9.00am to 5.30pm, Fri 9.00am to 6.00pm, Sat 9.00am to 6.00pm.

26

DIY SUPERSTORES

The recent expansion of DIY superstores (or "sheds", depending on your point of view) has been explosive. This retail phenomenon is based on a welcome upgrading of product quality and design, combined with more "user-friendly" service attitudes. Nevertheless, if you want detailed guidance and advice on DIY projects, you may be happier shopping at a smaller local store.

"Anything that is worth doing has been done frequently. Things hitherto undone should be given, I suspect, a wide berth."

Sir Max Beerbohm (1872–1936) British writer and caricaturist.

B and Q   Tel: 081-200 0200 for details of nearest branch. *Star store*: Hayes Bridge, Uxbridge Road, Hayes, Middx UB4 0JU. (Southall tube plus bus. The 207 stops outside.) *Tel*: 081-848 1898. *Open*: Mon to Sat, 8.00am to 8.00pm (all branches). Major DIY chain with 280 stores nationwide, most with garden centres. B and Q stocks over 20,000 products. Free deliveries. Kitchens with planning service. Bathrooms. Fitted bedrooms. Own-brand paints. Wallcoverings, tiles, floorings. Tools, tool hire. Telephone ordering. Guaranteed lowest prices. 10% discount for over 60s on Wed.
Also at: 2 Larch Drive, Gunnersbury Avenue, Chiswick Roundabout, W4. (5 mins Gunnersbury tube.) *Tel*: 081-995 8028.
And at: Sutton Court Road, Sutton, Surrey SM1 4RQ. (5 mins Sutton BR. Bus station opposite.) *Tel*: 081-643 8933.
And at: Alperton, Chadwell Heath, Chingford, Croydon, Eltham, Greenford, Ilford, Mitcham, New Malden, Ponders End, Sidcup, Stanmore, Staples Corner, Surbiton, Tottenham, Waltham Forest, West Norwood, Whetstone, Wimbledon.

Do It All   Tel: (0384) 456456 for details of nearest branch. *Star store*: Park Farm Industrial Estate, Frimley Road, Camberley, Surrey. *Tel*: (0276) 681678. Do It All/Payless DIY merged in 1990. Now they are the third largest DIY chain, with more than 235 stores. Usual DIY stocks, plus furniture and soft furnishing co-ordinates. Over 23,000 lines. Own brands for tiles, wallcoverings, tools, paint, garden furniture, peat and compost. Free DIY project leaflets available.
Also at: Peel Centre, Kiln Lane, Epsom, Surrey. *Tel*: (0372) 745344.

Open: Mon to Sat, 9.00am to 8.00pm, Sun 9.00am to 6.00pm.
And at: 113/117 Farnham Road, Slough, Berks. (5 mins Slough BR.) *Tel*: (0753) 822905.

✦ **Homebase**   *Tel*: 081-784 7200 for details of nearest branch. Star store: Syon Lane, Isleworth, Middx PW7 5NP. (Syon Lane BR.) *Tel*: 081-847 3687.
Fresh, clean approach to DIY. Light, airy stores. High display standards. Minimum 18,000 lines. Wide range of decorative products, DIY materials, tools etc. Outside stores for building materials. Outstanding house plants/garden centres, with resident horticulturists for advice. Laura Ashley boutiques. Tool hire. Timber/glass cutting. Paint-mixing service. Deliveries. Information desks. Free DIY project planners. Extra service for special/custom-made products to order. Interior design schemes available for £5.
• *Also at*: Warwick Road, Kensington W14 8PU. (5 mins Earl's Court tube.) *Tel*: 071-603 6397.
✓ *And at*: Weir Road, off Dunsford Road, Wimbledon SW19. (Wimbledon Park tube/Haydons Road BR.) *Tel*: 081-944 1044.
And at: Basildon, Basingstoke, Blackheath, Camberley, Catford, Chelmsford, Colchester, Crawley, Crayford, Croydon, Guildford, Harlow, Hatfield, Hendon, Ilford, Ipswich, Luton, Maidstone, Mill Hill, Milton Keynes, New Malden, New Southgate, Orpington, Oxford, Penge, Rayleigh Weir, Reading, Rochester, Romford, Waltham Cross, Walthamstow, Watford, Willesden..

Magnet   *Tel*: (0535) 661133 for details of nearest branch. *Star store*: 245/259 Kensington High Street, W8 6SA. (7 mins Kensington High Street tube.) *Tel*: 071-938 3377. *Open*: Mon to Sat, 9.00am to 6.00pm. Late night Thu and Fri, 8.00pm. Formerly a joinery firm, Magnet are particularly strong in windows/doors. Impressive kitchen range; computer-aided planning/installations. Also fitted bathrooms/bedrooms. Attractive, free colour catalogue available.
Also at: Pinkham Way, North

Circular Road, New Southgate N11 2UT. *Tel*: 081-368 5919.
And at: 4 Thames Street, Staines, Middx TW18 9SD. *Tel*: (0784) 466245.
And at: Cray Avenue, near Orpington, Kent BR5 3PU. *Tel*: (0689) 897707.
And at: Longfield Road, North Farm Industrial Estate, Tunbridge Wells, Kent TN2 3UR. *Tel*: (0892) 514427.

Texas Homecare   *Tel*: 081-200 0200 for details of nearest branch. *Star store*: Pipps Hill Retail Park, Gardeners' Lane South, Basildon, Essex SS14 3AP. *Tel*: (0268) 534921. *Open*: Mon to Sat, 9.00am to 8.00pm (all branches). Sun (where permitted), 9.00am to 6.00pm. 230 stores nationwide. The stores listed below are all new, or newly refurbished, and carry a full range of over 30,000 DIY products. Wrighton kitchens offer over 30 different designs. Own-brand contract kitchens available. Free planning/home surveys. Installations. Bathroom fittings/accessories. Bedroom/dining/occasional furniture. Over 360 wallcovering patterns. Vinyl/cork/carpet/ceramic tiles. Hand/power tools. Ladders, ironmongery, plumbing, hardware. Own-brand Square Deal paint. Dulux/Crown paints. Dulux Options colour-mixing systems. Own-brand Matchpoint co-ordinates. Small electricals. Decorative/exterior/ security lighting. Garden centres. Information bar/trained staff. Texas Pantry for refreshments. Children's play areas. Facilities for the disabled.
Also at: Winchester Road, Basingstoke, Hants RG22. *Tel*: (0256) 840464.
And at: Purley Way, Croydon, Surrey CR0 4RG. *Tel*: 081-667 1088.
And at: 123 London Road, Newbury, Berks RG13 1NF. *Tel*: (0635) 32032.
And at: Twinches Lane (on corner of Cippenham Lane), Slough, Berks SL1 5AD. *Tel*: (0753) 511120.

Wickes   *Tel*: 081-863 5696 for details of nearest branch. *Star store*: 53 Plough Lane, Wimbledon, SW19 0WB. (5 mins Haydon's Road BR.) *Tel*: 081-947 9818. DIY chain with 57 stores nationwide. Timber, building materials, ceramic tiles, bathrooms, kitchens, paint, electrical goods, plumbing, windows, doors, conservatories—even swimming pools! Made-to-measure doors/windows. Free "good ideas leaflets" for creative DIY. Free catalogues available. Deliveries with help from forklift trucks.

Also at: 850 High Road, Chadwell Heath, Essex RM6 4HX. (5 mins Goodmayes BR.) *Tel*: 081-590 1116.
And at: Invincible Road, Farnborough, Hants GU14 7QU. *Tel*: (0252) 510251.
And at: Weldale Street, Reading, Berks RG1 7BX. (5 mins Reading BR.) *Tel*: (0734) 588288. *Open*: Mon to Sat, 8.00am to 8.00pm.

And at: 1 Rat Lane, Rayleigh, Essex SS6 7UP. (5 mins Rayleigh BR.) *Tel*: (0268) 776262.
And at: Ashford, Aylesbury, Borehamwood, Canning Town, Catford, Cricklewood, Croydon, Dartford, Dunstable, Edmonton, Hanwell, Harlow, Hemel Hempstead, Maidstone, Merton, Ruislip, Slough, Tottenham.

27
MARKETS

Markets are legion and built into the British way of life. They are also top tourist attractions, so you will have to put up with crowds. You never know who you're going to meet at a market. As this book is concerned with the home, I have highlighted markets in London and the South East that offer home merchandise . . . if it isn't raining.

"This little piggy went to market,
This little piggy stayed at home . . ."

A domesticated piggy would miss the unequalled thrill of shopping at the market. You never know what you might find. Not just usual things, pretty things and (let's face it, the basic motivation) cheap things, but also wit, sparkle and thrills galore from the traders themselves and other shoppers.

London Markets

Bell Street Market   Bell Street, Lisson Grove NW1. (Edgware Road tube.) *Open:* Mon to Sat. Junk, secondhand furniture, antiques.

Beresford Square   Woolwich, SE18. (Woolwich BR.) *Open:* Tue to Sat, 9.00am to 5.00pm, Thu 9.00am to 1.00pm. General items and household goods.

Bermondsey Market   Bermondsey Square, SE1. (London Bridge tube/BR.) *Open:* Fri 3.00am to 4.00pm. Antique market. Main venue for dealers in London and the South East. 250 stalls selling furniture, silver, stuffed animals, glass, porcelain, pictures.

Berwick Street Market   Berwick Street (leading into Rupert Street), W1. (Leicester Square tube.) *Open:* Mon to Sat, 9.00am to 5.00pm. Mainly fruit/veg. Some cut-price clothing/household goods.

Bethnal Green Market   Bethnal Green Road, E1. (Bethnal Green tube.) *Open:* Mon to Sun, 8.00am to 1.00pm. Food/toys/household goods.

Brick Lane   Shoreditch, E1 and E2. (Liverpool Street/Aldgate East/Old Street tubes. Liverpool Street BR.) *Open:* Sun, 8.00am to 1.00pm. One of the more popular London markets. Serious collectors have been, shopped and gone before 9.00am. Antiques, crockery, electrical equipment, furniture, carpets.

Brixton Market   Electric Avenue, Pope's Road, Brixton Station Road, SW9. (Brixton BR.) *Open:* Mon to Sat, 8.00am to 6.00pm, Wed 8.00am to 1.00pm. Household, haberdashery, bric-à-brac.

Camden Lock   Commercial Place, Camden High Street, NW1. (Camden Town/Chalk Farm tubes.) *Open:* Sat and Sun, 9.00am to 6.00pm. Covered market open 7 days, 10.00am to 6.00pm. Seething, pulsating mass of tourists/locals: not for the faint-hearted/squeamish! Overflows into adjacent areas: Electric Ballroom, Canal Market, Chalk Farm market, The Old Stables. Particularly strong on homemade crafts: many craftspeople work to commission in the adjacent workshops. See **British Crafts 1. Craft Centres and Workshops**. Also ethnic clothing/rugs/home accessories. Bric-à-brac/pine.

Camden Passage   Camden Passage, Islington N1. (Angel tube.) *Open:* Wed 6.30am to 4.00pm, and Sat 8.00am to 4.00pm. Antiques, Art Nouveau, Art Deco, clocks, maps and prints, antique toys.

Church Street Market   Church Street, W2. (Edgware Road tube.) *Open:* Tue to Sat. Household goods, junk, antiques, bric-à-brac.

Columbia Road Market   Columbia Road, E2. (Shoreditch tube, plus bus.) *Open:* Sun 8.00am to 1.00pm. Plant and flower bargains.

Deptford Market   High Street, Douglas Way, Deptford SE8. (New Cross tube. Deptford BR.) *Open:* Wed and Sat. General household, bric-à-brac, secondhand, wickerwork, lampshades.

Earls Court Market   Lillie Road, SW6. (Earls Court tube.) *Open:* Sun 8.00am to 1.00pm. Bed linen, electrical goods, general household goods.

Greenwich Market   Church Street, Greenwich High Road, SE10. (Greenwich BR. Boat from Charing Cross or Westminster.) *Open:* Sat and Sun. Books, crafts, antiques, bric-à-brac.

Hackney Wick Car Boot Market   Hackney Wick Greyhound Stadium, Waterden Road, E15. *Open:* Sun 6.00am to 2.00pm. You never know what will turn up!

Hampstead Community Market   Hampstead High Street, NW3. (Hampstead tube.) *Open:* Mon to Sat, 9.30am to 6.00pm. Pictures, antiques, crafts, junk. Wonderful homemade cakes, etc.

Inverness Street Market   off Camden High Street, NW1. (Camden Town tube.) *Open:* Sat and Sun, 9.00am to 5.00pm. Bric-à-brac/junk. Browse for old tools/lighting/old kitchenware.

Jubilee Market   Covent Garden, WC2. (Covent Garden tube.) *Open:* Sat to Mon. Bric-à-brac and antiques Mon. Crafts and ceramics, Sat and Sun.

Kingsland Waste Market Kingsland Road, E8. (Dalston Junction BR.) *Open:* Mon to Sat. Large market selling a mixture of goods. DIY tools, house paints, electrical goods, secondhand furniture.

Lambeth Walk Market   Lambeth Walk, SE11. (Vauxhall/Lambeth North tubes.) *Open:* Mon to Sat, 8.00am to 6.00pm, Thu 8.00am to 1.00pm. Household goods.

Leather Lane Market   Leather Lane, EC1. (Chancery Lane tube.) *Open:* Mon to Fri, 12.00 noon to 2.30pm. Office workers throng this general lunchtime market: good for plants.

London Silver Vaults   Chancery Lane, EC2. (Chancery Lane tube.) *Open:* Mon to Fri and Sat am. Modern and antique silver.

Lower Marsh   Lambeth, SE1. (Waterloo tube/BR.) *Open:* Mon to Sat, 10.45am to 3.00pm. General household goods.

North End Road Market   North End Road, SW6. (Fulham Broadway tube.) *Open:* Mon to Sat, 9.00am to 5.00pm, Thu 9.00am to 1.00pm. Hardware, electrical goods, kitchen/bathroom ware, bedlinen, haberdashery.

Northcote Road Market Northcote Road, SW11. (Clapham Common BR.) *Open:* Mon to Sat, 7.00am to 6.15pm. General household goods.

Petticoat Lane Market Middlesex Street, E1. (Liverpool Street tube.) *Open:* Sun 9.00am to 2.00pm. Confusingly, you won't find Petticoat Lane on a map, as it's actually in Middlesex Street. Beloved for cheap clothing. Also china/household/junk. Go early for the best buys.

Portobello Road Market Portobello Road, W10 and W11. (Notting Hill Gate/Ladbroke Grove tubes.) *Open:* Sat. Bric-à-brac, junk, antiques.

Putney Flea Market Putney Hill, SW15. (East Putney tube/Putney BR.) *Open:* Fri and Sat. Bric-à-brac, junk.

Roman Road Market Roman Road, E3. (Mile End tube.) *Open:* Thu 8.30am to 2.00pm, Sat 9.00am to 5.30pm. Cut-price clothing. Designer seconds/samples. Household/linens/plants.

Shepherd's Bush Market Uxbridge and Goldhawk Roads, W12. (Goldhawk Road tube.) *Open:* Mon to Sat, 9.00am to 4.30pm, Thu 9.00am to 1.00pm. Crockery, bric-à-brac, kitchen utensils, carpets, rugs, vinyl flooring, bedding, furnishing fabrics, electrical goods, haberdashery.

Walthamstow Market High Street, Walthamstow E17. (Walthamstow Central tube/Walthamstow Queen's Road BR.) *Open:* Thu, Fri and Sat. Kitchenware, good quality crystal.

Well Street Market Well Street, Hackney E9. (Hackney Central/London Fields BR.) *Open:* Mon to Sat. General household goods.

Home Counties/ South East

▶ Bedfordshire

General Retail Market St Paul's Square, Bedford. *Open:* Wed and Sat. Bric-à-brac, clothing.

General Retail Market Arndale Centre, Luton. *Open:* Mon to Sat. Closed Wed pm. Undercover, at one end of vast Arndale complex. Clothing, fabric, jewellery, bric-à-brac, fruit, vegetables and general provisions.

▶ Berkshire

The Emporium Merchant's Place, Reading. *Open:* Mon to Sat. Junk, bric-à-brac, antiques.

General Retail Market Hosier Street, Reading. *Open:* Wed, Fri and Sat. Household goods, bric-à-brac, secondhand.

General Retail Market Rear of Town Hall, Wokingham. *Open:* Tue, Thu, Fri and Sat. General household items.

▶ Buckinghamshire

General Retail Market Friar's Square, New Town Centre, Aylesbury. *Open:* Wed, Fri and Sat 8.00am to 5.00pm. Large outdoor area and a covered underground section, stocking general household items, electrical goods, bric-à-brac.

Milton Keynes Market In front of Milton Keynes shopping centre. *Open:* Tue 9.00am to 5.00pm, Thu 9.00am to 4.00pm, Sat 9.00am to 5.30pm. Food, clothes, general household goods Tue and Sat. Antiques, bric-à-brac and crafts Thu.

▶ Cambridgeshire

Ely Market Market Place, Ely. *Open:* Thu 9.30am to 4.30pm. China, crockery, bric-à-brac, fabric, garden equipment.

▶ East Sussex

Saturday Market Upper Gardiner Street, Brighton. *Open:* Sat am. Antiques, junk, furniture, china, glassware.

Sunday Market British Rail Car Park, Brighton. *Open:* Sun 9.00am to 2.00pm. Various household items plus junk/treasures, antiques, furniture, pictures, bric-à-brac.

▶ Essex

General Retail Market Market Road, Chelmsford. *Open:* Thu. In the town centre, sells secondhand items.

General Retail Market High Street, Colchester. *Open:* Sat. General household goods.

Romford Market Market Place, Romford. *Open:* Wed, Fri and Sat. Antiques, bric-à-brac.

▶ Hampshire

General Retail Market High Street, Andover. *Open:* Thu and Sat. Household goods, bric-à-brac, clothing, fruit, vegetables and other foods.

▶ Hertfordshire

General Market St Peter's Street, St Albans. *Open:* Wed and Sat. Bric-à-brac, bedlinens, general household goods.

▶ Kent

The Brookman   Chatham. *Open:* Sat 9.00am to 5.00pm. General household goods.

Sydney Cooper Centre   St Peter Street, Canterbury. *Open:* Sat 9.30am to 5.00pm. Antiques and crafts.

Corporation Street   Rochester. *Open:* Sat 9.00am to 1.00pm. Fleamarket and Antiques.

General Retail Market   Kingsmead Road, Canterbury. *Open:* Wed and Sat. Large market stocking general household goods, haberdashery, bedding, towels, bric-à-brac, furnishing fabrics.

General Retail Market   King's Road, Herne Bay. *Open:* Sat 9.00am to 4.00pm. General household goods, furnishings, bric-à-brac, bedding.

Ivy Lane   Canterbury. *Open:* Mon to Sat. Bric-à-brac.

Maidstone Market   Maidstone. *Open:* Tue. Large market with indoor and outdoor area. Popular hunting-ground for dealers from all over the country. Antiques, bric-à-brac.

▶ Middlesex

Wembley Market   Wembley Stadium Car Park, Middx. (Wembley Park tube/Wembley Complex BR.) *Open:* Sun am. Large market. One of the busiest. Linens, general household goods, hardware.

▶ Oxfordshire

General Retail Market   Market Place, Banbury. *Open:* Thu and Sat. Clothing, fabric, flowers/plants, fruit/vegetables and general provisions.

The Covered Market   Between High Street and Market Street, Oxford. *Open:* Mon to Sat. Victorian, covered market building. Permanent shops and stalls. Clothing, footwear and foodstuffs.

▶ Surrey

The Covered Market   High Street, Epsom. *Open:* Mon to Sat (except Wed) 9.00am to 4.30pm. Wickerwork, crockery, cooking utensils, carpets, pictures, bric-à-brac, towels, linens, dried flowers.

St Peter's Street Indoor Market   St Peter's Hall, Ledbury Road, South Croydon. *Open:* Fri 10.00am to 4.00pm. Antiques, household items.

▶ West Sussex

General Market   Central Car Park, Burgess Hill. *Open:* Wed and Sat. Antiques.

28 AUCTIONS

Buying at auction requires nerve and practice: the latter is perhaps more easily acquired than the former. But be bold; the pickings are rich.

"Groucho: We're going to have an auction.
Chico: I came over here on the Atlantic auction."

From the Marx Brothers film, *The Cocoanuts*

Viewing an auction is essential: find out the times when this is permitted, and make thorough inspections. Check catalogue descriptions and lot numbers against goods. Many catalogues are available by mail order/subscription. Beware of the letters 'AF' beside the description of a lot; they stand for "as found", but may be a warning that something is wrong. The estimate in the catalogue may be a guide to the value of a piece, but always remember that value is only determined by what someone is prepared to pay. Fix an upper price limit firmly in your mind and stick to it.

Remember to take a tape measure and plans/measurements of the rooms you are furnishing with you to the viewing, and read the auctioneers' conditions of sale carefully. Buyers are usually charged a premium (the name given to the auctioneers' commission), which is usually 10% of the successful bidding price. VAT is charged on this. Find out the latest date for the collection of your goods: after that you may be charged storage.

Bid by raising your catalogue/ programme. Bids progress in even increments according to value, but may creep up by £1 when approaching a conclusion. Don't worry about dealers and special signs: let them get on with it. Blow your nose if you want to!

The following firms hold regular auctions. In all cases, please phone to check details before setting out on a journey.

London Postal Districts

Bonhams   Montpelier Street, Knightsbridge SW7 1HH. (5 mins Knightsbridge tube.) *Tel*: 071-584 9161. Regular sales: antiques, clocks, silver, tribal art, antiquities.

Specialist sales: fine furniture/ antiques/fine art. Catalogues available.
Also at: 65/69 Lots Road, SW10 0RN. (10 mins Fulham Broadway tube.) *Tel*: 071-351 7111. As a rough guide, items up to £2,000 in value. Sales on Tue at 10.30am: English/Continental furniture and furnishings. *Viewing*: Sun 11.00am to 4.00pm, Mon 8.45am to 7.00pm, Tue 8.45am to 10.30am. Also sales for ceramics/glass; silver; jewellery; Christmas presents. Phone to check details.

Frank G Bowen   15 Greek Street, W1V 6NY. (3 mins Tottenham Court Road tube.) *Tel*: 071-437 3244. Sales every 2/3 weeks on Thu: office furniture/ pictures etc. Phone to check details.

Christie's   8 King Street, SW1Y 6QT. (5 mins Green Park tube.) *Tel*: 071-839 9060. Regular sales: antique furniture, Victoriana, Art Deco, Art Nouveau. Chinese, Japanese, Persian works of art. Specialist sales: English/Continental furniture of all periods. Catalogues available.

Criterion Salerooms   53 Essex Road, Islington, N1 2BN. (5 mins Angel tube.) *Tel*: 071-359 5707. Sales weekly on Mon at 6.30pm: antique furniture/antiques/effects. *Viewing*: Sat and Sun, 11.00am to 3.00pm, Mon 10.00am onwards.

Dowell Lloyd and Co   118 Putney Bridge Road, SW15 2NQ. (10 mins East Putney tube.) *Tel*: 081-788 7777. Sales fortnightly on Sat at 9.30am: antiques/general goods. *Viewing*: Fri 9.00am to 7.30pm.

Forrest and Co   79/85 Cobbold Road, E11 3NS. (Leyton tube, plus bus.) *Tel*: 081-534 2931. Sales fortnightly on Thu at 11.00 am: "general goods", plus occasional sales of antiques. *Viewing*: Wed, 10.00am to 5.00pm.

General Auctions   63/65 Garrett Lane, SW18 4AA. (East Putney tube.) *Tel*: 081-870 3909. Sales on Mon at 11.00am: sales of bankrupt/ liquidated stock. *Viewing*: Sat

10.00am to 3.00pm. Also on-site sales. Phone to check details.

R F Greasby (London)   211 Longley Road, SW17. (7 mins Tooting Brodway tube. Opposite Tooting BR.) *Tel*: 081-672 2972. Sales on Mon at 10.00am. Also fortnightly miscellaneous sales (often more frequently, according to supply), including lost property for London Transport, and confiscated goods from Customs and Excise!

McGregor Nash and Co   Lodge House, 9–17 Lodge Lane, N12 8JH. *Tel*: 081-445 9000. (2 mins Woodside Park tube.) Sales on Mon at 5.00pm: general antiques. *Viewing*: Sun 9.00am to 1.00pm, Mon 9.00am to 5.00pm.

Thomas Moore Auctioneers   The Auction Rooms, 217/219 Greenwich High Road, SE10 8NB. *Tel*: 081-858 7848. Sales weekly on Thu at 10.00am: Georgian, Victorian and Edwardian furniture/antiques/ porcelain/glass. *Viewing*: Wed 2.00pm to 8.00pm, Thu 9.00am to 10.00am.

Phillips   101 New Bond Street, W1Y 0AS. (5 mins Green Park tube.) *Tel*: 071-629 6602. Sales on weekdays: antique furniture, rugs, works of art, ceramics, antique/ modern silver, jewellery, paintings, watercolours, drawings, prints. Also monthly specialist sales: books/ decorative arts. Catalogues available.

Phillips   10 Salem Road, Bayswater W2 4DL. (2 mins Bayswater/ Queensway tubes.) *Tel*: 071-229 9090. Weekly Wed sales: antique furniture/porcelain/*objets d'art*. Also toys, dolls, photographs, postcards, textiles etc. Special piano sales.

Rosebery's   The Old Booking Hall, Crystal Palace Station, Station Road, SE19. (Situated in Crystal Palace station.) *Tel*: 081-778 4024. Sales on Tue at 12.00 noon. Also fortnightly sales: antiques/art/fine furnishings. *Viewing*: Mon 10.00am to 8.00pm, Tue before auction, 10.00am to 12.00 noon.

Sotheby's   34/35 New Bond Street, W1A 2AA. (5 mins Green Park tube.) Tel: 071-493 8080. Regular sales: fine art/antiques, antique furniture, rugs, carpets, porcelain, glass, prints, works of art. Special sales: English and Continental furniture/ antiques. Catalogues available.

Southgate Auction Rooms   Cline Road, off Bounds Green Road, N11 2LZ. (5 mins Bounds Green tube.) Tel: 081-886 7888. Sales on Fri at 6.30pm: good prices for general household goods. Viewing: from 10.00am, day of sale.

Home Counties/ South East

William H Brown   Paskell Rooms, 11/14 East Hill, Colchester, Essex CO1 2QX. Tel: (0206) 868070. Sales on Tue at 10.00am: antique and general household effects/objets d'art/fine art. Viewing: Sat 9.00am to 7.00pm. Also on first Mon of month: china, glass, silver, jewellery, decorative items. Viewing: Sat prior, 9.00am to 1.00pm and Mon prior, 9.00am to 7.00pm.

Burstow and Hewett   Abbey Auction Galleries, Lower Lake, Battle, E. Sussx TN33 0AT. Tel: (0424) 62374. Monthly sales: antique furniture, silver, jewellery, modern oil paintings, engravings, watercolours, general household items/modern furniture/effects. Catalogues available.

Chancellors Fine Art   32 High Street, Ascot, Berks SL5 7HG. Tel: (0344) 872588. Sales on last Mon of month at 10.00am: English/ Continental antique furniture, paintings, porcelain, china,

jewellery. Viewing: Sat prior, 10.00am to 5.00pm.

Downer Ross (Auctioneers) Charter House, 426 Avenbury Boulevard, Milton Keynes, Bucks MK9 2HS. Tel: (0908) 679900. Sales every 4/6 weeks, also specialist sales: antiques.

GA Property Services   Worthing Auction Galleries, 31 Chatsworth Road, Worthing, W. Sussx BN11 1LY. Tel: (0903) 205565. Sales on Tue and Wed fortnightly at 9.30am: furniture/ china/glass/collectables. Six sales a year: antiques/Victoriana/fine art. Viewing: Sat prior, 9.00am to 4.00pm.

Hogg Robinson Auction Division 74 London Road, Kingston-upon-Thames, Surrey KT2 6PX. Tel: 081-541 4139. Three sales a month on Thu at 12.00 noon: antique furniture, Victoriana, general/household furniture/effects. Viewing: Wed prior, 2.00pm to 8.00pm, and morning of sale. Also monthly specialist sales.

Nationwide Anglia   Amersham Auction Rooms, 125 Station Road, Amersham, Bucks HP7 0AH. Tel: (0494) 729292. Sales weekly on Thu at 10.30am: quality antiques/ selected Edwardian and later furniture, antique china/glassware/ collector's items. Viewing: Wed 9.30am to 7.00pm, Thu from 9.00am.

Norris and Duvall   106 Fore Street, Hertford SG14 1AH. Tel: (0992) 582249. Monthly sales at Castle Hall, Hertford: antique furniture, china, glass, silver, jewellery, pictures, linen, lace, collector's items. Annual catalogue subscription £18.

Phillips   Baffins Hall, Baffins Lane, Chichester, W. Sussx PO19 1UA. Tel:

(0243) 787548. Sales fortnightly on Tue at 10.00am: household furniture, general antiques, household effects. Also fortnightly on Thu at 10.00am: reproduction and antique furniture, paintings, prints, clocks, carpets, rugs. Viewing: day prior.

Phillips Fine Art Auctioneers 49 London Road, Sevenoaks, Kent TN13 1AR. Tel: (0732) 740310. 10 sales a year: antiques, fine art, glass, porcelain, Eastern/Chinese/ Japanese works of art/artefacts. Catalogues available.

Reemans   Head Gate Auction Rooms, 12 Head Gate, Colchester, Essex CO3 3BT. Tel: (0206) 574272. Sales weekly on Wed: general household effects. Viewing: Tue 9.30am to 7.00pm. Also special sales on last Tue of month: fine art.

Rosan and Co   144/150 London Road, Croydon, Surrey CR0 2TD. (Adjoins Croydon General Hospital. 5 mins West Croydon BR.) Tel: 081-688 1123. Sales weekly on Sat at 10.00am and 2.00pm: general goods, including furniture and antiques. Viewing: Fri 10.00am to 5.00pm.

Thimbley and Shorland   31 Great Knollys Street, Reading, Berks RG1 7HU. Tel: (0734) 508611. Monthly sales on Sat at 10.00am: furniture/ antiques. Also quarterly sales: horse-drawn vehicles, etc.

Wilson Peacock   26 Newnham Street, Bedford MK40 3JR. Tel: (0234) 266366. Sales on Sat at 10.00am: household furniture, electrical goods, commercial machinery, bicycles, cars. Viewing: Fri 8.30am to 8.00pm. Also sales on first Fri of month: antiques. Viewing: Fri prior, 5.30pm to 8.00pm, Thu 8.00am to 6.00pm. Catalogue 50p.

29

SERVICES

The age of service is not dead. There is a host of skilled and willing people available to clean, mend and restore your household possessions. Of course you have to know where to find them, and very rarely is it cheap.

1. CARPETS AND UPHOLSTERY: CLEANING

Many firms advertise their services, but as carpets/upholstery can be ruined by inexpert cleaning, choose with care. Contact the National Carpet Cleaners' Association (tel: (0533) 554352), whose members have guaranteed professional standards and which operates an arbitration service if you have a complaint.

London Postal Districts

Pilgrim Payne Latimer Place, Latimer Road, W10. Tel: 081-960 5656. Holder of the Royal Warrant. All cleaning to highest standards.

Chemical and equipment firms licensing companies to use most products oversee standards carefully, so it's worth contacting them for operators in your area:

Bissell (Carpet Butler Deep Clean) Tel: 081-531 7241.
Prochem Tel: 081-549 0927.
Safeclean/Safeproof Tel: (0235) 833022.
Scotchcare Services (Scotchgard) Tel: (0494) 463825/463752.
ServiceMaster Tel: (0533) 610761. Hot water extraction (aka steam cleaning) is the newest method for carpet cleaning. Machines can be hired.
Trewax (Hydro-Mist machines) Tel: (0582) 599571.
Vibra Vac (Rug Doctor) Tel: (0903) 232019.

2. CHANDELIERS

London Postal Districts

Period Brass Lights See **Lighting 3. Chandeliers**. Cleaning, repairs, restorations on premises.

T Smith and Co See **18. Metal Repairs: Non-Ferrous** below.

Verdigris See **18. Metal Repairs: Non-Ferrous** below.

R Wilkinson See **12. Glass Repairs** below. Repair glass/replace missing parts.

Home Counties/ South East

Exquisite Interiors See **Furniture 12. Made to Measure and Commissioned**. Renovations of old brass fittings/chandeliers.

Voysey and Knapp See **18. Metal Repairs: Non-Ferrous** below.

3. CHINA REPAIRS

London Postal Districts

Ashton-Bostock 21 Charlwood Street, SW1V 2EA. Tel: 071-828 3656. Open: Tue, Wed and Thu, 9.30am to 5.30pm. Closed for lunch, 1.00pm to 2.00pm. Everyday china repairs

(allow 3 weeks). Fine china restoration. No glass.

Ceramic Restoration (John Parker) 7 Alwyne Villas, N12 2HG. Tel: 071-359 5240. Open: by appointment. Skilled repairs for fine decorative china (allow 3 to 4 months).

China Repairers 64 Charles Lane, NW8 7SB. Tel: 071-722 8407. Open: Mon to Thu, 9.30am to 5.30pm, Fri 9.30am to 4.30pm. Closed for lunch, 1.00pm to 2.15pm. General china repairs. Glass/porcelain.

Conservation Studio
17 Pennybank Chambers, 33/35 St John's Square, EC1M 4DS. Tel: 071-

251 6853. *Open:* Mon to Fri, 9.30am to 5.00pm. Team of three expert restorers: all fine ceramics.

Robin Hood's Workshop 18 Bourne Street, SW1W 8JR. *Tel:* 071-730 0425. *Open:* by appointment. Long waiting list for ceramic restorations. Tuition.

Lion, Witch and Lampshade See **Lighting 4. Table Lamps and Shades**   All china repairs (from 1

week to 1 month). Glass repairs/restoration. Tuition.

Studio 1D   Kensington Church Walk, W8 4NB. *Tel:* 071-937 7583. *Open:* Mon to Fri, 11.00am to 5.00pm. Ceramics. No glass.

Home Counties/ South East

Doreen Brown   1 Dunstan Terrace, Cockmouth Lane, Wadhurst, E. Sussx

TN5 6UF. *Tel:* (0892) 883432. *Open:* by appointment. Specialist in antique ceramic figure repairs.

A J Burford   Chislehurst, Kent. *Tel:* 081-467 9757. *Open:* by appointment. Skilled restoration of valuable ceramics.

Porcelain Collector   29 High Street, Shoreham Village, Sevenoaks, Kent TN14 7TD. *Tel:* (0959) 23416. *Open:* by appointment. High-quality repairs of antique porcelain/ stoneware.

4. CURTAINS AND BLINDS: CLEANING AND REPAIRS

Apart from the firms listed under **1. Carpets and Upholstery: Cleaning** there are also many dry cleaners who will accept curtains.

Bollom   *Tel:* (0273) 412111 for details of nearest branch.

Sketchley   *Tel:* (0455) 238133 for details of nearest branch.

London Postal Districts

The Cadogan Company   95 Scrubs Lane, NW10 6QU. *Tel:* 081-960 8020. All types cleaning/restoration

including unique service for reglazing chintz.

Centuryan Blinds   Service House, Mildmay Avenue, N1 4RW. *Tel:* 071-226 6600. *Open:* by appointment. In-home service for cleaning/mending blinds.

Churchill Curtain Cleaning Services 30 Kings Road, E4 7JE. *Tel:* 081-524 8824. Take down/clean/rehang. Guaranteed no shrinkage. Repairs/adaptations.

Cibenze Fabric Care 173 Hollydale Road, SE15 2SY. *Tel:* 071-639 4913. Curtains/all furnishing fabrics/rugs.

The Drycleaning Information Bureau   *Tel:* 081-863 8658. Can recommend cleaners for specific problems.

K's of Mill Hill   62 The Broadway, Mill Hill NW7 3TE. *Tel:* 081-959 6996. Curtains/blinds (all types): take down, clean, repair, alter, reline/adapt, rehang.

5. DYEING

London Postal Districts

Chalfont Cleaners and Dyers 222 Baker Street, NW1 5RT. *Tel:* 071-935 7316. 18 standard colours, or can match colour samples. Soft furnishings, but no carpets.

Thuro Clean   55 Bondway, SW8 1SJ. *Tel:* 071-582 6033. Carpet dyers.

6. FLOORS: STRIPPING AND REPOLISHING

Many of the wood specialists listed under **Floors 1. Wood** will also undertake sanding and sealing, and parquet renovations.

London Postal Districts

Andrew Keen Interiors   Flat 7, 7/9 The Heights, Beauchamp Road, SE19 3BZ. *Tel*: 081-771 6153. Repairs/ restorations/sanding and sealing. Stenciling.

Nimbus Wooden Floors   8 Garnies Close, SE15 6HW. *Tel*: 071-703 1177.

Restore/lay wooden floors. Sanding/ sealing/staining/bleaching. Special effects, including borders.

Tudor Flooring See **Floors 1. Wood**. Specialist parquet restorers. Sanding/sealing for old boards.

Victorian Pine See **Doors 1. Front and Interior**.   Well established. Sanding/sealing.

Victorian Wood Works See **Floors 1. Wood**.   Sanding/sealing/staining. Special borders.

World's End Stripping Company 9 Cork Street, W1X 1PD. *Tel*: 071-

439 3806. Lay new/restore old wood floors. Liming/bleaching/stencilled borders. Within M25.

Home Counties/ South East

Mike Smith   21 Oakfield Road, West Croydon, Surrey CR0 2UD. *Tel*: 081-680 3553. New wood floors. Restorations. Sanding/refinishing for boards/blocks.

Woodfloors and Woodstripping See **Floors 1. Wood**. Restoration of all wooden floors.

7. FRAMING AND FRAMES: PICTURE RESTORATION

Many specialist picture-framers can also restore frames/pictures. See also **Accessories 3. Frames**.

London Postal Districts

Blackman Harvey   36 Great Queen Street, WC2B 5AA. (5 mins Covent Garden tube.) *Tel*: 071-836 1904. *Open*: Mon to Fri, 9.30am to 6.00pm, Sat 10.00am to 4.00pm. High quality framing. Restore all frames. Expert picture restoration.

John Campbell Picture Frames 164 Walton Street, SW3 2JL. (10 mins South Kensington tube.) *Tel*: 071-584

9268. *Open*: Mon to Fri, 9.30am to 5.30pm, Sat 10.00am to 5.00pm. Conservation/restoration carved/ moulded frames. Gilding.

The Rowley Gallery 115 Kensington Church Street, W8 7LN. (5 mins Notting Hill Gate tube.) *Tel*: 071-727 6495. *Open*: Mon to Fri, 9.00am to 5.00pm. Late night Thu, 7.00pm. Restoration of frames/pictures.

Home Counties/ South East

The Hampton Hill Gallery 203/205 High Street, Hampton Hill, Middx

TW12 1NP. (5 mins Fulwell BR.) *Tel*: 081-977 5273/1379. *Open*: Tue to Sat, 9.00am to 5.30pm. Restoration of pictures.

Opal Frames   114 Imperial Parade, Brighton Road, Purley, Surrey CR2 4DB. (Purley BR, plus bus.) *Tel*: 081-668 8606. *Open*: Mon to Fri, 9.00am to 5.30pm, Sat 9.00am to 4.30pm. Oils, watercolours, etchings, lithographs, drawings, posters, prints.

8. FURNITURE: CANING AND RUSHING

Many firms listed under **10. Furniture: General repairs** (below) can also do caning and (less often) rushing.

London Postal Districts

The Cane Store 207 Blackstock Road, N5 2LL. *Tel:* 071-354 4210. *Open:* Mon, Tue and Wed, 10.00am to 7.00pm, Thu 10.00am to 1.00pm, Fri and Sat 10.00am to 6.00pm. Cane/willow/Lloyd Loom repairs, including conservatory furniture. Patching. Rerushing. Takes around 15 days.

Cliff Fuller 7 Kingsmere Park, NW9 8PJ. *Tel:* 081-205 0329. *Open:* Mon to Fri, 9.00am to 6.00pm, Sat 9.00am to 3.30pm (phone first). Antique/modern cane, rushwork. Seats/backs. Takes about five

weeks. Replacing modern cane panels takes ten days.

M and F Caners 22 Inks Green, E4 9EL. *Tel:* 081-527 5797. *Open:* by appointment. Sally Morgan and Joan Fisher have over 20 years' experience and "a lot of sore fingers!" More unusual patterns (eg spider back). Rerushing. Free collection/delivery for most of London.

Small Business Unit Royal National Institute for the Blind, 224 Great Portland Street, W1N 6AA. *Tel:* 071-388 1266. Can supply addresses of local cane/rush repair workshops.

Home Counties/ South East

Centre of Restoration and Arts 13/15 Victoria Street, St Albans, Herts AL1 3JJ. *Tel:* (0727) 51555.

Open: Mon to Sat, 9.00am to 5.00pm. Six experienced craftworkers repair cane/seagrass.

Country Chairmen Home Farm, Ardington, near Wantage, Oxon OX12 8PY. *Tel:* (0235) 833614. Tony Handley and his team even cut their own rushes! Restoration of antique/ modern furniture. Collection/delivery service in Thames Valley.

Patrick James Dodd 91 Merton Way, East Molesey, Surrey KT8 9PG. *Tel:* 081-979 6635. *Open:* by appointment. Mr Dodd is blind; he repairs cane/rush/seagrass/rattan. Takes about a month.

Wycombe Cane and Rush Works Victoria Street, High Wycombe, Bucks HP11 2QR. *Tel:* (0494) 442429. *Open:* Mon to Fri, 8.30am to 5.00pm. Traditional cane workshop, dating back to 1880. Cane/rush/ willow furniture. French polishing.

9. FURNITURE: FRENCH POLISHING

Many firms listed under **Furniture 10. General Repairs** below can also carry out French polishing.

London Postal Districts

Antiques and Piano Restoration 90 Lots Road, SW10 0QD. *Tel:* 071-

352 9876. *Open:* Mon to Fri, 8.30am to 6.00pm. All French-polishing of furniture/pianos. Antique furniture repairs. Piano restoration.

Brittania French Polishing 90 Teesdale Street, E2 6PU. *Tel:* 071-739 9842. *Open:* Mon to Fri, 8.00am to 7.00pm, Sat 8.00am to 12.00 noon. Experienced craftsmen. Estimates free.

E A Watts 82/84 Mitcham Lane, Streatham SW16 6NR. *Tel:* 081-769 2205. *Open:* Mon to Sat, 9.00am to 6.00pm. Late night Thu, 7.00pm. French polishing is a speciality at the repair workshop of this well-established, family furnishing firm. Also reupholstery/recaning/mirror resilvering.

10. FURNITURE: GENERAL REPAIRS

London Postal Districts

R S Banks and Son   98 Willesden Lane, NW6. *Tel*: 071-328 6147. *Open*: Mon to Sat, 10.00am to 5.00pm. Founded over 40 years ago by Chris Banks' father: team of six, with Luton workshop. Furniture repairs, antique/modern. Finishes/ French polish/spray paint renewed. Reupholstery.

Michael Foster   118 Fulham Road, SW3 6HU. *Tel*: 071-373 3636/5135. *Open*: Mon to Fri, 9.00am to 6.00pm, Sat 9.00am to 1.00pm. All antique restorations (and more humble jobs) in Putney workshop. Dining-tables stripped/repolished. Desks releathered. Chairs mended; broken legs replaced; weakened joints strengthened. Carving, lacquering, gilding, caning, rerushing. Painted furniture restoration. Glazing panels replaced. Reupholstery. Needlework restoration. Keyboard instrument repairs.

J T Grosse   12 Verney Road, SE16 3DN. *Tel*: 071-231 7969. *Open*: Mon to Fri, 7.00am to 6.00pm, Sat 7.00am to 12.00 noon. Founded by Albert Grosse in 1912: his sons, James and Albert, continue the family firm. Friendly workshop. All furniture repairs undertaken. Skilled antique restorations: marquetry, inlays, lacquer, gilding, French polishing.

S and H Jewell   26 Parker Street, WC2B 5PH. *Tel*: 071-405 8520. *Open*: Mon to Fri, 8.30am to 5.30pm. Large, friendly antique dealer, with restoration workshops. General furniture repairs. Specialist woodwork. Carving, gilding, repolishing, lacquerwork, upholstery.

Home Counties/ South East

Browns of West Wycombe   Church Lane, West Wycombe, Bucks HP14 3AH. *Tel*: (0494) 24537. *Open*: Mon to Fri, 8.00am to 6.00pm, Sat 8.00am to 12.00 noon. Family firm (seventh generation), who have owned the same premises for over 200 years. "Telephone for a friendly chat." Antique restorations. Small furniture repairs. Chair copies (estimates from photos). Regular London collections/ deliveries.

John Hartnett   2 Victoria Street, Brighton, E. Sussx BN1 3FP. *Tel*: (0273) 28793. *Open*: Mon to Fri, 9.00am to 6.00pm. Over 100 years old (established first in Paris, then London and now Brighton). General furniture repairs. Reupholstery. Specialist services: gilding/French polishing/carving/clocks.

Manor Antiques and Restorations 2 The New Shops, High Street, Old Woking, Surrey. *Tel*: (0483) 724666. *Open*: Mon to Sat, 10.00am to 5.30pm. All furniture repairs undertaken. French polishing, leather tops, caning, seagrass, rush. Pine stripping/waxing.

Phelps   133/135 St Margaret's Road, East Twickenham, Middx TW1 1RG. *Tel*: 081-892 1778/7192. *Open*: Mon to Sat, 9.00am to 5.30pm. Closed for lunch, 1.00pm to 2.00pm. Substantial furniture shop (founded 1890); friendly family firm. General repairs in own workshops: woodwork/repolishing/reupholstery/ recovering. Restoration of fine antiques.

11. FURNITURE: SPECIALISTS

London Postal Districts

Peter and Frances Binnington 65 St John's Hill, SW11 1SX. *Tel*: 071-223 9192. *Open*: Mon to Fri, 8.30am to 5.00pm. Specialist restorers of decorations on antique furniture. Goldwork, lacquer, paint, marquetry, veneers, boulle, ivory.

Carvers and Gilders   Unit 9, Charterhouse Works, Eltringham Street, SW18 1TD. *Tel*: 081-870 7047. *Open*: by appointment. Well-established workshop for carving/ gilding restorations. Furniture/ mirrors: no picture frames.

The Chair Man   1 Baronsmead Road, Barnes, SW13. *Tel*: 081-748 6816. *Open*: by appointment only. Richard Holmes specialises in chair repairs (no caning/rushing/ upholstery). London collections/ deliveries.

Serena Chaplin   32 Elsynge Road, SW18 2HN. *Tel*: 081-870 9455. *Open*: by appointment. Restoration gilt frames/mirrors/furniture. Also lacquerwork (screens/furniture).

M D Fisher   22 Sunbury Workshops, Swanfield Street, E2 7LF.

Tel: 071-739 9850. Open: Mon to Fri, 10.00am to 6.00pm. Marquetry/brass/tortoiseshell inlays on antique/reproduction furniture.

G D Warder and Sons   14 Hanway Place, W1P 9DE. *Tel:* 071-636 1867. *Open:* Mon to Fri, 9.00am to 5.00pm. Established over 40 years. Restoration of carving-gilding on period mirror frames/antique furniture.

Home Counties/South East

Angela Burgin Furnishing and Design   6/8 Gordon Street, Luton Beds LU1 1QP. *Tel:* (0582) 22563. *Open:* Mon to Fri, 8.00am to 5.00pm, weekends by appointment. Restoration/recovering all antique upholstery (traditional methods/

materials). Restoration antique draperies.

John Gould   Hampton Court Cottage, Sparepenny Lane, Farningham, Kent DA4 0JH. *Tel:* (0322) 864916. *Open:* by appointment. Repairs for classic modern plywood chairs, post 1920.

12. GLASS REPAIRS

Some china repairers will also tackle glass. See **3. China Repairs** above and also **Windows 2. Stained and Decorative Glass**.

London Postal Districts

Thomas Goode See **Accessories 11. Tableware and Table Linen**. Repair service for glass. Also china restoration. Silver cleaned/repaired/replated.

R Wilkinson and Son   5 Catford Hill, Catford, SE6 4NU. *Tel:* 081-314 1080. All domestic glass repairs. Stains/discolourations removed, chips ground down, decanter stoppers replaced. Blue liner replacement. Also chandelier restoration.

13. HIRING

Wickes and Homebase offer tool hire. See **DIY Superstores**. Local hire firms are numerous. The HSS chain of shops provides a comprehensive hire service. Branches in London/South East include:
Acton: 081-992 0101. Barking: 081-594 1042. Barnet: 081-440 3157. Beckenham: 081-658 5877. Cheam:

081-664 0026. Croydon: 081-689 3443. Fulham: 071-736 1769. Greenwich: 081-853 4114. Hackney: 081-533 3428. Hammersmith: 081-748 6740. Hayes: 081-573 1188. Kenton: 081-907 3614. Kilburn: 071-328 1798. Kingston: 081-546 1538. Lewisham: 081-314 5900. Leytonstone: 081-555 0293. Notting

Hill: 071-727 0897. Orpington: (0689) 834646. Purley: 081-660 6485. Richmond: 081-940 8441. Romford: (0708) 725029. Shepherds Bush: 081-743 6300. Stockwell: 071-720 6524. Tooting: 081-767 3127. Tottenham: 081-801 3261. Watford: (0923) 30545. Wembley: 081-903 9919.

14. KITCHENWARE REPAIRS

London Postal Districts

Buck and Ryan   101 Tottenham Court Road, W1P 0DY. *Tel:* 071-636

7475. *Open:* Mon to Fri, 8.30am to 5.30pm, Sat 9.00am to 4.00pm. Old-established ironmongers with exquisite tools selection. Can sharpen anything with a cutting edge: scissors, knives, shears, tools, blades.

Divertimenti See **Kitchens 9. Kitchenware**. Copper saucepans relined/knives resharpened.

Leon Jaeggi and Sons See **Kitchens 9. Kitchenware**. Retinning copper pans (about 48 hours).

15. LEATHER

London Postal Districts

Connolly Bros   Wandle Bank, Wimbledon SW19 1DW. *Tel:* 081-542 5251/081-543 4611. *Open:* by appointment only. Extensive services for leather cleaning/renovation/repair. Slashes mended/springs replaced. Can revive colours. Will recover if necessary. Leaflet available. Free estimates nationwide. Collections/deliveries.

K Restorations   1/3 Ferdinand Street, NW1 8ES. *Tel:* 071-482 4021. *Open:* Mon to Fri, 8.00am to 5.30pm. Desk/table releathering. DIY mail-order releathering kit. French polishing. Furniture repairs. Reupholstery. Cane/rush repairs. Oak liming. Collection/delivery.

Home Counties/ South East

Leathercare   Unit 5, Happy Valley Industrial Park, Primrose Hill, Kings Langley, Herts WD4 8HY. *Tel:* (0923) 268711/261851. *Open:* by appointment. Specialised service at works for leather furniture cleaning/restoration. Refurbishment of leather table/desk tops. Collection/deliveries. In-home estimates for a small fee (refundable on order).

16. LOOSE COVERS

Many firms listed under **Interior Design** and **Soft Furnishings 3. Made-to-measure** offer a loose-cover-making service.

London Postal Districts

Amoris Interiors   379 Harrow Road, Maida Vale W9 3NA. *Tel:* 081-968 0834. *Open:* Mon to Sat, 10.00am to 6.30pm. Loose cover/curtain-making/interior design service.

The Curtain Gallery See **Soft Furnishings 3. Made-to-measure**

In-home service for loose covers. Colour/design advice.

Highly Sprung   549 Battersea Park Road, SW11 3BL. *Tel:* 071-924 1124. *Open:* Mon to Sat, 10.00am to 6.00pm.
Factory Showroom: 12 Oakridge Road, High Wycombe, Bucks HP11 2PF. *Tel:* (0494) 439596. *Open:* Mon to Fri, 8.00am to 5.00pm, Sat and Sun 10.00am to 3.00pm. Your fabric or theirs. Furniture is collected and taken to the High Wycombe factory. Service takes about 10 days. Also reupholstery.

Let It Loose   The Front Room, 1 Windmill Row, Kennington SE11

5DW. *Tel:* 081-582 1437. *Open:* Mon to Sat, 10.00am to 6.00pm (summer 7.00pm). Consultant advises on colours/styles; fabric samples. Or use your own fabrics. Pattern-maker cuts template in your home. Service takes about three weeks.

Home Counties/ South East

Highly Sprung See **London Postal Districts** above.

17. METAL REPAIRS: IRON AND STEEL

London Postal Districts

Benbow's   Benbow Yard, Towneley

Street, SE17 1DZ. *Tel:* 071-701 0208. *Open:* Mon to Fri, 6.30am to 6.00pm. Irbin Benbow is the third generation of blacksmiths in his family, with a working forge on the same premises. Gates/railings

repaired. All iron/steel work: even pushchairs. Staircases/security grilles made.

J H Porter and Son   11 Pembroke Mews, off Earls Court Road,

Kensington W8 6ER. *Tel:* 071-937 1322. *Open:* Mon to Fri, 8.00am to 5.30pm. All iron/steel repairs. Saucepans, prams, gates, railings, balustrades, security grilles.

Smith and Rappold   Unit 12, 149 Roman Way, N7 8XH. *Tel:* 071-609 9591. *Open:* Mon to Fri, 8.00am to 5.30pm. Thomas Smith and Neville

Rappold repair/make gates, railings, fire escapes, staircases, balconies and so on.

Home Counties/ South East

Beaconsfield Forge   Kingfield

Road, Kingfield, Woking, Surrey GU22 9EG. *Tel:* (0483) 760313. *Open:* Mon to Fri, 8.30am to 5.00pm. Traditional blacksmiths. Mend gates, balustrades, railings. New ironwork to match old.

18. METAL REPAIRS: NON-FERROUS

See also **22. Silver Repairs** below.

London Postal Districts

T Smith and Co   35 Clerkenwell Close, EC1R 0AU. *Tel:* 071-253 7314. *Open:* Mon to Fri, 8.00am to 5.00pm. High-class restorations. Door furniture, window fittings, pots/pans repaired. Repolishing/re-plating.

Verdigris Art   Metal Restorers' Arch, 290 Crown Street, SE5 0UR. *Tel:* 071-703 8373. *Open:* Mon to Fri, 9.00am to 6.00pm. Expert bronze repair/restoration. Also pewter, brass, copper, spelter (lead/zinc mix). Sculptures/chandeliers/light fittings.

Home Counties/ South East

A Bartram   177 Hirings Hill,

Chesham, Bucks BP5 2PN. *Tel:* (0494) 783271. *Open:* by appointment. Specialist pewter repairs.

Voysey and Knapp   Erith Small Business Centre, High Street, Erith, Kent. *Tel:* (0322) 350032. *Open:* 8.00am to 5.30pm. Master metal workers Alfred Voysey and Walter Knapp have moved from Goodge Place to Kent. They mend chandeliers, lanterns, coffee tables, wall brackets. Speciality is brass. Also bronze/copper/silver. Re-plating.

19. ORIENTAL RUGS: CLEANING AND REPAIR

The firms below specialise in cleaning Oriental rugs. Specialist firms listed under **Accessories 8. Rugs** can also offer cleaning/restoration/valuation services.

London Postal Districts

Abercorn Carpet Specialists Abercorn Place, St John's Wood

NW8. *Tel:* 071-624 8365. Oriental carpets/rugs.

David Banks Services   20 Filmer Road, SW6 1BW. *Tel:* 071-385 9759/5701. Carpet relaid; Oriental carpets/rugs. Upholstery/curtains.

Behar Profex   The Alban Building, St Alban's Place, Upper Street, N1 0NX. *Tel:* 071-226 0144. Clean and restore Oriental rugs/tapestries.

Home Counties/ South East

Thames Carpet Cleaners   48/56 Reading Road, Henley-on-Thames, Oxon. *Tel:* (0491) 574676. Specialists in cleaning/restoring Oriental rugs.

20. REUPHOLSTERY

For further information, contact **The Association of Master Upholsters** Unit 1, Clyde Road, Wallington, Surrey SM6 8PZ. (*Tel:* 081-773 8069.)

London Postal Districts

ABC Upholstery 4 West Hill, Wandsworth SW18. *Tel:* 081-870 6996. *Open:* Mon to Fri, 9.00am to 5.00pm. Antique/modern upholstery. Also recaning/loose covers. Speciality is lining walls with fabric, which can be flat, pleated or gathered.

Michael Angell Upholstery Wellsbach House, The Business Village, Broomhill Road, Wandsworth SW18 4JG. (20 mins Wandsworth Town BR.) *Tel:* 081-871 5140/081-876 2157. *Open:* Mon to Sat, 8.30am to 6.00pm. Reupholstery, recovering. Antique/modern furniture repairs. Free local collection/delivery.

The Choumert Upholstery Co 131 Bellenden Road, SE15 4QY. (10 mins Peckham Rye BR.) *Tel:* 071-679 1775. *Open:* Mon to Fri, 9.00am to 5.30pm, Sat 9.00am to 12.00 noon. Reupholstery; new upholstered furniture to order.

Dhillon Upholstery 157a Malden Road, NW5 4HT. *Tel:* 071-267 4489. *Open:* Mon to Sat, 9.00am to 5.30pm. "No job too small." Specialist antique restorers. Repolishing.

A V Fowlds and Sons 3 Addington Square, Camberwell SE5 7JZ. (Elephant and Castle/Oval tubes, plus bus.) *Tel:* 071-703 2686. *Open:* Mon to Fri, 9.00am to 6.30pm. Established in 1870; traditional and modern reupholstery and repair service.

C H Frost Upholstery 67a Abingdon Road, Kensington W8 6AW. *Tel:* 071-937 0451. *Open:* Mon to Fri, 9.00am to 5.00pm, Sat 9.30am to 1.00pm. Charlie Frost (trading since 1955) is a reupholstery specialist. Also curtains/pelmets/loose covers. Furniture repairs/recaning.

Kingston Traditional Upholstery 185 Putney Bridge Road, Putney SW15 2NX. *Tel:* 081-870 0258. *Open:* Mon to Fri, 8.00am to 5.00pm, Sat 9.00am to 1.00pm. Recovering fabric/leather/kelim-covered upholstery. Frame renovation. Repolishing.

Jill Saunders See **Furniture 4. 20th-Century Classics: Originals and Copies**. Upholstery specialists; also make a range of reproduction Victorian/Edwardian upholstery. Plus furniture restoration, including French polishing, recaning and re-rushing.

Tulleys of Chelsea 289/297 Fulham Road, SW10 9PZ. (South Kensington tube, plus bus.) *Tel:* 071-352 1078. *Open:* Mon to Fri, 9.00am to 5.30pm. For other branches see **Upholstery and Suites 1. Chairs, Sofas and Suites**. Replacement seat/back cushions made-to-measure. Any shape, 4in deep. Feather or Dacron filling. Takes about six to eight weeks. Mail order.

Wallace Upholstery 8/10 Grange Road, E17. *Tel:* 081-520 7685. Complete reupholstery service. Home visits.

Mail Order

Foam for Comfort 401 Otley Old Road, Cookridge, Leeds, W. Yorks LS16 7DF. *Tel:* (0532) 678281 or 673770. Mail order service for replacement fire-retardant foam: soft/medium/firm. Existing covers can be refilled. Colour brochure available.

21. SILVER REPAIRS

See also **Metal Repairs: Non-Ferrous** above.

London Postal Districts

J H Bourdon-Smith 24 Mason's Yard, Duke Street, St James's, SW1Y 6BU. *Tel:* 071-839 4714/5. *Open:* Mon to Fri, 9.30am to 6.00pm. Cleaning/restorations/repairs.

Home Counties/South East

James W Potter and Sons 5 Stonemasons' Court, 67 Parchment Street, Winchester, Hants SO23 8AT. *Tel:* (0962) 840624. *Open:* Mon to Fri, 9.00am to 5.30pm, Sat 9.00am to 1.00pm. Family firm. Manufacturers of cutlery by hand. Antique copies. Antique cutlery repaired/restored.

22. STONE REPAIRS

London Postal Districts

H W Poulter 279 Fulham Road, SW10 9PZ. *Tel*: 071-352 7268. *Open*: Mon to Fri, 9.00am to 5.00pm, Sat 10.00am to 1.00pm. *Workshop*: 1a Adelaide Grove, off Uxbridge Road, W12. *Tel*: 081-749 4557. *Open*: Mon to Fri, 7.30am to 5.30pm. Family firm. Marble/stone cleaning and restoration.

30

HELP!

Whole books have been written on consumer rights. This chapter gives only the
briefest outline of them, to make shopping easier. Helpful places to visit,
leaflets to write off for, and useful organisations are also included.

1. YOUR RIGHTS

With thanks to Keith Richards, Senior Lawyer, The Consumers' Association.

Shops

You will be more effective as a shopper if you know your rights under the law. The Sale of Goods Act 1979 covers all goods (including food) bought from any form of trader—whether from shops, street markets, doorstep salesmen, in sales, at parties in private homes, or by mail order.

The Act covers goods bought with cash, or on credit. Once the seller accepts your offer to buy (whether verbally or in writing), a contract has been made. Under this contract, you have the right to receive goods of "merchantable quality" and fit for their normal purpose, bearing in mind the price paid, the nature of the goods, and how they were described. The goods must be "fit for any particular purpose" indicated by the seller, and they must be "as described".

If the seller has not fulfilled any of these obligations, your contract has been broken, and you are entitled to your money back or compensation. Make your complaint to the seller, not the manufacturer, as it is the seller who is responsible (whatever shops sometimes say). But see also the note below on manufacturers. You don't have to have a receipt to make a complaint. But matters run more smoothly if you have, so keep all bills/receipts carefully in a special place. When complaining, you must act quickly. If you cannot get back to the shop in person immediately, at least telephone or write, stating your complaint.

When a complaint is justified, you are entitled to your money back. You do not have to accept an exchange, or a credit note. But once you take a credit note, you cannot ask for your money back later.

Your rights apply even during sales. Notices that say "No money can be refunded" are illegal. But if the shop has drawn your attention to imperfections (with a "seconds" sign, for example), the onus is on you to make a good inspection of the goods before buying (though you can complain about imperfections that such an inspection cannot uncover).

Make complaints politely and calmly to the department or shop manager. Keep carefully copies of any correspondence. If you sign a contract for goods and services in your own home, you have seven days to change your mind.

The Supply of Goods and Services Act 1982 guards against poor workmanship: it states that "the supplier will carry out the services within a reasonable time and with reasonable care and skill". If you need help/advice, go to your local Citizens' Advice Bureau, or consult the Trading Standards Department at your town hall.

Manufacturers

The Consumer Protection Act 1987 makes manufacturers and importers liable for injury and damage caused wholly or partly by a defective product made after 1 March 1988. In the case of injury or death, anyone can claim, not just the purchaser. Seek advice if you have been harmed by a product.

2. CREDIT

Used sensibly, credit is a valuable aid, especially as a means to buying better-quality, longer-lasting furnishings that you could not otherwise afford. (This particularly applies to carpets, upholstery and beds.) Watch out for "interest-free" credit, which gives you more time to pay without costing you extra. You will probably have to spend over a certain amount with the shop in question to qualify.

Make sure you know the full cost of any other credit you are offered, and in particular check the Annual Percentage Rate (APR). If you sign a credit agreement in a shop, garage or finance company office, it is legally binding. But if you sign a credit agreement in your own home, you have five days in which to cancel or change your mind.

3. MAIL ORDER

In this book, mail order describes goods that are ordered by post or the telephone. They may then be delivered by post, carrier, the supplier's own transport, and so on. Shopping from home by mail order can be comfortable and convenient. Some merchandise is only available by mail order. And some goods may be cheaper when bought this way. On the other hand, you cannot inspect the goods before you buy.

Illustrations can be deceiving. Brochure colours may not be accurate. You may not get a fair idea of scale—of furniture in particular. And quality is hard to assess.

4. WHAT TO READ/WHERE TO GO

Free leaflets on consumer rights are available from your local library, or from The Office of Fair Trading, Field House, Bream's Buildings, EC4A 1PR. *The Fair Deal Guide to Shoppers' Rights and Family Budgeting* is a useful paperback published by HMSO for £1.95. Like any other subject, furnishing repays homework. Shops often do not have good stocks of manufacturers' literature/samples. Write off for these yourself. Get into contact with manufacturers before making major buys. A recommended stockist may offer the best service. Make the effort to visit manufacturers' showrooms: you cannot buy direct, but sight of the full product range, and access to specialist advice, are always helpful. There are numerous specialist magazines, containing the very latest news about suppliers. *Which?* is published by The Consumers' Association (2 Marylebone Road, NW1 4DX. *Tel:* 071-486 5544). It gives monthly comparative reports on tested products; you can consult back numbers at your local library.

London Postal Districts

The Building Centre   26 Store Street, WC1E 7BT. (Opposite Goodge Street tube.) Tel: 071-637 1022. *Open:* Mon to Fri, 9.30am to 5.15pm, Sat 10.00am to 1.00pm. Permanent exhibitions of building products/materials: bathrooms/kitchens, bricks, tiles and flooring, doors/windows to name but a few. Literature/leaflet distribution counter, plus technical centre, offering advice from two professionals. *For information on products, tel:* (0344) 864999. Good specialist book shop.

The Design Council   28 Haymarket, SW1Y 4SU. (2 mins Piccadilly Circus tube.) *Tel:* 071-839 8000. *Open:* 7 days, Mon to Sat, 10.00am to 6.00pm, Sun 1.00pm to 6.00pm. Designer Selection Service offers help with defining design requirements and provides names of three suitable firms (£80). Good bookshop with material on design history, furniture, interiors, product design, etc. Well worth a long browse.

The Design and Decoration Building 107a Pimlico Road, SW1W 8PH. (5 mins Sloane Square tube.) *Tel:* 071-730 2353. *Open:* Mon to Fri, 10.00am to 6.00pm. Late night Wed, 7.00pm. Open Sat and Sun, 11.00am to 5.00pm. Magnificent newly opened centre for interior design, with facilities for the trade and the public. Permanent showcase for manufacturers and small specialist shops. Frequent special exhibitions. Reference/advice available. Bookshop. Café.

5. HELPFUL PEOPLE

The trade associations listed below can provide help in various ways. Members in your area could be useful, as they should perform to at least the minimum professional standards. Most associations have an agreed code of practice, with a complaints/arbitration procedure if things go wrong. Some also have an agreed scale of fees and/or schemes protecting customers' deposits. Many publish useful general literature.

Building Employers' Confederation (BEC)   82 New Cavendish Street, W1M 8AD. *Tel:* 071-580 5588.

The Council for Registered Gas Installers (CORGI)

4 Elmwood, Chineham Business Park, Crockford Lane, Basingstoke, Hants RG24 0WG. *Tel:* (0256) 707060.

Draught-Proofing Advisory Association/External Wall Insulation Association/National Association of Loft Insulation Contractors/National Cavity Insulation Association *All at:* PO Box 12, Haslemere, Surrey GU27 3AH. *Tel:* (0428) 654011.

Electrical Contractors' Association (ECA) ESCA House, 34 Palace Court, Bayswater, W2 4HY. *Tel:* 071-229 1266.

Federation of Master Builders (FMB) 14/15 Great James Street, WC1N 3DP. *Tel:* 071-242 7583.

Fibre Building Board Organisation (FIDOR) 1 Hanworth Road, Feltham, Middx TW13 5AF. *Tel:* 081-751 6107.

Glass and Glazing Federation (GGF) 44/48 Borough High Street, SE1 1XB. *Tel:* 071-403 7177.

Guild of Master Craftsmen 166 High Street, Lewes, E. Sussx BN7 1XU. *Tel:* (0273) 478449.

Heating and Ventilating Contractors' Association (HVCA) ESCA House, 34 Palace Court, Bayswater W2 4JG. *Tel:* 071-229 2488.

Institute of Plumbing (IOP) 64 Station Lane, Hornchurch, Essex RM12 6NB. *Tel:* (04024) 72791.

Kitchen Specialists' Association (KSA) Information Office, 8 St Bernard's Crescent, Edinburgh EH4 1NP. *Tel:* 031-332 8884.

London and Provincial Antique Dealers' Association (LAPADA) 535 King's Road, SW10 0SZ. *Tel:* 071-823 3511.

National Federation of Roofing Contractors (NFRC) 24 Weymouth Street, W1N 3FA. *Tel:* 071-436 0387.

National Home Improvement Council 125 Kennington Road, SE11 6SF. *Tel:* 071-582 7790.

National Master Tile Fixers Association 44 Masons' Hill, Bromley, Kent BR2 9EQ. *Tel:* 081-464 0131.

Royal Institute of British Architects (RIBA) 66 Portland Place, W1N 4AD. *Tel:* 071-580 5533.

Royal Institution of Chartered Surveyors (RICS) 12 Great George Street, SW1P 3AD. *Tel:* 071-222 7000.

Thatching Advisory Service Rose Tree Farm, 29 Nine Mile Ride, Finchampstead, Bucks RG11 4QD. *Tel:* (0734) 734203.

6. LEAFLETS

Informative and inspirational leaflets/booklets are published by many trade organisations, furnishing and decorative equipment manufacturers, as well as some government departments. They are usually free, although you may be asked for postage. Below is a small selection (available in 1992) to get you started.

British Bathroom Council Federation House, Station Road, Stoke-on-Trent ST4 2RT. *Tel:* (0782) 747074. Fact sheets on planning a bathroom, including showers, and advice for the elderly/disabled.

British Carpet Manufacturers' Association Royalty House, 72 Dean Street, W1V 5HB. *Tel:* 071-734 9853. Hints/tips on buying and caring for carpets, plus a stain removal leaflet.

Department of Energy Energy Efficiency Office, Blackhorse Road,

SE99 6UB. Energy in Yor Home Pack (free). Ways to save money, increase comfort, and cut pollution.

Fibre Building Board Development Organisation See **5. Helpful People** above. DIY project leaflets.

Thomas French (Rufflette) Sharston Road, Wythenshawe, Manchester M22 4TH. *Tel:* 061-998 1811. Curtain-making/style details.

Glass and Glazing Federation See **5. Helpful People** above. Free leaflets on double/safety glazing, mirrors etc.

Home Woodwork Campaign 21/25 Carolgate, Retford, Notts DN22 6BZ. DIY instructions for panelling, shelving etc.

Homebase See **DIY Superstores**. Excellent free leaflets on DIY projects.

ICI Paints Division (Dulux) Wexham Road, Slough, Berks SL2 5DS. *Advice line,* Tel: (0753) 534225. Leaflets on painting techniques. £8 for personalised colour scheme service: send for details.

Ideal-Standard PO Box 60, National Avenue, Hull, HU5 4JE. *Tel:* (0482) 46461. Basic bathroom planning kit.

Kitchen Specialists' Association See **5. Helpful People** above. Advice folder on "Dos and Don'ts When Buying a Kitchen".

National Bed Federation 251 Brompton Road, SW3 2EZ. *Tel:* 071-589 4888. Advice sheets on choosing beds. Topics include children's beds, beds and bad backs, allergies and so on. Please send 34p stamp.

INDEX